W9-AMX-196

Student Study Guide

to accompany

L.R. Gay, Geoffrey E. Mills, and Peter Airasian's

Educational Research

Competencies for Analysis and Applications

Eighth Edition

Rayne A. Sperling
The Pennsylvania State University

PEARSON

Merrill
Prentice Hall

Upper Saddle River, New Jersey
Columbus, Ohio

Vice President and Executive Publisher: Jeffery W. Johnston
Publisher: Kevin M. Davis
Development Editor: Autumn Crisp Benson
Editorial Assistant: Sarah Kenoyer
Production Editor: Mary Harlan
Design Coordinator: Diane C. Lorenzo
Photo Coordinator: Lori Whitley
Cover Design: Jason Moore
Cover Image: SuperStock
Production Manager: Laura Messerly
Director of Marketing: Ann Castel Davis
Marketing Manager: Autumn Purdy
Marketing Coordinator: Brian Mounts

Copyright © 2006 by Pearson Education, Inc., Upper Saddle River, New Jersey 07458. Pearson Prentice Hall. All rights reserved. Printed in the United States of America. This publication is protected by Copyright and permission should be obtained from the publisher prior to any prohibited reproduction, storage in a retrieval system, or transmission in any form or by any means, electronic, mechanical, photocopying, recording, or likewise. For information regarding permission(s), write to: Rights and Permissions Department.

Pearson Prentice Hall™ is a trademark of Pearson Education, Inc.
Pearson® is a registered trademark of Pearson plc
Prentice Hall® is a registered trademark of Pearson Education, Inc.
Merrill® is a registered trademark of Pearson Education, Inc.

Pearson Education Ltd.
Pearson Education Singapore Pte. Ltd.
Pearson Education Canada, Ltd.
Pearson Education–Japan

Pearson Education Australia Pty. Limited
Pearson Education North Asia Ltd.
Pearson Educación de Mexico, S.A. de C.V.
Pearson Education Malaysia Pte. Ltd.

10 9 8 7 6 5 4 3 2 1
ISBN: 0-13-171669-7

To the Student

This student guide was developed to support the eighth edition of *Educational Research: Competencies for Analysis and Applications* by L. R. Gay, Geoffrey E. Mills, and Peter Airasian. Although I recognize some of you may be apprehensive about your course, this may very well be the best class you will ever take. The text is, and will remain, an excellent resource for you as you develop your expertise in research methods. An understanding of the content in your text and course as supported by this guide will open windows to your understanding of the discipline. This resource also provides you with the tools and language to understand and critique research as well as to conduct research in your field.

The guide includes several different types of activities and resources to facilitate your understanding of content and development of competencies in this course. For **Review the terms**, it is suggested that you write brief definitions of the terms (and check them against the text) to begin your review of the content in the text chapters. Writing definitions will help you to remember and clarify your understanding of the terms. However, you will not only want to know the terms, but you will also need to use and apply the information. As one way to facilitate application, it is suggested that in addition to defining the term, you generate novel examples for each of the concepts in the text. The general focus of the activities in this guide—**Checking what you know**, **For your own review**, **Practicing the Tasks**—is to provide you with a deeper understanding of and skill in research methods. Research is not always an exact science; sometimes it *just depends*. Some of your responses for activities in this guide will vary from the **Answers** I have provided at the end of each chapter. In many cases I have noted the salient parts of the answer or the thinking behind my answer so that you can judge your answer as appropriate or inappropriate. I also encourage you to work through the examples with your peers and consult with your instructor when necessary. The **Test-Like Events** (multiple-choice items) are included to give you the opportunity to assess yourself in chapter content and help you to perform better on the tests administered by your instructor. **Published articles, Portions of Published Work** and **Examples of Student Work** are also included to help you gain competency in evaluating and producing research. Refer to the Contents of this guide to see which examples complement Tasks in your text. Note that the line spacing of the student work examples has been changed to single-spaced, rather than double-spaced as is recommended by the APA, to conserve space in this guide.

Acknowledgments

In developing this resource, Hoi Suen at Penn State was helpful in connecting me with student work. He is an excellent mentor and an exceptional teacher of research methods and I really appreciate his assistance in obtaining some of the example student proposals found in this book. I also really respect the students who consented to share the work that is included throughout this student guide. When I told these students that I would be like to use their work to illustrate aspects of research methods all of these students enthusiastically sent their proposals along. Several noted that they would change aspects of their proposal if they were to write it again.

I really appreciate the opportunity to develop the activities within this work and thank Development Editors Autumn Benson and Julie Peters of Merrill/Prentice Hall as well as the staff at Merrill/Prentice Hall for their support in the development of this guide.

I hope you enjoy this guide and that it facilitates your understanding and appreciation of research methods.

Rayne A. Sperling

Contents

Chapter 1   Introduction to Educational Research

Chapter 1 Objectives

1. List and briefly describe the major steps involved in conducting a research study.
2. Describe the differences between quantitative and qualitative research.
3. Briefly define and state the major characteristics these research approaches: action, descriptive, correlational, causal-comparative, experimental, narrative, and ethnographic.
4. For each research approach in Objective 3, briefly describe two appropriate research studies.
5. Given a published article, identify and state the
   a. Problem or topic chosen to study
   b Procedures employed to conduct the study
   c. Method of analyzing collected data
   d. Major conclusion of the study

Review the Terms

Provide a succinct definition in your own words for each of the following terms.

Educational research: _____
_____

Inductive reasoning: _____
_____

Deductive reasoning: _____
_____

Scientific method: _____
_____

Hypothesis: _____
_____

Basic research: _____
_____

Applied research: _____
_____

Evaluation research: _____
_____

Formative evaluation: _____
_____

Ethnography: _____
_____

Summative evaluation: _____
_____

Research and development: _____
_____

Action research: _____
_____

Quantitative research: _____
_____

Qualitative research: _____
_____

Descriptive research: _____
_____

Correlational research: _____
_____

Variable: _____
_____

Correlation: _____
_____

Correlation coefficient: _____
_____

Causal-comparative research: _____
_____

Independent variable: _____
_____

Dependent variable: _____
_____

Experimental research: _____
_____

Generalizability: _____
_____

Single-subject experimental designs: _____
_____

Sample: _____
_____

Narrative research: _____
_____

For Your Own Review

1. State the steps of the scientific method

    _____
    _____
    _____
    _____

Checking What You Know

1. This activity requires you to apply your understanding of some of the Chapter 1 concepts.

    You are interested in comparing if business-run childcare or independent childcare better prepares preschoolers for kindergarten. You choose only 5-year-old children entering kindergarten who have been in the same childcare arrangement for at least 6 months to participate. You measure the preparedness for kindergarten by using standard kindergarten entrance exam questions and kindergarten CTBS (a standardized test) scores given during the spring of the school year.

    a. Write a research topic or question.

        _____
        _____
        _____

    b. Is this basic or applied research? _____

    c. Is this qualitative or quantitative research? _____

    d. Is this descriptive, correlational, or causal-comparative research?

        _____

    e. Is this study likely a true experimental research study? Why or why not?

        _____
        _____
        _____

2. Some research topics can be addressed from many different types of research. One example of such a topic might be standardized testing. Given the general topic of standardized testing, develop a research topic for each of the following approaches.

    a. Narrative _____
        _____

    b. Qualitative _____
        _____

c.   Descriptive _____

_____

d.   Correlational _____

_____

e.   Action research_____

_____

f.   Causal-comparative _____

_____

Practicing the Tasks

1.   Task 1-C in your text requires you to identify types of research by examining potential research topics. Consider each of the following potential topics and decide what type of research approach the topic likely illustrates.

a.   Should we fund the special reading program again next year? _____

b.   Does the developmental preschool have an effect on children's gross motor skills in kindergarten? _____

c.   What are the concerns of the local community regarding the proposed merger between two local smaller schools? _____

d.   What were the academic concerns of school personnel during desegregation?

_____

e.   What happens in a typical high school track practice? _____

f.   Is exposure to the arts as a child related to adult attendance at community arts performances?_____

g.   Are there differences in self-concept between men and women with eating disorders?

_____

h.   What are the social concerns of fully included high school students? _____

i.   Is there a relationship between number of books in the home and reading ability in second grade?

_____

j.   Are boys or girls more likely to engage in hands-on science displays in a local museum?

_____

k.   Is there a difference in amount of content learned between those learners who were randomly assigned to read on-line text versus those who read traditional textbooks?

_____

l. How do students feel about the new peer-tutoring program?

    _____

m. Are there gender differences in self-esteem in third grade students?

    _____

n. What is the experience of ethnic minorities in advanced placement high school classes?

    _____

o. Is birth order related to academic achievement? _____

p. What types of prior knowledge and beliefs do students bring to an introductory anthropology course? _____

q. What concerns do first-year teachers have regarding discipline in their classes?

    _____

r. Do high- and low-SES students differ in the number of school-based extra-curricular activities in which they participate? _____

s. How are age and persistence rates of graduate students related? _____

t. Are there differences among elementary, middle school, and high school students' reports of favorite occupational interests? _____

u. Is there a relationship between the number of hours of counseling provided free of charge by the university and client willingness to seek additional counseling? _____

2. Your text provides Task 1-A and Task 1-B, which require you to identify and briefly state several aspects of completed research studies. For additional practice on these Tasks, please consider the following three research reports, which appear at the end of this chapter: *Fifth-Graders' mathematical communications: Lessons from the field* (Perry, 2001), *Parents' and teachers' beliefs about children's school readiness in a high-need community* (Piotrowski, Botsko, & Matthews, 2000), and *Toward a Positive psychology of academic motivation* (Pajares, 2001). These three resources will be considered again in this guide. For Task 1-A and 1-B, however, consider the following for each:
    *   Topic
    *   Procedures
    *   Method of analysis
    *   Major conclusions

    At the conclusion of each of these three articles, write in the blanks provided.

Test-Like Event

1. When using scientific method, the step most similar to the discussion section of a research article is

    a. Recognize and identify a topic to be studied.
    b. Describe and execute research procedures.
    c. Analyze the collected data.
    d. State the results or implications.

2. Which of the following is an example of a quantitative study?

    a. Narrative
    b. Correlational
    c. Grounded theory
    d. Ethnography

3. Survey research is often considered _____ research.

    a. experimental
    b. correlational
    c. ethnographic
    d. descriptive

4. Medical research often is conducted to derive theory. This research is best described as

    a. applied research.
    b. action research.
    c. basic research.
    d. evaluation research.

5. Margarita decides to use a whole-language approach to reading instruction in her kindergarten classroom because she believes that children learn to read best when they are given a variety of experiences with books and print. She feels that teaching young readers skills makes them less interested in reading. Margarita is relying on which type of method of knowing?

    a. Tradition
    b. Expert authority
    c. Intuition and personal experiences
    d. Scientific and disciplined inquiry

6. Lei is interested in addressing the differences in academic success between fully-included and not fully-included middle school special education students. She is comparing the standardized test scores of both groups of students. Which type of research method below best describes Lei's study?

    a. Correlational
    b. Causal-Comparative
    c. Experimental
    d. Descriptive

7. The seventh-grade teachers are interested in whether rotating classes for mathematics benefits the students as opposed to staying in homeroom. They are unsure if the instructional time lost when changing rooms outweighs the benefits of more homogeneous ability grouping. They have conducted a meeting to gain more information about the problem and next they will analyze their data and then make a decision about which course to take. These teachers are best illustrating

    a. action research.
    b. experimental research.
    c. basic research.
    d. narrative research.

8. Raul is interested in teachers' perceptions of school safety. He administers an instrument to all of the teachers in his school district and then analyzes the data and presents the average responses and the most frequently cited concerns of the teachers. Raul is conducting which type of research?

    a. Correlational
    b. Causal-comparative
    c. Descriptive
    d. Experimental

9. Sandy, also interested in school safety, decides to conduct focus groups with the teachers. In addition, she conducts follow-up interviews with many of the teachers, parents, and students. She steps back from her data and considers how it is informing her questions. She allows the data to inform her next questions as she proceeds with the study. Sandy is conducting which type of research?

    a. Causal-comparative
    b. Grounded theory
    c. Ethnography
    d. Historical

10. Given the following research topic, *Is there a relationship between attendance in school and student popularity with peers?,* which type of study will likely be conducted?

    a. Correlational
    b. Descriptive
    c. Causal-comparative
    d. Experimental

11. Of the following, which illustrates a correlational study?

    a. Are there differences in self-esteem between students who are athletic and those who are not?
    b. Is self-esteem of students randomly-assigned to an intense physical training program higher than those learners not exposed to the training?
    c. Is there a relationship between self-esteem and athletic ability?
    d. How do students in high school Physical Education classes report their self-esteem?

12. Of the following, which illustrates a causal-comparative study?

    a. Are there differences in self-esteem between students who are athletic and those who are not?
    b. Is self-esteem of students' randomly-assigned to an intense physical training program higher than those learners not exposed to the training?
    c. Is there a relationship between self-esteem and athletic ability?
    d. How do students in high school Physical Education classes report their self-esteem?

13. Of the following, which best illustrates a descriptive (survey) study?

    a. Are there differences in self-esteem between students who are athletic and those who are not?
    b. Is self-esteem of students' randomly-assigned to an intense physical training program higher than those learners not exposed to the training?
    c. Is there a relationship between self-esteem and athletic ability?
    d. How do students in high school Physical Education classes report their self-esteem?

14. The type of research most directly interested in theory development is

    a. evaluation.
    b. applied.
    c. basic.
    d. descriptive.

15.-17. Manny is interested in investigating differences in spatial skills between middle school girls and boys enrolled in his computer graphics class. He administers two paper and pencil spatial ability measures and combines the scores and then compares them between boys and girls.

15. What type of research is Manny conducting?

    a. basic
    b. applied
    c. experimental
    d. evaluation

16. What research approach is Manny employing?

    a. narrative
    b. ethnographic
    c. correlational
    d. causal-comparative

17. Administering the spatial ability measure best illustrates which step of the research process?

    a. Selection and definition of a problem.
    b. Execution of research procedures.
    c. Analysis of the data.
    d. Drawing and stating conclusions.

18. Marlene recognized that some children in her 8th grade biology class are able to recite definitions but lack conceptual understanding of the course content she teaches. She decides to investigate the nature of her students' understanding with the intent to modify instruction as needed. Marlene is best illustrating

    a.   action research.
    b.   experimental research.
    c.   basic research.
    d.   deductive reasoning.

19. The local library conducts a summer reading program. This summer they have included a visiting author in the program. There has been some concern about the cost of the program, especially because both the PTA and the nearby university include a visiting author program during the academic year. Marcus, the librarian, has decided to collect data from program participants this summer in order to make a decision about whether to include the author program again next year. Marcus is engaging in which of the following types of research?

    a.   basic
    b.   experimental
    c.   evaluation
    d.   narrative

20. As a coach, Chris knows that all soccer players need strength training. Garrett is a soccer player, so Chris concludes that he is in need of strength training. Which type of reasoning is Chris displaying?

    a.   deductive
    b.   inductive
    c.   scientific and disciplined inquiry
    d.   reliance on tradition

21.-24. Rosita remembers that her college Educational Psychology professor mentioned that a strong relationship existed between the use of building toys in young children and later advanced mathematics and science achievement scores. During class, Rosita's interest was piqued so she has decided to pursue this topic for her Honor's thesis.

21. The other students in the class are not conducting further research on the topic but are taking the Educational Psychology professor's statement as true. These students are demonstrating which of the following ways of knowing.

    a.   Tradition
    b.   Expert authority
    c.   Scientific Method
    d.   Reasoning

22. In her study Rosita will rely on more than one type of data source. She will examine students advanced science and math standardized scores. She also will conduct a survey that asks high school students' parents to give a rating as to whether and how much their child played with certain toys. The study that Rosita is conducting is best characterized as

    a. applied
    b. basic
    c. evaluation
    d. research and development

23. The study as described above is best characterized as a(n)

    a. causal-comparative study.
    b. narrative study.
    c. experimental study.
    d. correlational study.

Companion Website

For more practice on becoming competent in this chapter's objectives, go to the Companion Website that accompanies this text at www.prenhall.com/gay. This site includes:

Objectives with links to:
- more multiple-choice questions in Practice Quiz
- Applying What You Know essay questions
- relevant Web sites

Custom modules to help you:
- calculate statistical tests (see "Calculating Statistical Tests")
- do research (see "Research Tools and Tips")
- practice analyzing quantitative data (see "Analyzing Quantitative Data")
- practice analyzing qualitative data (see "Analyzing Qualitative Data")
- practice evaluating published articles (see "Evaluating Articles")

Early Childhood Research Quarterly, 15, No. 4, 537–558 (2000)
ISSN: 0885-2006

© 2001 Elsevier Science Inc.
All rights of reproduction in any form reserved.

Parents' and Teachers' Beliefs About Children's School Readiness in a High-Need Community

Chaya S. Piotrkowski,
Fordham University

Michael Botsko,
Columbia University

Eunice Matthews
Eastern Connecticut State University

This study compared the beliefs of preschool teachers, kindergarten teachers, and parents in one mostly Hispanic and Black high-need urban school district to learn their views of what children should know and be able to do at kindergarten entry. Beliefs regarding the importance of 12 school readiness "resources" were assessed with the *CARES* survey designed for this study. Parents held remarkably similar beliefs, regardless of ethnicity or education. Parents and teachers also agreed that children must be healthy and socially competent, and be able to comply with teacher authority, although parents rated this latter resource higher. However, parents rated all classroom-related readiness resources as more important than teachers did. They believed it was necessary for a child to be able to communicate in English and to have basic knowledge and skills, which was more important than a child's approach to learning. Preschool teachers also believed that knowledge was more important than kindergarten teachers did. Directions for further research and implications for policy and practice are discussed.

Children living in poverty are at heightened risk for school failure, which has serious and long-lasting consequences. There is mounting evidence that school problems begin as early as kindergarten and first grade (Alexander & Entwisle, 1988; Lewitt & Baker, 1995; Luster & McAdoo, 1996). To address this problem, Goal 1 of the Educate America Act of 1993 states that "by the year 2000 all children in America will start school ready to learn" (US Department of Educa-

Direct all correspondence to: Chaya S. Piotrkowski, Fordham University, Graduate School of Social Service, 113 W. 60th Street, New York, NY 10023 <Piotrkowski@fordham.edu>.

537

Piotrowski, C. S., Botsko, M., & Matthews, E. (2001). *Early Childhood Research Quarterly, 15,* pp. 537-558, Copyright © 2001 by Elsevier Science, Ltd. Reprinted with permission.

538   **Piotrkowski, Botsko, and Matthews**

tion, 1993). In other words, to prevent school failure, communities need to facilitate children's school readiness.

Although universal school readiness has been embraced as a national education goal, the concept of children's "school readiness" remains highly controversial. It has been criticized for being thought of as a static attribute of children; for ignoring individual differences, inequities in children's experiences and opportunities, and the responsibility of schools to teach all children appropriately; for the downward shift of academic expectations to increasingly younger children; and for measurement-driven instruction, nonvalid testing, and an almost exclusive focus on cognitive/intellectual skills to the neglect of other competencies (e.g., May & Kundert, 1992; Meisels, 1992; National Association for the Education of Young Children, 1990; Shepard & Smith, 1986; Willer & Bredekamp, 1990). Not surprisingly then, the National Education Goals Panel Technical Planning Group for Goal 1 has tried to avoid the term "readiness" altogether (Kagan, Moore, & Bredekamp, 1995).

While experts debate the concept of school readiness, day-to-day decisions about how to prepare children for school are being made at the local level, for conceptions of school readiness are—in part—locally constituted (Graue, 1992; Smith & Shepard, 1988). Whether or not the term "school readiness" is used, helping young children be prepared for initial success in school is an extraordinarily important challenge that is especially pressing in high-need communities. Parents and preschool teachers struggle with this difficult problem, with little or no input from kindergarten teachers (Love, 1992). Absent generally accepted and empirically documented criteria of what young children should know and be able to do when they are 4 or 5 years old (Bredekamp, 1992), parents and preschool teachers must rely on their explicit and implicit *beliefs* regarding readiness as they prepare children for school.

Beliefs about School Readiness

Parents, preschool teachers, and kindergarten teachers share responsibility for the education of young children. Yet few studies have systematically compared their beliefs about what children should know and be able to do at school entry (Gredler, 1992; Lewitt & Baker, 1995). Beliefs influence child rearing (Okagaki & Sternberg, 1993; Segal, 1985; Stevenson et al., 1990) and educational practices (Bacon & Ichikawa, 1988; Fang, 1996; Farver, Kim, & Lee, 1995; Harvey, White, Rather, Alter, & Hoffmeister, 1966; Smith & Shepard, 1988; Vartuli, 1999). Without a shared vision of children's readiness, preschool teachers and parents may not encourage in children the skills, attitudes, and attributes that kindergarten teachers look for (Hains, Fowler, Schwartz, Kottwitz, & Rosenkoetter, 1989; West, Hausken, & Collins, 1993). When readiness expectations differ substantially, kindergarten teachers might view some children as "unready" and treat them differently (West et al., 1993). Teachers' views are particularly important because their early assessments of young children's readiness play an important role in special education placement, ability grouping, grade retention (e.g., Entwisle, 1995; Gredler, 1992; Powell, 1995; Rist, 1970; Shepard & Smith, 1986) and in shaping children's subsequent achievement trajectories (Alexander & Entwisle, 1988). Inconsistencies in what is expected also might confuse children, causing stress and maladaptive behaviors at kindergarten entry. Given the possible harms resulting from lack of clarity about what children are expected to know and do at kindergarten entry, it is important to learn more about the readiness beliefs of parents, preschool, and kindergarten teachers in high-need communities, where children are at increased risk of school failure.

The few studies examining parents' and teachers' readiness beliefs suggest that some substantial inconsistencies exist. Two studies comparing the readiness views of parents and kindergarten teachers found that parents emphasize academic-oriented skills more than teachers (Knudsen–Lindauer & Harris, 1989; West et al.,1993). Two studies compared the views of preschool and kindergarten teachers. One study found various differences in behavioral expectations (Foulks & Morrow, 1989), while the other study found that preschool teachers had greater expectations, both academic and behavioral (Hains et al., 1989). An important limitation of these two latter studies is that no statistical analyses of data were reported, leaving open questions of generalizability and reliability of findings. No studies have compared the beliefs of parents and preschool teachers, but Harradine and Clifford (1996) did compare childcare providers (including preschool teachers), parents of preschoolers, and kindergarten teachers. They found the groups had different concerns. For example, kindergarten teachers were more likely to emphasize a child's ability to not disrupt the class; families and providers emphasized school-like skills such as knowing English, knowing the letters of the alphabet, and counting; while childcare providers were most likely to emphasize problem-solving skills.

Current research is limited in helping us understand readiness beliefs in high-need communities, where children's school failure is a critical issue. Existing studies have aggregated data across socioeconomically diverse communities, so that we lack information regarding the readiness beliefs of parents and teachers *within* low-income communities (Holloway, Rambaud, Fuller, & Eggers–Pierola, 1995). Studies have not systematically examined ethnic variations in parents' views of children's readiness (Farver et al., 1995; Heaviside & Farris, 1993; Stevenson, Chen, & Uttal, 1990). Moreover, few studies have systematically examined beliefs regarding the multiple dimensions of children's school readiness, relying instead on lists of readiness characteristics. Finally, some studies used forced rankings, which may under- or overestimate beliefs about the importance of readiness characteristics.

The Present Study

The study reported here addresses these limitations. It examines consistencies and inconsistencies in parents', preschool teachers', and kindergarten teachers' beliefs about the multiple dimensions of children's readiness in one high-need urban school district in New York State. This city is similar to other urban centers in having large numbers of young children who live in poverty and disturbingly high rates of school drop-out, grade retention, and special education placement.

This study reports the first phase of a larger study examining the transition to kindergarten.

CONCEPTUALIZING CHILDREN'S SCHOOL READINESS

Despite its negative connotations, the term "school readiness" can be a useful concept if (a) it is not treated as a static attribute of children; (b) it incorporates the multiple aspects of children's functioning that are important for school success; and (c) it takes into account the joint responsibilities that families, communities, and schools have in providing caring environments that promote children's learning (Piotrkowski, in press). Piotrkowski conceptualizes school readiness as the social, political, organizational, educational, and personal *resources* that support children's success at school entry. At the neighborhood level, school readiness resources include affordable, high quality child care and preschool for all; well-stocked libraries that are welcoming to children and parents; safe playgrounds and streets, and so forth. Local school readiness resources include strong, accountable leadership; transition programming and parent involvement activities; on-going professional development and support for teachers; high quality, individualized instruction, and so forth (Shore, 1998). Family readiness resources include a rich literacy environment, nurturing parenting, financial resources, and social support for child rearing. Ideally, these resources are integrated to facilitate the optimal development of each child.

For the individual child, school readiness refers to the *personal readiness resources* (human capital) a child may bring to school to help him or her adapt successfully to the challenges of kindergarten. The Technical Planning Group for Goal 1 of the National Education Goals Panel identified five dimensions of children's readiness resources: physical well-being and motor development; social and emotional development; approaches to learning; language use; and cognition and general knowledge (Kagan et al., 1995). Building on this view, Piotrkowski (in press) has conceptualized a child's personal readiness resources as potentially consisting of: health and the age-appropriate ability to care for self; the ability to regulate emotion and behavior, interact appropriately with adults and children, and communicate needs and feelings effectively; an interest and engagement in the world around him or her, to motivate learning; motor skills; cognitive knowledge; and the ability to adjust to the demands of the kindergarten classroom setting. Thus, readiness resources consist not only of motor and cognitive skills and knowledge, but also social competencies (Raver & Zigler, 1997). Children use these more or less malleable resources to profit from the kindergarten experience, and meet societal expectations of competence there.

Graue (1992) and others have noted that beliefs about school readiness are locally-determined. But such beliefs are not mere social constructions. Rather, Piotrkowski (in press) proposes that beliefs vary systematically with local community, school, and family readiness resources. In high-need communities, where family and school readiness resources are limited, children's readiness resources may be viewed as especially critical, in order to compensate for resource-poor families and schools. Thus, children in these communities may be expected to have more extensive and concrete readiness resources at school entry than children in more affluent families and communities. Consistent with this view, kindergarten teachers in high-poverty and minority communities have higher expectations of children entering kindergarten than teachers in more affluent and majority communities (Heaviside & Farris, 1993). Ironically, those children who may be most in need of a wide array of personal readiness resources are also least likely to have them.

METHOD

Sampling

The community for the study was defined by the physical boundaries of a densely populated urban school district, covering about one square mile. The district was selected because almost 90% of elementary school students were eligible for federally funded free lunches, and it has large populations of Black and Hispanic families. Here, the term "Hispanic" is used for "those individuals. . . who were born in or trace the background of their families to one of the Spanish-speaking Latin American nations or to Spain" (Marin & Marin, 1991, p.1). Academically, the school district has significant problems, not unlike other school districts in low-income areas. Less than one year after data were collected, only 39% of children in Grade 3 scored at or above grade level on a city-wide reading test. The study population consisted of all parents[1] of children born in 1993 or 1994 attending community-based preschools in the district and their preschool teachers; all parents of preschoolers in two elementary schools in the district; and all kindergarten and preschool teachers in the district public schools.

Twenty-six out of 34 community-based preschool sites in the district agreed to distribute a parent survey from June through August of 1998. A "site" was defined as a physically distinct preschool setting serving 4-year-olds. Several sites could be under the auspices of a single agency. Directors or their designates distributed the surveys in English or Spanish to all parents of children who were in preschool classrooms with a substantial proportion of children eligible for kindergarten in the Fall of 1998. Directors and principals indicated that parents with limited literacy would be assisted to complete the surveys, but the extent to which this type of help was offered is unknown. To represent the views of preschool parents in the public schools, two public schools that had 50% of the prekindergarten classes in the district also were invited to distribute the surveys to parents. In June, the principal or assistant principal distributed parent surveys in Spanish or English to all 120 parents with enrolled children. Because data were gathered just one week before classes ended for the summer, we were unable to seek the participation of more public school prekindergartens or to do follow-up mailings with these parents. Parents returned surveys to school personnel in sealed envelopes; research staff picked up the sealed surveys.

Thirty-two preschool sites agreed to distribute surveys to preschool teachers of classes with four-year-olds. (At the request of Directors, surveys also were distributed to assistant teachers and classroom aides.) In addition, surveys were distributed by principals or through a one-time summer mailing to all 12 prekindergarten teachers in the public schools. From mid-June through December of 1998, surveys were distributed by principals or through a summer mailing to all kindergarten teachers in the 22 elementary school programs in the school district. Teachers returned surveys by mail.

With the exception of the public school prekindergarten sites, intensive follow-up procedures were used that included repeated visits by research staff to community-based preschools, multiple mailings to kindergarten teachers, and incentives (cash raffle prizes and children's books for the classrooms). Surveys were returned by 461 parents[2] in the sampling frame, representing 25 community-based preschools and two public schools. Their estimated response rate was 49%. Forty-six preschool teachers in 26 community-based preschools in the district returned surveys, a response rate of 73%. In the public schools, 6 out of 12 prekindergarten teachers returned surveys, a response rate of 50%. Of the 64 kindergarten teachers in the sampling frame, 57 teachers in 21 schools returned surveys, a response rate of 89%.

Measuring School Readiness Beliefs

When this study was conducted, no measure of school readiness beliefs was available that was appropriate for both teachers and parents with limited education and that tapped the range of school readiness resources children may bring to school. Therefore, the survey of *Community Attitudes on Readiness for Entering School (CARES)* was developed for the study. Beliefs about the importance of the following readiness resources were assessed: health; basic self-care; socioemotional maturity and self-regulation; interaction with peers; interest and engagement in the world; motor skills; cognitive knowledge; communication; and adjustment to the classroom setting, that is, complying with teacher directions and classroom routines. These were based on the five dimensions of school readiness identified by the National Education Goals Technical Planning Group for Goal 1 (Kagan et al., 1995), the conceptualization of school readiness as resources (Piotrkowski, in press), and a review of the literature.

Because specific indicators of these readiness resources have not been agreed upon (Bredekamp, 1992), behaviorally-anchored items were adapted from existing surveys that tapped school readiness beliefs or parents' and teachers' educational goals for young children (Freeman & Hatch, 1989; Hains et al., 1989; Harradine & Clifford, 1996; Heaviside & Farris, 1993; Johnson, Gallagher, Cook, & Wong, 1995; Knudsen-Lindauer & Harris, 1989; Okagaki & Sternberg, 1993; Stevenson et al., 1990). Included were some items that might be considered "developmentally inappropriate" to capture a broad range of readiness expectations (Hains et al., 1989). Items were reworded and simplified so parents with limited education could understand them. To refine items and the survey format, three focus groups were conducted with English-speaking Hispanic and Black parents. Drafts of the survey also were reviewed by preschool directors and

Beliefs About Children's School Readiness   **543**

teachers, Head Start education directors, special education staff, a reading specialist, and an administrator who had been a prekindergarten teacher in a public school in the district.

"Back-translation" was used with a draft version of the English instrument to create a Spanish version, followed by a "decentering" procedure (Marin & Marin, 1991) to make the English and Spanish versions comparable. In this latter approach, the English version is revised when the resulting translation results in confusing or awkward language. "Committees" composed of bicultural/bilingual staff and educators resolved differences of opinion.

The resulting *CARES* survey had 46 items on one page, grouped into seven sections with 4 to 8 items each. Respondents were asked: *"Think about a child who will BEGIN kindergarten in the fall. For each item below, enter one number to indicate how IMPORTANT or NECESSARY it is for a child starting kindergarten."* Respondents rated each item on a 4-point Likert-type scale as: not too important (1), somewhat important (2), very important, but not essential (3), and absolutely necessary (4). This response format was used to avoid the tendency of some parents in the focus groups to rate almost every item as "very important." The *CARES* also includes questions about respondent background characteristics. The survey takes less than 20 minutes to complete.

Assessing the Equivalence of the Spanish and English CARES   Marin and Marin (1991) suggest that Hispanic survey respondents may give more extreme responses and socially desirable answers and have more missing data than Whites. Moreover, the internal structure of an instrument may change when translated into Spanish, so that item meanings are not equivalent. Therefore, analyses were conducted to determine whether the Spanish and English versions of the *CARES* were equivalent. For these analyses, the data from parents in the school district were augmented by data from parents with 3- and 5-year-old preschoolers and from parents with children at a preschool site just outside the district ($N = 515$).

Analyses indicated that the language of the *CARES* was not significantly related to number of missing items, but that language was significantly related to response style. Those completing the Spanish version of the *CARES* ($n = 110$) were significantly more likely to use check marks ($n = 15$) rather than the four-point Likert scale (χ^2 (1, $N = 515$) $= 27.57$, $p = .0001$). Because those who used checks were more likely to have a ninth grade education or less (χ^2 (2, $N = 502$) $= 15.83$, $p = .0001$), the use of checks probably reflected a lack of familiarity with the four-point response format. Excluding those who used check marks, parents completing the Spanish *CARES* also were significantly less likely to endorse "4" (absolutely necessary) as a response (F (1,482) $= 4.28$, $p = .04$) and were significantly more likely to endorse "1" (not very important) as a response (F (1, 482) $= 68.40$, $p = .0001$).

Unfortunately, the limited item-to-respondent ratio for the Spanish *CARES* (46 items to 110 respondents) was insufficient to conduct a reliable factor analysis to determine if items have "equivalent meaning across ethnic groups" (Marin & Marin, 1991). Therefore, hierarchical regression was used to determine the impact of language of *CARES* on average ratings across all 46 items, controlling for background characteristics. The null hypothesis tested was that the language of the survey had no effect on parents' ratings, once background characteristics were controlled. Only Hispanic respondents were included in this analysis to allow us to focus on the language of the survey, while controlling for ethnicity. Those who used check marks as responses were excluded.

In step one of the regression model, age of respondent, educational attainment, acculturation as indicated by language used at home (Spanish/English/Spanish and English), income (indicated by a child's enrollment in Head Start), whether respondent was employed (yes/no), and whether respondent lived with a partner/spouse (yes/no) were entered as controls. In step two, language of the *CARES* (English or Spanish) was entered. The full regression model was statistically significant ($F (7, 205) = 49.70$, $p = .0001$), and the increment in R^2 when language of the *CARES* was entered was highly significant ($p = .0001$), accounting for an additional 18% of the variance in readiness beliefs, beyond the background variables. Therefore, the null hypothesis that the language of the *CARES* had no effect on responses could not be rejected, and those who used check marks or completed the Spanish version of the *CARES* were excluded from further analysis. Thus, only Hispanic parents who were able to read English were retained in the final sample. Excluded parents were poorer, less educated, less likely to be employed, and more likely to speak only Spanish at home than Hispanic respondents who completed the survey in English. This sample bias must be taken into account when interpreting findings.

Factor Analysis of the CARES   Exploratory factor analyses of the *CARES* (principal axis factor analysis with varimax rotation) were conducted separately for parents and teaching staff. To increase sample size, data from parents in the sample were augmented by data from parents with 3- and 5-year-old preschoolers, and from parents with preschoolers at a site just outside the district. Only parents who completed the English version of the *CARES* were included ($N = 397$). Data from 109 preschool and kindergarten teachers in the school district were augmented by data from teachers in two nearby public schools and the preschool outside the school district ($N = 152$). In the parent sample, 8 factors accounted for 57.3% of the variance. In the teaching sample, 10 factors accounted for 64.1% of the variance. This latter factor analysis must be treated cautiously because of the low respondent-to-item ratio (46 items to 152 respondents).

Results of both factor analyses were used to create eight multi-item subscales reflecting beliefs about children's school readiness resources.[3] These eight subscales approximated the *a priori* conceptualization and tapped beliefs regarding the importance of: Advanced Knowledge (10 items), Basic Knowledge (5 items), Compliance with Teacher Authority (3 items), Self-care (4 items), Emotional Maturity (5 items), Interest and Engagement to reflect approaches to learning (6 items), Compliance with Classroom Routines (5 items), and Motor Skills (3 items). No item was included in more than one subscale. For the parent sample, alpha coefficients for the subscales ranged from 0.74 to 0.90. For the teaching sample, alpha coefficients ranged from 0.77 to 0.92.

Four single items did not meet the criteria for inclusion in any subscale, but were retained because they tapped important readiness resources: Health ("Is rested and well-nourished. Health care needs are met"); Peer Relations ("Plays well with other children. Shares"); Communicates in Own Language ("Can Express feelings/needs in primary language"); Communicates in English (Can Express feelings/needs in English"). A fifth item ("Is interested in books and stories") was dropped from further analysis. Thus, the final *CARES* survey had 45 items that tapped beliefs about 12 school readiness resources children may have.

RESULTS

Sample Characteristics

The final sample of parents for data analysis consisted of the 355 parents of children born in 1994 or 1993 in the school district, who completed an English version of the *CARES* survey. (Children born in 1993 were eligible for kindergarten the coming fall.) Background characteristics of the parents are presented in Table 1. Most (91%) were parents; the others were guardians or foster parents. Only 8% were male. Over half (53%) were employed and 46% reported receiving government assistance. Most respondents spoke only English at home, but 10% spoke Spanish, 16% spoke both English and Spanish, and 2% spoke some other language.

Background characteristics of the teachers also are presented in Table 1. All kindergartens were full day classes. About 24% of the kindergarten teachers taught bilingual classes, 7% taught gifted and talented classes, and 7% taught special education or inclusion classes. Preschool teachers were significantly older, had more teaching experience, and were more likely to be members of ethnic minority groups than kindergarten teachers.

Beliefs about Children's School Readiness Resources

To simplify the analyses, an *a priori* conceptualization was used to divide the 12 beliefs about children's school readiness resources into two separate domains. Included in the first domain were beliefs regarding *General Readiness Resources* a child may have that pertain to a child's everyday life: Health, Peer Relations, Communicates in Own Language; Emotional Maturity; Self-care; Interest and Engagement; and Motor Skills. Table 2 presents the items within each subscale, as well as the percentage of respondents rating individual items in this domain as "absolutely necessary" for children starting kindergarten.

The second domain represents beliefs regarding the personal *Classroom-related Readiness Resources* a child may have that are especially pertinent to the classroom setting: Communicates in English; Compliance with Teacher Authority; Compliance with Classroom Routines; Basic Knowledge; and Advanced Knowledge. Table 3 presents the items within each subscale, as well as the percentage of respondents rating individual items in this domain as "absolutely necessary" for children starting kindergarten.

546   **Piotrkowski, Botsko, and Matthews**

Table 1. Demographic Characteristics of Parents, Preschool Teachers and Kindergarten Teachers

	Parents		Preschool Teachers		Kindergarten Teachers	
	N	(%)	N	(%)	N	(%)
Site						
Public elementary school	50	(14)	6	(12)	57	(100)
Head start	129	(36)	22	(42)	—	—
Head start collaboration	61	(17)	4	(8)	—	—
Religious-affiliated preschool	15	(4)	4	(8)	—	—
Other community-based preschool	100	(28)	16	(31)	—	—
Age (median)	29		40		35	
Sex						
Female	327	(92)	50	(96)	56	(98)
Male	28	(8)	2	(4)	1	(2)
Education						
Less than high school	96	(28)	0	(0)	0	(0)
High school diploma or GED	100	(29)	0	(0)	0	(0)
Some college, Assoc. Degree, or special training	137	(39)	5	(11)	0	(0)
4-year college degree	12	(3)	10	(21)	5	(9)
Some credits towards Masters	Not Asked		12	(26)	8	(14)
MA or MS degree	3	(1)	20	(43)	43	(77)
Ethnicity						
Hispanic (not Black)	152	(44)	14	(29)	20	(36)
Black (not Hispanic)	171	(49)	17	(35)	5	(9)
White	3	(1)	9	(19)	26	(47)
Other	20	(6)	8	(17)	4	(7)

Note: Percentages may not sum to 100% because of rounding.

Are There Differences among Parents?

We first determined if readiness beliefs varied by parental education (less than high school/high school diploma or equivalency/more than high school), ethnicity (Black/Hispanic), and age of preschool child (1993 vs. 1994 birth). Multivariate analyses of variance (MANOVA) were conducted separately for the General and the Classroom-related Readiness Resources. MANOVA accounts for the number of tests performed when assessing group differences across multiple dependent variables, so that the possibility of finding groups differences when none exist (Type I error) is reduced. Results of one-way analyses of variance (ANOVA) are reported where the MANOVA was significant (alpha = 0.05), along with Cohen's *d* (Cohen, 1988) to estimate effect sizes, using the POWPAL program (Gorman, Primavera, & Allison, 1995).

Neither MANOVA for educational attainment was statistically significant, indicating that parental education was unrelated to views about readiness in this sample. In the comparisons of Hispanic and Black parents, only the MANOVA

Beliefs About Children's School Readiness   **547**

Table 2.   General Readiness Resources: Percentage of Respondents Endorsing an Item as Absolutely Necessary

General Readiness Resources	Parents $N = 355$	Preschool Teachers $N = 52$	Kindergarten Teachers $N = 57$
1. Health			
Is rested and well-nourished. Health care needs are met.	87	83	96
2. Peer Relations			
Plays well with other children. Shares.	76	58	68
3. Communicates in Own Language			
Can express feelings/needs in primary language.	74	65	65
4. Emotional Maturity			
Does not hit/bite. Has self-control.	84	67	89
Has sense of right and wrong.	77	51	68
Is self-confident. Proud of his/her work.	74	64	53
Takes turns.	62	56	53
Shows independence.	60	58	42
5. Self-Care			
Feeds self with fork.	74	67	86
Buttons own clothes.	64	39	35
Finds own belongings.	64	54	65
Zips own jacket.	55	35	35
6. Interest & Engagement			
Asks lots of questions about how and why.	59	39	33
Is curious.	55	41	49
Is interested in world around him/her.	55	49	46
Starts things on his/her own.	43	49	28
Is eager to learn.	77	67	73
Likes to solve puzzles.	29	37	20
7. Motor Skills			
Can hold pencil. Can use a scissors.	58	44	33
Throws ball, skips, runs, hops, walks up/down stairs.	51	42	25
Stacks 5–6 blocks by him/herself.	47	37	18

for General Readiness Resources was statistically significant (Wilks's lambda = 0.92, $F = 3.31$ (7, 280), $p = .002$). Hispanic parents placed slightly more importance on a child being able to communicate needs and feelings in his or her own language (F (1, 286) = 7.69, $p = .006$, $d = 0.33$) and being emotionally mature (F (1,286) = 5.97, $p = .015$, $d = 0.29$) and somewhat stronger emphasis on children being interested and engaged (F (1, 286) = 17.34, $p = .0001$, $d = 0.49$). Similarly, when comparing parents by age of child, only the MANOVA for General Readiness was significant (Wilks's lambda = 0.93, F (7, 284) = 2.92, $p = .006$). Not surprisingly, parents of older children rated Motor Skills as slightly more important than parents of younger children (F (1, 290) = 5.93, $p = .015$, $d = 0.29$). Because there were few meaningful substantive differences in beliefs

Table 3.   Classroom-related Readiness Resources: Percentage of Respondents Endorsing an Item as "Absolutely Necessary" for Kindergarten

Classroom-related Readiness Resources	Parents N = 355	Preschool Teachers N = 52	Kindergarten Teachers N = 57
1. Communicates in English			
Can express feelings/needs in English.	71	33	28
2. Compliance with Teacher Authority.			
Pays attention to teacher.	89	79	74
Follows the teacher's directions.	87	59	70
Listens during group discussions/stories.	77	62	75
3. Basic Knowledge			
Knows names of body parts (eyes/nose/legs).	87	62	38
Knows ABCs.	82	33	19
Knows basic colors like "red, blue, yellow."	81	58	40
Can count to 10 or 15.	76	48	25
Understands big/small. Sorts by color/size.	65	39	21
4. Compliance with Classroom Routines			
Uses classroom equipment correctly.	62	41	30
Cleans up work space and spills.	61	37	30
Lines up and stays in line. Waits quietly.	60	29	30
Moves from one activity to the next with no problems.	55	46	42
Completes tasks on time.	42	14	21
5. Advanced Knowledge			
Knows own address/telephone.	70	42	19
Writes first name, even if some letters are backwards.	59	29	28
Understands yesterday/today/tomorrow.	49	19	9
Knows days of week in correct order.	44	17	5
Cuts simple shapes with scissors.	46	31	19
Recognizes words that rhyme like "cat, hat."	40	14	2
Can read a few simple words.	40	14	4
Can read simple stories.	30	8	4
Can count to 50 or more.	20	2	2
Can write on a line. Can color inside lines.	29	10	2

about children's school readiness resources, parents were treated as a single group for subsequent analyses.

Parents and Teachers' Beliefs about General Readiness Resources

Analyses were conducted separately for General and for School-related Readiness Resources. Within-group MANOVAs for the seven General Readiness Resources were statistically significant ($p < .05$), indicating that parents, preschool, and kindergarten teachers rated some resources as being relatively more important than others. Next, the parallelism procedure within profile analysis was

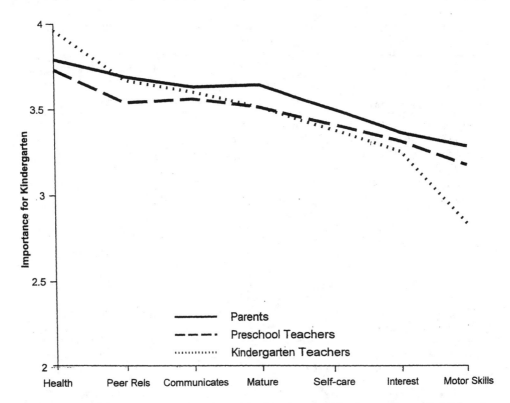

Figure 1. **Profiles of parents' and teachers' ratings of the importance of children's General Readiness Resources, where 4 represents "absolutely necessary," 3 represents "very important, but not essential," and 2 represents "somewhat important."**

used to determine if parents and teachers agreed on the *relative* rankings of the seven General Readiness Resources (Bray & Maxwell, 1985). Profile analysis refers to a series of multivariate tests to determine whether groups have the same pattern of response within and across all dependent variables. The parallelism procedure tests the null hypothesis that the mean distances between any dependent variables are equivalent for all groups.

Group profiles are presented in Figure 1. Without Motor Skills, the profiles are parallel (nonsignificant MANOVA), indicating the groups gave similar rankings to six of the General Readiness Resources. When Motor Skills was added to the model, the MANOVA achieved significance (Wilks's lambda = 0.92, F (12, 834) = 2.88, p = .001), indicating that the profiles diverge when that resource is entered into the model. Even when profiles are parallel, groups may differ in their absolute ratings of readiness resources. The MANOVA to test for such group differences was statistically significant (Wilks's lambda = 0.92, F (14, 832) = 2.63, p = .001).

Results of the follow-up ANOVAs (presented in Table 4, along with group means, standard deviations, and Cohen's d) and post hoc comparisons (Tukey's

Table 4. Analysis of Variance for Beliefs Regarding Children's General Readiness Resources

General Readiness Resources	Parents		Preschool Teachers		Kindergarten Teachers	
	M	SD	M	SD	M	SD
1. Health (1 item)	3.79	.62	3.73	.66	3.96	.19
F (2, 449) = 2.64 (d = .22)						
2. Peer Relations (1 item)	3.69	.61	3.54	.58	3.67	.51
F (2, 453) = 1.45 (d = .16)						
3. Communicates in Own Language (1 item)	3.63	.71	3.56	.70	3.60	.59
F (2, 449) = .30 (d = .07)						
4. Emotional Maturity (5 items)	3.64	.49	3.51	.46	3.51	.47
F (2, 444) = 2.87 (d = .23)						
Self-care (4 items)	3.50	.63	3.41	.49	3.38	.58
F (2, 453) = 1.37 (d = .16)						
6. Interest and Engagement (6 items)	3.36	.58	3.31	.62	3.25	.53
F (2, 450) = .96 (d = .13)						
7. Motor Skills (3 items)	3.28$_a$	.70	3.17$_a$	.70	2.83	.71
F (2, 447) = 10.28*** (d = .43)						

Notes: Means in the same row having the same subscript are not significantly different at $p < .05$ in the Tukey honestly significant difference comparison.
***$p < .001$

HSD, $p < .05$) revealed only one moderate group difference: kindergarten teachers rated Motor Skills as less important than parents and preschool teachers did. Otherwise, parents and teachers agreed that health and social competencies such as playing well with other children, communicating needs and feelings in their own language, and emotional maturity, were "absolutely necessary" (mean ratings of 3.5 or higher). They assigned lesser importance to self-care, being interested and engaged, and motor skills. These findings are consistent with the results presented in Figure 1.

Parents and Teachers' Beliefs about Classroom-related Readiness Resources

The same analyses were conducted for beliefs regarding the five personal Classroom-related Readiness Resources. Again, the within-group MANOVAs were statistically significant ($p < .05$), indicating that parents and teachers differentiated among the readiness resources. The parallelism test for the Classroom-related Readiness Resources was statistically significant (Wilks's lambda = 0.70, F (8, 870) = 20.93, $p = .0001$), indicating that the groups' relative ratings were different, as can be seen in the group profiles presented Figure 2. Further profile analyses indicated that the relative rankings of parents, preschool and kindergarten teachers all differed significantly from each other. The MANOVA to assess differences in absolute importance ratings also was statistically significant

Beliefs About Children's School Readiness   551

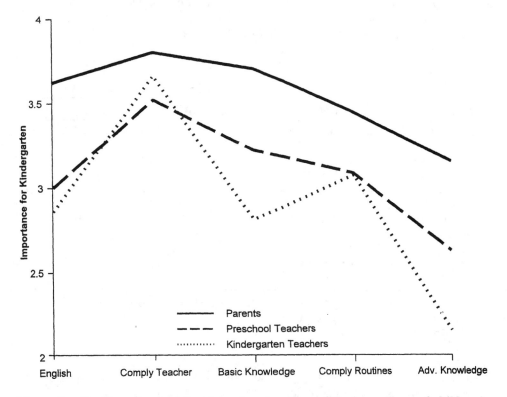

Figure 2. **Profiles of parents' and teachers' ratings of the importance of children's Classroom-related Readiness Resources, where 4 represents "absolutely necessary," 3 represents "very important, but not essential," and 2 represents "somewhat important."**

(Wilks's lambda $= 0.64$, $F(10, 868) = 21.58$, $p = .0001$). Results of the one-way ANOVAs (presented in Table 5, along with group means, standard deviations, and Cohen's d) indicate there were significant group differences for *all* five Classroom-related Readiness Resources.

All groups rated Compliance with Teacher Authority as "absolutely necessary" (mean ratings of 3.5 or higher), but the post hoc comparison (Tukey HSD, $p < .05$) revealed that parents tended to assign more importance than teachers to this resource. No group rated Compliance with Classroom Routines as "absolutely necessary," but post hoc comparisons revealed that parents rated this resource as somewhat more important than preschool and kindergarten teachers.

Three particularly large group differences, however, were identified ($d > 0.80$, Cohen, 1988). Seven out of 10 parents—Hispanic and Black alike—believed it was "absolutely necessary" for children to be able to express their feelings and needs in English. Further, a within-group ANOVA revealed no significant differences among Hispanic parents by language spoken at home (English/English and Spanish/Spanish). Post hoc comparisons indicated that teachers did not agree with

Piotrkowski, Botsko, and Matthews

Table 5.   Analysis of Variance for Beliefs Regarding Children's Classroom-related Readiness Resources

Classroom-related Readiness Resources	Parents		Preschool Teachers		Kindergarten Teachers	
	M	SD	M	SD	M	SD
1. Communicates in English (1 item) $F\ (2,\ 451) = 37.97^{***}\ (d = .82)$	3.62	.65	3.00_a	.91	2.86_a	.97
2. Compliance with Teacher Authority (3 items) $F\ (2,\ 448) = 8.55^{***}\ (d = .39)$	3.80_b	.46	3.52_a	.64	$3.66_{a,b}$	.54
3. Basic Knowledge (5 items) $F\ (2,\ 448) = 64.85^{***}\ (d = 1.08)$	3.70	.51	3.22	.70	2.81	.84
4. Compliance with Classroom Routines (5 items) $F\ (2,\ 443) = 16.87^{***}\ (d = .55)$	3.44	.55	3.08_a	.66	3.07_a	.62
5. Advanced Knowledge (10 items) $F\ (2,\ 437) = 71.14^{***}\ (d = 1.14)$	3.15	.61	2.62	.70	2.15	.67

Notes: Means in the same row having the same subscript are not significantly different at $p < .05$ in the Tukey honestly significant difference comparison.
$^{***}p < .001$.

parents; only about 3 out of 10 preschool and kindergarten teachers thought this resource was "absolutely necessary" (see Table 3).

Second, parents also believed that Basic Knowledge, such as knowing basic body parts, some colors, and the alphabet, was "absolutely necessary" at kindergarten entry. Again, post hoc comparisons revealed that teachers gave significantly lower ratings to this resource. Teachers disagreed with each other as well, with preschool teachers rating Basic Knowledge as significantly more important than kindergarten teachers did. For example, 76% of parents, 48% of preschool teachers, and only 25% of kindergarten teachers believed it was absolutely necessary that children be able to count to 10 or 15 when they entered kindergarten (see Table 3).

Finally, post hoc comparisons revealed similar differences with regard to Advanced Knowledge. Although this resource received the lowest mean ratings from all three groups, they disagreed on how important it was. Parents placed greater importance on children having Advanced Knowledge than teachers did, and preschool teachers believed that Advanced Knowledge was more important than kindergarten teachers did. For example, 70% of parents believed it was "absolutely necessary" for children to know their own address and telephone number, compared to 42% of preschool teachers, and 19% of kindergarten teachers (see Table 3).

Knowledge Versus Approaches to Learning

Many educators believe that curiosity and similar "approaches to learning" are especially important for learning (National Task Force on School Readiness,

1991). Therefore, paired t tests were used to compare each group's rating of Interest and Engagement to their ratings of Basic and Advanced Knowledge. All groups viewed Interest and Engagement as substantially more important than Advanced Knowledge ($p = .001$, $d > 0.80$). However, only kindergarten teachers believed Interest and Engagement to be substantially more important than Basic Knowledge ($t (55) = -4.44$, $p = .001$, $d = 1.97$). Parents rated Basic Knowledge as substantially more important than Interest and Engagement ($t (338) = 11.93$, $p = .0001$, $d = 1.30$), while preschool teachers believed they were of equal importance ($t (50) = -0.68$, $p = .50$).

DISCUSSION

This study has important limitations. Findings cannot be generalized to parents who stay home with their preschoolers or to Hispanic parents who speak only Spanish. Because survey items were behaviorally anchored to make them appropriate for parents with limited education, we were unable to ask directly about complex constructs such as phonemic and numeracy awareness. Furthermore, the study was conducted in only one school district. Despite these limitations and differences in samples and measures, the findings showed some consistencies with previous research in that parents and teachers agreed on the importance of children being healthy and socially competent; parents placed a greater emphasis on academically-oriented skills than teachers did; and preschool teachers had some higher expectations than kindergarten teachers (cf. Hains et al., 1989; Knudsen–Lindauer & Harris, 1989; Harradine & Clifford, 1996; West et al., 1993).

In this broad overall context, several findings from this study are particularly noteworthy. First, regardless of parental ethnicity, parents showed remarkable consensus about what children should know and be able to do at kindergarten entry, particularly with regard to Classroom-related Readiness Resources. In particular, Black and Hispanic parents believed that children should be able to communicate in English by the time they enter kindergarten, in marked contrast to the views of preschool and kindergarten teachers. This finding must be viewed cautiously, as non-English speaking parents were excluded from this analysis and only one item tapped this belief. Still, the idea that parents in this largely Hispanic community may lack confidence in the ability of schools to educate Spanish-speaking children adequately requires further research, especially in light of the public debate about the efficacy of bilingual education.

Second, in this community, parents at all educational levels agreed on how important the 12 children's readiness resources were and believed that basic knowledge is more important than how children approach learning. These results contrast with other studies that have found that parents with less education held higher expectations than more educated parents regarding academically-oriented skills (West et al., 1993), and that parents emphasized interest and curiosity over academic skills (Harradine & Clifford, 1996; West et al., 1993). It is possible that these inconsistencies result from differences in measurement and sampling. For

554   **Piotrkowski, Botsko, and Matthews**

example, in this study advanced and basic knowledge were measured separately whereas other studies combined them. In this study, school and community resources were controlled, whereas other studies aggregated data across communities with widely different school readiness resources.

One interpretation of low-income parents' heightened expectations regarding concrete classroom-related readiness resources is that education increases parents' knowledge of development (West et al., 1993), so that parents with limited education have developmentally inappropriate expectations. In this case, however, we also would expect parents to have significantly higher expectations with regard to self-care, emotional maturity, and peer relations, which they did not. Instead, the differences between parents and teachers centered on children's classroom-related readiness resources, particularly the importance of knowledge.

An alternative explanation is offered by Piotrkowski's resource model (Piotrkowski, in press). She has proposed that local school and family readiness resources influence beliefs about what children should know and be able to do at kindergarten entry. In economically depressed communities, like the one studied here, parents' elevated readiness beliefs regarding the resources children need for kindergarten may be a function not of developmentally inappropriate expectations but of realistic concerns that their children might not succeed in resource-poor local schools. Because of these concerns, parents might develop a compensatory strategy that de-emphasizes interest and curiosity and, instead, emphasizes the acquisition of concrete skills to help children adjust quickly and successfully to classroom demands. This resource model of school readiness beliefs needs to be systematically tested in future research.

Finally, several research questions are raised by the finding that the preschool teachers in the school district believed knowledge was more important for children entering kindergarten than the kindergarten teachers did. Does this disparity reflect the widespread lack of communication between preschools and kindergartens about curricula (Love, 1992), a perception by preschool teachers that kindergartens are becoming increasingly academic (Hains et al., 1989), pressures from parents, or preschool teachers' lack of confidence in local schools? Do kindergarten teachers' stated beliefs that basic knowledge and skills are not very important reflect their expectations that they will teach these academic skills (Hains et al., 1989), or are their stated beliefs more a reflection of their educational philosophy than their actual practices (Vartuli, 1999; West et al., 1993)? For example, Rimm–Kaufman, Pianta, and Cox (2000) found that kindergarten teachers identified lack of academic skills as one of the most frequent transition problems children had. Finally, we must ask how children fare who move from preschool to kindergarten settings with strikingly divergent expectations. Further research is needed to answer these questions.

Implications for Practice and Policy

Ensuring early school success requires that resources be committed to help low-income communities support children, rather than placing the burden on

28

Beliefs About Children's School Readiness   **555**

children themselves. Families and schools must be ready if children are to be ready. Part of becoming ready involves a meaningful commitment to the goal of early school success and a common vision of children's school readiness at the local level, especially in communities where children are at heightened risk of school failure.

The expansion of state-funded preschool initiatives offers important opportunities to bridge the gaps between preschool and kindergarten teachers regarding school readiness expectations. Providing funds for joint professional development and curriculum planning for preschool and kindergarten teachers within communities could result in a unified vision of what children should know and be able to do at school entry and articulated curricula between preschool and kindergarten, while improving teacher training. Also useful would be funding for local transition coordinators to institutionalize regular communication about children making the transition to kindergarten, visits by preschool and kindergarten teachers to each others' classrooms, and meetings between elementary school principals and directors of community-based preschools to engage in dialogue about school readiness, common problems, and solutions.

In all this, it is critical that the voices of parents in high-need communities be heard because it is their children who are at increased risk for failing in school. Involving parents in the community dialogue means that their emphasis on concrete academic skills should not be dismissed as developmentally inappropriate, but as an indicator of their legitimate concerns about failing schools and failing children. Educators have the responsibility of addressing parents' concerns by offering them empirically tested, developmentally appropriate pathways to literacy and numeracy education for preschoolers. Parents' high readiness expectations also offer an entree for intervention. Despite their high expectations, parents with limited education and those living in poverty are less likely than more affluent, educated parents to read to their children daily or take their children to the library (Zill, 1998). Instead, these parents may expect preschool teachers to take primary or even sole responsibility for arming their children with necessary school readiness resources (Holloway et al., 1995). Knowing that parents in high-need communities have high readiness expectations may provide a useful strategy in helping educate parents about the role they can play at home to help children develop the readiness resources parents themselves identify as essential.

As states become more involved in early childhood education, there is the danger that the negative aspects of the standards movement—particularly "high stakes testing"—will move downward to preschool to increase barriers to school entry. After all, asking what children should know and be able to do when they enter kindergarten is implicitly a way of asking about standards for preschool education. To avoid the pitfalls, while developing appropriate curricula and educational goals for preschool, it is important that local communities establish processes for consensus-building around common readiness goals for young children, develop continuity between preschool and kindergarten—including but not limited to integrated curricula–and assume joint responsibility for ensuring that all children be ready for success when they enter kindergarten.

556   **Piotrkowski, Botsko, and Matthews**

Acknowledgment: The work reported here was supported by a grant from a private foundation and PR/Award Number R307F970010-98 from the US Department of Education. The contents do not necessarily represent the positions or policies of the National Institute on Early Childhood Development and Education, the Office of Educational Research and Improvement, or the US Department of Education. We wish to thank the parents and staff in the preschools and elementary schools of the community in which the study was conducted, school district staff, members of the Universal Prekindergarten Advisory Board, and the Head Start Grantee for their unstinting support and generosity. We also wish to thank Pedro Laureano, Joanne Carrubba, Sondra Lee, Francesca Mercurio, Wanda Washington, and Pauline Sikat for their help in collecting and processing the data.

NOTES

1. As used here, "parent" includes other caregivers, such as guardians and foster parents.
2. A few surveys were returned by both parents, but decision rules were used to select one parent survey per child for inclusion in the sample.
3. For the results of the factor analyses and the decision rules used to create the multi-items subscales, please contact the first author.

REFERENCES

Alexander, K. L., & Entwisle, D. R. (1988). Achievement in the first 2 years of school: Patterns and processes. *Monographs of the Society for Research in Child Development, 53*(2, Serial No. 218).

Bacon, W. F., & Ichikawa, V. (1988). Maternal expectations, classroom experiences, and achievement among kindergartners in the United States and Japan. *Human Development, 31,* 378–383.

Bray, J. H., & Maxwell, S. E. (1985). *Multivariate analysis of variance.* Beverly Hills: Sage Publications.

Bredekamp, S. (1992). Discussion. Assessment alternatives in early childhood. In F. Lamb Parker, R. Robinson, S. Sambrano, C. S. Piotrkowski, J. Hagen, S. Randolph, & A. Baker (Eds.), *New Directions in Child and Family Research: Shaping Head Start in the 90's. Conference Proceedings,* (pp. 310–312). Washington, DC: ACYF, U. S. Department of Health and Human Services.

Cohen, J. (1988). *Statistical power analysis for the behavioral sciences, 2ⁿᵈ Edition.* Hillsdale, NJ: Lawrence Erlbaum Associates.

Entwisle, D. R. (1995). The role of schools in sustaining early childhood program benefits. *The Future of Children, 5*(3), 133–144.

Fang, Z. (1996). A review of research on teacher beliefs and practices. *Educational Research, 38*(1), 47–65.

Farver, J. A. M., Kim, Y. K., & Lee, Y. (1995). Cultural differences in Korean-and Anglo-American preschoolers' social interaction and play behaviors. *Child Development, 66,* 1088–1099.

Freeman, E. B., & Hatch, J. A. (1989). What schools expect young children to know and do: An analysis of kindergarten report cards. *The Elementary School Journal, 89*(5), 595–605.

Foulks, B., & Morrow, R. D. (1989). Academic survival skills for the young child at risk for school failure. *Journal of Educational Research, 82*(3), 158–165.

Gorman, B. S., Primavera, L. H., & Allison, D. B. (1995). POWPAL: A program for estimating effect sizes, statistical power, and sample sizes. *Educational and Psychological Measurement, 55,* 773–776.

Graue, M. E. (1992). Social interpretations of readiness for kindergarten. *Early Childhood Research Quarterly, 7,* 225–243.

Beliefs About Children's School Readiness **557**

Gredler, G. R. (1992). *School readiness: Assessment and educational issues.* Brandon, VT: Clinical Psychology Publishing Company, Inc.

Hains, A. H., Fowler, S. A., Schwartz, S. S., Kottwitz, E., & Rosenkoetter, S. (1989). A comparison of preschool and kindergarten teacher expectations for school readiness. *Early Childhood Research Quarterly, 4,* 75–88.

Harradine, C. C., & Clifford, R. M. (1996). *When are children ready for kindergarten? Views of families, kindergarten teachers, and child care providers.* Paper presented at the meeting of the American Educational Research Association, New York, NY (ERIC Document Reproduction Service No. ED 399044).

Harvey, O. J., White, B. J., Rather, M. S., Alter, R. D., & Hoffmeister, J. K. (1966). Teachers' belief systems and preschool atmospheres. *Journal of Educational Psychology, 5*(6), 373–381.

Heaviside, S., & Farris, E. (1993). *Public school kindergarten teachers' views on children's readiness for school.* Washington, DC: U.S. Department of Education, NCES 93–410.

Holloway, S. D., Rambaud, M. F., Fuller, B., & Eggers–Pierola, C. (1995). What is "appropriate practice" at home and in child care?: Low-income mothers' views on preparing their children for school. *Early Childhood Research Quarterly, 10,* 451–473.

Johnson, L. J., Gallagher, R. J., Cook, M., & Wong, P. (1995). Critical skills for kindergarten: Perceptions from kindergarten teachers. *Journal of Early Intervention, 19*(4), 315–349.

Kagan, S. L., Moore, E., & Bredekamp, S. (Eds.). (1995). *Reconsidering Children's Early Development and Learning: Toward Common Views and Vocabulary. National Education Goals Panel. Goal 1 Technical Planning Group.* Washington, DC: U. S. Government Printing Office.

Knudsen-Lindauer, S. L., & Harris, K. (1989). Priorities for kindergarten curricula: Views of parents and teachers. *Journal of Research and Childhood Education, 4*(1), 51–61.

Lewitt, E. M., & Baker, L. S. (1995). School readiness. *The Future of Children, 5*(2), 128–139.

Love, J. M. (1992). Connecting with preschools: How our schools help (and fail to help) entering kindergartners. In J. McRobbie, J. Zimmerman, & P. L. Mangione (Eds.), *Links to Success: New Thinking on the Connections Between Preschool, School, and Community.* A Regional Symposium, Proceedings Paper. San Francisco: Far West Laboratory for Educational Research and Development.

Love, J. M., & Logue, M. E. (1992). *Transitions to Kindergarten in American Schools. Executive Summary of the National Transition Study.* Washington, DC: U. S. Department of Education, Office of Policy and Planning.

Luster, T., & McAdoo, H. (1996). Family and child influences on educational attainment: A secondary analysis of the High/Scope Perry Preschool data. *Developmental Psychology, 32,* 26–39.

Marin, G., & Marin, V. O. B. (1991). *Research with Hispanic populations.* Newbury Park: Sage.

May, D. C., & Kundert, D. K. (1992). Kindergarten screenings in New York State: Tests, purposes, and recommendations. *Psychology in the Schools, 29,* 35–41.

Meisels, S. J. (1992). Doing harm by doing good: Iatrogenic effects of early childhood enrollment and promotion policies. *Early Childhood Research Quarterly, 7,* 155–174.

National Association for the Education of Young Children. (1990). NAEYC position statement on school readiness. *Young Children, 1,* 21–23.

National Task Force on School Readiness. (1991). *Caring communities: Supporting young children and families.* Alexandria, VA: National Association of State Boards of Education.

Okagaki, L., & Sternberg, R. J. (1993). Parental beliefs and children's school performance. *Child Development, 64,* 36–56.

Piotrkowski, C. S. (in press). A community-based approach to school readiness in Head Start. In E. F. Zigler & S. J. Styfco (Eds.), *The Head Start debates (friendly and otherwise).* New Haven: Yale University Press.

Powell, D. R. (1995). *Enabling young children to succeed in school.* Washington, DC: American Educational Research Association.

Raver, C. C., & Zigler, E. F. (1997). New perspectives on Head Start. Social competence: An untapped dimension in evaluating Head Start's success. *Early Childhood Research Quarterly, 12,* 363–385.

558   **Piotrkowski, Botsko, and Matthews**

Rimm–Kaufman, S. E., Pianta, R. C., & Cox, M. J. (2000). Teachers' judgments of problems in the transition to kindergarten. *Early Childhood Research Quarterly, 15*, 147–166.

Rist, R. C. (1970). Student social class and teacher expectations: The self-fulfilling prophecy in ghetto education. *Harvard Educational Review, 40*(3), 411–451.

Segal, M. (1985). A study of maternal beliefs and values within the context of an intervention program. In I. E. Sigel (Ed.), *Parental belief systems* (pp. 271–286). Hillsdale, NJ: Lawrence Erlbaum Associates.

Shepard, L. A., & Smith, M. L. (1986). Synthesis of research on school readiness and kindergarten retention. *Educational Leadership, 44*, 78–86.

Shore, R. (1998). *Ready schools*. Washington: National Education Goals Panel.

Smith, M. L., & Shepard, L. A. (1988). Kindergarten readiness and retention: A qualitative study of teachers' beliefs and practices. *American Educational Research Journal, 25*, 307–333.

Stevenson, H. W., Chen, C., & Uttal, D. H. (1990). Beliefs and achievement: A study of Black, White, and Hispanic children. *Child Development, 61*, 508–523.

U. S. Department of Education. (1993). *All Children Ready to Learn: Toward the National Education Goals and High Standards for All Students*. Washington, DC: Author.

U. S. Department of Health and Human Services. (1990). *Head Start Research and Evaluations: A Blueprint for the Future*. Washington, DC: Author.

Vartuli, S. (1999). How early childhood teacher beliefs vary across grade level. *Early Childhood Research Quarterly, 14*, 489–514.

West, J., Hausken, E. G., & Collins, M. (1993). *Readiness for Kindergarten: Parent and Teacher Beliefs*. Washington, DC: U. S. Department of Education, Office of Educational Research and Improvement, NCES 93–257.

Willer, B., & Bredekamp, S. (1990). Redefining readiness: An essential requisite for educational reform. *Young Children, 45*(5), 22–24.

Zill, N. (1998). Promoting educational equity and excellence in kindergarten. In R. C. Pianta & M. J. Cox (Eds.), *The transition to kindergarten* (pp. 67–105). Baltimore: P. H. Brookes.

Topic:

_____
_____
_____

Procedures:

_____
_____
_____
_____

Method of analysis:

_____
_____
_____

Major conclusions:

_____
_____
_____
_____
_____

Toward a Positive Psychology of Academic Motivation

FRANK PAJARES
Emory University

ABSTRACT   The purpose of this study was to integrate constructs from positive psychology with constructs from motivation theories that have received most of the attention in studies of academic motivation. Achievement goals, expectancy beliefs, and value were predictive of the positive psychology variables. Task goals were associated positively with optimism and with invitations, whereas performance-avoid goals were associated negatively with optimism and perceived authenticity. Expectancy and value constructs were associated positively with optimism, perceived authenticity, and invitations. Positive psychology variables were stronger in high-achieving students than in low-achieving students; boys had stronger perceived authenticity than girls did. Findings indicate that constructs drawn from positive psychology can help explain academic motivation and achievement.

Key words: achievement goals, motivation, optimism, positive psychology, self-efficacy

During the first half of the 20th century, psychologists who held either a behaviorist or psychoanalytic perspective were the dominant forces in American psychology. Apprehensive about what they considered the passive view of human functioning that behaviorism represented and dissatisfied with the focus on abnormality that characterized psychoanalytic interests, a third group of psychologists called for attention to inner experience, internal processes, adaptive functioning, positive life influences, and self-constructs. The writings of those theorists caught the attention of scholars and researchers, and, during the 1950s, the humanistic movement was born. The most powerful voice in the new movement was that of Maslow (1943, 1954), who proposed a dynamic theory of motivation in which internal and intrinsic motivating forces and affective processes lead to personal, social, and academic well-being. This was a view of academic functioning in which subjective experiences and positive attitudes play a prominent role.

Although widespread, the influence of humanistic psychology on education was erratic. The emphasis on self-processes encouraged a personal and cultural self-absorption that minimized the importance of collective well-being (Seligman & Csikszentmihalyi, 2000b). Moreover, the gap from theory to practice proved difficult to breach, and many laudable but misguided efforts to nurture the self-esteem of children fell prey to excesses and, ultimately, ridicule (Purkey, 2000). The goal of focusing on and fostering positive self-perceptions became mired in controversies over the value of self-processes in education—controversies that continue unabated to this day (see Kohn, 1994). Because research efforts were unsystematic and results were highly inconsistent, the tenets of humanistic psychology did not develop an empirical base (Pajares & Schunk, in press; Seligman & Csikszentmihalyi, 2000b). As a consequence, the humanistic movement waned during the 1980s as psychologists shifted their interest to cognitive processes and information-processing views of human functioning.

Recently, however, there has been another vigorous call within the discipline for a science of psychology grounded on positive experience (Bandura, 1998; Gilham & Seligman, 1999; Seligman & Csikszentmihalyi, 2000a; Vaillant, 2000). This *positive* psychology has been described as the study of human strengths and optimal functioning, and one of its key aims is to foster research on the positive personal traits and dispositions that are thought to contribute to subjective well-being and psychological health. Such research stands in contrast to the traditional study of people's distress, pathology, and maladaptive functioning that continues to characterize American psychology. Moreover, although positive psychology shares with the humanistic movement the aim of advancing human fulfillment, one of the key aims of positive psychology is that its methodology should be grounded firmly in systematic and scientific inquiry (Myers, 2001).

The American Psychological Association (APA) has embraced positive psychology's approach to the study of optimal human functioning by making its first 2000 edition of the *American Psychologist* a theme issue on positive psychology constructs (Seligman & Csikszentmihalyi, 2000a). In the area of education, researchers hope that insights available from investigations that emphasize a positive psy-

Address correspondence to Frank Pajares, Division of Educational Studies, Emory University, Atlanta, GA 30322. (E-mail: mpajare@emory.edu)

27

The Journal of Educational Research, 95, Sept./Oct., 2001, pp. 27-35. Reprinted with permission of the Helen Dwight Reid Educational Foundation. Published by Heldref Publications, 1319 Eighteenth St., N.W., Washington, D.C. 20036-1802. Copyright © 2001.

chology will alter the present focus of drawing inferences about adaptive functioning from students who are at risk or unmotivated to those who are resilient and resourceful (Bandura, 1998). For example, positive psychology seeks to shift the emphasis from research frequently conducted on concepts such as learned helplessness to the study of learned optimism and perseverance (Seligman & Csikszent-mihalyi, 2000b). To these ends, the new researchers urge that positive psychology constructs be integrated with those of traditional and established bodies of educational literature and lines of inquiry.

One of positive psychology's signature constructs is *optimism,* which is typically defined as holding a view of life events and situations that is characterized by positive thinking and maintaining a positive attitude toward the future (Peterson, 2000; Scheier & Carver, 1985, 1992; Seligman, 1991). Although optimism has received attention from social and personality psychologists who reported that it exercises a positive influence on human functioning, researchers have made few connections between this construct and either educational psychology or academic motivation. There is scant mention of optimism in the field's most popular motivation texts (e.g., Alderman, 1999; Brophy, 1998; Pintrich & Schunk, 1997; Stipek, 1998). Optimism warrants only three paragraphs in the 1,000-plus pages of the *Handbook of Educational Psychology* (Berliner & Calfee, 1996). Despite the neglect, researchers have found that possessing an optimistic explanatory style is related to adaptive academic benefits, including academic achievement, positive goal orientation, and use of learning strategies, whereas a pessimistic explanatory style is associated with negative outcomes and with learned helplessness (Buchanan & Seligman, 1995; Peterson, 1990; Seligman, 1991).

A second essential construct of a positive psychology that has received limited attention in motivation research centers on individuals' feelings of authenticity—the belief that one's achievements and attainments are deserved and that others recognize these achievements as being merited. The flip side of this belief has been called the *impostor syndrome,* the *impostor phenomenon,* or *perceived fraudulence,* defined as "a psychological syndrome or pattern based upon intense, secret feelings of fraudulence in the face of achievement tasks and situations" (Harvey & Katz, 1985, p. 3). Although perceived authenticity has special relevance to school settings, researchers have focused primarily on the areas of social and personality psychology (and especially business; see Fried-Buchalter, 1997). According to investigations conducted primarily with college students or adults, feelings of "inauthenticity" are often felt by high-achieving individuals, especially high-achieving girls (Clance, 1985). As has pessimism, the illusion of incompetence has been found to be associated with depression and anxiety (Kolligian & Sternberg, 1991) and with interpersonal inflexibility (Hayes & Davis, 1993).

A third construct provided by positive psychology theo-rists is grounded in invitational theory, which can be traced to a perceptual tradition in psychology maintaining that the beliefs persons develop about themselves and about others help form the perceptual lens through which they view the world and interpret new experiences (Purkey, 2000; Purkey & Novak, 1996). According to invitational theory, the messages that people send and receive play an important role in creating the beliefs that they develop, for it is these messages that often constitute the bridge on which perception, interpretation, and meaning travel (Valiante & Pajares, 1999). Theorists contend that people can intentionally send uplifting and empowering messages to themselves and others, and they define the *sending of invitations* as a process by which people are summoned to realize their own potential and to enhance the potential of others (Purkey & Novak, 1996). Positive invitations convey the message that people are able, valuable, responsible, and forgiving; negative invitations indicate that people are not valued and that they are incapable of participating positively in their own development.

Various mainstream motivation theories posit connections between academic motivation and the potential benefits that can accrue from optimistic beliefs, perceived authenticity, and invitations. One of the posited connections comes from a large body of research that has examined students' achievement goals, which are the reasons that students provide for engaging in academic tasks and activities. Students with a task-goal orientation engage in their academic work to master the material and ideas and seek academic challenge. For those students, learning is an end in itself. Students who hold a performance-approach goal orientation want to do better than their classmates so they will be recognized as competent by their peers, teachers, and parents. Students who hold a performance-avoid goal orientation do their academic work primarily because they fear appearing incompetent.

Researchers typically report that having a task-goal orientation has motivational benefits, whereas having a performance-avoid goal orientation can be detrimental (Urdan, 1997). Task goals are related positively to attributions of success to effort and persistence in the face of difficulty (both are components of optimism). Performance goals have been shown to be related to lack of persistence and to attributions of failure to lack of ability (a pessimistic view). Researchers have not established an empirical connection between achievement goals and positive psychology constructs. However, one can posit logically that students whose main reason for doing their academic work is grounded in fear of failure should be more likely to view their academic outcomes with pessimism and with a greater sense of inauthenticity. It also seems reasonable to posit that students who engage in academic work for intrinsic reasons should be more inviting and forgiving of themselves and of others than should students whose academic efforts are based on the sought approval or fear of disapproval from others.

A second body of motivation research that posits connections to the positive psychology constructs has focused on the expectancy and value beliefs that students hold about their academic work. *Expectancy beliefs* are judgments of capability to attain designated types of performances. Those beliefs that have received the bulk of attention in academic motivation studies have been self-concept (Marsh, 1990; Skaalvik, 1997), self-efficacy (Pajares, 1996; Schunk, 1991), and confidence to use self-regulatory practices (Zimmerman, 1989; Zimmerman & Schunk, 1989). A student's academic self-concept represents a composite view of him or herself as a student, a view formed through experience and feedback from others. The construct of self-efficacy is drawn from Bandura's (1986) social cognitive theory, and *academic self-efficacy beliefs* are defined as judgments of capability to succeed in academic pursuits. The key difference between the two constructs is that academic self-concept beliefs focus primarily on the feelings of *self-worth* associated with being a student, whereas academic self-efficacy centers on the *confidence* that students have to succeed in school. Students also possess judgments of their capability to use various self-regulated learning strategies required to accomplish academic work. This self-efficacy for self-regulated learning includes confidence judgments regarding how well students can motivate themselves to do schoolwork, finish their homework on time, or remember information presented in class or in their school books. In studies of academic motivation, *value* is defined in terms of students' perceived importance of, interest in, and enjoyment of school or an academic domain (Eccles, 1983).

Researchers with a self-concept or self-efficacy theoretical orientation would agree with invitational theorists that students' academic self-beliefs are created and developed, in part, by the messages—the invitations and "disinvitations"—that students send and receive (Bandura, 1997; Eccles, 1983; Marsh, 1990). For example, researchers have noted the conceptual relationship between invitations and self-concept—invitational theory and self-concept theory each grew out of the perceptual tradition in psychology (Purkey & Novak, 1996; Wiemer & Purkey, 1994). As regards self-efficacy, Pajares and Zeldin (1999) investigated the relationship between invitational messages and the sources of the self-efficacy beliefs of women with careers in mathematics, science, or technology. They found that the invitations the women reported receiving were important in their initial choice to pursue nontraditional careers and also formed the self-beliefs that nurtured the effort, persistence, and resilience required to overcome personal, social, and academic obstacles. The invitations from others that the women received early in their development reemerged at later points in their lives as self-invitations. Those findings support the contention of invitational theorists that significant others play a powerful role in the academic beliefs that students come to develop about themselves. Pajares (1994) suggested that the tenets of self-efficacy theory, self-concept theory, and invitational theory complement each other,

and he provided a model showing the hypothesized relationship between efficacy beliefs and invitations.

Theorists also have posited that students who value a domain and hold positive expectancy beliefs about their own competence, feelings of self-worth, and confidence in their self-regulatory strategies engage academic tasks with greater optimism than do students who devalue academics or doubt their abilities (e.g., Bandura, 1997; Eccles, 1983). Positive psychology theorists also would assert that there is a clear connection between expectancy beliefs, the belief that competence is authentic, and the tendency to be self- and other-inviting (Purkey, 2000; Seligman & Csikszentmihalyi, 2000b).

Although various motivation theories posit connections between academic motivation and constructs drawn from positive psychology, these constructs have not been included in studies of academic motivation. The purpose of the present study was to integrate the constructs from positive psychology with those that have received the bulk of research attention in the area of academic motivation. I sought to determine the degree to which each of the three types of achievement goals and each of the four types of expectancy-value constructs makes an independent contribution to the prediction of optimism, authenticity, and invitations in hierarchical regression models, controlling for previous academic achievement, gender, and age (see Middleton & Midgley, 1997; Pajares, Miller, & Johnson, 1999, for similar analyses in studies of academic motivation). I also was interested in testing the connection between the positive psychology variables and academic achievement, as well as the contention that high-achieving individuals, especially high-achieving girls, are especially susceptible to experiencing feelings of inauthenticity.

Participants and Data Source

Participants were 529 students in a public middle school in the Northeast (255 girls, 274 boys; 171 in Grade 6, 176 in Grade 7, 182 in Grade 8). The socioeconomic status of the school and of the area that the school served was largely middle class and students were primarily Caucasian. Students' ages ranged from 11 to 16 years. Instruments were group administered in individual classes during one period. All items were read aloud by the administrator. The study took place during the second semester of the academic year. The motivation variables were assessed with scales that have been used extensively in various studies. The teachers provided the students' grade point average in language arts and mathematics from the semester preceding the study. The averages were used as the GPA measure of academic achievement.

Achievement goals were assessed using a scale derived from the Patterns of Adaptive Learning Survey (PALS; Middleton & Midgley, 1997; Midgley et al., 1996) and adapted to reflect goals toward success in school. Task goals were assessed with 5 items (I like school assignments that really make me think); approach goals with 5 items (I want to do better than other students in my school); and avoid goals with 6 items (I do my school assignments so others in the class won't think I'm dumb). Students responded on a 6-point, Likert-type scale ranging from 1 (*definitely false*) to 6 (*definitely true*). In previous studies, the three types of goals loaded on separate factors with significant loadings ranging from .68 to .87 (Middleton & Midgley, 1997; Pajares, Britner, & Valiante, 2000). Alpha coefficients have ranged from .77 to .89 (Middleton & Midgley, 1997; Pajares et al., in press). In this study, Cronbach's alpha was .86 for task goals, .80 for approach goals, and .83 for avoid goals.

The *Academic Self-Efficacy* scale was drawn from Bandura's Children's Multidimensional Self-Efficacy Scale (see Zimmerman, Bandura, & Martinez-Pons, 1992), which assesses students' judgments of their capability to learn academic subjects and skills. Using a Likert-type scale that ranged from 1 (*not well at all*) to 6 (*extremely well*), students responded to questions that asked how well they believed they could learn mathematics, reading, and writing skills. Alpha coefficients ranging from .70 to .85 have been reported previously (Valiante & Pajares, 1999; Zimmerman & Bandura, 1994; Zimmerman et al., 1992). The higher coefficients have been reported with samples of college undergraduates. The coefficient for this study was .69. The modest reliability is not surprising, given that the self-efficacy assessment is the composite score of students' judgment that they can learn in academic areas in which they may view their capabilities differently. For example, some students may have great confidence that they can learn well in language arts courses but little confidence of their capabilities in mathematics.

Academic self-concept was assessed with 6 items from Marsh's (1990) Academic Self-Description Questionnaire that were transformed from subject-specific content into general academic content. For instance, an item such as "I get good grades in mathematics" was changed to "I get good grades in school." Students responded on a 6-point, Likert-type scale ranging from *definitely false* to *definitely true*. Reliability estimates for the self-concept instrument in various academic areas have ranged from .86 to .94 (Marsh, 1990; Pajares & Valiante, 1997, 1999; Skaalvik, 1997; Valiante & Pajares, 1999). The reliability estimate for the present study was .83.

The *Self-Efficacy for Self-Regulated Learning* scale is also a subscale from Bandura's Children's Multidimensional Self-Efficacy Scale that assesses student's judgments of their capability to use various self-regulated learning strategies. As with the Academic Self-Efficacy scale, students were asked to respond on a 6-point, Likert-type scale to items such as "How well can you motivate yourself to do schoolwork?" and "How well can you finish your homework on time?" A validation study by Zimmerman and Martinez-Pons (1988) revealed that a single factor underlay the items. Cronbach's alpha values ranging from .80 to .87

have been reported by Pajares and Graham (1999); Pajares and Valiante (1997, 1998); Valiante and Pajares (1999), Zimmerman and Bandura (1994), Zimmerman and Martinez-Pons (1988), and Zimmerman et al. (1992). The alpha value for this study was .81.

The degree to which students valued school was measured with 5 items assessing three indexes that contribute to perceived value of a domain: importance, interest, and enjoyment (see Eccles, 1983; Meece, Wigfield, & Eccles, 1990; Seegers & Boekaerts, 1996). Students were asked to rate how true or false statements were on a 6-point, Likert-type scale. (A sample item for importance was "It is important to me to get good grades in school"; for enjoyment, "I enjoy school"; for interest, "My schoolwork is interesting for me"). Researchers have reported alpha coefficients ranging from .69 to .92 when value has been assessed relative to a specific subject area or to school in general (Pajares & Graham, 1999; Pajares & Valiante, 1997, 1999; Valiante & Pajares, 1999). The alpha coefficient for this study was .89.

The Optimism Scale consisted of 12 items drawn from the Life Orientation Test, which is used extensively in the area of social and personality psychology (Scheier & Carver, 1985). Six of the items were worded positively and 6 items were worded negatively (e.g., "I'm always optimistic about my future"; "If something can go wrong for me, it will go wrong"). Because the scale has not been used in studies of academic motivation, I conducted exploratory factor analysis using the maximum likelihood method of extraction (Jöreskog & Lawley, 1968), a method believed to produce the best parameter estimates (Pedhazur, 1982). Criteria to determine the number of common factors to retain and analyze were Cattell's (1966) scree test; the percentage of common variance explained by each factor using the weighted, reduced correlation matrix; and the interpretability of the rotated factors. Because any factors that emerged from the analyses were expected to be intercorrelated, I used the oblimin method of oblique rotation. Results revealed that two factors underlay the items; they reflected the positive and negative wording. Factor structure coefficients from the rotated pattern matrix ranged from .49 to .75. Factor structure coefficients demonstrate the relationship between an item and a factor when holding all other items constant. Factor structure coefficients of .40 or higher were considered strong enough to demonstrate that the item indicated the common factor. Cronbach's alpha coefficient was .83.

Perceived authenticity was measured with a scale consisting of 5 items drawn from Clance's (1985) and Harvey and Katz's (1985) scales assessing inauthenticity and the impostor syndrome (e.g., "Sometimes I'm afraid other people will discover that I'm not very smart"). Reverse scoring of the items provides a measure of perceived authenticity. Because the scale has not been used in studies of academic motivation, I again conducted exploratory factor analysis using the procedures outlined in the previous paragraphs.

September/October 2001 [Vol. 95(No. 1)]

Results revealed that one factor underlay the items. Factor structure coefficients ranged from .42 to .83; Cronbach's alpha coefficient was .72.

Invitations of self and others were assessed with the Inviting/Disinviting Index-Revised (IDI), which consists of two subscales representing the degree to which individuals are inviting to themselves (e.g., "I pay attention to my own needs") or to others (e.g., "I like to include other people in enjoyable activities") (Schmidt, Shields, & Ciechalski, 1998; Valiante & Pajares, 1999; Wiemer & Purkey, 1994). Students responded on a 7-point, Likert-type scale that ranged from 1 (*never*) to 7 (*always*). In previous studies, test-retest reliability has ranged from .68 to .83 for the scales of the original IDI (Wiemer & Purkey, 1994) and .41 to .72 for those of adapted versions (Schmidt et al., 1998; Valiante & Pajares, 1999). Exploratory factor analysis results revealed that one factor reflecting inviting self and a second factor reflecting inviting others underlay the items. Factor structure coefficients ranged from .53 to .76. Cronbach's alpha coefficient for the present study was .81 for the inviting self scale and .76 for the inviting others scale.

Results and Discussion

Table 1 provides means and correlations for the variables in the study. Correlations among the motivation constructs were consistent with those of previous investigations, although that between self-efficacy and self-concept was higher than typically found ($r = .67$). That result likely was due to the domain similarity of the assessments. In previous studies, self-efficacy typically was assessed at the task level, that is, in terms of students' confidence that they could accomplish specific academic tasks (such as writing essays or solving mathematics problems). Self-concept is assessed

typically at the domain level, in terms of students' feelings of self-worth in academic areas. In the present study, I assessed self-efficacy at the academic domain level, that is, the composite score of students' confidence to succeed in their academic courses. Self-concept also was assessed at the academic domain level in terms of students' self-concept beliefs related to school in general. Note that academic achievement was correlated positively both with the positive psychology variables and with the motivation variables.

I conducted hierarchical regressions to determine the influence of the achievement goals and of the expectancy-value constructs on each of the positive psychology variables. Because achievement goals and expectancy-value beliefs represent differing theoretical frameworks, they were kept separate in the regression models predicting the positive psychology variables. Academic achievement (GPA), gender, and age were included at the first step. To determine the influence of the achievement goals, I added these at the second step. To determine the influence of the expectancy-value variables, I removed the achievement goals and included the expectancy-value constructs at the third step. Consistent with typical findings, the motivation variables were highly correlated (see Table 1). Consequently, I supplemented beta values for achievement goals and expectancy value variables with regression structure coefficients, which are not suppressed or inflated by collinearity (Thompson & Borello, 1985). (See Table 2 for the results.)

Each of the models testing the influence of achievement goals added a significant proportion of the variance to the positive psychology variables. A task-goal orientation was associated positively with optimism ($\beta = .399$), with being inviting to oneself ($\beta = .433$), and with inviting others ($\beta = .431$). Conversely, a performance-avoid orientation was associated negatively with optimism ($\beta = -.209$) and with

Table 1.—Means, Standard Deviations, and Zero-Order Correlations for Variables in the Study

Variable	M	SD	1	2	3	4	5	6	7	8	9	10	11	12
1. Optimism	4.0	0.8	—											
2. Authenticity	2.7	1.1	.30***	—										
3. Inviting self	4.5	1.0	.46***	−.01	—									
4. Inviting others	4.6	0.8	.39***	−.03	.53***	—								
5. Task goals	3.9	1.2	.39***	−.08	.47***	.47***	—							
6. Performance- approach	3.9	1.2	.10*	−.28***	.28***	.19***	.40***	—						
7. Performance- avoid	3.2	1.2	−.11*	−.49***	.14*	.05	−.18***	.57***	—					
8. Self-efficacy	4.6	0.9	.38***	.25***	.33***	.29***	.41***	.12*	−.10*	—				
9. Self-concept	4.5	0.9	.41***	.24***	.35***	.35***	.44***	.17***	−.07	.67***	—			
10. Self-regulation	4.3	0.9	.43***	.16**	.44***	.43***	.59***	.19***	−.05	.73***	.67***	—		
11. Value	3.5	1.2	.36***	−.07	.35***	.41***	.72***	.27***	.03	.34***	.42***	.53***	—	
12. GPA	2.9	0.8	.16**	.17***	.02	.13*	.16**	.04	−.04	.47***	.55***	.39***	.18***	—
13. Gender	—	—	−.01	.09*	.02	−.20***	−.13*	.07	.02	.01	−.10*	−.08	−.17***	−.10*
14. Age	12.6	1.1	−.04	.08	−.10*	−.01	−.09*	−.09*	−.08	−.10*	−.03	−.10*	−.10*	−.09*

Note. For gender, girls were coded −1 and boys were coded 1. Means for the motivation and positive psychology variables reflect the 6 points of the Likert-type scale. GPA scores ranged from 0 (F) to 4 (A). $N = 529$.
*$p < .05$. **$p < .001$. ***$p < .0001$.

Table 2.—Hierarchical Regression Analyses for Optimism, Authenticity, and Invitations—Beta Values and Structure Coefficients

Variables in equation	Optimism			Authenticity			Inviting self			Inviting others		
	Step 1	Step 2	Step 3	Step 1	Step 2	Step 3	Step 1	Step 2	Step 3	Step 1	Step 2	Step 3
Prior achievement	.15**	.08*	−.11**	.19***	.17***	.02	.12**	.06	−.09	.09*	.02	−.12*
Gender	.01	.06	.04	.10*	.11**	.06	.03	.08*	.08*	−.19***	−.14**	−.14**
Age	−.03	−.02	.00	.10*	.05	.09*	−.05	−.06	−.06	.01	.04	.04
Achievement goals												
Task		.40***			.00			.43***			.43***	
		(.827)			(−.160)			(.955)			(.949)	
Performance-approach		.05			−.02			.09			.06	
		(.219)			(−.548)			(.567)			(.385)	
Performance-avoid		−.21***			−.47***			.01			−.06	
		(−.251)			(−.943)			(.283)			(.098)	
Expectancy beliefs												
Academic self-efficacy			.11			.16*			−.01			−.01
			(.771)			(.694)			(.670)			(.562)
Academic self-concept			.25***			.21**			.12			.13*
			(.827)			(.665)			(.712)			(.675)
Self-efficacy for self-regulation			.14*			−.02			.31***			.27***
			(.861)			(.460)			(.911)			(.830)
Value			.17**			−.22***			.18**			.22***
			(.722)			(−.205)			(.728)			(.800)
R^2	.03**	.20***	.25***	.05***	.28***	.13***	.03**	.25***	.24***	.05***	.24***	.26***
Change in R^2		.17***	.22***		.23***	.08***		.22***	.21***		.19***	.21***

Note. Beta values are reported with significance indicators. Structure coefficients are reported within parentheses.
*$p < .05$. **$p < .001$. ***$p < .0001$.

perceived authenticity ($\beta = -.469$). The influence of holding a performance-approach goal orientation was nonsignificant. Results of the structure regression coefficients were consistent with the obtained effects.

Researchers who have been calling for investigations that discriminate between performance approach and performance avoid in studies of achievement goal orientation (e.g., Elliot, & Harackiewicz, 1996; Middleton & Midgley, 1997; Urdan, 1997) will be heartened by the finding that a performance-avoid orientation was associated negatively with optimism and with perceived authenticity, whereas a performance-approach orientation was not. It is not surprising that holding a performance-avoid orientation is associated with pessimism and with fears of inauthenticity. Students whose achievement efforts are grounded on the fear of appearing incompetent, being embarrassed, or looking stupid are naturally prone to view the fruits of their labors through the lens provided by that fear. There can be little psychological distance between the fear that others will think us incompetent and the suspicion that we may be so, the suspicion that our accomplishments are ill deserved. And how could fear and suspicion not be chaperoned by pessimism? In general, the findings support the contentions of researchers regarding the adaptive function played by task goals and the negative influence of performance-avoid goals.

Each of the expectancy-value models added a significant proportion of the variance to the positive psychology variables. Value of school predicted each of the outcomes ($\beta = .167$ for optimism; $\beta = .176$ for inviting self; $\beta = .219$ for

inviting others), although the influence on perceived authenticity was negative ($\beta = -.216$). Academic self-concept predicted optimism ($\beta = .244$), perceived authenticity ($\beta = .208$), and inviting others ($\beta = .131$). Self-efficacy predicted perceived authenticity ($\beta = .163$). Self-efficacy for self-regulation had a pronounced influence on being inviting to oneself ($\beta = .309$) and on inviting others ($\beta = .266$). The structure regression coefficients revealed that the influence of self-efficacy beliefs was attenuated by its collinearity with self-concept and with self-efficacy for self-regulation. The structure coefficients for self-efficacy suggest that it too was a noteworthy predictor of each of the positive psychology variables.

Finding that academic and self-regulatory confidence, as well as academic self-concept, are positively associated with optimism, authenticity, and invitations of self and of others is consistent with theoretical tenets from social cognitive theories and from self-concept theories (Bandura, 1997; Eccles, 1983; Marsh, 1985; Zimmerman, 1989). Although valuing school was one of the strongest predictors of optimism and of invitations of self and of others, results of the hierarchical regression analysis revealed a significant negative association between value and perceived authenticity. However, the correlation between these two variables was not significant and the structure regression coefficient was low. Clearly, the observed negative association is a function of value's covariation with one or more of the independent variables. Some expectancy-value theorists have posited that value and expectancies can interact in such a way that they can be inversely related, in the sense that expectations to succeed at difficult tasks is valued, whereas expectations to succeed at easy tasks is not valued (Atkinson, 1964). The nature of this covariation is not easily untangled, and additional research is warranted.

I conducted multivariate analyses of covariance to determine whether the positive psychology variables differed as a function of gender, academic capability, or age. The key point of interest was to determine whether, as some previous findings suggest, girls, especially high-achieving girls, report lower perceptions of authenticity than boys do. Dependent variables were the positive psychology constructs; gender was the independent variable and GPA and age were used as covariates. I tested the assumption of equal slopes by examining all possible interactions between gender, GPA, and age—they all proved nonsignificant. I reanalyzed the model with the interaction terms removed. Results revealed a significant multivariate effect for gender, Wilks's $\lambda = .93$, $F(4, 521) = 10.12$, $p = .0001$, for GPA, Wilks's $\lambda = .95$, $F(4, 521) = 7.27$, $p = .0001$, and for age, Wilks's $\lambda = .98$, $F(4, 521) = 3.14$, $p = .0145$. Analyses of covariance, followed by tests of the difference between the adjusted means, revealed that GPA was significantly associated with each of the positive psychology constructs. The age effects revealed that as students grew older they reported greater perceived authenticity but also grew less inviting of themselves. I found gender differences favoring boys on perceived authenticity; differences favoring girls were found on inviting others. The results are provided in Table 3.

As these results show, the contention that girls and high achievers, especially high-achieving girls, tend to have greater feelings of inauthenticity in school settings received mixed support in this investigation. Boys reported greater perceived authenticity than did girls, but academic achievement was associated positively with authenticity, and there was no significant interaction between gender and achievement on authenticity. The mean for girls was 4.2 and for boys, 4.4 on a scale from 1 to 6, suggesting that differences were modest and that all students rated themselves above the mean on this variable. Nonetheless, girls reported lower perceptions of authenticity even though their academic GPA was higher than that of the boys. As frequently reported in

the area of academic motivation, factors apparently continue to be at work to diminish the academic self-beliefs of some girls, and this warrants continued investigation and correction. The only other gender difference was that girls rated themselves stronger in being inviting to others, a finding consistent with previous research (Valiante & Pajares, 1999).

Conclusion

Results of this investigation reveal that integrating constructs prominent in traditional research on academic motivation with positive psychology constructs can yield valuable insights. Achievement goal theorists can add higher levels of optimism and a greater tendency to be inviting of oneself and of others as effects associated with holding a task goal orientation. Students whose academic efforts are grounded in love of the work and who prefer tasks from which they can learn, even if they make mistakes along the way, do not require that others validate their academic efforts and do not fear self-censure or the censure of others when errors are made. This social and psychological emancipation from need and fear frees individuals to more readily accept, appreciate, and forgive—to invite—themselves and others. And how could those personal and social invitations not be chaperoned by optimism and well-being?

In addition, findings support and extend the contentions of motivation theorists regarding the adaptive benefits of holding positive academic self-beliefs such as self-concept, self-efficacy, and self-efficacy for self-regulation, as well as valuing school. Although scholars have long known that these motivation constructs are related to positive academic outcomes, including academic achievement, it seems clear that they also are related to adaptive mental functioning and well-being. Clearly, dispositions such as optimism and authenticity are motivating. In addition, positive dispositions such as optimism, perceptions of authenticity, self-acceptance and regard, and acceptance and regard for others are themselves related to academic motivation and achievement.

Findings of any study are limited to the population from

Table 3.—Differences in Optimism, Authenticity, and Invitations, by Academic Achievement

Variable	Boys (n = 274)	Girls (n = 255)	GPA			Age		
			F	p	β	F	p	β
Optimism	4.0$_a$	4.0$_a$	13.16*	.0003	.154	0.46	.4948	−.029
Authenticity	4.4$_a$	4.2$_b$	17.52*	.0001	.189	4.94	.0266	.095
Inviting to self	4.5$_a$	4.5	8.87*	.0030	.121	4.36*	.0372	−.091
Inviting to others	4.5$_a$	4.8$_b$	4.18*	.0414	.088	0.07	.7946	.011

Note. Mean scores are adjusted lsmeans scores and are based on a Likert-type scale, ranging from 1 (*low*) to 6 (*high*) on the positive psychology variables. Adjusted group means for a dependent variable (row) that are subscripted by different letters are statistically different (experiment wise; $\alpha \leq .05$) computed on an effect identified by a multivariate analysis of covariance test of difference between adjusted means. GPA ranged from 0 to 4; age ranged from 11 to 16 years.

which the sample is drawn. In the present study, the sample consisted of Caucasian, middle class, middle school students. Researchers are urged to replicate the study using samples representative of other populations, socioeconomic strata, and academic grade levels. Moreover, the analyses conducted were correlational, and no causation should be inferred from the findings. Schunk (1991) and Pajares (1997) noted that, although quantitative methods typically have been used to study motivation constructs, qualitative methods such as case studies or oral histories are needed to gain additional insights and are especially relevant and appropriate to the study of academic self-beliefs.

Noddings (1992) observed that the ultimate aim of education should be "to produce competent, caring, loving, and lovable people" (p. 174). One need only cast a casual glance at the American landscape to see that attending to the psychological well-being of students is both a noble and necessary enterprise. The aim of education must transcend the development of academic competence. Schools have the added responsibility of preparing fully functioning and caring individuals capable of pursuing their hopes and aspirations. To do so, they must be armed with optimism, self-regard, and regard for others, and they must be shielded from doubts about the authenticity of their accomplishments. Teachers can aid their students by helping them to develop the habit of excellence in scholarship while nurturing the character traits necessary to maintain that excellence throughout their adult lives.

Results of this study reveal that students who value school, who view learning as an end in itself and believe that the purpose of learning is to master ideas and seek personal challenge, and who accompany these beliefs with confidence, positive self-feelings, and confidence in their self-regulatory practices also engage the world with optimism and view their accomplishments as merited and deserved. Such students also are more likely to regard themselves and to show regard for others. Those are attitudes and dispositions well worth nurturing in school. Moreover, they are the very elements with which a positive *educational psychology* should concern itself.

REFERENCES

Alderman, M. K. (1999). *Motivation for achievement*. Mahwah, NJ: Erlbaum.

Atkinson, J. W. (1964). *An introduction to motivation*. Princeton, NJ: Van Nostrand.

Bandura, A. (1986). *Social foundations of thought and action: A social cognitive theory*. Englewood Cliffs, NJ: Prentice Hall.

Bandura, A. (1997). *Self-efficacy: The exercise of control*. New York: Freeman.

Bandura, A. (1998, August). *Exercise of agency in accenting the positive*. Invited address delivered at the meeting of the American Psychological Association, San Francisco.

Berliner, D. C., & Calfee, R. C. (1996). (Eds.), *Handbook of educational psychology*. New York: Macmillan.

Brophy, J. (1998). *Motivating students to learn*. Boston: McGraw-Hill.

Buchanan, G. M., & Seligman, M. E. P. (Eds.). (1995). *Explanatory style*. Hillsdale, NJ: Erlbaum.

Cattell, R. B. (1966). The scree test for the number of factors. *Multivariate Behavioral Research, 1,* 245–276.

Clance, P. R. (1985). *The impostor phenomenon*. Atlanta, GA: Peachtree.

Eccles, J. S. (1983). Expectancies, values, and academic behavior. In J. T. Spencer (Ed.), *Achievement and achievement motivation: Psychological and sociological approaches* (pp. 75–146). San Francisco: Freeman.

Elliot, A. J., & Harackiewicz, J. M. (1996). Approach and avoidance goals and intrinsic motivation: A mediational analysis. *Journal of Personality and Social Psychology, 70,* 461–475.

Fried-Buchalter, S. (1997). Fear of success, fear of failure, and the imposter phenomenon among male and female marketing managers. *Sex Roles, 37,* 847–859.

Gilham, J. E., & Seligman, M. E. P. (1999). Footsteps on the road to a positive psychology. *Behaviour Research and Therapy, 37,* 163–173.

Harvey, J. C., & Katz, C. (1985). *If I'm so successful, why do I feel like a fake?* New York: Random House.

Hayes, K. M., & Davis, S. F. (1993). Interpersonal flexibility, Type A individuals, and the impostor phenomenon. *Bulletin of the Psychonomic Society, 31,* 323–325.

Jöreskog, K. G., & Lawley, D. N. (1968). New methods in maximum likelihood factor analysis. *British Journal of Mathematical and Statistical Psychology, 21,* 85–96.

Kohn, A. (1994). The truth about self-esteem. *Phi Delta Kappan, 76,* 272–283.

Kolligian, J., & Sternberg, R. J. (1991). Perceived fraudulence in young adults: Is there an "Impostor Syndrome"? *Journal of Personality Assessment, 56,* 308–326.

Marsh, H. W. (1990). The structure of academic self-concept: The Marsh-Shavelson Model. *Journal of Educational Psychology, 82,* 623–636.

Maslow, A. H. (1943). A dynamic theory of human motivation. *Psychological Review, 50,* 370–396.

Maslow, A. H. (1954). *Motivation and personality*. New York: Harper & Row.

Meece, J. L., Wigfield, A., & Eccles, J. S. (1990). Predictors of math anxiety and its influence on young adolescents' course enrollment and performance in mathematics. *Journal of Educational Psychology, 82,* 60–70.

Middleton, M. J., & Midgley, C. (1997). Avoiding the demonstration of lack of ability: An underexplored aspect of goal theory. *Journal of Educational Psychology, 89,* 710–718.

Midgley, C., Maehr, M., Hicks, L., Roeser, R., Urdan, T., Anderman, E., & Kaplan, A. (1996). *Patterns of Adaptive Learning Survey (PALS)*. Ann Arbor, MI: Center for Leadership and Learning.

Myers, D. G. (2001). *Psychology* (6th ed.). New York: Worth.

Noddings, N. (1992). *The challenge to care in schools: An alternative approach to education*. New York: Teachers College Press.

Pajares, F. (1994). Inviting self-efficacy: The role of invitations in the development of confidence and competence in writing. *Journal of Invitational Theory and Practice, 3,* 13–24.

Pajares, F. (1996). Self-efficacy beliefs in academic settings. *Review of Educational Research, 66,* 543–578.

Pajares, F., Britner, S., & Valiante, G. (2000). Writing and science achievement goals of middle school students. *Contemporary Educational Psychology.*

Pajares, F., & Graham, L. (1999). Self-efficacy, motivation constructs, and mathematics performance of entering middle school students. *Contemporary Educational Psychology, 24,* 124–139.

Pajares, F., Miller, M. D., & Johnson, M. J. (1997). Writing self-beliefs of elementary school students. *Journal of Educational Psychology, 91,* 51–60.

Pajares, F., & Schunk, D. H. (in press). Self-efficacy, self-concept, and academic achievement. In J. Aronson & D. Cordova (Eds.), *Psychology of education: Personal and interpersonal forces*. New York: Academic Press.

Pajares, F., & Valiante, G. (1997). Influence of writing self-efficacy beliefs on the writing performance of upper elementary students. *The Journal of Educational Research, 90,* 353–360.

Pajares, F., & Valiante, G. (1999). Grade level and gender differences in the writing self-beliefs of middle school students. *Contemporary Educational Psychology, 24,* 390–405.

Pajares, F., & Zeldin, A. L. (1999). Inviting self-efficacy revisited: The role of invitations in the lives of women with mathematics-related careers. *Journal of Invitational Theory and Practice, 6,* 48–68.

Pedhazur, E. J. (1982). *Multiple regression in behavioral research: Explanation and prediction* (2nd ed.). New York: Harcourt Brace.

Peterson, C. (1990). Explanatory style in the classroom and on the playing

September/October 2001 [Vol. 95(No. 1)]

field. In S. Graham & V. Folkes (Eds.), *Attribution theory: Applications to achievement, mental health, and interpersonal conflict* (pp. 53–75). Hillsdale, NJ: Erlbaum.

Peterson, C. (2000). The future of optimism. *American Psychologist, 55,* 44-55.

Pintrich, P. R. (1999, April). *Multiple goals, multiple pathways: The role of goal orientation in learning and achievement.* Paper presented at the meeting of the Society for Research in Child Development, Albuquerque, NM.

Pintrich, P. R., & Schunk, D. H. (1997). *Motivation in education.* Englewood Cliffs, NJ: Merrill-Prentice Hall.

Purkey, W. W. (2000). *What students say to themselves: Internal dialogue and school success.* Thousand Oaks, CA: Corwin.

Purkey, W., & Novak, J. (1996). *Inviting school success* (3rd. ed.). Belmont, CA: Wadsworth.

Scheier, M. F., & Carver, C. S. (1985). Optimism, coping, and health: Assessment and implications of generalized outcome expectancies. *Health Psychology, 4,* 219–247.

Scheier, M. F., & Carver, C. S. (1992). Effects of optimism on psychological and physical well-being: Theoretical overview and empirical update. *Cognitive Therapy and Research, 16,* 201–238.

Schmidt, J., Shields, C., & Ciechalski, J. (1998). The inviting-disinviting index: A study of validity and reliability. *Journal of Invitational Theory and Practice, 5,* 31–42.

Schunk, D. H. (1991). Self-efficacy and academic motivation. *Educational Psychologist, 26,* 207–231.

Seegers, G., & Boekaerts, M. (1996). Gender-related differences in self-referenced cognitions in relation to mathematics. *Journal for Research in Mathematics Education, 27,* 215–240.

Seligman, M. E. P. (1991). *Learned optimism.* New York: Knopf.

Seligman, M. E. P., & Csikszentmihalyi, M. (Eds.). (2000a). Positive psychology [Special issue]. *American Psychologist, 55*(1).

Seligman, M. E. P., & Csikszentmihalyi, M. (2000b). Positive psychology: An introduction. *American Psychologist, 55,* 5–14.

Skaalvik, E. (1997). Issues in research on self-concept. In M. Maehr & P. R. Pintrich (Eds.), *Advances in motivation and achievement* (Vol. 10, pp. 51–97). Greenwich, CT: JAI Press.

Stipek, D. (1998). *Motivation to learn: From theory to practice.* Boston: Allyn & Bacon.

Thompson, B., & Borello, G. M. (1985). The importance of structure coefficients in regression research. *Educational and Psychological Measurement, 45,* 203–209.

Urdan, T. C. (1997). Achievement goal theory: Past results, future directions. In M. Maher & P. R. Pintrich (Eds.), *Advances in motivation and achievement* (Vol. 10, pp. 99–142). Greenwich, CT: JAI Press.

Vaillant, G. E. (2000). Adaptive mental mechanisms: Their role in a positive psychology. *American Psychologist, 55,* 89–98.

Valiante, G., & Pajares, F. (1999). Invitations, motivation, and academic achievement. *Journal of Invitational Theory and Practice, 6,* 28–47.

Wiemer, D., & Purkey, W. (1994). Love Thyself as Thy Neighbor?: Self-other orientations of inviting behaviors. *Journal of Invitational Theory and Practice, 3,* 25–33.

Zimmerman, B. J. (1989). A social cognitive view of self-regulated academic learning. *Journal of Educational Psychology, 81,* 329–339.

Zimmerman, B., & Bandura, A. (1994). Impact of self-regulatory influences on writing course attainment. *American Education Research Journal, 31,* 845–862.

Zimmerman, B. J., Bandura, A., & Martinez-Pons, M. (1992). Self-motivation for academic attainment: The role of self-efficacy beliefs and personal goal setting. *American Educational Research Journal, 29,* 663–676.

Zimmerman, B. J., & Martinez-Pons, M. (1988). Construct validation of a strategy model of student self-regulated learning. *Journal of Educational Psychology, 80,* 284–290.

Zimmerman, B. J., & Schunk, D. H. (1989). (Eds.). *Self-regulated learning and academic achievement: Theory, research, and practice.* New York: Springer-Verlag.

Topic:

_____

_____

_____

Procedures:

_____

_____

_____

_____

Method of analysis:

_____

_____

_____

Major conclusions:

_____

_____

_____

_____

_____

Fifth-graders' mathematical communications: Lessons from the field
The Educational Forum; West Lafayette; Fall 2001; Jill A Perry;

Volume: 66
Issue: 1
Start Page: 71
ISSN: 00131725
Full Text:

Copyright Kappa Delta Pi Fall 2001

I had the privilege of spending six months during the winter of 2000 and spring of 2001 in a fifth-grade, public school classroom with 23 children and their teacher, Kelly Richards. I entered their classroom with a blue rollerball pen, a yellow pad, and a question: What is the nature of children's communications as they engage in mathematical tasks individually, in small groups, and in whole-class situations? The question evolved out of my interests in the connections among mathematics and literacy, language, and communication-interests that began to emerge when I was a high school mathematics teacher.

SITUATING THE STUDY

In 1989, the National Council of Teachers of Mathematics (NCTM) published the Curriculum and Evaluation Standards for School Mathematics. This document began a widespread shift in the way many educators think, write, and talk about mathematics education in the United States. NCTM suggested that educators should approach the teaching of mathematics in new ways and proposed changes in both content (e.g., number sense and numeration, geometry, and probability) and processes (e.g., problem solving, communication, reasoning, and connections). Suggesting a broader definition and use of communication in the mathematics classroom, NCTM (1989,6) called for an increase in students' reading, writing, discussing, representing, and modeling mathematics, because, "as students communicate their ideas, they learn to clarify, refine, and consolidate their thinking." Teachers who embraced the standards sought ways to shift the emphasis in their classrooms from talking and writing as answer-giving to talking and writing as sense-making.

In April 2000, NCTM released its revised "standards document," Principles and Standards for School Mathematics (PSSM). In PSSM, communication as a standard maintained its prominent status. Now, however, the forms emphasized in the communication-process standard are verbal and written, while the symbolic, graphic, pictorial, and gestural forms are emphasized separately in a representation-process standard (NCTM 2000). The separation is not a true bifurcation; instead, it underscores the important role that representation plays in the communication of and about mathematics. NCTM (2000, 67) explicitly acknowledged the link between the two: "Representations should be treated as essential elements ... in communicating mathematical approaches, arguments, and understandings to one's self and to others." Representation can, but does not have to, have a communicative purpose.

An interest in communication and representation in mathematics education is also evident in the projects of a number of researchers (Alro and Skovsmose 1998; Cobb and Bauersfeld 1995; Cobb, Yackel, and McClain 2000; Durkin and Shire 1991; Lampert 1990; Pimm 1987; Rowland 2000; Sfard 2000; and Steinbring, Bartolini Bussi, and Sierpinska 1998). In seeking to understand the nature of communication in the mathematics classroom, these and other researchers have provided insight into the complexities of mathematics learning and teaching, classroom cultures, and mathematical language, representations, and communications.

SCRATCHING THE SURFACE

At the start of my study, I knew very little about the children in the fifth-grade classroom. Kelly Richards gave me some of the demographic information during the first week of my visits. Of the 23 children in Ms. Richards class, 3 were African American, 1 was Haitian, 1 was Hispanic, 1 was Middle Eastern, and 17 were European American. This was representative of the school population. There were 13 girls and 10 boys. Four of the children were identified as having at least one "specific learning disability" (SLD) and were "pulled out" for their SLD classes in

---

Perry, J. (2001). Fifth-graders' mathematical communications: Lessons from the field. *The Educational Forum, 66(1).* West Lafayette, IN: Kappa Delta Pi. *Copyright Kappa Delta Pi Fall 2001. Reproduced with permission of the copyright owner. Further reproduction or distribution is prohibited without permission.*

the morning. Four of the children were identified as "gifted." These students were pulled out for their gifted class for most of one day each week. The other 13 children included in this study had not been identified as having exceptionalities and were considered "typical" students.

Kelly Richards is a "reform-inspired" (Sfard 2000) teacher who provides activities and problems in which her students explore mathematical ideas individually, in small groups, and as a whole class. Because she considers children's oral, written, and pictorial forms of communication important to the learning of mathematics, she encourages her students to use these multiple forms as they work. With the exception of two one-day activities, I did not alter the curriculum. Ms. Richards was open to allowing me a greater involvement in planning and teaching, but I wanted to study children in a real classroom and did not want the responsibilities of a teacher. I wanted to have the freedom to lose myself in the children's interactions.

METHODOLOGY

During the six months I spent with these fifth-graders, I immersed myself in their words, pictures, voices, laughter, and frustrations. I gathered myriad images, sounds, words, and emotions in multiple forms-field notes, videotapes, audiotapes, students' work, and memories-and immersed myself in them at home. I continuously cycled through the materials, questioning them and myself to make sense of the patterns that emerged. Through this process, I engaged in qualitative inquiry as Janesick (2000) described it. Because I was with them over time and collected multiple forms of data, I came to know the children as individuals and as a class-to go beyond the surface (Janesick 2000).

DATA COLLECTION

At all stages of the study, I observed students as they worked alone as well as in pairs, small groups, and whole-class settings. Handwritten field notes (Emerson, Fretz, and Shaw 1995; Sanjek 1990; Patton 1990), a reflective journal (Janesick 2000), audio- and videotapes of the children in whole-class and smallgroup settings, and notes and transcriptions of portions of audio- and videotapes were my data. In addition, because written and other forms of mathematical communications were of interest in this study, I collected, date stamped, photocopied, scanned, printed, or photographed student and classroom artifacts (Hodder 2000; Patton 1990).

During the third month of the study, I began to interview the children informally about their mathematical thinking, intentions, and communications as my curiosities arose, recording their responses in my field notes and capturing some on tape. I tried not to interrupt the children as they worked; instead, I talked to them during pauses in and transitions between activities, during the last ten minutes of class (at the end of their mathematics time), and before mathematics time began on the following day. I hoped for these interviews to be light and conversational in tone (Heath 1983; Patton 1990), something like the "unstructured interviewing" Fontana and Frey (2000) described.

The children adjusted quickly to this type of interviewing; it became a normal, unforced part of our interactions throughout the remainder of the study. Some of the children became comfortable enough that at times we were able to engage in conjecturetesting, wherein I would tell them what I conjectured about their mathematical communications and thinking and they would agree with, refute, or revise my conjectures (Popper 1963; Lakatos 1976). My interactions with the children, especially after I had been with them for five months, suggested that they responded honestly, that they were not just trying to tell me what they thought I wanted to hear. In addition to looking for patterns and relationships in my assumptions about their intentions and understandings, I looked for patterns and relationships among the children's self-reported intentions and understandings.

DATA ANALYSIS

I analyzed data throughout the study, using "inductive analysis," letting the categories, themes, and patterns emerge from the data rather than forcing them into preconceived categories (Janesick 2000). By writing analytical commentaries, I made my assumptions and impositions visible, "capturing... ruminations, reflections, and insights and mak[ing] them available for further thought and analysis" (Emerson, Fretz, and Shaw 1995, 100). These also provided a place for me to make sense of what I was observing and thinking-the interpretive-separate from my descriptive field notes and post-observation notes.

I learned to rely on and trust my intuitions about students and my classroom. In addition, I learned to be open to adjustments in those intuitions as situations changed, as I gathered new information. Intuition is intangible; analysis began the day I entered the classroom. The depth and richness of my analysis grew as I gathered more data-empirical and ephemeral-as I stayed with the children and the data over time.

PRIMARY FINDINGs

Eventually, three broad themes emerged from the data (Perry 2001). First, children negotiate meaning individually. Second, they also negotiate meaning with their peers. Finally, children demonstrate their understanding to others.

Negotiating Meaning Individually

There were many indications that the children were actively engaged in negotiating meaning individually. Through observing the children as they worked, I learned that the children regularly engaged in this process with themselves. Indeed, they preferred to try to make sense of the mathematics for themselves before they engaged in negotiation of meaning with others. When the children created visuals as part of their individual negotiation of meaning, their erasures and cross-outs made visible their attempts at sensemaking.

Creating Visuals. Most of the children perceived creating visuals as a part of doing mathematics rather than as external to the process. I use the term visuals in the broad sense in which Cobb (2000, 18) used the term symbols, to include conventional mathematical symbols along with pictures and "physical materials as well as charts, tables, graphs, and nonstandard notations." The children's primary intention in creating visuals was to help themselves understand the mathematics, to negotiate meaning with themselves. In Ms. Richards class, some of the children drew pictures to help themselves understand their mathematical tasks only when the task was visual in nature, while others created pictures to negotiate meaning of the mathematics individually even when the task was not visual in nature. These findings are consistent with Presmeg's (1986) conclusions from her study of high school students. One student extended individual negotiation in a way atypical of most of the children's work: she used color even when it was not a part of the task. Clearly, the children negotiated meaning with themselves in many ways, but some had more strategies than others.

There are some fascinating implications of these findings. Sfard (1994, 49) found that the mathematicians she interviewed said "they just could not think without making pictures." If we wish to help children become a part of the larger mathematical community, we should foster children's use of multiple forms of representation and communication of and about mathematics by providing experiences and problems that can be approached using several different forms of representation. In addition, having children work together on problems and asking them to provide at least two different approaches to solving those problems might extend the children's repertoires. Critical to this process is a whole-class debriefing in which the children share their approaches.

Crossing-Out and Erasure. The visuals the children created as they worked out problems and tested their ideas tended to be sloppy and unorganized (to an interloper), revealing the spontaneous nature of this type of communication. To the children, what self-communications looked like did not matter as much as the meaning made during the process of creating and revising them. When the children drew pictures and symbolized as part of their individual negotiation of meaning, their erasures and cross-outs made visible their attempts at sense-making. They did this crossing-out after they thought they had "finished the math," as they were looking back over it to see if it made sense. They crossed out the work that they had concluded was not "right." Students often left trails of erasures, revealing the starts and stops that they made as they continuously revisited their work and thinking in making sense of the mathematics. They were privately engaged in the self-questioning that we, as math teachers, hope children pursue.

Again, important implications can be derived from this study. In addition to looking at the children's answers (and the work neatly rewritten in a "Show your work" section), teachers should look at the children's private scratch work and drawings. We should value this messiness as an assessment tool and use such draft work as a starting point for interviews with individual children about their mathematical thinking.

Self Time. When given a small-group task, the children seemed to prefer to try to make sense of the mathematics for themselves before they engaged in negotiation of meaning with others. This "self time" seemed necessary for most of the children, who used it to negotiate meaning with themselves in two primary ways: creating visuals and verbalizing their self-talk. In addition to working independently within their small groups, children talked to themselves as they sought to make sense of the mathematics. Sometimes, the children reached a point at which they could no longer negotiate meaning with themselves, due to a conceptual lacking or failure because they did not have an understanding of the conventional notation necessary to record the answer. When the negotiation process broke down, they either tried to go on to the next task, asked their teacher, or turned to a group mate. Because this process seemed important for so many of the children, a few minutes of "self time" should be worked into small group activities. The children did this on their own, and there seemed to be a bit of autonomy to the process, which is what we want to foster. If "self time" becomes a regular part of class time, teachers may send the message that this kind of time is valuable. Regular allocation and expectation of "self time" might also give teachers

an opportunity to help those children who do not seem to self-talk figure out what to do with that kind of time. Teachers could use this as a "learning strategies" time.

Negotiating Meaning with Peers

Negotiation of meaning with their peers occurred most often in the form of talk during small-group discussions. The children talked, wrote, symbolized, drew, gestured, and built their mathematical understanding into being, but the children's talk was central to their mathematical activity. Whether as an entire class or in small groups, students used talk most often when communicating with others about their mathematical problems and activities. They talked to find out what others were thinking, to explain their own thinking and to clarify tasks. Talk was the medium through which they almost exclusively engaged in negotiations of mathematical meaning and tasks with others.

Need for Time. The time it took children to come to a shared meaning varied greatly, ranging from only a few minutes to the entire class period. We cannot know how much time it will take children to reach a shared meaning for the mathematics in which they are engaged, but children must have sufficient time to work together to negotiate meaning.

Visuals and Peer Negotiations. The children supported their talk with pictures and scratch work, but typically only if they had created them prior to coming to the discussion. They created these visuals for themselves before they used them in their discussions with others. They did not create visuals spontaneously as they worked in groups. Their already-created visuals clarified and amplified their arguments, thinking, and questions, which differs from Sfard's (1994,49) findings that mathematicians drew pictures when they were "trying to explain" concepts to her.

Negotiating the Task. Moreover, before the children could come to a shared meaning of the mathematics at hand, they first had to develop a shared understanding of the task. Methods of task negotiation ranged from simple questions from one student to another-such as "What are we supposed to do?"-to a direct explanation by the teacher to the class or group in an attempt to be sure that all understood the task. As teachers, we often take for granted that children are working on the teacher-assigned task. Yet children spend varying amounts of time negotiating their tasks. Sometimes, only a few details are needed; at other times, the entire math period might consist of trying to figure out what to do. Children trying to engage in a sensemaking activity will find one.

Christiansen (1997) contended that students must have a common understanding of the goal of and directions for a task before they are able to negotiate a common meaning for the mathematics content. It is essential that students engaged in mathematical tasks together share a common "context" for the task, as Christiansen (1997) found with high school freshmen. Ms. Richards's fifth-graders needed a common understanding of the task before they were able to come to a shared meaning for the mathematics. Sometimes, children merely asked one another what they were to do. Other times, it was a matter of reading the directions together. Ms. Richards directions and explanations were usually detailed enough that the children could figure out with their group mates what she wanted them to do. Sometimes, they called her over to tell her what they thought they were supposed to do, testing their ideas about the task. Sometimes, they just asked her. If a whole group was uncertain, she answered their questions and guided them through the first few minutes of a discussion to make sure that they knew what she wanted them to do. There were also times when they had just forged ahead in a wrong direction; she would gently redirect

them. Though the children might begin group work with a few minutes of procedural talk, they generally let their understanding of the task emerge as they worked.

What does this information imply? First, teachers must be mindful of giving their students clearly defined tasks. Still, however well-defined the task, children may engage in negotiating it. They may engage in talking before they get to work. Children, like adults, are social beings. In addition, they may not have been listening when the directions were given. Of course, they may not understand the mathematics, so they do not understand how to approach the task. Knowing that children spend time negotiating the task, however, teachers might allot more time for small-group activities than they think the task itself should take.

Failure to Reach Shared Meaning. Unfortunately, at times, no shared meaning emerged from small-group discussions. Sometimes, children were not respectful of one another; at other times, someone in the group took on the role of "teacher." Reasons for this failure depended on the children's perceptions as well as the situation. Lampert (1990,55) identified this same type of behavior in her students' interactions, considering it a "nonmathematical way of knowing." Negotiation of shared meaning was most successful when respect was equal among group members and when there was no "teacher-talk" present-even when the lecturing came from the teacher.

When Ms. Richards entered a group, the task of the group changed from attempting to negotiate a shared meaning to searching for only the right answer and receiving her approval. Even when Ms. Richards was just proximal to the group, the flow reverted back to having her as the audience, with the burden of probing and directing on her shoulders. The shift was palpable and often had the effect of shutting down negotiations.

Because negotiating a shared meaning was most successful when respect was shared equally among group members and when there was no teacher-talk present, explicit discussion of the mathematics as well as small-group interactions should be part of debriefing sessions. Negotiating a shared meaning was also most successful when children engaged in a mathematically rich task that required divergent thinking. When these types of activities were provided, the focus became negotiating meaning rather than solely memorizing and applying preexisting definitions and formulae.

Demonstrating Understanding to Others

Ms. Richards's students perceived their primary goal to be demonstrating their thinking and understanding to their teacher. They displayed this goal both in whole-class discussions and in writing.

Whole-Class Discussions. In contrast to their general perception that small-group work provided a forum for work with others to understand the mathematics, the children perceived the wholeclass discussion as a forum for explaining their thinking and strategies to and test their ideas with their intended audience-their teacher. These findings differ from Yackel's (1995) analysis of second-graders' talk in small-group and whole-class interactions. As Yackel (1995,132) concluded, "From the student's point of view, the purposes for talking in the classroom are to explain their thinking to others and to challenge and question the thinking of others."

During whole-class discussions, Ms. Richards's students experienced a kind of "fishbowl" phenomenon-they perceived that their peers were observing and judging all comments. In whole-class situations, Ms. Richards led the discussions, asking the students for answers, ideas, questions, strategies, and explanations. The flow of these discussions was fairly consistent: she would pose a question, call on individual children to answer, and then follow up their responses with a request for an explanation, a probing question, or a redirection. Often, the children listened to one another and then responded to Ms. Richards about how their solutions and strategies were similar or different.

In these interactions, the children seemed to be seeking teacher validation of their own thinking rather than seeking to validate others' thinking. Also, they would change their answers and adopt different strategies throughout the course of a discussion. They knew that this happened to them but did not seem to think that it happened to their classmates, too. In general, they did not perceive that a purpose for talking during whole-class discussions was to contribute to others' learning.

Students did not perceive such discussions as opportunities for two-way negotiation of meaning. However, the children listened to one another, considered other approaches and answers, and sometimes modified their thinking or commented on a peer's contribution. This was almost always done through Ms. Richards, however. Only one student viewed this time differently and consistently tried to engage her peers in discussion. However, they did not think it was their responsibility in this forum; relegating that onus to Ms. Richards. In that light, they did not address each other directly. Their goal in whole-class discussions was to demonstrate their understanding rather than to test or build others'. It was like a showcase.

Like most teachers, Ms. Richards used this time to assess the children's individual understandings of the mathematics. However, the richness of their small-group discussions suggests that providing class time in which children engage in whole-class negotiations of meaning with their peers and their teacher could be a great learning tool. Yet this type of engagement did not seem natural to the children; it had to be taught (or re-taught). Making whole-class negotiation an object of discussion could help children become independent thinkers and negotiators.

Writing. Writing, too, seemed to be a showcase. Just like whole-class discussion tended to happen after students had worked on the mathematical tasks alone or in groups, so did the children's writing. It was a written form of whole-class talk: they gave answers, explained their thinking, and showed their work. Their overarching goal was to demonstrate their thinking and understanding to their teacher.

Most children saw writing as having two purposes: explaining and showing work. In contrast to their perception of drawing pictures and symbolizing as integral to doing mathematics, the children perceived writing as external to the process. When the children tried to make sense of the mathematics they were doing, they did not "write" except to record answers and do scratch work using numerals and other conventional mathematical symbols. They did not see justifying, reflecting, or testing ideas as purposes for writing. One explanation might be that they are not developmentally ready for these other kinds of writing, though they did use these types periodically. In an age of standardized testing gone amuck, it is not surprising that the children would be inundated with this type of writing prompt.

Because children use familiar communicative and conceptual tools, providing experiences with tools they do not have is important. Children should have multiple and frequent experiences with writing for different purposes, such as justifying, testing ideas, reflecting, explaining, and showing work.

LEARNING FROM THE KIDS

We have much to learn about mathematics and mathematics education from the students sitting in mathematics classrooms-from what they create, say, draw, write, symbolize, graph, and gesture. To learn this, we must be present with students as they go about their daily routines of work and play. From spending six months with these fifth-graders and conducting hundreds of those "informal interviews" (known as conversations outside the realm of formal research), I learned that talking with students is important. I learned the importance of talking with them about the mathematics and about themselves as learners, thinkers, doers, and people.

By watching, listening, taking notes, tape recording, videotaping, and collecting children's creations, teachers and researchers have a better chance of finding out about children's mathematical understandings and interactions. Paying attention to their social interactions is important as well, looking in on individual students as they work in small groups, individually, and in whole-class settings. We must go beyond observing students to learn their interpretations of settings and their expectations from those settings. For classroom teachers, this stretch is difficult, because time is often very limited.

However, the value of restructuring time so that this type of observing is possible seems to linger in the voices of the fifth-graders. Research partnerships between college faculty members and classroom teachers can also prove to be invaluable. Ultimately, the responsibility to bridge the gap between the two rests on the shoulders of the college faculty members. They must stay current-and, to do that, they must be in the classroom with children and their teachers.

REFERENCES

Alro, H., and 0. Skovsmose. 1998. That was not the intention! Communication in mathematics education. For the Learning of Mathematics 18(2): 42-51.

Christiansen, 1. 1997. When negotiation of meaning is also negotiation of task. Educational Studies in Mathematics 34(1): 1-25.

Cobb, P. 2000. From representations to symbolizing: Introductory comments on semiotics and mathematical learning. In Symbolizing and communicating in mathematics classrooms, ed. P. Cobb, E. Yackel, and K. McClain, 17-36. Hillsdale, N.J.: L. Erlbaum Associates.

Cobb, P., and H. Bauersfeld, eds. 1995. The emergence of mathematical meaning: Interaction in classroom cultures. Hillsdale, N.J.: L. Erlbaum Associates.

Cobb, P., E. Yackel, and K. McClain, eds. 2000. Symbolizing and communicating in mathematics classrooms. Hillsdale, N.J.: L. Erlbaum Associates.

Durkin, K., and B. Shire, eds. 1991. Language in mathematical education: Research and practice. Bristol, Pa.: Open University Press.

Emerson, R. M., R. I. Fretz, and L. L. Shaw. 1995. Writing ethnographic fieldnotes. Chicago: University of Chicago Press.

Fontana, A., and J. H. Frey. 2000. The interview: From structured questions to negotiated texts. In Handbook of qualitative research, 2d ed., ed. N. K. Denzin and Y. S. Lincoln, 645-72. Thousand Oaks, Calif.: Sage.

Heath, S. B. 1983. Way with words: Language, life, and work in communities and classrooms. New York: Cambridge University Press.

Hodder, 1. 2000. The interpretation of document and material culture. In Handbook of qualitative research, 2d ed., ed. N. K. Denzin and Y. S. Lincoln, 703-15. Thousand Oaks, Calif.: Sage.

Janesick, V. J. 2000. The choreography of qualitative research design: Minuets, improvisations, and crystallization. In Handbook of qualitative research, 2d ed., ed. N. K. Denzin and Y. S. Lincoln, 379-99. Thousand Oaks, Calif.: Sage.

Lakatos, 1. 1976. Proofs and refutations: The logic of mathematical discovery. New York: Cambridge University Press. Lampert, M. 1990. When the problem is not the question and the solution is not the answer: Mathematical knowing and teaching. American Educational Research Journal 27(l): 29-63.

National Council of Teachers of Mathematics. 1989. Curriculum and evaluation standards for school mathematics. Reston, Va.: NCTM.

National Council of Teachers of Mathematics. 2000. Principles and standards for school mathematics. Reston, Va.: NCTMPatton, M. Q. 1990. Qualitative evaluation and research methods, 2d ed. New bury Park, Calif.: Sage.

Perry, J. A. 2001. Negotiating meaning, demonstrating understanding: Perceptions and intentions in fifth-graders' mathematical communications. Ph.D. diss., University of Central Florida.

Pimm, D. 1987. Speaking mathematically: Communication in mathematics classrooms. New York: Routledge.

Popper, K. R. 1963. Conjectures and refutations: The growth of scientific knowledge. New York: Routledge.

Presmeg, N. C. 1986. Visualization in high school mathematics. For the Learning of Mathematics 6(3): 42-46.

Rowland, T. 2000. The pragmatics of mathematics education: Vagueness in mathematical discourse. New York: Falmer. Sanjek, R., ed. 1990. Fieldnotes: The makings of anthropology. Ithaca, N.Y.: Cornell University Press.

Sfard, A. 1994. Reification as the birth of metaphor. For the Learning of Mathematics 14(1): 44-55.

Sfard, A. 2000. On reform movement and the limits of mathematical discourse. Mathematical Thinking and Learning 2(3): 157-89.

Steinbring, H., M. G. Bartolini-Bussi, and A. Sierpinska, eds. 1998. Language and communication in the mathematics classroom. Reston, Va.: National Council of Teachers of Mathematics.

Yackel, E. 1995. Children's talk in inquiry mathematics classrooms. In The emergence of mathematical meaning: Interaction in classroom cultures, ed. P. Cobb and H. Bauersfeld, 131-62. Hillsdale, N.J.: L. Erlbaum Associates.

I like mathematics because it is not human and has nothing to do with this planet or with the whole accidental universe—because, like Spinoza's God, it won't love us in return.

BERTRAND RUSSEL, British philosopher, 1872–1970

Jill A. Perry is Assistant Professor of Secondary Education/Foundations of Education at Rowan University in Glassboro, New Jersey, where she teaches general and mathematics pedagogy courses. Her research interests include mathematics and literacy education.

Chapter 1 Answers
For Your Own Review
1. 1. Recognize and identify a topic to be studied
    2. Describe and execute procedures to collect information about the topic being studied
    3. Analyze the collected data
    4. State the results or implications based on analysis of the data.

Checking What You Know
1. a. Are there differences in preparation for kindergarten between students enrolled in either business-run or independent childcare? (Your answer may differ.)
    b. Applied (not deriving theory)
    c. Quantitative (test scores are data)
    d. Causal-comparative (comparing two groups)
    e. It is likely difficult to do experimentally because cannot randomly select and assign participants

2. Your answers to this exercise will likely differ. The following are examples.
    a. What content was included in standardized tests in 1960?
    b. How do teachers feel about administering standardized tests? (Assuming data collection through observation or interviews)
    c. How do administrators use the results of standardized test to improve decision-making? (Assuming data collection through survey)
    d. Is there a relationship between standardized test performance and teacher reports of student progress? (Note that there is relationship being examined and quantitative data.)
    e. How can we as teachers decrease the pressure students feel regarding standardized test taking? (Note that teachers are seeking to examine and act on a problem.)
    f. Are there differences in standardized test performance between different ethnic and racial groups? (Note that differences are being addressed and that the groups are predetermined so it is not experimental.)

Practicing the Tasks
1. a. This is an evaluation study because it entails decision-making
    b. This is an applied study that would likely be quantitative and would be conducted with a causal-comparative approach, comparing the gross motor skills of students both who were enrolled and those who were not enrolled.
    c. This study is applied and would likely be done with a descriptive survey design. It might be conducted with a qualitative approach, however.
    d. This study topic is an example of historical research.
    e. This is likely a qualitative study conducted through observations and interviews, perhaps ethnographic.
    f. Applied, correlational –seeks to address relationship between two variables
    g. Applied, causal-comparative—differences between two existing groups
    h. This is an applied descriptive study that would likely be done quantitatively through a survey or qualitatively through interviews.
    i. Applied, correlational (Note the relationship and quantitative data)
    j. Applied, causal-comparative
    k. Applied, experimental
    l. applied, likely survey
    m. Applied, quantitative, causal-comparative
    n. Likely qualitative although might be conducted as a descriptive survey study.
    o. Correlational
    p. Likely qualitative although might be conducted as a descriptive survey study.
    q. Descriptive, applied study that would likely be conducted either as a descriptive survey or as a qualitative interview study.
    r. Causal-comparative
    s. Correlational
    t. Causal-comparative
    u. Correlational

2.   **Tasks 1-A and 1-B:** The following answers provide the minimum amount of information you should be able to identify after reading the first chapter of the text.

Piotrowski, Botsko, & Matthews (2001)

Topic: How do parents, preschool teachers, and kindergarten teachers evaluate school readiness? (See manuscript page 539.)

Procedures: This study used survey methods. The CARES survey was administered.

Method of analysis: The study used descriptive statistics (means, standard deviations, percentages), ANOVAS and MANOVAS, and visual analyses (graphs)

Major conclusion: Generally, teachers in this study had lower expectations for school readiness than did parents of these young children.

Pajares (2001)

Topic: (See page 29 left column): To integrate constructs from positive psychology with academic motivation and to investigate relationships between these two areas of research.

Procedures: Several instruments were administered to a sample of middle school students.

Method of analysis: Correlations were presented to show relationships among variables.

Major conclusions: Several connections between positive psychology and academic motivation were apparent.

Perry (2001)

Topic: The study investigates communication within a fifth-grade mathematics classroom.

Procedures: This study included observations, interviews, and other data sources from the classroom (e.g. video, audio, student work).

Method of analysis: Inductive—some with conjecture testing with the participants.

Major conclusions: The author reports three themes: Negotiating meaning individually, negotiating meaning with peers, and demonstrating understanding to others. In presenting each of these three themes, Perry provides examples and support from her data.

Test-Like Event

1.	d	20.	a
2.	b	21.	b
3.	d	22.	a
4.	c	23.	d
5.	c		
6.	b		
7.	a		
8	c		
9.	b		
10.	a		
11.	c		
12.	a		
13.	d		
14.	c		
15.	b		
16.	d		
17.	b		
18.	a		
19.	c		

Chapter 2   Selecting and Defining a Research Topic

Chapter 2 Objectives

1.   Make a list of at least three educational topics on which you would be interested in conducting a research study.
2.   Select one of the topics and identify 10 to 15 complete references (source works) that directly relate to the selected problem. The references should include a variety of multiple source types (e.g., books, periodicals, Internet reports, etc.).
3.   Distinguish the difference between quantitative and qualitative methods of starting a research study.
4.   Read and abstract the references you have listed.
5.   Formulate a testable or descriptive hypothesis for your problem.

Review the Terms

Provide a succinct definition in your own words for each of the following terms.

Research topic: _____
_____

Theory: _____
_____

Replication: _____
_____

Review of literature: _____
_____

Library search: _____
_____

Keywords: _____
_____

Primary sources: _____
_____

Secondary sources: _____
_____

ERIC database: _____
_____

Abstracting: _____
_____

Hypothesis: _____
_____

Inductive hypothesis: _____
_____

Deductive hypothesis: _____
_____

Null hypothesis: _____
_____

Non-directional hypothesis: _____
_____

Directional hypothesis: _____
_____

Meta-analysis: _____
_____

For Your Own Review

1.   List the steps to abstracting presented in your text.

   _____
   _____
   _____
   _____
   _____
   _____
   _____
   _____
   _____

2.   State the five characteristics of a good topic.

   _____
   _____
   _____
   _____
   _____

3.   Recall the four characteristics of a good hypothesis.

   _____
   _____
   _____
   _____

4.   Your test suggests stating hypothesis in terms of P, X, & Y. Where P represents _____, X represents _____, and Y represents _____.

5. What functions might the review of related literature serve in a qualitative research study?

_____

_____

_____

_____

Other Sources for Review

To assist you with accessing resources, the AERA Special Interest Group (SIG) on Communication of Research has developed a Web site that provides links to educational research journals that are available online with no charge. Those included are peer-reviewed scholarly journals. This site can supplement the sources you access to find articles for your research topics. See http://aera-cr.ed.asu.edu/links.html.

Just for Practice

For each of the following sample research topic statements, determine if the study is qualitative or quantitative, and circle the correct term. If it is quantitative identify the P (participants), X (independent variable), and Y (dependent variable) by underlining and then labeling each in the statement. If it is qualitative, briefly describe the context and focus of the study.

1. The purpose of the current study is to identify if there are gender differences in self-esteem in fourth grade children.

    Quantitative   Qualitative

    _____

2. Research has consistently indicated that the transition to college life is difficult. The purpose of this study is to describe the typical first year experience for women at a small liberal arts college.

    Quantitative   Qualitative

    _____

3. For decades researchers have questioned the effects of pictures on learning from text. Some suggest that pictures distract the reader, while others indicate that pictures assist the reader in comprehension of the text. This study compares ninth-grade readers' comprehension of science text with and without pictures.

    Quantitative   Qualitative

    _____

4. As children age and gain experiences their ideas of future occupations changes as well. The purpose of this study is to discuss occupational interests with children of varying ages.

    Quantitative   Qualitative

    _____

5. The purpose of this study is to compare children's motivation for reading before and after enrollment in a summer reading program designed to teach phonemic awareness to struggling learners.

    Quantitative   Qualitative

    _____

Checking What You Know

1. Chapter 2 of your text suggests that some research ideas come from our everyday experiences. Have you ever wondered about cable subscriptions? It seems that cable companies are always sending advertisements, offering free previews, offering different enticements, and utilizing various forms of telemarketing! Consider the following research topic statement and answer the follow up questions.

    The current study investigates the differences in number of new cable subscriptions between those households that are offered a free preview and those who are given a first month discount.

    a. Is this likely a qualitative or quantitative topic statement? _____

        State the null, non-directional, and directional hypotheses that correspond with this topic statement.

    b. Null hypothesis: _____
        _____

    c. Non-directional hypothesis: _____
        _____

    d. Directional hypothesis:_____
        _____

2A. Thousands of SAT preparation programs exist to help future college and university students prepare to take the exam or to better their exam scores. Assume for a minute that you want to research SAT programs. For each of the following research topics related to research that might address SAT preparation programs, state a null hypothesis, a non-directional hypothesis, and a directional hypothesis. Then go back and label the participants (P), the treatments (X), and the outcome (Y) in your statements.

    Are there increases in SAT scores between those learners that take the "*We will make you smarter*" SAT preparation program over the course of two weeks and those who take the intensive weekend version?

    1. Null hypothesis: _____
        _____
        _____

    2. Non-directional hypothesis: _____
        _____
        _____

3. Directional hypothesis: _____
_____
_____

B. Are there increases in SAT scores between those students who are taught the "*We will make you smarter*" SAT preparation program by specially trained instructors or students who have been taught the program by certified, but not specially trained, high school teachers?

   1. Null hypothesis: _____
_____
_____

   2. Non-directional hypothesis: _____
_____
_____

   3. Directional hypothesis: _____
_____
_____

C. Is there a relationship between attendance in the SAT preparation program and increases in second administrations of the SAT?

   1. Null hypothesis: _____
_____
_____

   2. Non-directional hypothesis: _____
_____
_____

   3. Directional hypothesis: _____
_____
_____

Applying What You Know

1. Objective 2 in this chapter requires that students identify references that relate to their selected problem (*Select one of the topics and identify 10 to 15 complete references that directly relate to the selected problem. The references should include multiple sources (e.g., books, periodicals, Internet reports, etc).* As your text notes, it is not advisable to have a topic that is too broad, but often learners' initial topics <u>are</u> too broad. Further, sometimes students have difficulty applying search terms. For practice in narrowing a search use the following example. Suppose that you are interested in the effects of teaching children strategies to learn from text. After an initial ERIC search on *strategies and children* that yielded over 18,000 sources you know you have to narrow your search. You thought about it and realize that you are mostly interested in the effects of teaching learners to summarize text information. Go to the ERIC Database at <u>http://www.eric.ed.gov</u> and conduct the following search using the simple search function.

a. Use *strategy training* as a keyword search term. How many sources did you get? _____ (Note that the new ERIC site places the Boolean operator AND between terms. Just think of how many there would be if the search had been *strategy* OR *training*)

b. Well, strategy training is not a better search! Let's use the Narrow My Search option and only include sources since 1990. How many did you get? _____

c. Well, that is clearly still too many. Let's narrow further and include *reading* as a search term. Results? _____

d. Let's target only journal articles as well. _____

e. Still too broad! Let's also include children _____

This search should have yielded about 50 or so sources (depending on how many entries were in ERIC's database the particular time you conducted your search), which is a small enough number to start evaluating those sources.

2. In a recent search, I was looking for articles that address student learning from animation in science. I used the advanced search option in the ERIC database and used the terms *animation*, and *science* and *learning*.

Below are three of the citations and abstracts that resulted from that search. Your text refers you to suggestions for evaluating sources. While you cannot completely evaluate these sources without looking through the manuscripts, you can tell a lot from reading the abstracts. Answer the following questions for each of the three following abstracts.

- Is this a journal article?
- Is this a primary source, secondary source, or other source?
- Is this source from a scholarly journal?
- Is the source current?
- Does the source appear to be objective?

ERIC #: ED480531

Title: Discovering Nature with Young Children.
Authors: Chalufour, Ingrid; Worth, Karen;
Descriptors: Environmental Education; Inquiry; Integrated Curriculum; Learning Activities; Mathematics Education; Outdoor Education; Play; Preschool Curriculum; Preschool Education; Science Education; Scientific Literacy; Young Children
Journal Name: N/A
Journal Citation: N/A
Publication Date: 2003-00-00
Pages: 167
Pub Types: Guides - Classroom - Teacher
Abstract: Young children's curiosity about nature and their need to make sense of the world presents an opportunity to incorporate science as a natural and critical part of children's early learning. This guide, part of a preschool science curriculum, uses an inquiry approach to encourage young naturalists to observe life more closely, build an understanding of what is living and nonliving, and develop science inquiry skills and scientific dispositions. The guide's introduction describes the rationale and curriculum goals, details supportive characteristics of the classroom environment and culture, discusses the fundamental role of play, and offers suggestions for involving families. The remainder of the guide is organized into six sections. Section 1 provides tips for preparing the physical environment. Section 2 presents the open exploration of plants and animals, during which children learn to use basic tools and describe characteristics, behaviors, and needs of living things in their

natural environment. Section 3 involves more focused exploration of plants whereby teachers create opportunities for discussion and reflection as children are involved in growing plants, monitoring plant growth, studying plants and their parts, and conducting monthly observations. Section 4 involves more focused exploration of animals as children search for animals, create a terrarium for animal visitors, observe animals and their body parts, and study animal behavior and life cycles. Included throughout these sections are teaching plans and preparation steps. Sidebars provide examples, reminders, and sample teacher notes to illustrate how the curriculum may be implemented effectively. Section 5 presents extension activities to broaden learning experiences through field trips, guest naturalists, and books/videotapes. Section 6 highlights teachers' role in the inquiry process; describes observation, documentation, and assessment procedures; contains instructions for plant and animal care; details suggestions for involving families; and lists recommended books and videotapes. The guide's seven appendices include suggestions for long-term representational projects, guidelines for creating documentation panels, and forms for documenting learning activities and outcomes. (KB)

Identifiers:	Nature; Scientific Thinking
Source:	RIE
Level:	2
Institutions:	N/A
Sponsors:	N/A
ISBN(s):	ISBN-1-929610-38-6
ISSN(s):	N/A
Audiences:	Administrators; Practitioners; Teachers
Languages:	English
Geographic	Source: U.S.; Minnesota

Government Level: N/A

Publisher: Redleaf Press, 450 North Syndicate, Suite 5, St. Paul, MN 55104-4125 ($25.95). Tel: 800-423-8309 (Toll Free); Fax: 800-641-0115 (Toll Free); Web site: http://www.redleafpress.org.

a. Is this a journal article? _____

b. Is this a primary source, secondary source, other source? _____

c. Is this source from a scholarly journal? _____

d. Is the source current? _____

e. Does the source appear to be objective? _____

ERIC #:   EJ404224

Title:	The Effects of Computer Animated Elaboration Strategies and Practice on Factual and Application Learning in an Elementary Science Lesson.
Authors:	Rieber, Lloyd P.
Descriptors:	Analysis of Variance; Computer Assisted Instruction; Drills (Practice); Elementary Education; Elementary School Science; Hypothesis Testing; Learning Processes; Pretests Posttests; Science Instruction; Time on Task; Transfer of Training

Journal Name: Journal of Educational Computing Research

Journal Citation: v5 n4 p431-44 1989

Publication Date: 1989-00-00

Pages:	N/A
Pub Types:	Journal Articles; Reports - Research

Abstract:	Describes study that was conducted to examine the effects of animation and practice on factual and application learning in elementary science computer-based instruction (CBI). The extent to which animation and practice promoted near and far transfer of learning outcomes is explored, and effects on processing time are examined. (31 references) LRW

Identifiers:	Computer Animation
Source:	CIJE

Level: N/A
Institutions: N/A
Sponsors: N/A
ISBN(s):   N/A
ISSN(s):   N/A
Audiences: N/A
Languages: English
Geographic Source: N/A
Government Level: N/A
Publisher: N/A

    f.   Is this a journal article? _____

    g.   Is this a primary source, secondary source, or other source? _____

    h.   Is this source from a scholarly journal? _____

    i.   Is the source current? _____

    j.   Does the source appear to be objective? _____

ERIC #:   ED468892

Title: Teaching Science Online: Hands Off Is Not Minds Off!
Authors: Schoenfeld-Tacher, Regina; McConnell, Sherry; Schultheiss, Patricia; Bowen, Richard; Jones, Robert
Descriptors: Discourse Analysis; Distance Education; Higher Education; Instructional Design; Instructional Effectiveness; Online Courses; Science Instruction; Web Based Instruction
Journal Name: N/A
Journal Citation: N/A
Publication Date: 2002-00-00
Pages: 14
Pub Types: Reports - Research

Abstract: This study used Bloom's Taxonomy in conjunction with new and emerging research paradigms, such as discourse analysis, to examine the outcomes of online science instruction in various biomedical science courses (i.e., histology, histopathology, physiology, microbiology, and farm animal anatomy). By combining quantitative and qualitative data, a fuller picture of how distance delivery affects student learning in the context of various science courses is developed. Data sources included chat transcripts, course exams, direct observations, and student surveys. Results show that it is possible to teach a science course, including laboratories, entirely online without any adverse effects on academic outcomes. By addressing the effects of a delivery system on classroom interactions and academic performance for science content, the study makes a contribution to the body of knowledge about distance education. (Contains 24 references.) (MES)

Identifiers: Blooms Taxonomy
Source: RIE
Level: 2
Institutions: N/A
Sponsors: N/A
ISBN(s):   N/A
ISSN(s):   N/A
Audiences: N/A
Languages: English
Geographic Source: U.S.; Colorado
Government Level: N/A
Publisher: N/A

    k.   Is this a journal article? _____

    l.   Is this a primary source, secondary source, or other source? _____

    m.   Is this source from a scholarly journal? _____

n. Is the source current? _____
o. Does the source appear to be objective? _____

Test-Like Event

1. According to your text the first step in selecting a topic is

    a. identifying a general topic or problem of interest to you.
    b. going to the library to conduct a hand search of recent articles.
    c. generating a research hypothesis statement.
    d. identifying the variables you will examine in the study.

2. Of the following, which is considered an important characteristic of a good research topic?

    a. The topic can be answered through opinion.
    b. The topic can be investigated within a year.
    c. The topic contributes to theory or practice.
    d. The topic requires a measure of student learning.

3. According to your text, there are three main sources best used to identify research topics. Which of the following is NOT a source promoted by your text?

    a. theories
    b. library search
    c. personal experiences
    d. replications

4. According to characteristics of good topics presented in your text, which of the following is the best example of a good topic?

    a. Should teachers rely on ability grouping in classrooms for reading instruction?
    b. Of all the ways children learn in school, do they best learn through observation?
    c. Are there increased math skills of those involved in the peer-tutoring program?
    d. Should parents read to their children prior to school enrollment so that they become better readers?

5. Jessica needs a research topic for her thesis. She goes to the library and goes through all of the journals searching for ideas. Evaluate Jessica's strategy for finding a research topic.

    a. The strategy will likely work well because she will be familiar with current research.
    b. The strategy will likely not work because she will find too narrow of a topic.
    c. The strategy will likely not work because libraries are better used after the topic is identified.
    d. The strategy will work well because she will find something in which she is both interested and skilled.

Use the following research topic to answer questions 6-8: *Is there a significant difference in sixth grade student achievement as measured by classroom tests between learners taught via overhead and those taught via slides?*

6.   Given the following examples, the null hypothesis is

   a.   There is a significant difference in student achievement between those taught via overhead and those taught via slides.
   b.   There is no difference between student achievement between those taught via overhead and those taught via slides.
   c.   Those taught via slides will outperform those taught via overhead on student achievement as measured by classroom tests.

7.   The non-directional hypothesis is

   a.   There is a significant difference in student achievement between those taught via overhead and those taught via slides.
   b.   There is no difference between student achievement between those taught via overhead and those taught via slides.
   c.   Those taught via slides will outperform those taught via overhead on student achievement as measured by classroom tests.

8.   The directional hypothesis is

   a.   There is a significant difference in student achievement between those taught via overhead and those taught via slides.
   b.   There is no difference between student achievement between those taught via overhead and those taught via slides.
   c.   Those taught via slides will outperform those taught via overhead on student achievement as measured by classroom tests.

9.   Which of the following is a primary source regarding the effects of attention on learning?

   a.   A research report published in the *Elementary School Journal*.
   b.   A summary of a study in Willingham's (2001) <u>Cognition</u> textbook.
   c.   A review article published in *Educational Psychology Review*.
   d.   A website that summarizes the findings from attention studies conducted in the last three years.

10. Given the following hypothesis, which of the following represents the independent variable?
   Graduate students who study statistics concepts with computer-generated simulations perform better on application problems than those students who learn statistics with text examples.

   a.   Statistics concepts
   b.   Application problems
   c.   Graduate students
   d.   Instructional method

11. Wen, a special educator, recently read a research study about a behavior modification strategy used to decrease eating speed in a normal functioning adult. She decides to conduct a study to see if the intervention might be used successfully with one of her students, a middle school student with mental retardation. Wen's research topic is best described as a study that

    a. tests theory.
    b. is a replication.
    c. is developed through a library search.
    d. comes from questions we generally ask ourselves.

12. Which of the following is a researchable survey research topic regarding standardized testing?

    a. Should standardized tests be administered?
    b. What is the relationship between scores on two different standardized tests?
    c. What strategies do teachers use to decrease parent anxiety over standardized test scores?
    d. How do learning outcomes, such as course grade, relate to standardized test scores?

13. Of the following, which is likely a qualitative research topic about academic motivation?

    a. The purpose of the study is to compare properties of two motivation inventories.
    b. An examination of differences in academic motivation based upon SES.
    c. Description of the motivation of several students in an advanced placement high school history class.
    d. Research study of the relationship between motivation and standardized test scores.

14. Pedro is conducting a literature search on instructional methods for teaching mathematics concepts to rural high school students. Of the following, which is likely the best search term(s) for Pedro to use for an electronic database search?

    a. Mathematics instruction and high school
    b. Instructional methods
    c. High school students or mathematics instruction
    d. Students and rural education

15. Kelly's teacher suggested that he start with secondary sources to get a sense of the existing literature for his research topic. Which of the following is likely a secondary source?

    a. A previous student's dissertation
    b. An article in *Review of Research and Instruction*
    c. A paper that describes a study that was presented at a national conference
    d. An article in *American Educational Research Journal*

16. After conducting a literature search in ERIC, Maja found herself with three studies that directly relate to her topic. One of the studies had a research label of ED43180. Given this label, what is one conclusion that can be drawn about the source?

    a. It is not a review paper.
    b. It is a secondary source.
    c. It is not a journal article.
    d. It is a peer-reviewed source.

17. When organizing a research manuscript, the references most directly related to your study

    a. appear in the review first.
    b. appear in the review last.
    c. are interspersed with other related literature.
    d. appear primarily in the interpretation of your findings.

18. Josie turned in her *research topic* and her professor turned it back and asked for her to redo the assignment. Given the topic, *My study will address differences in children's learning from varying types of instructional materials*, why was it likely returned?

    a. The topic is not researchable.
    b. The topic is not relevant to educational research or theory.
    c. Her research procedure is unclear.
    d. Her variables are not operationally defined.

19. Ling proposed to study whether there are differences between standardized test scores in fifth- grade children who were taught mathematics in same gender versus mixed gender mathematics classrooms. Which of the following is an accurate label for this research topic?

    a. Experimental
    b. Correlational
    c. Qualitative
    d. Quantitative

20. Given Ling's study above, which of the following is the non-directional hypothesis?

    a. There will be no differences in standardized mathematics scores between fifth grade children in same gender versus mixed gender classrooms.
    b. There will be a difference in standardized mathematics scores between fifth grade children in same gender versus mixed gender classrooms.
    c. Fifth grade learners in same gender mathematics classes will perform better on standardized tests than those enrolled in mixed gender classrooms.
    d. Fifth grade learners in mixed gender mathematics classes will perform better on standardized tests than those in same gender classrooms.

21. Marcy is a qualitative researcher who is interested in studying the thoughts and strategies that people have and use when they solve complex problems. Marcy's committee suggested that she conduct a literature review. Of the following, based upon your text, why might Marcy's committee make such a recommendation?

    a. A literature review could assist Marcy in refining her research questions.
    b. A literature review must be conducted before starting a qualitative research study.
    c. A literature review is the only way to determine if Marcy's study is meaningful.
    d. A literature review is necessary to justify that her study is valid.

22. Tafare must complete a term paper for his research class. He remembers that he read a study recently that examined the relationship between self-efficacy for sport and academic self-concept in college first-year athletes. He wonders if the relationship between these constructs is similar in high school students. The source of this research topic is derived from

    a. library immersion.
    b. personal experience.
    c. theory.
    d. replication.

Practicing the Tasks

The following two examples are portions taken from previous students' Task 2 activities. Both these examples are sections from students' drafts of their research proposals that were later modified based upon content covered later in the course, increased knowledge and experience, and their instructor's feedback. One place both students substantially modified their proposals was in the hypotheses section. Note in both, however, how the literature is reviewed and the research topic is defined from the literature, or the 'V' as mentioned in your text. Although full proposals are not provided, to support Chapter 2 content and Task 2, consider the portions of the proposals, located at the end of this chapter, as you consider each of the following questions.

Cindy Bochna's *Treating Autism*
Given the introduction to Cindy's proposal, answer the following questions.

1. Is this a qualitative or quantitative research topic? _____

2. Restate the research topic: _____
    _____

3. Your text indicates criteria for a good research topic. Given the following criteria, is Cindy's topic a 'good' research topic? For each, answer yes or no and explain your answer.

    a. Is it interesting, or at least is it likely interesting to the researcher and potential others?
        Yes   No   _____
        _____

    b. Can the topic be addressed through data collection?   Yes   No   _____
        _____

    c. Is the topic significant to theory, research, or practice?   Yes   No   _____
        _____

    d. Does the project appear to be manageable to a novice researcher?   Yes   No
        _____
        _____

    e. Is the topic an ethical research topic to study?   Yes   No   _____
        _____

4. If you were going to expand the literature reviewed in Cindy's proposal, suggest a database to search for literature and two keywords you might use to initiate your search.

    _____   _____   _____

Monica Wright's *Effects of Mental Imagery Training*
Given the introduction to Monica's proposal answer the following questions.

1. Is this a qualitative or quantitative research topic? _____

2. Restate the research topic: _____
    _____

3. Your text indicates criteria for a good research topic. Given the following criteria, is Monica's topic a 'good' research topic? For each, answer yes or no and explain your answer.

    a. Is it interesting, or at least is it likely interesting to the researcher and potential others?
        Yes   No   _____
        _____

    b. Can the topic be addressed through data collection?   Yes   No   _____
        _____

    c. Is the topic significant to theory, research, or practice?   Yes   No   _____
        _____

    d. Does the project appear to be manageable to a novice researcher?   Yes   No   _____
        _____

    e. Is the topic an ethical research topic to study?   Yes   No   _____
        _____

4. If you were going to expand the literature reviewed in Monica's proposal, suggest a database to search for literature and two keywords you might use to initiate your search.

    _____   _____   _____

Companion Website
For more practice on becoming competent in this chapter's objectives, go to the Companion Website that accompanies this text at www.prenhall.com/gay. This site includes:

Objectives with links to:
- more multiple-choice questions in Practice Quiz
- Applying What You Know essay questions
- relevant Web sites

Custom modules to help you:
- calculate statistical tests (see "Calculating Statistical Tests")
- do research (see "Research Tools and Tips")
- practice analyzing quantitative data (see "Analyzing Quantitative Data")
- practice analyzing qualitative data (see "Analyzing Qualitative Data")
- practice evaluating published articles (see "Evaluating Articles")

The following student-created research proposal is reprinted with the permission of Cindy Bochna.

Treating Autism: An Investigation of the Young Autism and TEACCH Projects

Cindy Bochna

Introduction

Autism is classified by the American Psychiatric Association's *Diagnostic and Statistical Manual of Mental Disorders* (DSM-IV) as a pervasive developmental disorder, a term meant to indicate, "severe and pervasive impairment in several areas of development: reciprocal social interaction skills, communication skills, or the presence of stereotyped behavior, interests, and activities" (APA 1994, 65). The Autism Society of America estimates that there about 400,000 people in the United States with some form of autism. Once considered a low-incidence disorder, autism is now referred to as one of the most common childhood conditions within the category of childhood disorders. However, this may be due in part to children being misdiagnosed as something other than autistic in the past. Unlike Down's syndrome, the cause of autism is still unknown, making the battle to treat the afflicted an uphill one. As of yet, there is no cure.

Autism is usually present within the first year of life, but about one-third of the time it appears to have its onset within the second or third year. Around the age of three, the parents of a child who is still, "lacking in meaningful speech," and the child's pediatrician usually agree upon the need for a diagnostic evaluation by a specialist in childhood disorders (Cohen, 1998). Once a child is determined to exhibit symptoms of autism, extensive research (Lovaas, 1987; Smith, Eikeseth, Klevstrand, and Lovaas, 1997; Sheinkopf and Siegel, 1998; Smith and Lovaas, 1998; Cattell-Gordon and Cattell-Gordon, 1998) has proven early and intensive educational intervention invaluable. "Intensive" refers to the number of hours a day and week of intervention, the amount of time directly focused on the individual child's learning during those hours, and the duration of weeks, months, or years during which the intervention continues (Cohen, 1998).

While researchers agree upon early and extensive intervention for autistic children, the exact nature of this intervention varies greatly depending upon whom one talks to. There are two major approaches to treatment, the behavioral approach and the developmental approach. While there are a multitude of intervention programs that can be classified as falling into one of these two categories, addressing all of these programs is beyond the scope of this study. Therefore, this study will attempt to evaluate two of these intervention techniques, the first following a behavioral approach and the second a developmental approach to treatment. These are the Lovaas method, also known as the Young Autism Project, and TEACCH, or Treatment and Education of Autistic and Related Communication-Handicapped Children.

The Lovaas Method

In 1970, O. Ivar Lovaas began to conduct a study whose method was later to become known as the Young Autism Project. It was a behavioral-intervention project that sought to maximize behavioral treatment gains by treating autistic children, "during most of their waking hours for many years" (Lovaas, 1987). Treatment included all, "significant" people involved in the very young (below the age of 4 years) autistic child's environment. The treatment consisted of an average of 40 hours per week of instruction conducted by an outside therapist for 2 or more years (Smith and Lovaas, 1998). Lovaas hypothesized that construction of a, "special, intense, and comprehensive learning environment" for very young autistic children would allow some of them to catch up with their normal peers by first grade (1987).

The Young Autism Project followed the process of Applied Behavioral Analysis (ABA) (Cattell-Gordon and Cattell-Gordon, 1998). ABA is a method of teaching that focuses on the systematic development of skills by breaking down each desired skill or goal into small parts and then teaching each part individually using a precise cue. The parts are then chained together to produce the whole, and each correct response to each cue receives positive and functional (i.e., serve the intent of increasing behavior) reinforcement. Examples of reinforcers are small bites of food, sensory and perceptual reinforcers, play, access to favorite activities, and social praise involving verbal praise, kisses, and hugs (Smith and Lovaas, 1998). The emphasis is on teaching the child to learn in a normal environment and, "acting on that environment to produce successful outcomes for the child" (Cattell-Gordon and Cattell-Gordon, 1998).

In 1987, Lovaas reported that at the start of his study, there were no significant differences between the experimental group and the control groups. Following the study, Lovaas stated that 47% (9 of the 19 children) were "recovered," a statement he based on their improved IQ scores and placement in regular education first grade classrooms (1987). Studies done by the May Institute in Massachusetts, the Princeton Child Development institute in New Jersey, the Douglass Developmental Center at Rutgers University, the Early Intervention Program at Murdoch University in Australia, and the Pervasive Developmental Disorders Clinic at the University of California, San Francisco have also found that early intervention that is intensive, one to one, precise, and behavioral (the Lovaas' method) can significantly help children who are diagnosed with autism (Cattell-Gordon and Cattell-Gordon, 1998).

The main criticism of the Young Autism Project is of its financial burden. Smith and Lovaas (1998) estimated the cost of treatment to be between $40,000 and $60,000 per year, or an average of $120,000 to $180,000 for the 2 to 3 years of treatment that the project entails. The caregivers may be able to convince their school district to cover part of the cost if they are persistent in their efforts. Smith and Lovaas justify the cost by claiming that the long-term benefits of reducing the need for services in the children they help will more than compensate for the initial financial investment (1998).

TEACCH-based home program

TEACCH is a statewide comprehensive intervention system that provides a variety of services to autistic individuals and their families across age periods. Since 1972 the system has operated out of the department of psychiatry of the University of North Carolina, Chapel Hill, with state funding. It has an extensive training program for professionals and is also in use in other areas of the country as well as other parts of the world. The TEACCH model is mostly used in classroom settings, but there is a home intervention component as well.

The primary educational goal of TEACCH is to increase the student's level of skill. Recovery is not a term used in this system, and while the Lovaas program is based on the premise that the child must overcome his autistic characteristics so as to adapt to the world around him, in TEACCH the child is provided with an environment designed to accommodate the characteristics of autistic children (Cohen, 1998).

TEACCH makes use of many visual organizers or cues because, "visual processing is a strength of many autistic children" (Cohen, 1998). Spontaneous functional communication is the language goal of TEACCH, and alternative modes of communication such as pictures, manual signs, and written words are used when speech is particularly difficult for the child. "Such strategies neutralize or deemphasize deficits common in children with autism and minimize behavioral problems" (Cohen, 1998).

In their 1998 study, Ozonoff and Cathcart evaluated the effectiveness of using the TEACCH intervention model of home programming, in which parents are taught to serve as their child's "co-therapist," implementing treatment in the home setting. The typical home program lasted 10 weeks, during which therapists first trained the parents once a week for an hour and then sent the caregivers home with specific activities, materials, and techniques. The development of the home program was unique to each child, however, most interventions shared the same components of structured teaching, capitalization on visual strengths to teach more difficult skills, a schedule to help the child anticipate future events, a communication system of some type (gestures, pictures, signs, or words), and preacademic-prevocational activities that helped prepare the child for entry into the public school system (e.g., colors, numbers, shapes, drawing, writing, assembly, and packaging tasks). Therapists observed the parents administering the treatment once during the course of the study, but outside of the modeling done by the therapist with the child to instruct the parents in the clinic, the treatment was administered by the parents alone. Ozonoff and Cathcart found that the children in the treatment group demonstrated significant improvement in the areas of cognitive and developmental skills over the control group.

The main criticism of the TEACCH project is of its lack of published outcome data. While its creators have published several books documenting their data on the project, journal publications regarding the project are scarce.

Hypothesis

It is hypothesized that use of the TEACCH home intervention program will yield the same results as those of the Lovaas Young Autism Project with young at a fraction of the financial cost.

Effects of mental imagery training combined with visual literacy training on reading comprehension of third grade elementary students

Monica L. Wright

Reading comprehension is a fundamental aspect to the general and overall education of all children. The ability to comprehend what was read improves the child's educational potential dramatically. Reading involves an interaction with the text which allows for an overall understanding of what the text is trying to say. Some children tend to be better at comprehending what they have read than do other children.

Research presented by Pressley (1997) explains the nature of "good readers" and how they tend to proceed through the reading process. First, "good readers" will actively look for information relevant to their reading goal. Another characteristic of skilled readers is the development of hypotheses and conclusions during reading; they make inferences during the reading process. They tend to integrate ideas from different parts of the story or text.

Pressley (1997) asserts that good readers activate prior knowledge in an attempt to relate certain points in the text to one another. This assumption supports the literature concerning visual literacy. Ferro and Weller (1989) state that visual literacy involves accessing stored knowledge and skills and using prior knowledge to make interpretations of novel visual stimuli. Heinich, Molenda, Russell, and Smaldino (1993) define visual literacy as the person's learned ability to create, interpret, and store messages accurately. James (1989) states that using visual images from prior knowledge facilitates reading comprehension via increased memory retention. Schallert-Lawrie (1989) also advocates for adopting visual literacy framework into the curriculum. Thus, for some readers, visual literacy skills may improve reading comprehension. However, these skills may need to be formally taught.

Another important characteristic of "good readers" involves constructing some sort of mental image or representation of the meaning of the text. This allows for an overall comprehension and understanding of the reading material (Pressley, 1997). Gambrell and Jawitz (1993) mention three theories that support the notion of mental imagery, "Paivio's (1971, 1991) dual-coding theory, Wittrock's (1981) theory of generative learning, and Rosenblatt's (1978, 1985) transactional theory." The dual-coding theory assumes that verbal and nonverbal information are coded in two distinct and interrelated mental systems. It is theorized that the verbal subsystem involves language, abstract thoughts, and sequential processing. The nonverbal subsystem is primarily concerned with concrete and parallel processing. These two systems can work independently of each other but they can also work inconjunction with one another. The integration of these two systems reveals the concept that language can elicit mental imagery, and imagery can elicit language. Dual-coding theory is supported by many researchers in this field (Anderson, 1995; Paivio, 1971; and Hodges, 1994). The implications of this theory help to support the notion of imagery as a potential memory strategy.

Much research supports the idea that mental imagery promotes comprehension of the text because it allows the reader to produce images that connect prior knowledge to the current text (Couch & Moore, 1992; Gambrell & Jawitz, 1993; Hodges, 1994; Pressley, 1997; Schirmer, 1995). Using mental imagery as a reading comprehension strategy can be beneficial for both novice and expert readers (Pressley, 1997; Couch & Moore, 1992; Drake, 1996; Gambrell & Jawitz, 1993; Hodges, 1994; Oakhill & Patel, 1991; Parente & Herrman, 1996). Research also suggests that mental imagery is most beneficial when the image retained is concrete (Oakhill & Patel, 1991; Parente & Herrman, 1996; Pressley, 1997; Schirmer, 1995). The more concrete the text the better the reader will comprehend because he or she is able to make concrete representations instead of abstract ones. For example, it is easier to create a mental image of a car driving down the road, then it is to create a mental image of what love is. This line of research plays a significant role in training students how to utilize mental imagery as a reading comprehension strategy.

How can we, as educators, improve a child's reading comprehension? Current research supports the notion of visual literacy (Rezabek, 1989) and mental imagery as a reading comprehension strategy to improve understanding and memory of any text, especially concrete texts. However, none of the studies combined visual literacy and mental imagery to determine if an interaction exists. The purpose of the current proposed study is to create a "real life" paradigm that utilizes mental imagery training and visual literacy training to increase the reading comprehension (measured by memory retention) of elementary age students. It is hypothesized that mental imagery traning combined with visual literacy training will improve reading comprehension in third grade elementary students.

This research proposal is reprinted with the permission of Monica L. Wright.

Chapter 2 Answers
For Your Own Review
1. Check relevancy
    Skim article
    Record bibliographic information
    Classify/code and record code
    Abstract (Summarize)
    Record thoughts and opinions, note questions
    Indicate direct quotes
    Make a second copy

(Your text also noted the abstracting process was one that included: *Locating, Reviewing, Summarizing*, and *Classifying*.)

2. Interesting to the researcher
    Researchable through data collection
    Significant (contributes to theory/practice)
    Manageable based upon researcher's skill, time, resources
    Ethical (won't harm or embarrass participants)

3. Based upon sound reasoning
    Reasonable explanation for predicted outcome
    States expected relationship between variables
    Is testable within a reasonable time frame

4. P=Participants
    X=Independent Variable
    Y=Dependent Variable

5. To demonstrate the underlying assumptions behind the research questions
    To indicate to reviewers that the researcher is knowledgeable about intellectual traditions
    To provide the researcher with an opportunity to identify any gaps in the body of literature and how the proposed study may contribute to existing literature
    To help refine the research questions

Just For Practice
1. Quantitative, P= 4th grade children, X=Gender, Y=self-esteem
2. Qualitative, context includes women at small liberal arts school their transition is the focus
3. Quantitative, P= 9th grade readers, X=text with or without pictures, Y=Comprehension
4. Qualitative, context is children of various ages their occupational interests are the focus.
5. Quantitative, P=struggling readers, X=with or without summer program, Y=motivation

Checking What You Know
1. a. Quantitative
    b. There is no difference in the number of new cable subscriptions between those given a free preview and those given 1st month discount.
    c. There is a difference the number of new cable subscriptions between those given a free preview and those given 1st month discount.
    d. Those given a free preview are more likely to subscribe to cable when compared to those given a 1st month discount. (You may have picked the other way around! They never really show anything good in the preview anyway.)

2.A 1. There are no increases in SAT scores between those learners who take the *We will make you smarter* SAT preparation program over two weeks and those who take the intensive weekend version.
    2. There are increases in SAT scores between those learners who take the *We will make you smarter* SAT preparation program over two weeks and those who take the intensive weekend version.

3. Students enrolled in the intensive weekend version of the *We will make you smarter* SAT preparation program will have greater gain scores than those enrolled in the program over a two week time period. (Again, your direction might have been that the spaced program works better.)

B 1. There are no increases in SAT scores between those learners who take the *We will make you smarter* SAT preparation program from a specially trained instructor and those who take the program from a certified but not specially trained teacher.
  2. There are increases in SAT score between those learners who take the *We will make you smarter* SAT preparation program from a specially trained instructor and those who take the program from a certified but not specially trained teacher.
  3. Students enrolled in the *We will make you smarter* SAT preparation program with a specially trained instructor will have greater gain scores than those enrolled in the program with a certified but not specially trained teacher. (You may have hypothesized the teachers were better instructors even without training.)

C 1. There is no relationship between attendance in the SAT preparation program and gain scores in a second a administration of the SAT.
  2. There is a relationship between attendance in the SAT preparation program and gain scores in a second administration of the SAT.
  3. As student attendance in the SAT preparation program increases, scores in a second administration of the SAT increase. (You may have hypothesized attendance decreases scores, perhaps because it increases anxiety or something.)

Applying What You Know
1. a. 18000+. (These search numbers will vary as database entries change often).
   b. 9300+
   c. 940+
   d. 200+
   e. Approximately 50

2. a NO
   b. Other (curriculum guide)
   c. No
   d. Yes, 2003
   e. Unsure. It is hard to tell with only the abstract and it is not data driven.
   f. Yes
   g. Primary
   h. Yes
   i. Maybe not. The article was published in 1989 and used computer animation (This article, however, is still heavily referenced)
   j. Yes
   k. No, ERIC document
   l. Primary
   m. No
   n. Fairly, 2002
   o. It seems to be based upon the abstract

Test-Like Event
1.	a	10.	d	19.	d
2.	c	11.	b	20.	b
3.	b	12.	c	21.	a
4.	c	13.	c	22.	d
5.	c	14.	a		
6.	b	15.	b		
7.	a	16.	c		
8.	c	17.	b		
9.	a	18.	d		

Answers to Article Examinations

Cindy Bochna's *Treating Autism*:

1.   Quantitative

2.   Are there differences between the outcomes of the TEACCH program when compared to the Lovaas method when working with young autistic children.

3.   a.   yes, this project would be very interesting to many special educators, therapists, school personnel
     b.   yes, Data collection will help Cindy answer her research question.
     c.   yes, although I am not a content expert, from the literature review it seems this study will contribute to research and practice and perhaps theory too.
     d.   maybe. This is a big project to manage. It would depend upon the number and nature of the children and the degree of their autism. To conduct this study Cindy would have to work closely with families, organizations, schools, and children. I would discourage a student of mine from doing this study for a thesis. I know Cindy though and she has experience with the school district she has identified, and has been a teacher of autistic children and worked within that environment. She could likely do this study for a dissertation, perhaps. Without the skills in the specific area of autism, many advanced researchers would not be able to manage this project.
     e.   yes, The study could be conducted ethically. The study would undergo strict review (you will learn about this soon) because of the nature of the participants. If one program was found to be much better, the design of the study should allow for those participants who did not receive the 'best' program to receive access to the better program.

4.   Cindy might use ERIC or a psychology database to extend her literature review. Cindy notes in the proposal that there are not many research studies, so perhaps psych web might provide some additional resource information for her study. Keywords might include autism, intervention and autism, Lovaas, TEACCH, Cindy might also use an author search of those authors she has already cited.

Monica Wright's *Effects of Mental Imagery Training*:

1.   Quantitative

2.   Are there benefits of mental imagery training and visual literacy training for the reading comprehension of third grade learners?

3   a.   yes, the research topic is of interest to many researchers, educators, educational psychologists, and reading specialists.
     b.   yes, the topic can be examined through data collection and analysis.
     c.   yes, the project can inform research and practice.
     d.   yes, the project appears to be manageable. It would take time to develop rapport with the schools and to get IRB and parental permissions. It would also take time and skills to develop the training, instructional, and testing materials. I would expect Monica to do a pilot study with college learners and a pilot study with younger learners prior to conducting this research. The project would be 'doable' as a thesis but it would take about a year or so to complete.
     e.   Yes, The topic is an ethical, and important, research topic to study. Of course, Monica would need to obtain IRB permission to conduct the study and would need to strictly follow the protocol submitted and approved by the IRB. Her participants should be aware of the level of anonymity and confidentiality afforded by her study procedures and she would need to obtain consent from her participants to conduct the study.

4.   ERIC, reading comprehension strategies, mental imagery and learning, visual elaborations.

Chapter 3   Preparing and Evaluating a Research Plan

Chapter 3 Objectives

1.   Briefly describe three ethical considerations involved in conducting and reporting educational research.
2.   Describe two major pieces of legislation affecting educational research.
3.   Briefly describe each of the components of a quantitative research plan.
4.   Briefly describe each of the components of a qualitative research plan.
5.   Briefly describe two major ways in which a research plan can be evaluated.

Review the Terms

Please provide a succinct definition in your own words for each of the following terms.

Research plan: _____

_____

Informed consent: _____

_____

Protection from harm: _____

_____

Confidentiality: _____

_____

Anonymity: _____

_____

Deception: _____

_____

Human subjects review (IRB): _____

_____

The Family Education Rights and Privacy Act of 1974: _____

_____

The National Research Act of 1974: _____

_____

Population: _____

_____

Instrument: _____

_____

Parental consent: _____
_____

Design: _____
_____

Assumption: _____
_____

Limitation: _____
_____

For Your Own Review

1. What is the difference between anonymity and confidentiality? Provide an example of each.

   _____
   _____
   _____

2. State two major pieces of legislation affecting educational research as presented in your text. Briefly describe each.

   _____
   _____
   _____

3. List at least two general ethical principles presented in your text.

   _____   _____

4. State the two major ways that qualitative research differs from quantitative research that produces additional ethical concerns.

   _____
   _____
   _____

Other Sources for Review

Recently, many research institutions have developed training modules to assure that those interested in conducting research with human subjects are aware of ethical standards. Some IRB's now require successful completion of the training prior to approval of a research study. Your university or college might require you to complete a training course. The National Institutes of Health (NIH) also has developed a training module that you can take via the web. The training module reviews much of the content presented in Chapter 3 and can be accessed through http://cme.nci.nih.gov/. Upon completion you will be awarded a certificate.

Two examples of university ethics homepages are those for Duke University's Medical center: http://researchethics.mc.duke.edu/clinethics.nsf/webpages/home, and Oregon State University's: http://oregonstate.edu/research/RegulatoryCompliance/index.html. In addition, you are encouraged to examine your own institution's web page or printed ethics documents.

While your text addresses ethics with human subjects, and professional ethics, an additional area of research ethics is in reporting results and publishing findings. Two additional resources can support your understanding of this content. The first, Uchiyama, K., Simone, G., & Borko, H. (1999). "Publishing Educational Research: Guidelines and tips." AERA.Net Electronic Publications is available online through the American Educational Research Association (AERA) at http://35.8.171.42/aera/epubs/howtopub/intro.htm. This site is VERY useful for emerging educational researchers. Not only are ethics addressed, but in addition, many other insights into the research process are included.   The second is an ERIC document published by Syrett, K. L., & Rudner, L. M. (1996). Authorship Ethics. ED 410318

Applying What You Know

1. Your text suggests that the human subjects review board is concerned about informed consent and potential risks to participants. Identify concerns that the board might have regarding each of the following examples.

    a. A friend of yours is interested in studying a new treatment for counseling young women with anorexia nervosa.

    _____

    _____

    b. Samuel wants to investigate how children respond to negative feedback. In his design children complete difficult puzzles. Some of the children are informed erroneously that they are worse than their peers at solving these problems. Others are told they perform better than their peers.

    _____

    _____

    c. Denise studies teacher burnout. She proposes to study teachers firsthand by posing as a teacher and working in a school facing many difficult issues for a year. Only in this way can she really appreciate what it is like for teachers 'in the trenches' and she feels she can get honest answers from teachers with burnout.

    _____

    _____

    d. As a kinesiologist interested in the relationship between physical activity and academic performance, Danny proposes to limit the exercise of one group of children in his study while allowing the other group to exercise as they normally would.

    _____

    _____

e. Robert is studying a new strategy to teach reading that, by indications in other countries, works much better than the methods currently used. He proposes to try it in one classroom for a full year while in the other classrooms in the school the children get reading instruction as they normally would.

_____

_____

f. Jane is a college professor interested in students' beliefs about typical classroom management strategies of teachers. As part of her ongoing research agenda, she requires students in her research methods course to fill out questionnaires.

_____

_____

g. Josephine is conducting a study that examines emotional response by calculating heart rate in young children. To do this she must design a situation where the children emotionally react. The heart rate is measured by electronic monitors.

_____

_____

h. Priya is interested in studying the effects of parenting strategies on middle school students' self-concept. She asks parents to report their parenting strategies and measures students self-concept via self-report.

_____

_____

Practicing the Tasks

Task 3a in the text requires that students develop a research plan for a quantitative study. Task 3b in the text requires that students develop a research plan for a qualitative study. Each student's plans will be individual and different from all others. To assist you in completing Task 3a and Task 3b, consider the following research proposals developed by students at Penn State. Sometimes research plans include a time schedule and a budget. While these two components were not required for these students' assignment, indicate how long you think the study might take and identify potential costs of conducting the research. In addition to the required components of the plan for Task 3a and Task 3b, also consider any ethical concerns of the proposal. Therefore, for the example plans, describe each of the following components

For task 3a:
*   Participants
*   Instruments/materials used
*   Design
*   Procedure
*   Data analyses procedures (you can simply summarize the techniques that might be used)
*   Potential time line
*   Budget items
*   Ethical considerations

The following research plan is written by Susan McClellan, a doctoral student at Penn State University, and is reprinted with her permission. She studies teaching statistics and research methods and conducts research on instructional design manipulations for learning from text. Typically this plan would be typed double-spaced, but is printed single-spaced to conserve space in this guide.

The effects of technology resources on achievement in statistics
Susan McClellan

Few people would refute the huge impact of technology on what we do in our everyday lives, including the world of education. More specifically, technology has greatly influenced mathematics education over the last 30 years due to increased uses of computers and calculators in schools. Bratton (1999) indicated that the impact of technology in the teaching and learning of statistics has been especially strong since the availability of statistical software (i.e., Fathom and Minitab) and statistical calculators (i.e., TI-83) increase the possible data exploration and analyses within a classroom environment.

Ben-zvi (2000) asserted that the role of technological tools in students' statistical learning is crucial for developing statistical reasoning and conceptual understanding. One of the most important aspects of Ben-zvi's theory is that "multiple linked representations and simulations [improve a student's ability] to construct meanings for statistical concepts and ideas" (p. 151). Multiple linked representations refer to simultaneous presentation of more than one representation (i.e., numbers, symbols, and graphs) within a technology environment, such as on a computer or calculator screen. Through the creation, manipulation, and transformation of these multiple [visual] representations of statistical concepts, students gain more powerful statistical reasoning and conceptual understanding than by working with single representations or ones that are not multiply linked through the technological tool.

According to Ben-zvi (2000), another significant feature of current technological tools is the dynamic nature of some of the statistical software programs that are available. A multirepresentational dynamic statistical computer-based environment typically involves manipulation tools that allow a user to physically manipulate data, physical line markers (i.e., to mark the median or mode), statistics, or distributions and graphs and see the resulting effects as they occur. The linked feature further enhances the user's learning experience and deepens the user's understanding and reasoning ability because the effects from the user's manipulation of one representation (say, adding an outlier to a set of data) can be observed in the representations of the descriptive statistics and displays of the dotplot, boxplot, and histogram, for example.

Some of the technological tools currently available include the TI-83 graphing calculator and two statistical software program called Minitab and Fathom. The TI-83 has statistical and graphical capabilities that rival the software programs, but the viewing screen is only a few square inches. The TI-83 links representations (like data and its graph), but they are not viewable on the screen at the same time; the user can only view one at a time. Minitab, on the other hand, features multiple linked representations and can simultaneously display many windows of data, statistics, and graphs. Minitab is only dynamic in the sense that you can change the data and rerun the commands for new displays. The other program called Fathom is fully dynamic by Ben-zvi's definition and features simultaneously displayed, linked multiple representations. The dynamic feature in Fathom allows the user to see the effects of data manipulation in continuous and real-time manner. For example, if a user drags a dot on a dotplot for a few seconds, the user can see the corresponding data number, descriptive statistics, line markers, boxplot, and histogram change in their respective effects.

This study has two objectives. One is to study the effect of technology-based multiple representations on statistical reasoning, and the other is to examine the influence of dynamic features in statistical software packages on statistical reasoning. I predict that the linked multiple representations and the dynamic features of the technology can positively impact statistical reasoning since a user's experiences with these features should lead to development of uniquely rich and powerful understanding and reasoning ability. The following two research hypotheses will be proposed:

1) Students who learn statistics by utilizing Fathom will have higher levels of statistical reasoning than those who utilize Minitab, and

2) Students who use either Fathom or Minitab will have higher levels of statistical reasoning than the students who use only the TI-83 calculator.

Methodology

The subjects will be 96 high school students enrolled in a one-semester Introductory Probability and Statistics course at a large suburban public high school. The goal of the course is oriented toward developing statistical reasoning ~~is~~ in students and less toward developing computations and skills than the traditional introductory course in statistics. Each of the 96 students will be randomly assigned to one of three course sections of 32 students taught by the same teacher—a control group in one section and two treatment groups, one in each of the other two sections. The design will be a randomized Posttest Only Control Group Design. This design was selected in order to avoid pretest contamination.

The independent variable will be the technology (TI-83, Minitab, or Fathom) used for the lab assignments. The control group (Group C) will access the TI-83 calculators for regular use and via lab assignments. The first treatment group (Group M) will access the Minitab statistical software (via lab assignments) and the TI-83 calculators for regular use. The second treatment group (Group F) will access the Fathom dynamic statistics software (via lab assignments) and the TI-83 calculators for regular use.

(So, your study is not comparing M & F against C; rather it is either 1) comparing the use of M or F *in addition to the use of TI-83*; i.e., the use of a M-TI83, an F-TI83 vs. a TI83-TI83 combo; or 2) comparing the effect of the use of M or F against C in *lab assignments only*. Your theoretical background does not support either of these two approaches.)

The students' statistical reasoning will be measured by an instrument administered at the end of the course called the *Statistical Reasoning Assessment* (SRA), developed by Garfield and Konold (Garfield, 1998) as a part of the ChancePlus Project to assess high school students' levels of statistical reasoning and application of statistical reasoning. Scoring will be calculated using the test's Correct Reasoning Skills Scales and the Misconceptions Scales. The SRA is a 20-item multiple-choice test of probability and statistics items focusing on reasoning about data, representations of data, statistical measures, uncertainty, samples, and association and common misconceptions that lead to incorrect statistical reasoning. Content validity was determined through a process involving consulting with content experts, revisions of items, pilot testing and other administrations, and more revisions. Low criterion-related validity was reported, "suggesting that statistical reasoning and misconceptions are unrelated to students' performance in a first statistics course" (p. 7). Test-retest reliability calculations were reported of .70 for the total correct score and .75 for the scores of incorrect reasoning. The test designers acknowledged that the reliability and validity analyses did not yield "impressive results" (p. 13). This instrument was chosen since it is the only one that currently exists for assessing statistical reasoning and has been used elsewhere. An additional criterion-related validity analysis could be conducted within this study, looking at the correlations of student scores from assignments, tests, labs, and the course final exam.

This research design essentially has no classical validity problems. There are no external validity problems, and mortality could potentially be a threat to internal validity if either of the treatments makes people drop out of the study. There will be some hesitation to depend on randomization to indicate group equivalence and a realization that randomization is often difficult in educational settings.

Additional potential threats to validity are also considered. The Hawthorne Effect is minimized because the treatment should be long enough to remove novelty effect. The study will be conducted by double blind method in the sense that neither the subjects nor the teacher will know the research hypotheses. All three groups will be advised that opportunities will be given after the study to work with the Minitab and Fathom statistical software packages to minimize experimental diffusion and resentful demoralization. Additionally, the groups will also be advised not to discuss the labs with students outside of a particular section of the class since separating the students completely (i.e., in different buildings) is not practical. The researcher will perform random checks of the teacher's implementation of the different labs and of the regular class instruction to deal with treatment fidelity as a possible threat. Any changes or departures from the original design will be described in the final publication of the results.

References

Ben-zvi, D. (2000). Toward understanding the role of technological tools in statistical learning. *Mathematical Thinking and Learning 2*(1&2), 127-155.

Bratton, G. (1999). The role of technology in introductory statistics courses. *The Mathematics Teacher 92* (8), 666-669.

Garfield, J. (1998, March). *Challenges in assessing statistical reasoning.* Paper presented at the Innovative Assessment Strategies for Improving the Teaching and Learning of Statistics Symposium at the AERA 1998 Annual Meeting, San Diego, CA.

Garfield, J. & Gal, I. (1999). Teaching and assessing statistical reasoning. In L. Stiff & Curcio, F. (Eds.), *Developing Mathematical Reasoning in Grades K-12: 1999 Yearbook* (pp. 207-219). Reston, VA: NTCM.

1a. Statement of topic:_____

_____

b. Review of related literature (summarize the key points):_____

_____

_____

c. Statement of the hypothesis: _____

_____

d. Participants: _____

_____

e. Design: _____

_____

f. Instruments/materials used: _____

_____

g. Procedure: _____

_____

h. Data analyses procedures (you can simply summarize the techniques that might be used)

_____

_____

i. Potential time line: _____

_____

j. Budget items: _____

_____

k. Ethical considerations: _____

_____

Carlee Pollard is a doctoral student at Penn State in Educational Psychology. Her interests include measurement, evaluation, and testing.

The Effect of Review Options on Computerized Test Scores

Carlee K. Pollard

Introduction

Answer changing behaviors have been studied in great detail in paper-and-pencil tests and to some extent in computer adaptive tests. One area that has yet to be explored is whether or not there is an impact of *variation* in review options on computerized test scores. With web-based testing becoming more popular in education it is important to look at how review options may impact scores on computerized tests. If there is an effect, it is important that it be considered in high stakes testing situations.

Review of the Literature

Answer changing behaviors have attracted the interest of researchers for many years. The focus of these studies has been first on paper-and-pencil tests and then shifted to computer adaptive tests. Several results have been found consistently. What has been found is that given the option, participants prefer the opportunity to review and change their answers. For example, according to one study by Vispoel (1993), 81% of the participants favored the review option. It has also been shown that most examinees will review and change their answers only on a small portion of items. Wrong-to-right changes normally outnumber the right-to-wrong changes (Vispoel, 1998) showing that these changes typically result in an improvement of the examinees' scores. In addition, answer changes have been found to be beneficial to those who have a logical reason behind the change. Those who change answers based upon guessing do not benefit from it (Shatz and Best, 1987).

It is important to note that students are accustomed to and often encouraged to review answers in typical testing situations. According to Lunz, Bergstrom and Wright (1992), "educators have trained students from elementary school to medical school to review responses after completing a test to catch careless errors and thus render a more accurate demonstration of competence (p. 39)." They also point out that "the testing goal is not to penalize an examinee for clerical errors in the name of psychometric integrity, but rather to measure their ability as accurately as possible (p. 39)." Finally, they add that better performance with review options may be related to the "familiarity and comfort associated with the knowledge that review and correction of careless errors was allowed" (p. 39).

It is virtually impossible to exclude review options on traditional paper and pencil tests. In these formats, while test designers determine the actual items, the test-taker determines the order that the final answers are worked through (Stocking, 1997). Therefore it seems reasonable that for computerized versions of these traditional tests to be equivalent the option should be included (Vispoel, 1998).

The equivalence of paper-and-pencil tests and computerized tests has been extensively studied but without consideration of the review options. While most studies show that computerized formats and paper-and-pencil formats are typically equivalent, one study suggests that each test and each use of those tests should first be tested for equivalence (Buchanan and Smith, 1999). Hoffman and Lundberg (1976) found that while their test was equivalent for multiple choice and true-false items, the matching items found significant difference depending on mode of presentation. One study, by Federico (1991), found that "the relative reliability of computer-based and paper-based measure depends on the specific criterion assessed" (p. 345).

One major difference between paper-and-pencil tests and computer-based tests is that one group is reading from paper and the other is reading from a computer screen. Heppner, Anderson, Farstrup, and Weiderman (1985) found that on a speed test, reading from a computer screen resulted in worse performance than reading from paper.

Even groups who regularly used computers performed worse on the computer form. They attribute these differences to slower reading on the part of the computer test-takers leading to a higher amount of unanswered items.

The research on review in computer adaptive tests seems to focus on whether or not review options will effect the efficiency of the test (Lunz et. al., 1992). Some researchers are concerned about the use certain strategies that may increase a student's score if review is permitted in an adaptive test (Vispoel, 1998). For example, is it possible for a student to answer all of the questions wrong (which would lead to an easy test) then go back and answer all of the questions correctly leading to an exaggerated test score (Stocking, 1997)? Basically, the adaptive review research is used to determine if offering review options in an adaptive setting is feasible. None of this research explores different variations in review options.

The focus of the relevant literature appears to be based on two ideas: 1. the use of review options in paper-and-pencil tests as well as computer adaptive tests and 2. on the equivalence of paper-and-pencil and computerized test formats. One reason for the lack of literature in the area of variation in review options may be that the technology when many of these studies were conducted did not allow for easy incorporation of different review formats. Today there are many testing companies that offer programs for developing tests to be administered via the Internet. These different programs are designed to allow the test administrator to customize the test to their needs. The basis for this study is to use one of these programs to design several formats of same test.

Present Study

The purpose of this study is to examine whether including review options on a computerized test impacts the total score. More specifically the research questions are: does including review options lead to an increase in the total score and which option leads to the highest scores? Tests are now being offered on-line and eventually it seems as though paper-and-pencil tests will be obsolete. As computers are being used more and more for testing, it is important to study the format of these tests to see if it impacts the test-taker's score.

It is believed that for this study, scores will be highest on a format that allows maximum flexibility for review. The hypothesis is that the no review option will yield the lowest mean scores while the two formats allowing review will have total scores approximating that on the paper-and-pencil version.

Participants will be recruited through a course in the statistics department. These participants will be randomly split into four groups, one for each of the test formats. Each group will be given instructions specific to the testing situation that they will be encountering. For example, those not given the review option shall be informed that once an answer is given they will not have the opportunity to go back and change it later. Prior to starting the study, each participant will be asked to give informed consent before continuing with the procedure. They will be assured of anonymity and confidentiality of their individual scores. They also will be informed that they may withdraw from the study at any time.

The equipment that is needed for this study will be computers that are connected to a web-based test administration program such as Test Pilot. Different computers will be set up for different formats. The test chosen for this experiment will be examining knowledge of basic statistics through problem solving and knowledge of statistical terms in a multiple-choice format. A pilot sample will be run to ensure the equivalence of the paper-and-pencil and computerized testing situations. A Cronbach's alpha on this data will assess the reliability of the test itself.

This study will approximate a posttest only control group design. The participants will be randomly assigned to a condition and only a posttest will be used. The groups receiving the review option will be considered treatment groups while the no review option group and paper-and-pencil group will serve as control groups. This design will reduce the threats to external and internal validity.

Each group of participants will complete a test with the format depending on the group assignment. One group will complete the paper and pencil format. This is based upon Buchanan and Smith's (1999) recommendation that each test being adapted to computer version should be compared against the traditional version to ensure equivalence. A second group will complete the same test items on computer in a linear fashion presented one at a time without the opportunity to later review the answers. A third group will again use a computer to complete the same test items using a format that presents the items one at a time but with the option of back tracking/skipping ahead to change answers at any point. The final group will be administered a computerized version of the same items comparable to the paper-and-pencil format in that all the items will be presented on the screen all at once with a scroll bar on the side. The participants given the review options will be able to review their answers at any point in the test. This opportunity contrasts studies such as that done by Vispoel (1998) where the participants were only permitted to review their previous answers after completing the test.

A One-way ANOVA will be used to analyze the mean scores from each of the four groups to determine whether or not the means are statistically different. A Tukey test will be run to determine which (if any) of the means are different.

If it is determined that one computerized testing format leads to higher scores than the others, it is important that this information be used when developing high stakes exams to be administered by computer.

Bibliography

Buchanan, T. and Smith, J.L. (1999). Using the internet for psychological research: Personality testing on the world wide web. *British Journal of Psychology, 90,* 125-144.

Federico, P. (1991). Measuring recognition performance using computer-based and paper-based methods. *Behavior Research Methods, Instruments, & Computers, 23* (3), 341-347.

Heppner, F.H., Anderson, J.G.T., Farstrup, A.E., and Weiderman, N.H. (1985). Reading performance on a standardized test is better from print than from computer display. *Journal of Reading, 28*(4), 321-325.

Hoffman, K.I. and Lundberg, G.D. (1976). A comparison of computer-monitored group tests with paper-and-pencil tests. *Educational and Psychological Measurement, 36,* 791-809.

Lunz, M.E., Bergstrom, B.A., and Wright, B.D. (1992). The effect of review on student ability and test efficiency for computerized adaptive tests. *Applied Psychological Measurement, 16*(1), 33-40.

Shatz, M.A. and Best, J.B. (1987). Students' reasons for changing answers on objective tests. *Teaching of Psychology, 14* (4), 241-242.

Stocking, M.L. (1997). Revising item responses in computerized adaptive tests: a comparison of three models. *Applied Psychological Measurement, 21* (2), 129-142.

Vispoel, W.P. (1993). Computerized adaptive and fixed-item versions of the ITED vocabulary subtest. *Educational and Psychological Measurement, 53,* 779-788.

Vispoel, W.P. (1998). Reviewing and changing answers on computerized and self-adaptive vocabulary tests. *Journal of Educational Measurement, 35* (4), 328-347.

2a. Statement of topic:_____
_____

b. Review of related literature (summarize the key points):_____
_____
_____

c. Statement of the hypothesis: _____
_____

d. Participants: _____
_____

e. Design: _____
_____

f. Instruments/materials used: _____
_____

g.   Procedure: _____

_____

h.   Data analyses procedures (you can simply summarize the techniques that might be used)

_____

_____

i.   Potential time line: _____

_____

j.   Budget items: _____

_____

k.   Ethical considerations: _____

_____

Chapter 21 provides Joel D. Galbraith's example research study that was conducted for a class. We will visit this study several times throughout the study guide. Joel's paper can support your understanding for Task 3b. For now, please use Joel's study to address the following components of Task 3b.

3a. Is a research purpose presented? Describe_____

_____

b.   Is the researcher's identity described? _____

_____

c.   Is there a presentation of entry and access? _____

_____

d.   What was the data collection method(s)? _____

_____

e.   Are limitations presented? _____

_____

Test-Like Event
1.   Your text suggests that time schedules are effective for

   a.   qualitative researchers.
   b.   quantitative researchers.
   c.   neither qualitative or quantitative researchers.
   d.   both qualitative and quantitative researchers.

2. A research plan generally includes all EXCEPT which of the following?

    a. nature of the participants
    b. type of data to be collected.
    c. tables of descriptive statistics.
    d. techniques to analyze data.

3. A researcher obtains IRB approval to conduct a research study

    a. before a plan is developed.
    b. before data collection.
    c. after data collection.
    d. after data analysis.

4. The privacy act of 1974 is designed to protect

    a. students' educational records.
    b. students from deceptive research studies.
    c. minors from involuntary research participation.
    d. research participants from physical or mental harm.

5. Qualitative research raises more ethical concerns than quantitative research because

    a. qualitative researchers more often deceive participants.
    b. qualitative researchers more often violate confidentiality.
    c. qualitative researchers are generally more personally involved with participants.
    d. qualitative research is often more physically dangerous.

6. Susan would like to conduct a study in a local preschool. The most crucial individual or group she will likely need to gain permission from to collect data at the school is

    a. the children.
    b. the parents.
    c. the teachers.
    d. the director.

7. In a research plan, the limitations of the study are included in the _____ section.

    a. literature review
    b. hypothesis
    c. design
    d. procedures

8. When comparing quantitative and qualitative research approaches, a quantitative plan differs from a qualitative plan in that quantitative research

    a. requires a statement of topic and qualitative research does not.
    b. participants are generally larger in number than in qualitative research.
    c. hypotheses are stated later in the research process than in qualitative research.
    d. includes a description of the proposed data analysis methods and qualitative does not.

9. The ethical principle that dictates that psychologists attend to differences in power between themselves and others and they do not exploit clients is the principle of

    a. professional and scientific responsibility.
    b. concern for others' welfare.
    c. respect for people's rights and dignity.
    d. social responsibility.

10.-14   Terrell violated ethical procedures when, as a high school English teacher, he conducted a study on the relationship between standardized test scores and birth order. Her accessed students' standardized test scores and family composition data from their school files. Terrell has already written the study up and he doesn't understand why he has violated Ethical procedures because in the publication of the data there are no student names.

10. Terrell has violated Federal Acts. The violation regarding a lack of informed consent is a directly related to the

    a. The National Family Research and Privacy Act.
    b. National Family Rights Act.
    c. Family Educational Rights and Privacy Act.
    d. National Research Act.

11. The violation of accessing student records is directly related to

    a. The National Family Research and Privacy Act.
    b. National Family Research Act.
    c. Family Educational Rights and Privacy Act.
    d. National Research Act.

12. Terrell did not share student names in his report. The participants in Terrell's study were afforded

    a. anonymity
    b. confidentiality
    c. Neither anonymity or confidentiality
    d. Both anonymity and confidentiality

13. Terrell's research study is best described as

    a. qualitative, grounded theory.
    b. quantitative, correlational.
    c. qualitative, ethnography.
    d. quantitative, experimental.

14. Dale wants to do a study on second-graders' math self-efficacy. To conduct the study he will have to gain entry into the school. Of the following, the most likely procedure Dale will use is to obtain

    a. parental consent and then contact the school district.
    b. teacher consent and then contact the superintendent or principal.
    c. consent from the district and then contact the teachers.
    d. children's assent and then gain consent from the district.

15. One difference in research plans between qualitative and quantitative research is that

    a. qualitative researchers generally develop the topic earlier in the research process than quantitative researchers.
    b. qualitative researchers generally develop generalizations from larger samples than quantitative researchers.
    c. qualitative researchers generally conduct reviews of literature earlier in the research process than do quantitative researchers.
    d. qualitative researchers develop hypotheses later in the research process than do quantitative researchers.

16. Amy gained entry into a residential facility for juvenile offenders to measure their possible selves (a motivational construct). In her research plan, the section in which Amy will report the process she used to gain entry into the research site is the

    a. Introduction.
    b. Hypotheses.
    c. Method.
    d. Discussion.

17. Maria does measurement studies with large pre-existing datasets, such as those found in the NELS data or data from ETS. These datasets have only identifying numbers and participant characteristics. Maria can provide the participants in this research study

    a. anonymity
    b. confidentiality
    c. neither anonymity or confidentiality
    d. both anonymity and confidentiality

Companion Website

For more practice on becoming competent in this chapter's objectives, go to the Companion Website that accompanies this text at www.prenhall.com/gay. This site includes:

Objectives with links to:
- more multiple-choice questions in Practice Quiz
- Applying What You Know essay questions
- relevant Web sites

Custom modules to help you:
- calculate statistical tests (see "Calculating Statistical Tests")
- do research (see "Research Tools and Tips")
- practice analyzing quantitative data (see "Analyzing Quantitative Data")
- practice analyzing qualitative data (see "Analyzing Qualitative Data")
- practice evaluating published articles (see "Evaluating Articles")

Chapter 3 Answers
For Your Own Review

1. Anonymity means that the researcher does not know the identity of the participant. Confidentiality means the researcher knows who the participant is but agrees not to tell anyone. Confidentiality is more common in educational studies. Some surveys are conducted without any identifying information and would be anonymous. An example of confidentiality is when a researcher conducts an interview study, and knows participants and what they have said, but does not disclose who the participants were nor identify individual participants with their responses.

2. National Research Act of 1974 provides protection for human subjects and that proposed research is reviewed and approved by an authorized group prior to the execution of the research. This act also notes that no harm (physical or mental) comes to participants and informed consent by the participant or their parents of legal guardian if under age is obtained. The Family Educational Rights and Privacy Act of 1974 (Buckley Amendment) was designed to protect the educational records of students.

3. Competence, integrity, professional and scientific responsibility, respect for peoples' rights and dignity, concern for others' welfare, social responsibility.

4. The research plan is in progress and changing thereby adding the likelihood that additional ethical concerns arise and the qualitative researcher may observe illegal or unprofessional behavior.

Applying What You Know

1. a. This study would likely raise concerns about risks because of the age of the participants and about the physical, mental, and emotional health of the participants. The board would likely review this study as a Category III study because the risks are so great. Note, however, that this study could potentially be very important research so the risks might be warranted.

    b. A board would likely be concerned because of the age of the participants and because this study involves a form of deception. It might also harm the children's sense of ability and may cause emotional risk.

    c. This study involves deception and as presented does not include informed consent.

    d. Limiting the exercise of children could cause physical, mental, and emotional harm. The participants' age will also pose more risks than a study with adults.

    e. When a treatment is known to work or believed strongly to work it is unethical to withhold it from those who might benefit. Generally in a study like this, if the treatment is really believed to be better, the ethical design of the study would include all learners being exposed to the treatment at some point.

    f. This study would raise concerns because it may involve coercion and may limit participants ability to decline to participate. Most IRB's have stricter review for those researchers' conducting research on their own, even adult, students.

    g. This study is one that my son actually participated in. This study would undergo a stringent review because the children are minors, 'medical' equipment is being used, and they are placed in a situation of emotional distress.

    h. This study involves children's self-concept at a vulnerable time. The researchers might also uncover inappropriate parenting strategies and will have to have a mechanism for that possibility in their IRB proposal.

Practicing the Tasks

1. McClellan's research proposal

    a.   Statement of topic: Are there differences in statistical reasoning between those learners who complete class assignments via statistical calculators, or two types of statistical software?

    b.   Review of related literature (summarize the key points): The problem of the study is derived from everyday experiences and this proposal does not review as much research as many might. The literature reviewed supports that technology has changed mathematics education, and that the capability for dynamic instructional displays can support understanding.

    c.   Statement of the hypothesis: The hypotheses proposed are set out from the text and enumerated: They include students who learn statistics by utilizing Fathom will have higher levels of statistical reasoning than those who utilize Minitab, and students who use Fathom or Minitab will have higher levels of statistical reasoning than the students who use only the TI-83 calculator.

    d.   Participants: 96 high school students in an introductory statistics and probability course in a suburban pubic high school. In your design, if you know more about the potential participants it is good to include it. You may not at this point.

    e.   Design: (This will mean more to you later in the course): A randomized post-test only control group design. Note that Susan provided a brief rationale for the design (pretest contamination and a discussion of validity threats.)

    f.   Instruments/materials used: the course materials, assignments, and tests, and the SRA

    g.   Procedure: It is assumed that the participants in the study will complete assignments in their classes consistent with their treatment condition. The SRA will be administered after the treatments. This study most closely resembles a causal-comparative study. Susan did a nice job discussing the potential threats to validity within the procedures of her proposal.

    h.   Data analyses procedures (you can simply summarize the techniques that might be used). Susan did not mention her analysis procedures but it is assumed she would likely use differences between group analyses that might include ANOVA or Chi Square tests.

    i.   Potential time line: The study is to be conducted over the course of one semester. The time line, however, would include time to gain permission at the research site, time to obtain human subjects approval and consent, time to develop instructional materials, time to conduct the study, and score and analyze data, as well as time to interpret the data and write up the study.

    j.   Budget items: To conduct this study the researcher might need to purchase license to the statistical packages used and TI-83 calculators. The assessment instrument used might also need to be purchased. The researcher might compensate the school in the form of instructional materials or training that might add additional costs. The researcher might also pay someone to develop materials, or to score and analyze data. Copy costs for materials and tests might also be needed.

    k.   The participants are under-age and the study will likely need parental consent and student assent.

2.   Pollard's research proposal:

    a.   The role of review options on a computerized test score. Research questions are: Does including review options lead to an increase in the total score and which option leads to the highest scores?

    b.   Carlee addresses the recent reviewed literature and also summarizes that the most crucial literature addresses the use of review options in paper and pencil tests and computer adaptive tests and the equivalence of paper and pencil and computerized test formats.

    c.   Hypotheses include that a group with a no review option will perform lowest on the test, the two review options will have scores similar to those obtained by participants in the paper and pencil condition.

    d.   It appears that the participants are university students in statistics. Note, also how nicely Carlee adds the ethical considerations and informed consent procedures in her plan. She placed that information in the participants' section. Your text notes that sometimes this information is included in the procedures section.

    e.   Four group random post-test only design (You might know at this point only that she has four groups that are randomly assigned to condition)

    f.   Instruments include the computerized testing software (she mentions web pilot as an option), computers, and the actual tests.

    g.   Procedure: Carlee describes the conditions that participants will be assigned to as part of her procedures. There is not a complicated procedure in this study as there is only one test administration across different conditions.

    h.   Data analyses procedures (you can simply summarize the techniques that might be used). ANOVA with Tukey follow-ups.

    i.   Potential time line: The time line would include time to gain human subjects' approval and consent, time to develop instructional materials (this might be the longest phase but it should be relatively short compared to many studies), time to conduct the study, and time score and analyze data, as well as time to interpret the data and write up the study.

    j.   Budget items: The main budget items would be the software. Sometimes in studies like this the participants are paid but that does not appear to be the case in this proposal.

    k.   The participants are college students (and are generally not minors) so can provide informed consent. There would be ethical concerns if the scores were being counted toward their class grade and some participants were at a disadvantage.

3.   Galbraith's research study

    a.   A research purpose is clearly described. The study is grounded in related literature as well as the study context.

    b.   The researcher's identity is clearly elaborated.

    c.   Yes, Joel presents a discussion of how he gained access as well as a discussion of the IRB procedures.

    d.   Interviews, observations, informal conversations were the primary data collection measure. In addition Joel reflects about notes and entries in his journal as informative to his study.

    e.   Some limitations are noted, and a large section of lessons learned and recommendations for the novice qualitative researcher from Joel's perspective are included.

Test-Like Event

1.	d	8.	b	15.	d
2.	c	9.	b	16.	c
3.	b	10.	d	17.	d
4.	a	11.	c		
5.	c	12.	a		
6.	d	13.	b		
7.	d	14.	c		

Chapter 4 Selecting a Sample

Chapter 4 Objectives

1.   Identify and describe four random sampling techniques.
2.   Select a random sample using a table of random numbers.
3.   Identify three variables that can be stratified.
4.   Select stratified samples, cluster samples, and systematic samples.
5.   Identify and describe three nonrandom sampling technique.
6.   Identify and briefly describe two major sources of sample bias.
7.   Describe quantitative and qualitative sampling strategies.

Review the Terms

For each of the following terms provide a succinct definition in your own words.

Sample: _____

_____

Population: _____

_____

Sampling: _____

_____

Target Population: _____

_____

Accessible (Available) population: _____

_____

Random sampling: _____

_____

Simple random sampling: _____

_____

Stratified sampling (strata): _____

_____

Proportional Stratified Sampling: _____

_____

Cluster sampling (Cluster): _____

_____

Demographics: _____

_____

Systematic sampling: _____

_____

Table of random numbers: _____

_____

Multistage sampling: _____

_____

Sampling error: _____

_____

Sampling bias: _____

_____

Non-random samples: _____

_____

Convenience sampling: _____

_____

Purposive sampling: _____

_____

Quota sampling: _____

_____

Intensity sampling: _____

_____

Homogeneous sampling: _____

_____

Criterion sampling: _____

_____

Snowball sampling: _____

_____

Random purposive sampling: _____

_____

Probability sampling techniques: _____

_____

Qualitative sampling: _____

_____

For Your Own Review

1.   List the steps of simple random sampling.

_____
_____
_____
_____
_____
_____
_____
_____
_____

2.   State three types of qualitative sampling.

_____
_____
_____

3.   Provide and describe below one type of sampling bias.

_____

Checking What You Know

1.   You have decided to determine if first-year, undergraduate student grades are affected by living on-campus or off-campus. You know that you can't use only University A because the majority of first-year students are required to live on campus. You are concerned about using another school as a comparison to University A. Why? List at least 2 reasons. Then, suggest three ways to combat these concerns. (You do not have to use University A in all of the options.)

a. _____
    _____

b. _____
    _____
    _____

Applying What You Know

1.   A recent article in the popular press suggested that Americans have horrible diets and that university students have the worst diets of all Americans. The article had no data to support that claim. Let's imagine that we are going to conduct a survey study that examines university students' diets. We have a tight budget so we are going to sample from our University population of 7,000 students.

a.   What is our potential target population? _____

b.   What is our accessible population? _____

c. What additional characteristics of the population would be of interest to us?

_____
_____

d. If we were going to use simple random sampling, what would we do?

_____
_____
_____
_____
_____
_____
_____
_____

e. If we want to sample representatives from engineering, education, and nutrition what type of sampling would we now use? _____

f. What are the benefits of such sampling? _____

_____
_____

g. Generate an example of how we could implement each of the following types of sample bias (Of course, we wouldn't want to do this!).

1. Convenience: _____

_____

2. Purposive: _____

_____

3. Quota: _____

_____

2. Shaireen is an elementary education teacher. She is interested in examining if there are differences in third grade student achievement scores based upon whether the class has a student teacher or not. She proposes to compare two of the classrooms in her school to answer her research question.

a. What is our potential target population? _____

b. What is our accessible population? _____

c. What additional characteristics of the population would be of interest to us?

_____
_____

d. What type of sampling is Shaireen proposing? _____

_____

e. What are some drawbacks of this sampling technique? _____

_____

f. How might Shaireen combat these drawbacks? _____

_____

Practicing the Tasks

Task 4 of your text requires that you describe a sample appropriate for evaluating your hypotheses and your research questions. To get ready to complete this task on your own research questions, consider the eight samples in the following Participants sections of student proposals and published articles. For each of these examples, identify sampling technique, characteristics of the sample (e.g., size, demographics), the target population, and the accessible population. Some of these participant sections are from research proposals for which the student may not have secured entry into a research site or was still in planning stages. For each, also consider other characteristics of the sample that might be helpful to report if the study had been conducted. Identification of these other characteristics will help you consider potential bias.

1. Monica Wright's proposal, *Effects of Mental Imagery Training*, through the hypotheses was presented in Chapter 2 of this guide. Below is her Participants' section.

Four third grade classrooms from a rural elementary school in central Pennsylvania will participate in the study. Each classroom has an average of 25 students (with varying reading comprehension abilities). The majority of the students will be Caucasian (approximately 80%), the remaining students may include students from varying races and ethnic backgrounds. All four classes currently use the same reading text that includes brief tests (for comprehension) at the end of each story.

a. Sampling technique: _____

_____

b. Characteristics of the sample: _____

_____

c. Target population: _____

d. Accessible population: _____

e. Other characteristics of interest: _____

_____

2. Cindy Bochna's proposal, *Treating Autism,* up through the hypotheses was presented in Chapter 2 of this student guide. Below is her Participants' section.

Subjects will be children pre-diagnosed as autistic by a medical doctor and approximately 3 years of age enrolled in special education preschool classes at two locations in the Los Angeles Unified School District.

a. Sampling technique: _____

_____

b. Characteristics of the sample: _____

_____

    c. Target population: _____

    d. Accessible population: _____

    e. Other characteristics of interest: _____

    _____

Susan McClellen and Carlee Pollard's proposals were presented in the last chapter. Let's review their participants sections provided below.

3.   Susan McClellan's Participants' Section of *The Effects of Technology Resources on Achievement in Statistics*

The subjects will be 96 high school students enrolled in a one-semester Introductory Probability and Statistics course at a large suburban public high school. The goal of the course is oriented toward developing statistical reasoning in students and less toward developing computations and skills than the traditional introductory course in statistics. Each of the 96 students will be randomly assigned to one of three course sections of 32 students taught by the same teacher—a control group in one section and two treatment groups, one in each of the other two sections. The design will be a randomized Posttest Only Control Group Design. This design was selected in order to avoid pretest contamination.

    a. Sampling technique: _____

    _____

    b. Characteristics of the sample: _____

    _____

    c. Target population: _____

    d. Accessible population: _____

    e. Other characteristics of interest: _____

    _____

4. Carlee Pollard's Participants' Section of *The Effect of Review Options on Computerized Test Scores*

Participants will be recruited through a course in the statistics department. These participants will be randomly split into four groups, one for each of the test formats. Each group will be given instructions specific to the testing situation that they will be encountering. For example, those not given the review option shall be informed that once an answer is given they will not have the opportunity to go back and change it later. Prior to starting the study, each participant will be asked to give informed consent before continuing with the procedure. They will be assured of anonymity and confidentiality of their individual scores. They also will be informed that they may withdraw from the study at any time.

    a. Sampling technique: _____

    _____

    b. Characteristics of the sample: _____

    _____

    c. Target population: _____

    d. Accessible population: _____

    e. Other characteristics of interest: _____
       _____

5. Pajares (2001) was presented in Chapter 1 and the participants' section is reproduced below.

Participants were 529 students in a public middle school in the Northeast (255 girls, 274 boys, 171 in Grade 6, 176 in grade 7, 182 in grade 8). The socioeconomic status of the school and of the area that the school served was largely middle class and students were primarily Caucasian. Students' ages ranged from 11 to 16 years.

    a. Sampling technique: _____
       _____

    b. Characteristics of the sample: _____
       _____

    c. Target population: _____

    d. Accessible population: _____

    e. Other characteristics of interest: _____
       _____

6. Perry (2001) was presented in Chapter 1 of this guide, and its participants' section is reproduced below.

During the six months I spent with these fifth-graders, I immersed myself in their words, pictures, voices, laughter, and frustrations. I gathered myriad images, sounds, words, and emotions in multiple forms-field notes, videotapes, audiotapes, students' work, and memories-and immersed myself in them at home. I continuously cycled through the materials, questioning them and myself to make sense of the patterns that emerged. Through this process, I engaged in qualitative inquiry as Janesick (2000) described it. Because I was with them over time and collected multiple forms of data, I came to know the children as individuals and as a class-to go beyond the surface (Janesick, 2000).

    a. Sampling technique: _____
       _____

    b. Characteristics of the sample: _____
       _____

    c. Target population: _____

    d. Accessible population: _____

    e. Other characteristics of interest: _____
       _____

7. The following Participants' section is from Ma, X (2001). Bullying and being Bullied: to what extent are Bullies also victims. *American Educational Research Journal, 38*(2), 351-370.

Data were collected from all students in grades 6 and 8 as well as their teachers in the English sector throughout the province. Students completed several achievement tests and a student questionnaire. Teachers also completed a teacher questionnaire. The current study used student data that included all of the sixth graders (N=6,883) from 147 schools, and all of the eighth graders (N=6868) from 92 schools in the province. Therefore, the sixth and eighth graders represented two populations rather than samples.

    a. Sampling technique: _____
        _____

    b. Characteristics of the sample: _____
        _____

    c. Target population: _____

    d. Accessible population: _____

    e. Other characteristics of interest: _____
        _____

8. The following Participants' section is from Hogan, K, & Corey, C. (2001). Viewing classrooms as cultural contexts for fostering scientific literacy. *Anthropology and Education, 32*, 214-233.

This study occurred with one class of fifth graders in a high-poverty urban school in New York state. There were 21 students in the class (eight girls, 13 boys, 16 African American, four Hispanic, and one Euro-American). The teacher had chosen several of the boys to be in his class that year to prevent them from being tracked into special education for problems that he believed were more situational than psychological. The overall academic performance of the class was quite low, and the teacher was under enormous pressure to help the school raise its standing in the states' ranking of schools, based upon students standardized test achievement in reading, writing, and mathematics. Therefore, a large portion of the school day was dedicated to regimented direct instruction, practice, and drill in these subjects imbued with reminders about test performances. When teaching subjects such as social studies, the teacher engaged his students in provocative moral discussion of issues such as religion and crime, so the students were used to sharing their opinions in open discussions and debates during some portion of the school day.

    a. Sampling technique: _____
        _____

    b. Characteristics of the sample: _____
        _____

    c. Target population: _____

    d. Accessible population: _____

    e. Other characteristics of interest: _____
        _____

Test-Like Event

1. You are given a random list of all graduating seniors at the university. You decide to survey every five names on the list to ask them what types of activities they participated in while they were at the university. What type of sampling are you displaying?

   a. Random
   b. Stratified
   c. Cluster
   d. Systematic

2. You wish to do a comparison study between two outpatient physical therapists' success rates. Instead of assigning patients to go to one or the other, you divide your sample into two groups and randomly sample based upon which therapist individuals attend. Which type of sampling are you displaying?

   a. Random
   b. Stratified
   c. Cluster
   d. Systematic

3. You wish to do a study to examine the effects of socio-economic status on diet. You can randomly sample all of the people that work or are patients at a local hospital for the study.   You are concerned about the disproportionate number of your sample with higher socio-economic status, while not representing the lower socio-economic groups well. How would you sample to control for this problem?

   a. Random
   b. Stratified
   c. Cluster
   d. Systematic

4. You go to the mall next weekend to study how people spend their spare money. You ask all passersby to participate. Which type of bias are you illustrating?

   a. Convenience
   b. Purposive
   c. Quota
   d. Demographic

5. Which of the following is an example of qualitative sampling technique?

   a. Cluster
   b. Random Purposive
   c. Stratified
   d. Systematic

6. Of the following, which is a type of random sampling?

    a. Quota
    b. Systematic
    c. Convenience
    d. Purposive

7. When it is not possible to list all members of a population, researchers often use which of the following types of sampling?

    a. Simple Random
    b. Systematic
    c. Stratified
    d. Quota

For items 8-16 consider the following general situation.Principal Meyer's school has 2,000 elementary children. She wants to obtain information from parents regarding school homework policies in order to make decisions about future school policy.

8. Principal Meyer takes a numbered list of all students in the school and randomly selects a sample to participate. Which sampling technique is she best illustrating?

    a. Systematic
    b. Simple random
    c. Cluster
    d. Stratified

9. Principal Meyer wants to be sure she has a proportionate sample of parents based upon the grade level of their children. Which sampling method should she consider using?

    a. Systematic
    b. Simple random
    c. Cluster
    d. Stratified

10. Principal Meyer decides she will send out surveys to the entire school and then will analyze the first 200 responses. In this case she is illustrating which of the following types of sampling?

    a. Convenience
    b. Traditional
    c. Quota
    d. Purposive

11. Principal Meyer has decided to consider changes to her policy because the PTO president suggested some parents had concerns about the current policy. She leaves a stack of surveys at the main office desk and as parents come to pick up their children, volunteer, or as they enter the school on any other business she asks them to take the time to complete the survey. Which of the following does this strategy best illustrate?

    a. Purposive
    b. Intensity
    c. Convenience
    d. Coercion

12. Of the following, which type of research is Principal Meyer conducting?

    a. Basic
    b. Experimental
    c. Evaluation
    d. Correlational

13. Given the general guidelines presented in your text and her population, which of the following represents an approximate sample size she should collect?

    a. 20-50
    b. 100-200
    c. 300-400
    d. 1500-2000

14. The target population in her study is

    a. children in her school.
    b. parents of children in her school.
    c. elementary children in her district.
    d. parents of children in America.

15. Suppose Principal Meyer decides to approach her study differently. She identifies children as either those involved in extra-curricular activities or those not involved in extra-curricular activities. She samples about 20 parents of children from each group and collects data with a short interview. Which of the following best illustrates the sampling technique she is now using?

    a. Homogeneous
    b. Intensity
    c. Snowball
    d. Criterion

16. Principal Meyer decides to do phone interviews. She selects a few parents to start with and at the end of her brief interview she asks if the participant knows anyone else that might want to have input into the decision. She then lists those names and contacts them to participate. In this case which type of sampling is she is illustrating?

   a. Homogeneous
   b. Intensity
   c. Snowball
   d. Criterion

17. Mia studies the experiences of Asian women enrolled in American Universities. She selects a sample of eight single women from Asian countries who traveled to the United States for study. Which type of sampling is Mia illustrating?

   a. Homogeneous
   b. Intensity
   c. Snowball
   d. Cluster

18. Mia's study is an example of

   a. Quantitative research.
   b. Qualitative research.
   c. Basic research.
   d. Evaluation research.

Companion Website
For more practice on becoming competent in this chapter's objectives, go to the Companion Website that accompanies this text at www.prenhall.com/gay. This site includes:

   Objectives with links to:
   • more multiple-choice questions in Practice Quiz
   • Applying What You Know essay questions
   • relevant Web sites

   Custom modules to help you:
   • calculate statistical tests (see "Calculating Statistical Tests")
   • do research (see "Research Tools and Tips")
   • practice analyzing quantitative data (see "Analyzing Quantitative Data")
   • practice analyzing qualitative data (see "Analyzing Qualitative Data")
   • practice evaluating published articles (see "Evaluating Articles")

Chapter 4 Answers
For your own review

1. Identify population
   Determine sample size
   List all members of the population
   Assign all on list a consecutive number
   Select arbitrary number in table of random numbers
   Look at number of digits assigned to each member
   If number corresponds to an assigned number that individual is in the sample
   Go to next number and repeat
2. Intensity, homogeneous, criterion, snowball, random purposive sampling
3. Quota, convenience, purposive (judgment)

Checking What You Know
1. a. There are many possible answers to this question. The schools could differ on strata of some type (e.g., majors, hs gpa, SES, type of school), different policies, availability of on-campus and other food services, location of school, number of on-off students, number of commuters, varying school policies about food in residence life. There are many other possible answers.

   b. There, again, are many possible answers. Three include to 1.) randomly sample University A, 2.) change the target population and randomly select across more than one school, and 3.) change the nature of the study and sample a small purposive sample.

Applying What You Know
1. a American University students
   b Students at our University
   c. Demographics of our university, SES, geographic location of the university, population of international students, number of those who live in student housing versus off campus or at their family homes, type of University (private, public,) among other characteristics, would make a difference in the generalizability of our study.
   d. Identify and define the population: Our university has 7000 students.
      400 participants are needed. We would send about 700 to assure we obtained our desired representative sample size.
      It might be difficult to get a list of all the population and number it. The registrar would likely be the best source of this information.
      Number each person in the population
      Pick a number from the random number table and examine—
      Select participants into the sample based upon the number corresponding from the table to your list.
      Repeat the last step until you have your sample.
   e. Use a stratified sampling procedure.
   f. Stratified sampling allows for the correct proportion in the sample on some characteristic in the population
   g. 1. Convenience: One way to bias this sample via conveniences to simply 'hang out' at a highly populated place, say the student union, or a university function like a sporting events and collect information from those students who will participate when approached.
      2. Purposive: One way to bias this sample with purposive sampling is, for example, if as a faculty member at the university you think that you can get a range of responses by going to the residence life dining hall, the most popular local pizzeria, and the local market, and sampling at these locations. You are making a judgment, based upon what you know about the population, as to how to get a representative sample.
      3. Quota: One way that quota sampling might happen in this study is that you might have a hard time obtaining a list of all of the population members. You could bias your sample by suggesting that you would collect data until you had at least 100 participants from each academic level (first-year, sophomore, junior, senior, and graduate), with 25 each who live on campus and off.

2. a. Our potential target population could be all of elementary school children everywhere in the US? But..realistically, we might target in the district or schools that have student teachers from the same university, for example.
    b. We would need student level information such as SES and prior achievement. We also would need to know about the characteristics of the teacher, student teacher, etc.
    c. A convenience sample—with nonequivalent groups—you know now this is a bad sampling strategy. Later you will learn it is also a horrible research design.
    d. Shaireen, with additional classrooms would best use appropriate cluster sampling as found describe in your text.
    e. Increase the number of classrooms. Randomly assign student teachers to a larger number of classrooms.

Practicing the Tasks
1. a. It is not clear if these classrooms were randomly selected, as in a cluster sample, or if they were convenience sampled.
    b. 80% white, 4 classrooms of 25 each, rural PA
    c. Likely the true target population is all elementary students
    d. The accessible population is classrooms in this rural school (your text noted it is sometimes difficult to get into schools to do studies).
    e. Reading ability of the students would be helpful to know for this study as would SES or ethnicity information. This is a proposal and if Monica had conducted the study she likely would include such information.

2. a. The tample is purposively selected.
    b. Diagnosed with autism, at one of two L.A. Unified Schools, number not presented and would likely vary year to year
    c. Autistic preschoolers
    d. Autistic preschoolers in L.A. Unified School District who participate
    e. SES and functioning level of the students. Again, this is a general research proposal for a course and all information about the participants might not be known.

3. a. Cluster
    b. 96 students, in three sections, at a large suburban high school.
    c. Introductory statistics students Susan would probably like to generalize to introductory statistics instruction overall (hs, college, graduate school, even middle school).
    d. Introductory statistics instruction in this high school
    e. When Susan writes up the study, after it is conducted, it would be nice to know the students' ability, SES, past use of technology

4. a. Convenience, from existing statistics courses with random assignment to groups.
    b. University statistics students, number not noted
    c. The target of this study would be computerized-test takers
    d. The accessible population is students enrolled in statistics courses at this university.
    e. In this case, when Carlee reported the study she would likely add characteristics of her sample to include general ability, GPA, prior statistics or mathematics experience. She might also consider collecting information about their interest in statistics or opinions about perceived value of statistics.

5. a. This information is not entirely clear. It appears the entire school population may have been sampled.
    b. Over 500 Public middle school students in the Northeast
    c. Middle school learners and perhaps a broader target that included
    d. Students enrolled in this Northeastern middle school
    e. Some limited amount of information about ages and some limited demographic and characteristics of the sample are included.

6. a. This qualitative study describes the context in narrative form. It is not clear how the class was selected from this section of the report.
   b. Fifth grade students
   c. & d. The target and accessible population are less relevant in this study because of the nature of the inquiry the researchers will not be using inferential statistics and will not be generalizing their findings.
   e. As you will later see when we revisit this article, other characteristics of the participants are presented as well as more about the setting of the study as their perspectives are presented.

7. a. This sampling strategy was to select all of the population in a province for the sample. This happens, sometimes, as noted in your text with very small populations, it also sometimes is a strategy used for large prediction studies. Census.
   b. 6,883 and 6,868 from 92 schools in a province in Canada.
   c. The target population might middle school learners generally. If the target population is those middle schoolers in the province, then the target and accessible populations are the same
   d. The accessible population is province middle school children
   e. Other characteristics of the province might be nice to know. Demographic data from province sources might be used to supplement.

8. a. This qualitative study was done similar to a case study with the sample being the class in the case.
   b. 21 students in a large suburban school, high poverty, many minority, low academic performance
   c-d. As a qualitative study the researcher is not really interested in target population or accessible population because there is an intention to generalize findings from this study to other contexts.
   e. The authors provide a lot of information about the setting of the study (the class and some school information)

Test-Like Event

1.   d
2.   c
3.   b
4.   a
5.   b
6.   b
7.   d
8.   b
9.   d
10. c
11. c
12. c
13. c
14. b
15. b
16. c
17. a
18. b

Chapter 5   Selecting Measuring Instruments

Chapter 5 Objectives

1. State the links or relationships among a construct, a variable, and an operationalized variable.
2. Describe different types of variables: nominal, ordinal, interval, and ratio; categorical and quantitative; dependent and independent.
3. Explain various testing terms: standardized test, assessment, measurement, selection, supply, performance assessment, raw score, norm-and criterion-referenced scoring.
4. Describe the purposes of various types of tests: achievement, aptitude, attitude, interest, value, personality, projective, nonprojective and self-report.
5. Describe various scales used to collect data for cognitive and affective variables.
6. Familiarize yourself with measuring instrument and select instruments suited for varied research needs.
7. Describe the purposes of and ways to determine content, criterion-related, construct, and consequential validity.
8. Describe the purposes of and ways to determine stability, equivalence, equivalence and stability, internal consistency, and scorer/rater reliability.
9. Define or describe standard error of measurement.
10. Know useful sources for finding information about specific tests.
11. State a strategy for test selection
12. Identify and briefly describe three sources of test information.

Review the Terms
Provide a succinct definition in your own words for each of the following terms.

Data: _____

_____

Construct: _____

_____

Variable: _____

_____

Instrument: _____

_____

Nominal variable: _____

_____

Ordinal variable: _____

_____

Quantitative variable: _____

_____

Measurement scale: _____

_____

Interval variable: _____

_____

Ratio variable: _____

_____

Independent variable: _____

_____

Dependent variable: _____

_____

Nonprojective instruments: _____

_____

Projective instruments: _____

_____

Test: _____

_____

Cognitive characteristic: _____

_____

Affective characteristic: _____

_____

Assessment: _____

_____

Standardized test: _____

_____

Measurement: _____

_____

Selection methods: _____

_____

Supply methods: _____

_____

Performance assessment: _____

_____

Raw score: _____

_____

Norm-referenced scoring: _____

_____

Criterion-referenced scoring: _____

_____

Self-referenced scoring: _____

_____

Cognitive test: _____

_____

Achievement test: _____

_____

Diagnostic test: _____

_____

Aptitude test: _____

_____

Attitude scale: _____

_____

Likert scale: _____

_____

Semantic differential scale: _____

_____

Rating scale: _____

_____

Validity: _____

_____

Response set: _____

_____

Content validity: _____

_____

Sampling validity: _____

_____

Face validity: _____

_____

Bias: _____

_____

Projective test: _____

_____

Interest inventory: _____
_____

Values test: _____
_____

Personality inventory: _____
_____

Criterion-related validity: _____
_____

Concurrent validity: _____
_____

Predictive validity: _____
_____

Construct validity: _____
_____

Consequential validity: _____
_____

Reliability: _____
_____

Stability: _____
_____

Test-retest reliability: _____
_____

Equivalence: _____
_____

Internal-consistency reliability: _____
_____

Split-half reliability: _____
_____

Interjudge reliability: _____
_____

Intrajudge reliability: _____
_____

Scorer/rater reliability: _____
_____

Reliability coefficients: _____

_____

Standard Error of Measurement: _____

_____

Mental Measurements Yearbook: _____

_____

Tests in Print: _____

_____

For Your Own Review

1. State one measure used to calculate internal consistency reliability.

    _____

2. List the four measurement scales

    _____
    _____
    _____
    _____

3. Contrast the terms instrument, assessment, and measurement.

    _____
    _____
    _____
    _____
    _____
    _____

4. Elaborate or explain your response to each of the following T/F items.

    a. All things being equal: Supply items are more reliable than select items.

        _____
        _____
        _____

    b. Researcher constructed instruments are more reliable and valid than existing instruments.

        _____
        _____
        _____

    c. Norm-referenced tests are more valid than are criterion referenced tests.

        _____
        _____
        _____

Just for Practice

1. Use the following list of descriptors for each of the following assessments. Some are examples from the text and some are novel examples and require application. You may use more than one descriptor for each assessment listed.

Standardized test   Cognitive test   Aptitude measure
Projective instrument   NonProjective instrument   Affective test
Personality test   Norm-referenced   Criterion-referenced
Self-referenced   Achievement test   Attitude scales

   a. The Iowa Test of Basic Skills _____
   b. Teacher made math test _____
   c. Preschool Reading motivation scale _____
   d. GRE _____
   d. Weschsler Intelligence Scale for Children-Revised (WISC-R) _____
   f. House-Tree-Person (child draws a HTP, used by psychologists) _____
   g. MMPI _____
   h. Swim team training times _____
   i. SAT _____
   j. Perceived interest questionnaire _____
   k. Spatial ability measure _____

2. For each of the following, indicate the scale of measurement:

   a. Class rank _____
   b. Gender _____
   c. Achievement test score _____
   d. Employment status _____
   e. Temperature _____
   f. Height _____
   g. Raw score on a teacher made test _____
   h. Distance _____
   i. Age _____
   j. Major _____
   k. Time of race completion _____
   l. Political party affiliation _____

Checking What You Know

1. Which type of reliability or validity is best illustrated by the following examples? The answer may be used more than once. Some answers may not be used at all.

    Criterion-related validity   Concurrent validity   Construct
    Consequential validity   Content validity   Predictive validity
    Alternate-forms reliability   Sampling validity   Scorer/rater reliability
    Internal consistency reliability   Split-half reliability   Test/retest reliability

    a. Pauline administers motivation to learn inventory on Monday and again one week later to indicate the correlation between the scores. _____

    b. Drake administers a tolerance for pain measure before training and then correlates the score on the measure with persistence in triathlon training. _____

    c. This is estimated by Cronbach's alpha _____

    d. Max administers a physics test. When he looks at it he is concerned that it measures advanced mathematics, not physics. Max is concerned about _____

    e. Ms. Cable, a secondary biology teacher, is concerned that the new state-wide test for advanced biology only seems to test the first semester of the standard curriculum. Her concern is most related to _____.

    f. Lisa administers both group-administered and an individually-administered measures of self-confidence and examines the relationship between them. Lisa is best illustrating _____.

    g. Equivalence is tested through an estimate of _____.

    h. Dan has developed a new measure of motivation. He examines the relationship among items on each of his scales. Dan will examine _____.

2. For each of the following, identify the variables by placing a V over them. When possible identify them as either dependent (or criterion) (DV) or independent (predictor) (IV) variables.

    a. Are there differences in college learners' choice of science careers between those exposed to laboratory classes in the late elementary grades and those who were not exposed to lab classes?

    b. Is there a relationship between age and interest in music education?

    c. Is there a relationship between size of family and feelings of social competence in middle school girls?

    d. What are the variables that best predict completion of an initiated doctoral dissertation?

    e. Are there gender differences in average time of homework completion?

    f. Does kindergarten misbehavior relate to sixth grade attendance and achievement?

Applying What You Know

Bruce is studying the benefits of different types of instructional materials for learning science content. Some previous research suggests that diagrams and pictures can be helpful to learning, but that often learners do not attend to them. Other previous research suggests that animations can be helpful to learning, but that they sometimes serve to distract the reader from important information. Some say that having students draw or including inserted questions helps science learning. Given Bruce's general area of research (i.e., science learning) develop the following. You may elect to use any type of instruction or go with a survey study or a qualitative study.

a.   Research topic: _____
   _____

b.   Variables (identify types if appropriate): _____
   _____
   _____

c.   What data source will you use? How will you assure reliability and validity? _____
   _____
   _____

d.   Who will be in the sample (include characteristics as well as size)? _____
   _____
   _____

Practicing the Tasks

1.   Task 5 requires that you describe three instruments appropriate for collection of data pertinent to your study and include

   a.   Name, publisher, cost
   b.   A brief description of the purpose of the instrument
   c.   Validity and reliability data
   d.   The group for which the instrument is intended
   e.   Administration requirements
   f.   Information regarding scoring and interpretation
   g.   Reviewers overall impressions

To practice parts of this task, let's suppose that we are interested in measuring young children's motivation for reading. As your text indicates there are several ways to obtain measures. Among others, several means include examining reviews of instruments in Buros' Institute of Mental Measurements, PRO-Ed, Tests in Print and Educational Testing Service to find a measure that will meet the requirements. Another strategy is to use some literature based searches to find instruments that might work.

The research topic of our hypothetical study is *Is there a relationship between urban first grade children's motivation for reading and school attendance?* Of course there are probably a number of extraneous variables in a study of this nature, such as Socio-Economic Status variables such parents' education and family income, general health of the child, transportation, even age of the child, not to mention reading ability! However, for our study, personnel at the school have requested attendance and reading motivation because the school is experiencing attendance problems and feels that if more is done to motivate young learners they will want to be at school. The school would like us to use a student-based measure that can be group administered because there will be several hundred students participating and they would like to administer the measure in school as a cross sectional survey (You will learn about that in Chapter 6. For now just know it is going to be administered all at once.). Further, since reading is such a large component of the first grade curriculum, they would like to focus on reading motivation.

Before we start let's review a little.

1. What type of study are we planning? _____

2. What type of instrument are we trying to find (personality, cognitive, attitude, aptitude, supply, selection, projective?)
    _____
    _____

3. List two considerations we should think about before we start to investigate.

    _____   _____

Okay, now we are ready to roll.

4. Conduct a search online through Buros Institute of Mental Measurements (you can use this as a keyword) to find potential instruments. Use the search term *reading motivation*. How many did you find? _____

5.   Several of the hits are instruments for older learners, or not reading contexts. Below is brief information on three of the instruments that the search yielded: the MRP, the Children's Academic Intrinsic Motivation Inventory, and the MAT. Given these three examples, summarize, from the information provided, some strengths and weaknesses of each for use in our current study.

5a. The MRP

Motivation to Read Profile (MRP).

Gambrell, Linda B. Palmer, Barbara Martin Codling, Rose Marie Mazzoni, Susan Anders

Table of Contents

Descriptive information
Contact information
Suggestions to extend your search

Descriptive Information

Title: Motivation to Read Profile (MRP).
Author: Gambrell, Linda B. Palmer, Barbara Martin Codling, Rose Marie Mazzoni, Susan Anders
Abstract: The Motivation to Read Profile (MRP) is a two-part instrument designed to assess the reading motivation of second through sixth grade students. The group-administered Reading Survey consists of 20

items, 10 of which measure students' self concept as readers and 10 of which measure the value students place on reading. Students respond to the items on a four-point, Likert-type scale. The Conversational Interview is individually administered. It is designed to provide information about individual students' reading motivation, for example, favorite authors, books, and stories, and how students locate reading material. A total score and two subscale scores may be computed for each student. The profile may be used for several applications, including monitoring and documenting reading motivation after implementation of a reading motivation intervention program, or administering the instrument at the beginning of the year and monitoring changes in reading motivation throughout the school year. Technical data are included. (KM)
Test Acronyms: MRP
Material Notes: 1. Article reprint. See availability source.
Publication Date: 1996
Most recent update to the database: May 1997
ETS Tracking Number: TC020075

Contact Information

For more detailed information about this measure and its related materials, please contact or consult:
Reading Teacher, 0034-0561, v49 n7 p518-33, Apr 1996.

Strengths/weaknesses:

_____
_____
_____
_____
_____
_____
_____
_____
_____

5b. *Children's Academic Intrinsic Motivation Inventory.*

Gottfried, Adele Eskeles

Table of Contents

Descriptive information
Contact information
Suggestions to extend your search

Descriptive Information

Title: Children's Academic Intrinsic Motivation Inventory.
Author: Gottfried, Adele Eskeles
Abstract: Measures children's intrinsic motivation for school learning in the subject areas of reading, mathematics, social studies, and science and also provides a general scale of academic intrinsic motivation not distinguished by subject area. Academic intrinsic motivation concerns children's enjoyment of learning, interest in novelty, curiosity, persistence in difficult tasks, and feeling of competence, mastery and challenge. May be group or individually administered. An individual administration is recommended for children with learning, reading or perceptual difficulties and problems. Items 45-56 are supplementary and may be excluded from administration of the inventory. They are not to be included in scoring, in any event.
Test Acronyms: CAIMI TIM (I)
Grade Level(s): 4; 5; 6; 7; 8.
General Notes: See also Children's Academic Anxiety Inventory (TC012171). TIME: 45; approx. ITEMS: 56.
Publication Date: 1982

Most recent update to the database: Apr 1983
ETS Tracking Number: TC012172

Contact Information

This measure is archived in the Tests in Microfiche Collection at the Educational Testing Service. Contact: Educational Testing Service (ETS) Test Collection Library
Rosedale and Carter Roads
Princeton, NJ 08541
(609) 734-5689
In order to assist you, ETS will require their document tracking number: TC012172. As of January, 1998, the cost was $11.00, plus $3.00 shipping and handling.

Strengths/weaknesses:_____

_____

_____

_____

_____

_____

_____

_____

5c. *Motivation Analysis Test (MAT)*

Cattell, Raymond Bernard, 1905- Horn, John L Sweney, Arthur B

Table of Contents

Descriptive information
Contact information
Suggestions to extend your search

Descriptive Information

Title: Motivation Analysis Test (MAT)
Author: Cattell, Raymond Bernard, 1905- Horn, John L Sweney, Arthur B
Abstract: The Motivation Analysis Test (MAT) assesses person's interests, drives, and the strengths of sentiment and value systems. Measures adult motivational patterns. Material is written at a reading level of 6.9. Five scales measure basic drives including mating, assertiveness, fear, narcism-comfort, pugnacity-sadism. Five scales measure sentiments including self concept, superego, career, swetheart-spouse, and home-parental.
Test Acronyms: Satisfaction
Material Notes: 1. Test, Form A (1964) 2. Key, Form A, U1 (unintegrated) 3. Key, Form A, U2 (unintegrated) 4. Key, Form A, I1 (Integrated) 5. Key, Form A, I2 (Integrated) 6. Example to illustrate scoring procedure (AS & Profile) 7. Administration Instructions for Motivation Analysis Test 8. Handbook (1959 & 1964) 9. Answer Sheet, Form A (1964) 10. MAT Dynamic Structure Profile 11. Preliminary Description manual for individual assessment with/MAT
Publication Date: 1964
Most recent update to the database: Aug 1994
ETS Tracking Number: TC000609

Contact Information

For more detailed information about this measure and its related materials, please contact or consult:
Institute for Personality and Ability Testing, Inc.

Strengths/weaknesses:

_____
_____
_____
_____
_____
_____
_____
_____
_____

6. Armed with this information, let's conduct an ERIC database search and see what else we can find. Use the search term *reading motivation* and *children*. This will allow us to examine how other researchers measure reading motivation and also look at current literature. Although this project is a school-based evaluation, almost action oriented, the current literature can help us find instruments as well. How many did the search yield? _____

7. Looking through these, some look as if they are programs to increase motivation. Our school might need those later. Some also look as if they are opinion pieces on the importance for motivation. Let's change our search a bit and add *measurement* to our search terms. What did this search produce?

    _____

8. Okay, let's change gears a little and conduct a literature search by Gambrell as author. Remember, she is the lead author of the MRP we found through Buros. Are we on the right track? How many did you get? _____

9. Find the reference for the article published in *The Reading Teacher* as indicated in our review from Buros and check out the abstract. What do you think?

    _____
    _____

Task 5 requires that you find three potential instruments. We don't have all the information but we are definitely on the way with one and we have ruled out several others.

Let's go back to ERIC. There is another instrument used in schools to measure motivation to read and I remember there was a bit of research on it. The author's name was Wigfield. Let's see what that turns up. (If you didn't have that knowledge reading abstracts would have gotten you there pretty quickly. He has done a fair bit of research.)

10. What did you find? _____
     _____
     _____

11. Search Allan. How many articles? _____

12. What is the instrument? _____

13. Reading abstracts, does it appear to be one we might want to use? _____ Why or why not?_____
    _____
    _____

14. How can we get the questionnaire? _____
    _____
    _____

Well, we still need another. Perhaps we need to try different search terms. Maybe motivation is too narrow. In reading the abstracts from Wigfield, it appears that attitude was used a lot. Let's try that. We can either try Buros again (okay idea), search in ERIC some more with reading attitudes as a search term (okay idea) or we can browse through hundreds of abstracts until we find what other measures might be used (not a good idea; it may take forever.)

15. Let's try both the ERIC and the Buros search.

    An ERIC search of reading attitudes is huge: _____. Let's narrow a little, reading attitudes and assessment yields several possibilities. List two: _____; _____. At first glance neither seem great but the PRAS might work. (It has been used with first graders as indicated by a little further research.)

16. Let's go back to Buros with the attitude search. It seemed consistent with our needs from the ERIC search. What did this search turn up? Any possibilities?
    _____
    _____

(Note the MRP came up again in this search.)

Well, Task 5 for our study is not completely done, but we are well on our way. We have access to at least 4 instruments that might work for us that do not cost anything, have been used for similar samples, and can be easily group administered and appear to have reliability and validity data. You can use similar strategies to find additional instruments for your own research topic for Task 5.

Test-Like Event

1. Given the research topic, "Are there differences in apparent fatigue in third grade learners who are either given homework, or not given homework?" The independent variable has

    a. no levels
    b. one level
    c. two levels
    d. three levels

Consider the following scenario for items 2-9.

    Nadine conducts research on superintendents' decision making. Her research question is, "Are there gender differences in decision making?" and "Are there differences in decision making based upon whether or not the superintendent spent a minimum of 5 years in school-based settings as either a teacher, specialist, or principal?" In her study, participants respond to a few demographic items (including gender and years of school-based experiences) by recording in their responses in a computer scan sheet. Participants then complete a multiple-choice assessment that measures their knowledge of decision-making strategies. Nadine next administers a Likert-Scale that measures personal decision-making style. The last task is for participants to answer their reaction to a problem scenario that a superintendent might face. In their answer they must include their decision given the scenario and their reasons why they would make that decision.

2. In Nadine's study which of the following represents a *supply* method for collecting data?

    a. decision-making style survey
    b. multiple-choice test
    c. answers to problem scenarios
    d. demographic items

3. Nadine's study represents a

    a. causal-comparative study.
    b. correlational study.
    c. experimental study.
    d. descriptive study.

4. Nadine's variable 'gender' represents a _____ level variable.

    a. nominal
    b. ordinal
    c. interval
    d. ratio

5. Data collected from the decision-making style inventory represents _____ level data.

    a. nominal
    b. ordinal
    c. interval
    d. ratio

6. In Nadine's study, years of teaching is measured as a _____ level variable.

    a. nominal
    b. ordinal
    c. interval
    d. ratio

7. The multiple-choice test that measures knowledge of decision making strategies is best described as a

    a. personality test.
    b. cognitive assessment.
    c. performance assessment.
    d. attitude instrument.

8. The problem scenarios best represent

    a. aptitude measure.
    b. personality test.
    c. attitude instrument.
    d. authentic assessment.

9.   Of the following, which represents an independent variable in Nadine's study?

    a.   Years of teaching
    b.   Problem scenarios
    c.   Multiple-choice assessment
    d.   Decision-making style inventory

10. Of the following, which represents a quantitative variable?

    a.   gender
    b.   state of birth
    c.   ethnicity
    d.   age

11.-14. Mildred conducted a forty-item Likert survey study of all the teachers, principals, and specialists in the state regarding opinions about block scheduling options. Her research question is *"What are our state educators' opinions regarding block scheduling?"*

11. In her study, *type of educator* represents

    a.   nominal data
    b.   ordinal data.
    c.   interval data.
    d.   ratio data.

12. Given her sampling technique, Mildred's sample is

    a.   biased.
    b.   not representative.
    c.   a census.
    d.   invalid.

13. Mildred's research topic is an example of

    a.   correlational research.
    b.   causal-comparative research.
    c.   experimental research.
    d.   descriptive research.

14. Which of the following DOES NOT represent a variable in Mildred's study?

    a.   type of school personnel
    b.   opinion
    c.   survey
    d.   the state

Companion Website

For more practice on becoming competent in this chapter's objectives, go to the Companion Website that accompanies this text at www.prenhall.com/gay. This site includes:

Objectives with links to:
- more multiple-choice questions in Practice Quiz
- Applying What You Know essay questions
- relevant Web sites

Custom modules to help you:
- calculate statistical tests (see "Calculating Statistical Tests")
- do research (see "Research Tools and Tips")
- practice analyzing quantitative data (see "Analyzing Quantitative Data")
- practice analyzing qualitative data (see "Analyzing Qualitative Data")
- practice evaluating published articles (see "Evaluating Articles")

Chapter 5 answers
For Your Own Review

1. Cronbach alpha, Kuder-Richardson

2. Nominal, Ordinal, Interval, Ratio

3. A test is a systematic, usually formal, paper and pencil procedure for gathering information about peoples' cognitive and affective characteristics. Assessment is a broader term than test and includes the collection, synthesis, and interpretation of formal, informal, numerical or textual information. One type of assessment is a test. Measurement is the process of giving a score or quantifying performance on assessment.

4. a. False. All things being equal, selection items are more reliable than supply items because selection items have a correct answer so there is not subjectivity (which decreases reliability) in scoring. In addition, in practice we generally can provide a greater number of selection items than supply items which also helps the reliability of our measure.
    b. False. As noted in your text, it is often better to go with existing instruments that have known psychometric properties. Such existing instruments have undergone testing and have often been created by very capable psychometricians. Many researchers are not well-trained enough to create effective, valid instruments.
    c. False. Criterion referenced tests can be as reliable and valid as norm-referenced tests. It depends on what it is we are measuring and the characteristics of the individual assessments. For example, a norm-referenced vocabulary test might not include the vocabulary necessary for your schools' curriculum, rendering the assessment invalid—whereas a criterion referenced vocabulary test that was constructed, piloted, and previously tested on the vocabulary actually found within the curriculum would be more valid.

Just for Practice

1. a Cognitive, standardized, achievement, norm-referenced,
    b. Cognitive, achievement, criterion-referenced
    c. Affective; hard to know anything else by the title
    d. Achievement (aptitude some argue), norm-referenced, standardized, cognitive
    e. Aptitude, standardized, norm-referenced, cognitive
    f. Personality, projective
    g. Personality, standardized, norm-referenced
    h. Likely self-referenced scores although the coach or swimmer might set a criterion or know a norm-referenced time
    i. Achievement (aptitude some argue), norm-referenced, standardized, cognitive

  j. Affective test or an attitude scale
  k. Generally these are norm-referenced, cognitive tests

2. a. Ordinal
  b. Nominal
  c. Interval
  d. Ordinal
  e. Ratio
  f. Interval
  g. Interval
  h. Ratio
  i. Depends on how you would measure: interval or ratio
  j. Nominal
  k. Ratio
  l. Nominal

Checking What You Know

1. a. test/retest reliability
  b. predictive validity
  c. internal consistency reliability
  d. content validity
  e. sampling validity
  f. concurrent validity
  g. sampling validity
  h. internal consistency reliability

2. a DV = choice of science career; IV=type of class (2 levels: Lab/no lab)
  b. Age (PV) and interest in music education (CV)
  c. Size of family (PV) and feelings of social competence (CV)
  d. Unknown predictor variables (PV); completed doctorate (CV)
  e. DV=homework completion time; IV= gender (2 levels m/f)
  f. Kindergarten misbehavior (PV) and sixth grade attendance (CV) and achievement (CV)

Applying What You Know

There is too much variance in this exercise to be able to provide potential answers. Check them with a peer or with your instructor.

Practicing the Tasks

1. Correlational

2. Attitude, likely selection (because of the children's reading ability and also because of time and administration constraints)

3. Among others, cost might be a consideration, sample type (urban kids), reliability and validity are certainly important, time to administer is likely a consideration, skill needed to administer is a concern (an expert couldn't administer them all realistically)

4. My search of *reading motivation* provided 12 hits.

5. a. Some MRP notes: The MRP appears to include a group administered component, it is fairly current, it is intended for use with children of our sample's age, it was published in a practitioner journal and may be appropriate. Additional technical data are available which likely means reliability and validity data are available. It might be good to get the Issue of the Reading Teacher where it appears and investigate further.
  b. Some notes for the Children's Academic Intrinsic Motivation Inventory: It appears to measure more than just reading motivation for older children. It might cost to use it, and it may be a little dated. Positive aspects of the inventory indicate that it measures a motivation the school might be interested in and it can

be group administered. However, it seems less a fit than the MRP so perhaps looking into that inventory first is warranted.

    c.   Notes about the MAT. This instrument does not appear to fit our needs for the current study. It measures more personality than motivation and several scales don't fit our needs. IT is also written for older, more able readers. For this study, the MAT should not be considered.

6. Mine provided 63—yours may be slightly different based upon updates to the database between the time I conducted the search and when you do.

7. Not much help!

8. Gambrell (narrowed to Linda and selected by author) provides about 36—looking through the titles we can tell we are on the right track.

9. The abstract indicates that the instrument is included in the manuscript as well as additional data. We need that article!

10. Right track—looks like Allan is the author and that he has several articles. Click his name.

11. Approximately 26

12. The instrument is the Motivations for Reading Questionnaire (MRQ) .

13. From reading the abstracts I think we would be interested in the instrument.   It appears that it has been used with similar-aged populations and appears to have some information on reliability and validity. In addition, there are published articles that have used the instrument which also lends credibility to the instrument.

14. The questionnaire is available from the ERIC document (ED394137) which is a grant report. Includes both the instrument information and a copy of the instrument. We should access that report! The abstract is copied and pasted below from the ERIC search:

11 of 26
TI: Title
    A Questionnaire Measure of Children's Motivations for Reading. Instructional Resource
    No. 22.
AU: Author
    Wigfield, Allan; And Others
AF: Author Affiliation
    National Reading Research Center, Athens, GA.; National Reading Research Center,
    College Park, MD.
AG: Agency
    Office of Educational Research and Improvement (ED), Washington, DC.
AV: Availability
    EDRS Price - MF01/PC01 Plus Postage.
SO: Source
    24p. 1996.
NU: Other Numbers
    Clearinghouse: CS012441; Contract or Grant: 117A20007
AB: Abstract
    This paper describes the Motivations for Reading Questionnaire (MRQ), including
    information on how the MRQ can be used and how to administer and score it. The MRQ
    assesses 11 possible dimensions of reading motivations. It can be used with children in late
    elementary school and middle school. Scores on the MRQ have been shown to relate to
    children's reported reading frequency, and their performance on different standardized tests.
    It can be used in various ways in schools: for instance, to generate profiles of children's

motivations change over the course of a school year, or to see how boys' and girls' reading motivations differ. Contains 13 references and 2 tables of data. The Motivations for Reading Questionnaire is attached. (Author/RS)

LA: Language
English

PY: Publication Year
1996

PT: Publication Type
141 Reports: Descriptive; 160 Tests/Questionnaires

CO: Country of Origin
U.S.; Georgia

DE: Descriptors
Evaluation Methods; Intermediate Grades; Junior High Schools; Middle Schools; *Questionnaires; *Reading Attitudes; *Reading Motivation; Sex Differences; *Student Attitudes

ID: Identifiers
*Motivations for Reading Questionnaire

SF: Subfile
ERIC, Resources in Education (RIE)

AN: Accession Number
ED394137

15. a. Provides around 2000 references.
    b. Ortiz and colleagues BRISC (abstract below from ERIC):
    c. Saracho's PRAS (abstract follows the Ortiz et al. abstract below from ERIC):

TI: Title
A Brief Rating Scale of Preschool Children's Interest in Shared Picture Book Reading.

AU: Author
Ortiz, Camilo; Arnold, David H; Stowe, Rebecca M

AV: Availability
EDRS Price - MF01/PC01 Plus Postage.

SO: Source
11p. 1997.

NT: Notes
Portions of paper presented at the Annual Meeting of the Association for the Advancement of Behavior Therapy (31st, Miami Beach, FL, 1997).

NU: Other Numbers
Clearinghouse: PS026711

AB: Abstract
Despite its supposed importance, children's emergent interest in literacy has been seldom studied. As a result, no easy-to-use and psychometrically sound measure of children's emergent interest in literacy exists. This study made an initial attempt at validating such a measure. On three separate occasions, 24 parents and their 2- to 3-year-old children completed the Brief Reading Interest Scale (BRISC), a measure of preschool children's interest in reading. In addition, parents reported how often their child asked to be read to at home, and they filled out reading logs to record how well their child's interest was maintained when read to at home. Finally, parents were videotaped in the lab reading picture books with their child. The reliability of the BRISC, as well as its ability to predict the other measures of child interest in reading, were examined. BRISC scores at the initial visit correlated .78 with BRISC scores collected 1 week later and .71 with BRISC scores that were collected 4 weeks after the initial visit. BRISC scores correlated -.23 with videotaped interest, .45 with parent reading logs, and -.49 with parents' report of how often

their child asked to be read to. All correlations were in the expected direction as a lower score on the BRISC indicated more interest in shared reading. While the validity of the BRISC needs improvement, it appeared to have potential as a cost-effective measure of young children's interest in shared reading that might facilitate research on the influences and effects of interest. (Author/EV)
LA: Language
English
PY: Publication Year
1997
PT: Publication Type
143 Reports: Research; 150 Speeches/Meeting Papers
CO: Country of Origin
U.S.; Massachusetts
DE: Descriptors
Childhood Attitudes; Childrens Literature; *Measurement Techniques; *Picture Books; *Preschool Children; Preschool Education; Reading Aloud to Others; *Reading Attitudes; Test Reliability; Test Validity
SF: Subfile
ERIC, Resources in Education (RIE)
AN: Accession Number
ED421247

TI: Title
The Development of the Preschool Reading Attitudes Scale.
AU: Author
Saracho, Olivia N
SO: Source
Child Study Journal; v16 n2 p113-24 1986
NU: Other Numbers
Clearinghouse: PS514564
AB: Abstract
Describes the construction of a nonreading instrument (Preschool Reading Attitudes Scale) designed to assess attitudes toward reading in young children, aged three through five years. Demonstrates the scale to be valid and reliable with these age groups. (HOD)
LA: Language
English
PY: Publication Year
1986
PT: Publication Type
080 Journal Articles; 143 Reports: Research
TA: Target Audience
Researchers
DE: Descriptors
*Attitude Measures; Early Reading; *Measurement Techniques; *Preschool Children; *Reading Attitudes; Reading Interests; Reading Research; Research Methodology; *Test Reliability; *Test Validity
ID: Identifiers
*Preschool Reading Attitudes Scale
SF: Subfile
ERIC, Current Index to Journals in Education (CIJE)
AN: Accession Number
EJ342943

16. The Buros search for *Attitudes* brings up dozens. Several might work. I would suggest we start with what we already have found though.

Test-Like Event

1.	c	6.	a	11.	a
2.	c	7.	b	12.	c
3.	a	8.	d	13.	d
4.	a	9.	a	14.	d
5.	c	10.	d		

Chapter 6 Descriptive Research

Chapter 6 Objectives

1. Briefly state the purpose of descriptive research.
2. List the major steps involved in designing and conducting a descriptive research study.
3. Briefly describe the main types of self-report research.
4. List and briefly describe the steps involved in conducting a questionnaire study.
5. Identify and briefly describe four major differences between an interview study and a questionnaire study.

Review the Terms

Provide a succinct definition in your own words for each of the following terms.

Descriptive research: _____
_____

School survey: _____
_____

Sample survey: _____
_____

Developmental survey: _____
_____

Cross-sectional survey: _____
_____

Longitudinal survey: _____
_____

Trend survey: _____
_____

Cohort survey: _____
_____

Panel survey: _____
_____

Follow-up survey: _____
_____

Questionnaire: _____
_____

Interview: _____

_____

Cover letter: _____

_____

Interview guide: _____

_____

Structured item: _____

_____

Unstructured item: _____

_____

Interview study: _____

_____

Census Survey: _____

_____

For Your Own Review

1. Restate three of the criteria presented in your text regarding questionnaire items.

   _____
   _____
   _____

2. State one important characteristic of a cover letter.

   _____

3. State one purpose of pilot studies. _____

4. List a benefit and two drawbacks of interview studies.

   _____
   _____
   _____

Additional Sources for Review

The American Statistical Association, provides several online sites to assist survey researchers including the Survey Research Methods Site http://www.amstat.org/sections/srms/ and an excellent resource on mail surveys. An additional cite, http://members.bellatlantic.net/~abelson/ provides a number of links to other survey research information and strategies. Similarly, for interview research, one great source is the award-winning Sage publication, Handbook of Interview Research edited by Gubrium & Holstein.

Checking What You Know

Chapter 1 presented a research study, Piotrowski, Botsko, & Matthews (2000), that used survey methods to study how parents, preschool teachers, and kindergarten teachers evaluate school readiness.

Go back to that article and answer the following questions in support of Chapter 10 content.

1. Restate the research question or topic._____
    _____

2. Briefly describe the sampling strategies used.
    _____

3. What type of survey design was employed? _____

4. How was the instrument developed? _____
    _____

5. Describe the nature of the instrument (e.g., length, type of item) _____
    _____

6. How was the reliability and validity of the instrument established?
    _____
    _____

7. What was the response rate? What strategies were used for increasing response rate?
    _____
    _____

8. Does the study report if confidentiality or anonymity was addressed with the participants?
    _____

Practicing the Tasks

Task 6 requires that after stating a problem, you formulate hypotheses, describe a sample, select how to collect data, and develop the methods section of your research report. Maja Aleksic's proposal for a graduate student research award is included at the end of this chapter as a student example that supports Task 6 requirements. In this brief proposal Maja provides a brief literature framing, and a clear, albeit very concise, method section. Her design section very clearly illustrates the design and her conditions. Also note the budget in her proposal. Although not required for Task 6, as the text indicated budgets are often found in proposals. Maja was awarded the funds to do this study, which turned out to be the pilot for her dissertation study. Her advisor, Peggy Van Meter, helped her develop this proposal.

Test-Like Event

1. Which of the following sampling methods is *most often* used in survey research?

    a. stratified.
    b. snowball.
    c. homogeneous.
    d. cluster.

2. When analyzing descriptive survey data one suggested strategy is to report

    a. raw data by participant.
    b. percentage of response.
    c. item by item descriptive statistics
    d. inferential statistics by item.

3. When compared to surveys, which is <u>NOT</u> a disadvantage of interviews?

    a. response rates.
    b. experimenter effects.
    c. time of administration.
    d. skill needed.

4. According to your text if you were to receive a 60% response rate after a first mailing of a survey you should

    a. analyze your data, your sample of responses is representative.
    b. send out another mailing to your sample to increase your response rate.
    c. start with an entirely new sample, your response rate is too low.
    d. consider your survey complete for the first sample and select a second sample.

5. According to your text one of the drawbacks of interview studies is that

    a. interview data is less accurate than survey data.
    b. the depth of response is too shallow.
    c. getting enough participants.
    d. interviews are time consuming.

6. When constructing an interview guide, the researcher should

    a. have questions that relate to a specific study topic.
    b. be memorized by the researcher' to increase flow.
    c. include a number of unstructured questions.
    d. include leading questions to establish rapport with participants.

7. Of the following, which is an example of a survey research topic?

    a. Are there differences between the groups' performance based upon our treatment variable?
    b. Does SES predict academic achievement at large state universities?
    c. Are there differences in spatial ability based upon gender?
    d. How do teachers in the state feel about the proposed modified school year?

8. The first step in a quantitative survey study is

    a. select an appropriate sample.
    b. review the literature.
    c. identify a problem to study.
    d. examine the research context.

9. The local park agency is conducting a survey to determine if the county parks should be open year round or if they should close during the long winter months when they get fewer visitors. This type of study is best described as a (n)

    a. school survey.
    b. opinion poll.
    c. developmental survey.
    d. follow-up survey.

10. Joleen investigates the perceived benefits that parents report regarding their children's experiences with her interactive dinosaur display. This type of research can be classified best as a(n)

    a. school survey.
    b. opinion poll.
    c. developmental survey.
    d. follow-up survey.

11. Marcus is conducting a cross section survey of all the men who were promoted to eagle scout in the state during 1992 and 1993. Marcus's strategy can be best be described as

    a. A trend study.
    b. A panel study.
    c. A census study.
    d. A cohort study.

12.-16. Consider the questionnaire items below as you answer the following questions.

    1. Gender M   F
    2. Educational level: Less than high school degree___HS degree or GED ___ BS or BA_____
        post graduate degree _____

    3. Annual salary _____

    4. Number of children in your home _____

    5. Rate your agreement that the county needs a new park.

        SA   A   U   D   SD

    6. Why do you want to have a new park built in the county? _____
        _____

12. The item that will provide the most reliable data is likely

    a. item 1.
    b. item 2
    c. item 4.
    d. item 6.

13. Data collected from item 1 will be _____ level data.

    a. nominal
    b. ordinal
    c. interval
    d. ratio

14. Item 5 is an example of a(n) _____ type of item.

    a. open-response
    b. Likert
    c. semantic differential
    d. checklist

15. The most biased item is likely

    a. item 2.
    b. item 3.
    c. item 4.
    d. item 6.

16. Participants are most likely to find _____ the most sensitive item.

    a. item 1
    b. item 2
    c. item 3
    d. item 4

Companion Website

For more practice on becoming competent in this chapter's objectives, go to the Companion Website that accompanies this text at www.prenhall.com/gay. This site includes:

Objectives with links to:
- more multiple-choice questions in Practice Quiz
- Applying What You Know essay questions
- relevant Web sites

Custom modules to help you:
- calculate statistical tests (see "Calculating Statistical Tests")
- do research (see "Research Tools and Tips")
- practice analyzing quantitative data (see "Analyzing Quantitative Data")
- practice analyzing qualitative data (see "Analyzing Qualitative Data")
- practice evaluating published articles (see "Evaluating Articles")

Chapter 6 Answers
For Your Own Review

1. Among the answers: define ambiguous terms, know what information you need, avoid leading questions, organize items from general to specific, pretest the questionnaire, word questions in positive terms

2. The cover letter should explain what is being asked, should be addressed to specific participants, explain the purpose of the study, might include endorsement from a relevant group or organization, anonymity and confidentiality might be addressed, and a deadline for response should be included.

3. Pilot studies are important for several reasons, including for item revision and for assuring the resulting data will be quantifiable.

4. Benefits would include in depth data and drawbacks would include expensive and time consuming.

Checking What You Know

1. To examine perceptions of parents, preschool teachers and kindergarten teachers regarding children's readiness for school.

2. Schools were approached and asked to participate. It is unsure how the region was selected. It could be convenience or judgment. An attempt was made to collect data from some locations that did not participate.

3. A cross-sectional design was used for each of the groups.

4. The instrument was developed from previous measures. Deference was given to reading level of the instrument. Focus groups of those similar to sample were held to facilitate instrument development, the instrument was back-translated and procedures were used to assure that two versions of the instrument (Spanish and English) were equivalent. The instrument was pilot tested.

5. The instrument had 46 four-point Likert items divided into two main sections as well as demographic items. The 46 items represented seven sections with 4-8 items per section.

6. The samples were checked for equivalence. Factor analytic techniques were used to examine reliability of the instrument.

7. Response rates varied by participant group. Parents were estimated at 49%, preschool teachers at 73%, prekindergarten teachers at 50%, and kindergarten teachers at 89%. There is mention of incentives and intense follow-up procedures to increase response rate. It is also noted that time of year precluded some follow-up strategies.

8. Teachers responded via mail, which suggests perhaps anonymity. No names are disclosed in the report. It is unclear how incentives may have affected anonymity.

Note: Also note how the study reported the data as percentages as discussed in Chapter 6.

Test-Like Event

1.a	10.d
2.b	11.c
3.b	12.a
4.b	13.a
5.d	14.b
6.a	15.d
7.d	16.c
8.c	
9.b	

Questioning as a method of improving illustration processing, learning, and student interest

Maja Aleksic

Proposal awarded the "Graduate Student Alumni Society Research Initiation Grant" December, 2001-2002, Penn State University, State College, PA.

Problem Statement and Literature Review

There is little debate that the reading of textbooks is a dominant learning mode in education. Diagrams, charts, maps and other methods of spatially representing information are often incorporated into textbooks as ways of potentially increasing learning. Aside from illustration facilitative effect on learning, Levie & Lentz (1982) noted that illustrations can have a variety of additional effects. For example, they may add to reader enjoyment and interest. Even though there is a growing research base indicating that text illustrations can positively impact learning (Mandl & Levin, 1989) and interest (Holliday, Brunner & Donais, 1977; Rigney & Lutz, 1970; Sewell & Moore, 1980), too little of that potential is realized in daily educational practices (Weidenmann, 1989). Text illustrations are often undervalued and encoded at a superficial level, thus minimizing their contribution to the instructional process (Peeck, 1994). This study is designed to examine one possible method of promoting systematic processing of spatial aids, by instructing readers to pay close attention to the provided text illustration. It is hypothesized that the presence of adjunct questions, questions requiring processing of pictured content, would enhance learning from illustrated text and would extend illustration processing beyond the surface, superficial level.

Facilitative effects of specific instructions, instructions that guide the learner to specific areas in the picture, have been demonstrated in a number of studies (Bernard, 1990; Peeck, 1994; Reinking, Hayes & McEneaney, 1988; Weidenmann, 1989). Although the results of several studies have demonstrated that the instructional benefits of illustrations can be enhanced (e.g., Bernard, 1990; Peeck, 1994; Reinking, Hayes & McEneaney, 1988; Weidenmann, 1989), one concern is that learners may ignore these instructions when conditions permit. In their efforts to improve text learning with illustrations, Scevak & Moore (1998) were unsuccessful until a specific written response was required. In short, unsuccessful research in this area (e.g., Iding, 1997; Rasco, Tennyson & Boutwell, 1975) suggests learners may ignore processing instructions and thus instructional interventions are considerably less effective.

In an earlier study supported by this grant, Zecevic & Van Meter (2000) found that groups receiving specific illustration processing instructions received higher problem solving score means, compared to learners receiving either global or no processing instructions. Furthermore, of the two groups receiving specific illustration processing instructions, the highest mean problem solving score was obtained by learners required to give an active response and place a mark in the appropriate section of the illustration. Even though the pattern of results supported the studies predictions no statistically significant results were obtained. Further manipulation of the materials used in this study may lead to more obvious significant differences between the experimental conditions.

In this study two levels of specific illustration processing instructions will be employed. The fist level of instructions, selection questions, will focus student attention on specific portions of the illustration. The second level of instructions, integration questions, will focus student's attention on the relationship and function of structures within the illustrated systems. Additionally, in this study, two levels of student active response will be employed. The first level of active response will require learners to place a check mark on the appropriate portion of the illustration. Because the nature of this type of response is primarily selection, it has been termed selection response. The second level of active response will require learners to write down their response, thus forcing the learner to process the information to a greater degree. Because students will need to select, organize, and integrate material in order to provide an adequate answer, this response has been named integration response.

One aspect not examined this far is the impact of illustration processing instructions on affective variables, specifically interest. Levin and Mayer (1993) proposed that illustrations improve learning as a result of making text information more concrete by providing a more picturable representation of the text content. Illustrations are believed to make text more concrete, better organized, more coherent, and informationally complete for the reader. Research indicates that just this type of text will lead to increased text-based interest. Given that specific integration questions may lead to better and more effective illustration processing, this in turn may lead to observable benefits not only in learning but also levels of text based interest.

In this study, five main hypotheses will be examined. First, it is predicted that learners perceiving integration questions will learn more from illustrated text than learners presented with selection questions. Second, of the two groups receiving integration questions, those students required to give a written response to the instructions will learn more than those required to simply place a check mark on the illustration. Third, learners receiving integration questions will rate the text as more interesting then learners presented with selection questions.

133

Fourth, of the two groups receiving integration questions, those students required to give a written response to the instructions will rate the text as more interesting then those required to simply place a check mark onto the illustration. Finally, because processing of illustrations is believed to enhance the construction on internal mental models (e.g., Mayer, 1989, 1994) it is predicted that learning differences will be revealed on a higher order problem solving posttest but not a lower order recognition posttest.

Methods

Participants. One hundred and twenty undergraduates enrolled in an introductory class at Penn State University would participate in this study. By means of a screening pretest, participants of low prior knowledge would be selected.

Design. This study will employ a hierarchical design, with instructions as the independent variable. The conditions will be: selection questions-selection response (SS), selection questions – integration response (SI), integration questions-selection response (IS) and integration questions-integration response (II). In the (SS) condition, subjects will receive specific selection questions as well as instructions to place a check mark on the illustration in the area(s) where the answer can be found. In the (SI) condition, subjects will receive specific selection questions as well as instructions to write down their response in the provided space next to the appropriate illustration. In the (IS) condition, subjects will receive specific integration questions as well as instructions to place a check mark on the illustration in the area(s) where the answer can be found. In the (II) condition, subjects will receive specific integration questions as well as instructions to write down their response in the provided space next to the appropriate illustration. In addition, two comparison control conditions will be employed. The first one will be a text-only condition while the second one will be a text plus illustrations condition.

Materials. In order for learning to be demonstrated in this study, a topic about which students have little prior knowledge must be selected. A prior knowledge screening test will be used to assess students level of familiarity with the topic of the learning material. Additionally, no student scoring above 50% will be included as a research participant. The prior knowledge assessment will require learners to rate their knowledge of biology and marine biology on a 5-point scale, ranging from very poor to excellent. In addition, learners will be asked to complete a knowledge checklist, assessing their reading behavior in the area of biology. Materials will include four versions of a text on the topic of the Starfish, interest questionnaire and a posttest. Each subject will be presented a packet with materials appropriate for their assigned condition. Packets will contain a six-page, 1237 word text on the Starfish, eight illustrations and instructions. Illustrations will provide an organizational framework for the reader by representing various structures of the starfish's water-vascular system and their appropriate connections and relationships. Illustrations will appear on the right side of the text page, across their corresponding paragraphs. Four types of instructions will be used. The SS group will receive selection questions specifying what to look for in the illustration. In addition learners will also be required to "put a check mark on the illustration in the area(s) where the answer can be found". The SI group will receive the same selection questions as the SS group but will be required to "write down the answer in the provided space next to figure 1". The IS group will receive integration questions specifying what to look for in the illustration as well as the specific function of the illustrated structures. In addition learners will also be required to "put a check mark on the illustration in the area(s) where the answer can be found". The II group will receive the same integration questions as the IS group but will be required to "write down the answer in the provided space next to figure 1". In the text only condition students will receive the text without any illustrations while students in the text plus illustration condition will receive the text with the appropriate illustrations. Following the study period, students will complete a 10 item perceived interest questionnaire, assessing their overall interest in the text. Ratings will be made on a five-point scale and will ask participants to indicate the degree to which they agree or disagree with each statement. Finally, students will be asked to complete a two-part posttest. The first part will consist of four problem solving tasks that will ask students to consider what would happen if one of the structures of the system were missing as well as determine the cause of a specific system failure. The second part of the posttest will be a multiple-choice test assessing recognition of definitions and structures within the system.

Procedure. Students will be randomly assigned to one of the six experimental conditions. First, students will complete the pretest. Second, packets appropriate for assigned conditions will be handed out and instructions will be read aloud. Subjects will be instructed to read the text carefully, follow the provided instructions, and then try to remember as much as they can of the text because they will be asked to answer some questions later on. There will be no time limit on the passage. Following reading, subjects will be instructed to complete the perceived interest questionnaire, assessing their overall interest in the text. The two-part posttest will be handed out shortly after learners finish with experimental materials.

Data Analysis. Two one-way analysis of variance will be used. With problem solving scores as the dependent variable, groups receiving integration questions are expected to outperform groups without such questions. In addition, those students required to give a written response to the questions will outperform the group required to simply place a check mark on the illustration. No significant differences are expected on the multiple-choice posttest. Because it is difficult to assess the meaningfulness of nonsignificant statistical results, effect sizes will be calculated. Finally, learners receiving integration questions are expected to rate the text as more interesting then groups without such questions. In addition those students required to give a written response to the questions will rate the text as more interesting then those required to simply place a check mark onto the illustration.

Budget. In an earlier study conducted by Zecevic & Van Meter (2000) the awarded 390$ were used to prepare the experimental packets. In this study the awarded funds will primarily be used for photocopying of research materials (text, illustrations, instructions and posttest measures). It is estimated that approximately 2400 pages will need to be copied, costing 600$. A portion of the funds will also be used to provide compensation to a rater that will be recruited to score the problem-solving portion of the posttest.

References

Bernard, R.M. (1990). Using extended captions to improve learning from instructional illustrations. *British Journal of Educational Technology,* 21, 215-225.

Hayes, D.A., & Readance, J.R. (1982). Effects of cued attention to illustrations in text. In J.A. Niles & L.A. Harris (Eds.), *New inquires in reading: Research and instruction.* Rochester, N.Y: National Reading Conference.

Iding, M.E. (1997). Can questions facilitate learning from illustrated science texts? *Reading Psychology: An International Quarterly*, 18, 1-29.

Mandl, H., & Levin, J.R. (1989). Knowledge acquisition from text and pictures. Amsterdam: Elsevier.

Mayer, R.E. (1989). Models for understanding. *Review of Educational Research*, 59, 43-64.

Mayer, R.E. (1994). Visual aids to knowledge construction: building mental representations from pictures and words. In W. Schnotz & R.W. Kulhavy (Eds.), *Comprehension of Graphics*, North Holland: Elsevier.

Moore, P.J., & Skinner, M.J. (1985). The effects of illustrations on children's comprehension of abstract and concrete passages. *Journal of Research in Reading*, 8, 45-56.

Peeck, J. (1994). Enhancing graphic-effects in instructional texts: influencing learning activities. In W. Schnotz & R.W. Kulhavy (Eds.), *Comprehension of Graphics*, North Holland: Elsevier.

Rasco, R.W., Tennyson, R.D., & Boutwell, R.C. (1975). Imagery instructions and drawings in learning prose. *Journal of Educational Psychology,* 67, 188-192.

Reinking, D.R., Hayes, D.A., & McEneaney, J.E. (1988). Good and poor reader's use of explicitly cued graphic aids. *Journal of Reading Behavior*, 20, 229-247.

Scevak, J.J., & Moore, P.J. (1998). Levels of processing effects on learning from texts with maps. *Educational Psychology*, 18, 133-155.

Weidenmann, B. (1989). When good pictures fail: An information processing approach to the effects of illustrations. In H. Mandl & J.R. Levin (Eds.), *Knowledge acquisition from text and pictures.* North Holland: Elsevier.

Chapter 7   Correlational Research

Chapter 7 Objectives

1. Briefly state the purpose of correlational research.
2. List and briefly describe the major steps involved in basic correlational research.
3. Describe the size and direction of values associated with a correlation coefficient.
4. Describe how the size of a correlation coefficient affects its interpretation with respect to (1) statistical significance, (2) its use in prediction, and (3) its use as an index of validity and reliability.
5. State two major purposes of relationship studies.
6. Identify and briefly describe the steps involved in conducting a relationship study.
7. Briefly describe four different types of correlation and the nature of the variables they are used to correlate.
8. Describe the difference between a linear and a curvilinear relationship.
9. Identify and briefly describe two factors that may contribute to an inaccurate estimate of relationship.
10. Briefly define or describe predictor variables and criterion variables.
11. State purposes of prediction studies.
12. State the major difference between data collection procedures in a prediction study and a relationship study.

Review the Terms

For each of the following terms provide a succinct definition in your own words.

Correlational research: _____

_____

Scatterplot: _____

_____

Correlation coefficient: _____

_____

Statistical significance: _____

_____

Attenuation: _____

_____

Relationship study: _____

_____

Pearson R: _____

_____

Spearman rho: _____

_____

Linear Relationship: _____

_____

Curvilinear relationship: _____

_____

Predictor: _____

_____

Criterion: _____

_____

Cross-validation: _____

_____

Multiple regression equation: _____

_____

Artificial dichotomy: _____

_____

Error of measurement: _____

_____

Coefficient of determination: _____

_____

Path analysis: _____

_____

Canonical Correlation: _____

_____

Shrinkage: _____

_____

Shared variance: _____

_____

Intervening variable: _____

_____

Prediction studies: _____

_____

For Your Own Review

1. The text gives guidelines for interpreting correlations. Provide an example of a low, moderate, and high correlation.

    Low: _____   Moderate _____   High _____

2. Draw a scatter plot that illustrates the relationship between standardized test scores and teacher grades in the following dataset. Estimate the correlation.

Teacher grade	Standardized test score
80.00	85.00
92.00	88.00
75.00	80.00
70.00	74.00
65.00	60.00
84.00	80.00
68.00	72.00
72.00	68.00
78.00	82.00
84.00	90.00

3. Compare and contrast Spearman Rho and Pearson r correlations.

    _____

    _____

4. What is the equation that represents single variable predictions?

    _____

Applying What You Know

For each of the following, interpret the correlation coefficient provided. None of these examples has one 'right' answer.

1. a. A recent publication reported an internal consistency reliability of $r = .65$ for a measure of new measure of children's self-esteem. Your friend Catherine wanted to use the measure for her dissertation, and asked your opinion. What do you suggest? Why?

    _____

    _____

    b. Your class was discussing a large study of self-concept and grades. The researchers reported that grades predict self-concept and reported that grades accounted for 36% of the sample variance in self-concept. Your classmate suggested that is not a relevant finding. What is your opinion? Explain.

    _____

    _____

c. Several legislators want to do away with standardized testing. They suggested a recent study with a large national sample found that SES variables are a significant predictor of standardized test scores. They suggest, therefore, that test scores are not a relevant indicator of achievement because they are measuring SES. How do you react? Is there anything else you would like to know? _____

_____

_____

_____

d. Your university requires that you take an English Language Usage (ELU) exam upon entry into a major. The test is costly to the institution so a group of researchers were commissioned to determine if it is worthwhile to administer the test. Their findings included that ELU scores were correlated $r=.89$ with GPA. What do you recommend about administration of the ELU? Why?

_____

_____

_____

e. You are a new member on Diana's research team. The team is starting a new study that will examine social skills of primary -aged children that have been involved in an empathy-training program and those who have not. The group is determining which measures to use to study social skills and Diana suggests to her team that they use teacher ratings, student self-ratings, peer-ratings, and parent ratings as well as student scores on the "I am nice to my friends" inventory that is administered by the teacher aloud. Ardell, another team member suggests that there really is not a need to use all of the instruments. He notes that the teacher rating scales and the parent rating scales are correlated $r=.95$, and the peer-ratings are correlated $r=.21$ with the teacher ratings. Further, he wonders if the self-rating scale, never used before, will be appropriate because it requires the student to do some reading and they are not very able readers. He says, "Let's just use the teacher ratings and the 'I am nice to my friends' inventory." Diana asks you what you think. Provide a response for the team.

_____

_____

_____

_____

_____

_____

Test-Like Event

1. Which of the following is one purpose for correlational research?

    a. To examine differences in treatment conditions
    b. To understand participants' perspectives
    c. To report how past events occurred
    d. To examine the strength of variables in predicting an outcome

2. Of the following, which best illustrates a correlational study?

    a. Are there differences in parents' reports of how much their children learn between children with a 'strict' teacher and those with teacher who is perceived as 'easy-going'?
    b. Is there a relationship between time on task in a classroom and parents' reports of student learning?
    c. What are the characteristics of a teacher who parents perceive as 'strict'?
    d. How do students behave in a classroom of a teacher who is perceived as strict?

3. In Jiri's study, GRE score was negatively correlated with high school class size. Which of the following is an accurate statement according to Jiri's findings?

    a.   Students who attended large high schools are more likely to have higher GRE scores.
    b. Students who attended smaller high schools are more likely to have higher GRE scores.
    c. Students with high GRE scores are equally likely to have attended smaller or larger high schools.
    d. Going to a small high school will cause learners to have higher GRE scores.

4. Kenji reported a correlation of $r=.08$ between interest in reading and academic self-confidence. This correlation indicates that interest in reading and academic self-confidence are

    a. strongly related.
    b. relatively independent.
    c. moderately related.
    d. meaningfully related.

5. Darrell studies school violence. His research indicated that size of school was positively related to incidence of school violence $r=.25$, and SES was negatively related to incidence of school violence, $r=-.32$. Regarding Darrell's findings, one can conclude that

    a. Size of school is a much better predictor of school violence than SES.
    b. SES is a much better predictor of school violence than size of school.
    c. Both size of school and SES similarly predict school violence.
    d. Both size of school and SES are strong predictors of school violence.

6. Given the graph below, what is the most likely correlation between these variables?
    a. -.90
    b. -.50
    c. .60
    d. .85

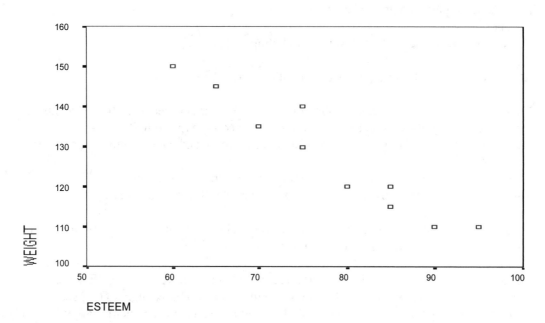

7. The graph below most likely represents a correlation of

    a. -.80
    b. -.40
    c. 0.0
    d. .30

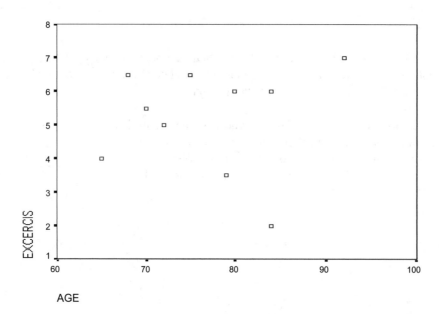

8. Which of the following cannot be a correlation coefficient?

   a. -1.0
   b. 0.0
   c. .68
   d. 3.1

9. Correlation studies must include

   a. a treatment condition and a control group.
   b. levels of independent variables.
   c. three groups and one dependent variable.
   d. one group and two variables.

10. Which of the following represents the strongest correlation?

   a. -1.0
   b. -.03
   c. 0.0
   d. .83

11. When compared to correlation coefficients for achievement measures, to be considered adequate, correlation coefficients for affective measures

   a. are often lower.
   b. are often higher.
   c. must be lower.
   d. must be higher.

12. Wakar examines the relationship between spatial ability and test scores in advanced physics classes. He correlates test scores with a 100-point measure of spatial ability. Which type of correlation should Wakar calculate?

   a. Kendall's tau
   b. Phi coefficient
   c. Pearson *r*
   d. Biseriel

13.-14. Ewen and Ryan both study correlations between self-esteem and persistence on difficult problem solving tasks. Persistence in their work is measured by length of time on a given problem. Self-esteem is measured by a self-report self-esteem measure. Ewen has 148 participants in his study and found a significant correlation between the two variables. Ryan studied 84 participants and also found a significant correlation between the two variables.

13. The researchers used the same significance level to test their findings. Of the following which can one conclude?

    a. Ryan needed a higher correlation coefficient for his findings to be significant.
    b. Ewen needed a higher correlation coefficient for his findings to be significant.
    c. Both researchers need the same correlation coefficient for their findings to be significant.
    d. Neither of the researchers had enough participants to conduct the correlation study.

14. Which of the following correlation coefficients is appropriate for these researchers' studies?

    a. Phi
    b. Biserial
    c. Pearson *r*
    d. Kendall tau

15. Victoria has 24 students in her math class. She wants to examine the relationship between their math scores and their science scores. She ranks her students from 1 to 24 and then ranks them in science from 1 to 24. She correlates the rankings. Which correlation coefficient should she use?

    a. Spearman rho
    b. eta
    c. Pearson *r*
    d. Tetrchoric

16. Mu-Ping found a correlation of .70 between achievement and motivation in her study of fourth- grade history students. What is the coefficient of determination in Mu-Ping's study?

    a. 14%
    b. 49%
    c. 70%
    d. 92%

17. For Shannon's dissertation she proposed a prediction study. She was using several variables to predict willingness to participate in experimental nutrition research. She proposed to randomly sample 100 adults and to examine age, weight, gender, occupation, and proximity to the research center as predictor variables. Her committee members did not accept her proposal. What is the likely reason why they asked Shannon to modify ?

    a. She proposed to randomly sample for a survey study.
    b. Her proposed sample is too small for the number of variables.
    c. Her variables do not appear to be related to her research topic.
    d. Her variables are not measurable to be used in research.

18. Ian conducted a path analysis for his dissertation . His findings indicated that motivation and self-confidence accounted for 41% of the variance in course grades in a large sample of university students enrolled in introductory English courses. He replicated his study with a second group of participants. In the second sample, the variance Ian predicted was likely

   a. lower because of attenuation.
   b. higher because of replication.
   c. lower because of shrinkage.
   d. higher because of restriction of range.

19.-20. Tian correlated attitude toward science using a standard measure and standardized test scores in a gifted, high achieving sample (n=100). The internal consistency reliability of the attitude measure was r=.84. The internal consistency of the standardized test was r=.90.

19. Tian did not find significant correlations. What is the most likely reason?

   a. attenuation
   b. restriction of range
   c. unreliable measurement
   d. sample size

20. Given the two measures in Tian's study, what can be inferred from the reliability coefficients?

   a. They both have low reliability.
   b. They both have adequate reliability.
   c. The standardized test score reliability is too low.
   d. The attitude toward science reliability is too low.

Companion Website

For more practice on becoming competent in this chapter's objectives, go to the Companion Website that accompanies this text at www.prenhall.com/gay. This site includes:

Objectives with links to:
- more multiple-choice questions in Practice Quiz
- Applying What You Know essay questions
- relevant Web sites

Custom modules to help you:
- calculate statistical tests (see "Calculating Statistical Tests")
- do research (see "Research Tools and Tips")
- practice analyzing quantitative data (see "Analyzing Quantitative Data")
- practice analyzing qualitative data (see "Analyzing Qualitative Data")
- practice evaluating published articles (see "Evaluating Articles")

Chapter 7 Answers
For Your Own Review
1. While the acceptability of a correlation would vary based upon the purpose and use, an example low correlation might be r= .25, moderate, r= 50, and high r=.90

2. The actual correlation is *r*= .869.

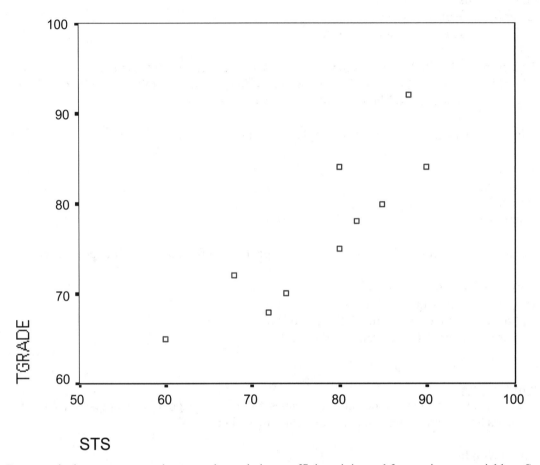

STS

3. Pearson r is the most commonly reported correlation coefficient, it is used for continuous variables. Spearman Rho is the appropriate correlation coefficient to report when the data are rank or ordinal level.

4. Y=a + bX

Applying What You Know
1. a.   The internal consistency reliability for this instrument is really pretty low. However, it IS an affective measure, is one of the most used instruments in children's self esteem, and has a well-documented correlation of *r*=.68, so it might be okay. If Catherine is really set on the inventory she might use the inventory as well as an additional inventory that is established as reliable and/or one that has been often used in her area of study. If this internal consistency correlation was reported for an achievement measure, she should likely actively look for a different measure.

    b.   This is actually a common finding in research that measures large constructs such as self-concept, motivation, self-regulation. A 36% of accounted variance might be considered very different by different researchers. For example, some say if it doesn't predict at least 40% it isn't worth considering as an important relationship. Accounting for 36% of the sample variance might not seem like much, so your classmates point is well taken. However, consider all of the components of someone's self-concept. That one variable, grades, can account for 36% might be important. The truth is, on this one, you could ask

146

several different researchers and get several different answers. If the construct being measured was not as nebulous a construct as self-concept, 36% would likely not be much to talk about.

c.   A large national sample might be a very large number. I would want to know how big the sample was, what the actual correlation between the variables was, and I would want to know how much unique variance SES accounted for. So what if it is significant if it is only a correlation of $r=.18$, for example. To state that Standardized test scores are a measure of SES is likely a reach, as well. That would suggest a perfect correlation and causation , which is not an appropriate assumption .

d.   The ELU does not appear to be adding much information over that found by GPA. Unless there is an additional reason to administer the exam, and because it is costly it might be something to discontinue administering. There may be a valid reason to administer the exam and it may provide more information to those using the test scores than GPA alone can provide.

e.   There may be logistical reasons not to administer all of the measures that Diana suggests. For example, maybe parents don't return the instruments. Maybe the IRB is concerned about the peer-ratings. Maybe the school doesn't want to use so much class time to assess the empathy training. There are numerous logistics that might affect this problem. Let's examine Ardell's points.   If there are high correlations between parent and teacher ratings, teachers are accessible and might have a higher response rate. Maybe he is right to not use the inventory. If the parents are a part of the empathy training and it might help the program if they are involved, maybe they should send them out anyway. The peer-ratings don't seem correlated with the teacher ratings. Hmmm. This might mean that they are providing additional information in addition to what the teacher ratings can or it might mean that they will not provide anything relevant and the peers are rating each other based upon variables other than social skills. Why would someone want to use a new scale? It sounds like this scale could be group administered (maybe better reliability) and the teacher administers it (perhaps more valid because the students don't yet read well.) and using it with other measures might provide the team data for arguing its use in the future. If it is really highly correlated with the other measures, for example, perhaps in the future it will be a viable measure. All things being equal it is a good idea to include several measures, as your text indicates, for reliability and validity. For this problem, among other concerns, the team will have to consider the validity of the instruments being considered, contextual variables, time of administration, cost, and other issues and barriers as well. What fun!!

Test-Like Event

1. d	8. d	15. a
2. b	9. d	16. b
3. b	10. a	17. b
4. b	11. a	18. c
5. c	12. c	19. b
6. a	13. a	20. b
7. c	14. c	

Chapter 8   Causal-Comparative Research

Chapter 8 Objectives

1. Briefly state the purpose of causal-comparative research.
2. State the major differences between causal-comparative and correlational research.
3. State one major way in which causal-comparative and experimental research are the same and one major way in which they are different.
4. Diagram and describe the basic causal-comparative design.
5. Identify and describe three types of control procedures that can be used in a causal-comparative study.
6. Explain why the results of causal-comparative studies must be interpreted very cautiously.

Review the Terms

For each of the following terms provide a succinct definition in your own words.

ex post facto: _____

_____

Retrospective causal-comparative research: _____

_____

Prospective causal-comparative research: _____

_____

Matching: _____

_____

Extraneous variable: _____

_____

Homogeneous groups: _____

_____

Factorial analysis of variance: _____

_____

Analysis of covariance: _____

_____

Organismic variables: _____

_____

Control group: _____

_____

For Your Own Review

1. Describe how causal-comparative research is different from experimental research.

    _____
    _____
    _____

2. Describe the benefits of causal-comparative studies over experimental studies. Address specifically the role of independent variables in your response.

    _____
    _____
    _____
    _____
    _____
    _____

3. List and describe one common control procedure used with causal-comparative studies.

    _____
    _____

Checking What You Know

1. Given the following research topic, answer the questions below: Are there differences in third grade reading scores between children who attended independent preschool, district provided preschool, or no outside preschool?

    a. What is the dependent variable (s)? _____

    b. What is the independent variable? Identify any levels of the variable.

        _____

    c. Why is this an example of ex post facto research and not correlational?

        _____
        _____

    d. Why is this an example of ex post facto research and not experimental?

        _____
        _____

    e. What extraneous variables might there be in this study? Identify and describe at least three.

        _____ _____ _____
        _____
        _____
        _____

    f. Select one of the potential extraneous variables and suggest one way to 'control' that variable.

        _____
        _____

2. Given the following research topic, answer the questions below: Are there differences in university GPA and persistence rates between students who enrolled in first year seminars compared to those who did not enroll in first year seminars?

    a. What is the dependent variable(s)? _____

    b. Are there any other dependent variables that might be of interest in this study?
        _____

    c. What is the independent variable? Identify levels of the variable.
        _____

    d. Why is this an example of ex post facto research?
        _____
        _____

    e. Consider the extraneous variable high school (HS) GPA. Describe how you could control this extraneous variable through ANCOVA.
        _____

    f. Consider the extraneous *variable academic major*. Describe how you could control this extraneous variable through homogeneous grouping.
        _____
        _____

    g. Consider the extraneous variable *campus living arrangement*. Describe how you could control this extraneous variable through matching.
        _____
        _____

    h. Suggest one additional extraneous variable and one way to control it.
        _____

3. Given the following research topic, answer the questions below: Are there differences between higher- and lower- achieving sixth-grade students' value of mathematics?

    a. What is the dependent variable(s)? _____

    b. Are there any other dependent variables that might be of interest in this study?
        _____

    c. What is the independent variable(s)? Identify levels of the variable(s).
        _____

    d. Why is this an example of ex post facto research?
        _____
        _____

4. Given the following research topic, design two different ex post facto studies in accord with the designs provided (See Table 8.1 in your text). Identify the components of the design in your topic.

    You are interested in the use of different instructional strategies (e.g., drill and practice note cards, instructional diagrams, mnemonics, or others you might consider) for learning anatomy concepts.

    a.   In the space below provide a research topic that illustrates this design.

Group	Independent Variable	Dependent Variable
E	(X)	O
C		O

    b.   Suggest one extraneous variable in your design. How would you control it?

    c.   In the space below provide a research topic that illustrates this design.

Group	Independent Variable	Dependent Variable
E	(X_1)	O
C	(X_2)	O

    d.   Write a null hypothesis for your topic.

    e.   Write a directional hypothesis for your topic.

Test-Like Event

Circle the best answer in each of the following items.

1. Which of the following is the best example of a causal-comparative research topic?

    a. Are there gender differences in kindergartners' fine motor skill proficiency?
    b. What are the characteristics of fine motor skills in kindergartners?
    c. Is there a relationship between fine motor skills and academic skills in kindergartners?
    d. What strategies do kindergarten and first-grade teachers use to develop fine motor skills?

2. Which is an example of a prospective casual-comparative study? For each consider that Susan is interested in differences between groups that use cooperative learning.

    a. At the beginning of the year, Susan groups her science classes into one that will use cooperative learning and peer tutoring, and one that will not. At the end of the year she compares the class grades.
    b. Susan compares the class grades between one teacher that used cooperative learning in her science classes and one who did not.
    c. Susan randomly assigns students to one study session that will learn new science concepts with cooperative learning and peer tutoring and one group that will be taught the science concepts by the science teacher. At the end of the session she assesses how much they have learned.
    d. Susan observes two different science classes for several months. One of the classes uses cooperative learning and peer tutoring and the other class does not. At the end of the year she reports her findings comparing the cases in a narrative form.

3. Miguel is studying the use of mnemonics on second language acquisition. Which of the following best illustrates a causal-comparative study?

    a. Is there a relationship between mnemonics and vocabulary acquisition?
    b. Are there differences in vocabulary acquisition between students who use mnemonics and those who do not?
    c. What types of spontaneous mnemonic strategies do students use for vocabulary acquisition?
    d. How many different mnemonic strategies does the average teacher suggest to students to help vocabulary acquisition?

4. Marissa studies the benefits of review on test taking. Which of the following is a possible causal-comparative study in Marissa's research?

    a. Does number of hours of review prior to an exam predict exam performance?
    b. Do students who attend a review session do better on exams than students who do not attend?
    c. What happens in a typical review session for a large enrollment university course?
    d. How many faculty in higher-education hold review sessions for entry-level courses?

5. Goro is interested in language disfluencies and birth order. Of the following, which best represents a causal-comparative research topic?

    a. What are the typical social characteristics of first-born children with language disfluencies?
    b. Is there a relationship between number of children in the home and frequency of disfluencies?
    c. Do first-born children have more disfluencies than later-born children?
    d. Does birth order predict type of identified language disfluencies in primary grade children?

6.-8   Debbie plans to compare interest in music and end-of-year course grades between three of her fourth-grade music classes. In one of her classes she will use primarily instrumental music as a vehicle for instruction, in another she will use primarily vocal music. In the third she will use both.

6. What is the independent variable in Debbie's study?

    a. interest
    b. fourth graders
    c. course grades
    d. type of instruction

7. The independent variable in this example has how many levels?

    a. There are no levels.
    b. 1 level
    c. 2 levels
    d. 3 levels

8. Debbie's study is best described as

    a. projective causal-comparative.
    b. retrospective causal comparative.
    c. prospective causal-comparative.
    d. retrojective causal-comparative.

9. One limitation of causal-comparative research is that findings from causal-comparative studies

    a. are not descriptive.
    b. do not allow examination of relationships.
    c. can not identify causes.
    d. can not compare groups.

10. One reason that causal-comparative studies are done in schools when compared to correlational studies is that causal-comparative studies

    a. can identify causes for outcomes.
    b. allow for random assignment.
    c. require fewer participants.
    d. allow for group comparison.

11. Of the following, the most common descriptive statistic reported in causal-comparative research is the

    a. variance.
    b. mean.
    c. standard error or the mean.
    d. quartile deviation.

12. The statistic used to compare group frequency differences is the

    a. mean.
    b. standard deviation.
    c. t-test.
    d. chi square.

13. Causal-comparative research includes at least

    a. one group and one outcome variable.
    b. two groups and one outcome variable.
    c. two groups and two outcome variables.
    d. three groups and one outcome variable.

14. Of the following, which is NOT an example discussed in your text as a strategy used to control for group differences in a causal-comparative study?

    a. Path modeling
    b. Matching
    c. Homogeneous grouping
    d. ANCOVA

Companion Website
For more practice on becoming competent in this chapter's objectives, go to the Companion Website that accompanies this text at www.prenhall.com/gay. This site includes:

Objectives with links to:
- more multiple-choice questions in Practice Quiz
- Applying What You Know essay questions
- relevant Web sites

Custom modules to help you:
- calculate statistical tests (see "Calculating Statistical Tests")
- do research (see "Research Tools and Tips")
- practice analyzing quantitative data (see "Analyzing Quantitative Data")
- practice analyzing qualitative data (see "Analyzing Qualitative Data")
- practice evaluating published articles (see "Evaluating Articles")

Chapter 8 Answers
For Your Own Review

1. Causal comparative and experimental studies are similar in that both attempt to establish cause-effect relationships and both involve group comparisons. In experimental research, the researcher manipulates the independent variable, and can randomly assign participants.

2. Causal-comparative research allows study of independent variables that cannot, should not, or have not for some reason been manipulated. One salient benefit given this characteristic is that it is often unethical to manipulate variables researchers might want to study. For example, consider fetal alcohol syndrome. It is unethical to experimentally conduct a study of fetal alcohol syndrome but causal-comparative research allows us to study (but not identify cause and effect) children of mothers who consumed considerable amounts of alcohol while pregnant.

3. ANCOVA, matching, or homogeneous grouping

Checking What You Know

1. a. Third-grade reading scores
   b. This study has one independent variable, type of preschool, with three levels (independent, district, none).
   c. This study examines difference between groups. Correlational studies address relationships in one group.
   d. This study is done after the fact, retrospectively, children are not randomly assigned to the treatment conditions (in this case, preschool) as they would have to be in an experimental study.
   e. There are many extraneous variables in this study (yours may differ here). They might include time in preschool, previous childcare arrangements, level of education or experience of the preschool teacher, curriculum differences, size of preschool class, SES variables (e.g., family income, education level), number of educational experiences in the home, the list is pretty long!
   f. Your answer to this question should include some form of matching, ANCOVA, or homogenous grouping. For example, one could match children in each of the conditions by family income. For another example, one could control the variable level of teacher experience and education level, as well as class size, through homogeneous grouping by only selecting sites that have a certain teacher-to-child ratio and teachers with a minimum of 3 years teaching experience and a BS degree.

2. a. University GPA; persistence rates
   b. There are many others that might be of interest. School satisfaction is one example.
   c. Enrollment in First Year Seminar (2 levels-yes or no)
   d. The enrollment has already happened. Some universities have tried to control this type of study and examine the effects of first year seminars through an experimental design. Most times, however, this type of topic would be studied through a casual comparative study.
   e. ANCOVA could be used by statistically controlling for HS GPA in the analyses.
   f. To control for academic major through homogeneous grouping one could select only one major and examine the differences between students with or without FYS in that major.
   g. To control for campus living arrangement (which might be a extraneous variable especially for persistence) through matching, one could select stratified numbers of participants in the two groups based upon living arrangement.
   h. There are many other potential extraneous variables. Some examples include size of university, content of FYS, cost of living, extra-curricular activities, and prestige of university. These can be addressed through matching, ANCOVA, or homogeneous grouping.

3. a. The dependent variable is value of mathematics.
   b. Other dependent variables that might be of interest include course selection. Other (extraneous—control) variables of interest might include gender and prior knowledge (among a host of others).
   c. The independent variable is achievement. There were two levels: higher and lower
   d. Learners were divided based upon prior achievement

4. a. Your research question will vary a little but for this design there is one dependent variable, such as test score, number of concepts learned. In this first design the independent variable is one where one group would get a treatment (or has received a treatment). Perhaps an anatomy instructor implements flash cards in one class or not in another. Or maybe in one class the instructor uses the song mnemonic (the hip bone is connected to the…) while in the other he or she does not. Differences in the dependent variable are then compared. The C in this design might be considered the business as usual condition. A research question might be *"Are there differences between students anatomy test scores between those who learned through a song mnemonic and those who did not learn the song?"*

    b. There are numerous extraneous variables that might be important in this study. Although your answer will likely differ, one extraneous variable might be previous anatomy courses. Homogeneous grouping by selecting only those who have or have not taken a previous anatomy course would be one way to control for that extraneous variable.

    c. For this design two comparison groups are being compared. In this case, perhaps one group gets flash cards and one group gets drawings (your instructional manipulation could be different). One class, for example, might get flash cards to remember terms while the other could get labeled drawings. The outcome measure might be the same as in the previous example, such as test score, or number of concepts recalled.

    d. Null: There are no differences in student test scores between those given flashcards or those given labeled drawings. (Note for the null in your answer there should be no differences between the groups (X_1, X_2) you have on the outcome measure (O) you have.)

    e. Directional: Students provided flash cards will perform higher on the test than those who were provided labeled drawings. (Note for the directional in your answer there should be differences between the groups (X_1, X_2) you have on the outcome measure (O) you have and you state which will be better.)

Test-Like Event
1. a
2. a
3. b
4. b
5. c
6. d
7. d
8. c
9. c
10. d
11. b
12. d
13. b
14. a

Chapter 9   Experimental Research

Chapter 9 Objectives

1.   Briefly state the purpose of experimental research.
2.   List the basic steps involved in conducting an experiment.
3.   Explain the purpose of control.
4.   Briefly define or describe internal validity and external validity.
5.   Identify and briefly describe eight major threats to the internal validity of an experiment.
6.   Identify and briefly describe six major threats to the external validity of an experiment.
7.   Briefly discuss the purpose of experimental design.
8.   Identify and briefly describe five ways to control extraneous variables (and you better not leave out randomization!).
9.   For each of the pre-experimental, true experimental, and quasi-experimental group designs discussed in this chapter, (a) draw a diagram, (b), list the steps involved in its application, and (c) identify major problems of invalidity.
10.   Briefly describe the definition and purpose of a factorial design.
11.   Briefly explain what is meant by the term *interaction*.

Review the Terms

Provide a succinct definition in your own words for each of the following terms.

Random assignment: _____

_____

Experimental research: _____

_____

Experimental group: _____

_____

Control: _____

_____

Environmental variable: _____

_____

Random selection: _____

_____

Internal validity: _____

_____

External validity: _____

_____

Pre-experimental design: _____

_____

True experimental design: _____

_____

Quasi-experimental design: _____

_____

History: _____

_____

Participant variable: _____

_____

Maturation: _____

_____

Testing: _____

_____

Instrumentation: _____

_____

Statistical Regression: _____

_____

Differential selection of participants: _____

_____

Mortality: _____

_____

Multiple-treatment interface: _____

_____

Unobtrusive measures: _____

_____

Interaction: _____

_____

Selection-maturation interaction: _____

_____

Pretest-treatment interaction: _____

_____

Selection treatment interaction: _____

_____

Active variable: _____

_____

Specificity of variables: _____
_____

Reactive arrangements: _____
_____

Assigned variable: _____
_____

Manipulation: _____
_____

Treatment diffusion: _____
_____

Experimenter effects: _____
_____

Experimenter bias effect: _____
_____

Hawthorne effect: _____
_____

John Henry effect:_____
_____

Novelty effect: _____
_____

Placebo effect:_____
_____

Confounding:_____
_____

Single-variable designs: _____
_____

One-group pretest—posttest design: _____
_____

Static-group comparison: _____
_____

Pretest-posttest control group design: _____
_____

Posttest-only control group design: _____
_____

Solomon four-group design: _____
_____

Nonequivalent control group design: _____
_____

Time-series design: _____
_____

Multiple time-series design: _____
_____

Counterbalanced design: _____
_____

For Your Own Review

1. Discuss the relationship between internal and external validity.

    _____
    _____
    _____
    _____
    _____
    _____

2. List two ways, other than randomization, to control extraneous variables

    _____
    _____

3. What are the three usual types of experimental comparison?

    _____
    _____
    _____

Checking What You Know

Review the sections in the text on internal and external validity threats. On the lines provided, write the term that best answers each question

1. Internal validity threats.

    a. Justin is conducting a study that examines motivation of young athletes. He randomly selects a group of baseball players during tournament season. During the season, however, they all play together and a group of negative kids seems to have affected the groups' motivation to play. This illustrates which type of validity threat in Justin's study? _____

b. Roberto examines the benefits of a new vocabulary program. He randomly assigns very low achieving readers either to his program or an alternative program. He finds that students in both programs demonstrate increases in reading achievement. This is most likely due to what type of validity threat? _____

c. Mildred is comparing two programs for stress-reduction for patients with cardiac problems. One group has an intensive three-day training while they are recovering in the hospital. The other group has the training every other Friday for the first three months of their recovery. She finds that students in the Friday program often drop out of the study. Mildred's problem is best categorized as _____.

d. When measuring self-esteem as part of her study on victims of violent crimes, Laura finds that participants are inconsistent in their answers on the inventory she uses. Laura conducts an internal consistency test and finds that the reliability of the measure is $r=.45$. Laura's study is threatened by _____.

2. External validity threats

a. Gregg has designed a new treatment for impulsive behavior. He conducts developmental studies individually with young children that compare his treatment with other programs. Gregg must be particularly careful when he interacts with the children that he presents the treatments in a standardized manner. Gregg is most worried about which external validity threat?

_____

b. As part of his experimental program, Andrew measures self-efficacy before and after a training on a new skill in industrial arts class. He recently wrote a paper on his work and sent it out for peer review. The reviewer examined the self-efficacy measure and questioned if the study examined self-efficacy or self-concept. The reviewer has questioned the validity of his study due to _____.

c. In a recent study that Dana was conducting that compared weight loss programs, she randomly assigned participants to two different weight loss programs--one that focused on fewer calories and one that focused on fewer fat grams. During the pre-screening questionnaire, Dana overheard one of the participants share with the person sitting next to her, "Oh, this study must be about how many calories you eat a day." Dana has a threat of _____.

d. In Roberto's reading study, he is concerned about the 'true' measure of his training because he can not control the reading children do at home or the instruction and reading that they get in their classrooms at school. Roberto is most concerned about which validity threat?

_____

3. Diagram the design for each of the following examples in the blank spaces provided below:

a. Lori randomly assigns her volunteer students to one of three conditions in her study about learning anthropology in authentic environments. One group receives a guided museum tour, one group receives a computer-based tutorial, and the third group receives a cooperative group experience. She measures their understanding of anthropology concepts at the end of the training.

b. Ginger took three classrooms of fourth-grade learners and gave them weekly spelling tests for three weeks. During the fourth week each group received a different spelling training program. One group received the *Phonics for Intermediate Grades* lessons, one group received *Latin Roots Help Us Spell* program and the third group received a prefix-suffix training program at the beginning and the end. Ginger then measured their spelling scores for four weeks and compared the groups.

c. Ken conducts a study to test out a new mathematics program. One class he teaches with the old textbook and the other group he teaches with the new program. At the end of the year he compares their standardized test scores.

Applying What You Know

1. You are interested in the benefits of different types of technology training on teachers' technology skills, use, and their attitude regarding instructional technologies. You are in the unique position to be able to study all of the teachers in a regional unit that houses several districts. You therefore can conduct the research any way that you would like to (We are fantasizing a little!).

a. Given this scenario: what are some of the potential extraneous variables we need to be careful to consider? List three_____   _____   _____

b. Given this scenario: what are the likely dependent measures in a study you would design?

    _____   _____   _____

c. What is the independent variable this study will manipulate? _____

d. Describe how you would conduct this study as a Pretest-Posttest control group design. *Diagram the design and label.*

    _____
    _____
    _____
    _____
    _____

e. Describe how you would conduct this study as a nonequivalent control group design. *Diagram and label.*

_____
_____
_____
_____
_____

f. Describe how you would conduct this study as a Time Series Design. *Diagram and label.*

_____
_____
_____
_____
_____

g. Describe how this study could be conducted as a factorial design.

_____
_____
_____
_____
_____

2. You may have considered some different science learning study, but do you remember from Chapter 5 that Bruce is studying the benefits of different types of instructional materials for learning science content? He is interested in the effects of pictures, diagrams, illustrations, animations, simulations, adjunct questions, required multiple choice questions, marginal notes, student note taking while learning, etc. There are too many choices of things he can study to help learners learn from text! Design a study for Bruce given his general topic area. Diagram and label the design. What is one threat that this design controls for?

_____
_____
_____
_____
_____

Test-Like Event

Circle the best answer in each item.

1. In experimental research, unlike in other types of research, groups are equated on variables other than the independent variable by

    a. matching.
    b. randomization.
    c. homogeneous sampling.
    d. ANCOVA.

2. In an experimental study another name for the outcome variable is the

    a. independent variable.
    b. dependent variable.
    c. extraneous variable.
    d. mediating variable.

3.-4. In a recent study, Barbara measured the benefits of a ten-minute afternoon rest period in full day kindergarten for on-task behavior and reading ability. She had two kindergarten classes of approximately 28 each and conducted t- tests to examine differences between the groups. She found benefits for behavior but not for reading ability (Note that this is NOT really an experimental study).

3. One LIKELY reason for her findings is that

    a. her measures did not measure behavior.
    b. her sample is too small.
    c. she conducted the wrong analysis.
    d. her groups were too similar.

4. The treatment variable in Barbara's study is

    a. on-task behavior.
    b. kindergarteners.
    c. rest period.
    d. parent's occupation.

5. The first step in an experimental study is

    a. selection and definition of a problem.
    b. execution of procedures.
    c. formulation of conclusions.
    d. analysis of data.

6. The type of validity concerned with whether extraneous variables have been adequately controlled is referred to as

    a. internal validity.
    b. consequential.
    c. content validity.
    d. construct validity.

7. Dave and Doug are designing a new study that measures the effects of sport on self-esteem in young children. They were alarmed to find that high achieving children elect not to participate in the study. This effect represents which of the following types of validity?

    a. Experimenter effects
    b. Reactive effects
    c. Selection effects.
    d. Interaction effects.

8. Rosemary is testing a new problem solving strategy in her study. She finds, however, that when students take the pretest they learn some of the strategy. Even if they don't later receive the intervention, their strategy score increases. Rosemary is best illustrating a threat of

    a. history.
    b. testing.
    c. instrumentation.
    d. reactive effects.

9. The primary drawback of the Solomon Four-Group design is

    a. it does not control for mortality.
    b. it requires more participants.
    c. it requires more time.
    d. it is less ethical than other designs.

10. Given the following notation, which design is illustrated?

    O   X   O

    a. One shot case study
    b. One group pretest-posttest design
    c. Posttest only control group design
    d. Static group comparison

11. Mary Beth's study compared persistence of those students who enrolled in a first year seminar and those who did not enroll in the seminar. He found that those who had the First Year Seminar had greater persistence. Since students volunteered to be in the Seminar, with which validity threat should Mary Beth be most concerned?

    a. Multiple treatment interference
    b. Instrumentation
    c. History
    d. Selection-Treatment Interaction

12. Which of the following is a threat to internal validity?

    a. history
    b. reactive effects
    c. specification of variables
    d. treatment diffusion

13. The threat to validity that occurs when participants in different conditions talk about the study with each other is known as

    a. experimenter effects.
    b. reactive effects.
    c. instrumentation.
    d. treatment diffusion.

14. Kate was conducting a study on two treatment interventions to decrease test anxiety. During her study, she found out that the English teacher was covering test anxiety in her advanced classes. Some of the students in the English classes were also in Kate's study. Kate's situation illustrates a threat by

    a. statistical regression.
    b. multiple treatment interference.
    c. specificity of variables.
    d. selection-maturation interaction.

15. Of the following, which is an example of an experimental design?

    a. Soloman four group design .
    b. Static group comparison.
    c. Posttest only control group design.
    d. Nonequivalent control group design.

16. When diagrammed, how many cells does a 2x3 factorial design have?

    a. 2
    b. 4
    c. 6
    d. 8

17. A study that investigates the effects of two different types of therapy for anxiety by gender would be symbolized as a

    a. 2x2 factorial design.
    b. 3x2 factorial design.
    c. 2x3 factorial design.
    d. A Solomon four-group design.

18. Given the following research topic, indicate why this is NOT an example of experimental research.*Are there gender differences in fourth grade learners' spatial ability as measured by a computer-delivered assessment.*

    a. The IRB does not let us do experimental work with such young minors.
    b. By examining gender differences the study is ex post facto research.
    c. Experimental research can not be done with computer delivered mechanisms.
    d. Experimental research is not done with cognitive outcomes such as spatial ability.

19. According to your text what is one problem that experimental studies in education commonly encounter.
    a. An inability to secure enough participants.
    b. A lack of sufficient exposure to treatments.
    c. The questions asked in education mostly concern relationships.
    d. Educational settings do not allow for experimental research.

20. Gender is an example of an _____ variable.

    a. assigned
    b. adjunct
    c. active
    d. *a priori*

21. Ecological validity refers to

    a. external validity.
    b. internal validity.
    c. construct validity.
    d. content validity.

22. Maxine conducted a study that includes a pretest-post test control group design. She randomly assigned students to treatment groups for an intervention. Unfortunately, her participants did fabulously on the pretest. This will most directly cause which of the following threats for Maxine?

    a. History
    b. Mortality
    c. Statistical regression
    d. Selection effects

23. Krista decides to test her summer environmental camp participants to see if they learned during her program. She, therefore gives them a knowledge test the last day of camp. Which type of design did Krista use?

    a. Time Series
    b. Single subject
    c. One-shot case
    d. One group pretest-posttest

Companion Website

For more practice on becoming competent in this chapter's objectives, go to the Companion Website that accompanies this text at www.prenhall.com/gay. This site includes:

Objectives with links to:
- more multiple-choice questions in Practice Quiz
- Applying What You Know essay questions
- relevant Web sites

Custom modules to help you:
- calculate statistical tests (see "Calculating Statistical Tests")
- do research (see "Research Tools and Tips")
- practice analyzing quantitative data (see "Analyzing Quantitative Data")
- practice analyzing qualitative data (see "Analyzing Qualitative Data")
- practice evaluating published articles (see "Evaluating Articles")

Chapter 9 Answers
For Your Own Review
1. Internal validity is control; external validity is generalizability. The more you control extraneous variables the less you can generalize. As you design a study to allow for generalizability, you lose internal control. Both are important to consider as you design a study and the balance is sometimes difficult. As noted in the text, sometimes researchers conduct very controlled studies and then conduct a second study to address external validity.
2. There are several potential answers: Pre-test, matching, control of experimental setting, limit treatment times
3. A versus B; A versus no A; Little of A versus a lot of A

Checking What You Know
1. a. History
   b. Statistical Regression
   c. Mortality
   d. Instrumentation

2. a. Experimenter
   b. Specificity of Variables
   c. Reactive effects
   d. Multiple Treatment interference

3 a. R X_1 O
       R X_2 O
       R X_3 O

   b. O O O X1 O O O
       O O O X2 O O O
       O O O X3 O O O

   c. X1   O
       X2   O

Applying What You Know

1. a. Among others: how much technology teachers already use, how much technology is available, previous training, age of student, level of teacher, school district they are from, educational level of the teachers
    b. attitude measure, skill test, delayed skill test
    c. Types of technology training
    d. Your answer will vary some:

> R   O   X1   O
> R   O   C   O

> In this case, the X1 might be any one of types of training, I placed a C for control group, and the Os are pre and post test—one could elect attitudes or one of the skills measures.

    e. X1   O
        X2   O

> There are a number of potential answers to this question. In any of these answers there are two pre-exisiting groups (X1, X2) that are compared on a single outcome (O). For example perhaps attidude after training (O) is compared between one group (X1) that receives a technology-specific training where they learn a specific type of application and the other group (X2) receives a general training where they are briefly exposed to several different types of applications

    f. O   O   O   X1   O   O   O

> There are several potential answers to this question. For example, perhaps time in minutes of instructional technology use per week is measured for three weeks prior to a training (each of the first three O), participants are exposed to a training (X1), and then their time in minutes of instructional technology use is again measured for a subsequent three weeks (the last three O).

    g. There are many ways one could conduct a factorial design for this example. One is to group participants by some variable (e.g. level of instruction) and also by region or by available technology. The possibilities are nearly endless.

2. Share your answer with a peer or with your instructor. There is too much variance to provide a model answer. However, keep in mind that a dependent variable is needed for an experimental design as well as randomization. The number of groups would dictate your design as well as potential consideration of other factors to make it factorial design.

Test-Like Event

1.	b	18.	b
2.	b	19.	b
3.	d	20.	a
4.	c	21.	a
5.	a	22.	c
6.	a	23.	c
7.	c		
8.	b		
9.	b		
10.	b		
11.	d		
12.	a		
13.	d		
14.	b		
15.	c		
16.	c		
17.	a		

Chapter 10 Single Subject Experimental Research

Chapter 10 Objectives

1. For each of the A-B-A single-subject designs discussed in this chapter, (1) draw a diagram, (2) list the steps involved in its application, and (3) identify major problems with which it is associated.
2. Briefly describe the procedures involved in using a multiple-baseline design.
3. Briefly describe an alternating treatments design.
4. Briefly describe three types of replication involved in single-subject research.

Review the Terms

Provide a succinct definition in your own words for each of the following terms.

Single-subject experimental design: _____

_____

Baseline measures: _____

_____

Interobserver reliability: _____

_____

Intraobserver reliability: _____

_____

Baseline stability: _____

_____

Single variable rule: _____

_____

Case study: _____

_____

A-B design: _____

_____

Additive design: _____

_____

A-B-A design: _____

_____

Changing criteria design: _____

_____

A-B-A-B design: _____

_____

Multiple baseline designs: _____

_____

Alternative treatment designs: _____

_____

Direct replication: _____

_____

Simultaneous replication: _____

_____

Systematic replication: _____

_____

Clinical replication: _____

_____

For Your Own Review

1. In a single subjects design the A represents the _____ and B represents the
   _____.

2. Discuss external validity and internal validity in single-subjects designs. _____
   _____
   _____

3. State one reason single subjects designs might be preferable over group designs.
   _____
   _____
   _____
   _____

4. State the three types of replication used in single subjects designs.
   _____
   _____
   _____

Applying What You Know

1. To practice our knowledge of single subject designs let's consider the following scenario.
   Jessica is a somewhat difficult learner in your life skills class. As a special needs learner she needs
   the content you teach in your class however she refuses to attend in class or participate in class
   activities. You would like to put an intervention in place to increase her participation. Before you
   introduce the intervention you need to ascertain her current level of participation. You ask the school
   psychologist to come by class and observe.

a. This strategy is called _____.

b. How many observations should be the minimum you would consider? _____.

c. Given this scenario, how might an A-B design be used?

_____

_____

_____

_____

d. What is one drawback of the A-B design above?

_____

e. Given this scenario, how might you employ an A-B-A-B design?

_____

_____

_____

f. What is one benefit of the A-B-A-B design in this case compared to the A-B design? What is one drawback? How might you modify the design to combat the drawback?

_____

_____

_____

g. Given this scenario, let's assume that you have two possible treatments that you would like to use with Jessica. What single subjects design would allow you to try both treatments? Briefly describe how this design could be implemented.

_____

_____

_____

h. What is one drawback of the design you selected above?

_____

Test-Like Event

1. Compared to single subjects designs, group design

    a. more often generalize.
    b. require more rigor.
    c. are more valid.
    d. are more reliable.

2. One benefit of single subjects designs is

    a. increased validity.
    b. lack of a necessary control group.
    c. the ability of their findings to generalize.
    d. ease of administration.

3. Missy wants to start a new program with an autistic child she is working with but thinks she needs to collect baseline data first. How many data points does Missy need for baseline?

    a. two data points
    b. three data points
    c. four data points
    d. five data points

4. Ron is a child who has a difficult time staying awake in class. His therapist has decided to try a new program with him. First the therapist observes his behavior during his afternoon classes for a week. Next Ron employs the strategies his therapist has provided for a week. The therapist then observes his afternoon classes for another week to see if the program helped.

    a. A-B
    b. A-B-A
    c. B-A-B
    d. A-B-A-B

5. One ethical benefit of single subjects designs is that

    a. no deception occurs.
    b. class time is not wasted
    c. anonymity is protected
    d. every participant can receive the treatment.

6. Of the following which is the most concerning threat to internal validity in single subject designs?

    a. Instrumentation
    b. History
    c. Maturation
    d. Selection

7. Maddy is a second grade special needs learner who has difficulty staying on task in the classroom. Her teacher and a paraprofessional are collecting baseline data regarding her off-task behaviors during reading class. They decide to collect data at the same time for a 15 minute period and correlate their recordings. These professionals are using which of the following strategies?

    a. Test-retest reliability
    b. Interobserver reliability
    c. Intraobserver reliability
    d. Alternate forms reliability

8. One means to increase reliability of single subjects designs is to assure that

    a. only one person conducts the treatment.
    b. the treatment is standardized.
    c. that numerous children are receiving treatment at the same time.
    d. assure that replication is conducted.

9. Jeb is collecting baseline data on Cynthia's self-stimulation behavior in class. He observes her for several class periods and notes her behavior is getting worse. She is now banging her head on her desk repeatedly during class, when only three days ago she was tapping her arm with her pencil. Cynthia's behavior is indicating a trend. In this case the trend will

    a. increase the number of data points needed.
    b. decrease the necessity of an intervention phase.
    c. decrease the number of data points needed.
    d. increase the length of time of the treatment phase.

10. Nuzhat is receiving treatment for hitting behaviors in class. It would be detrimental to remove the treatment. Which of the following single-subject designs would be most appropriate to use under this circumstance?

    a. A-B-A
    b. A-B-A-B
    c. Alternating treatments
    d. Multiple baseline

11. Iftakar has employed an alternating treatments design in his work with James. He is using either reinforcement or ignoring strategies and alternates them daily. Given what you know about alternating treatment designs. What is a major concern with this strategy?

    a. It poses internal validity threats.
    b. It poses control threats
    c. It poses external validity threats.
    d. It poses history threats.

12. Patsy is convinced the only 'good' single subjects designs are alternating treatment designs. Which of the following is a drawback of alternating treatment designs that Patsy seems to be ignoring?

    a. All learners will not get a treatment.
    b. Carry over effects may be a problem
    c. Only one treatment can be studied at once
    d. Treatment must be withdrawn.

13. Which of the following illustrates an additive design for an A-B-A study?

    a. A-A-B-B-A-A
    b. A-B-A-B
    c. Multiple baseline study
    d. Alternating treatments design

14. Mrugan wants to use a single subjects design to present three treatments for three behaviors with his student Darla. Which of the following is the best design for him to use?

    a. A-B-A-B
    b. Alternating treatments
    c. Multiple baseline
    d. An additive design

15. As a rule when conducting single–subjects designs the number of observations in the treatment phase should

    a. Be smaller than the number in the observation phase.
    b. Be approximately the same as the number in the observation phase.
    c. Be larger than the number in the observation phase.
    d. Be double the number in the observation phase.

16. The representation OOOOXOXOXOXOOOOOXOXOXOXO best illustrates a
_____design.

    a. A-B
    b. A-B-A
    c. A-B-A-B
    d. Multiple baseline

Chapter 10 Answers
For Your Own Review Answers

1. A represents the nontreatment condition; B represents the treatment condition

2. External validity in single-subject designs is not the same as group designs. Findings from single subject designs do not generalize. However, replication can be used to generalize the findings. Internal validity of single subjects designs is generally a strength when proper controls are used. Instrumentation is often a challenge for single subjects designs.

3. Ethical concerns, some children do not get treatment; small sample sizes are problematic

4. Direct, Systematic, Clinical

Applying What You Know

1. a. Collecting baseline data

    b. This will vary but a minimum of three is recommended. It often takes more observations due to variance in people's behavior.

    c. In an A-B (not a great design!) baseline data would be collected and then a treatment phase would be introduced, such as reinforcement for participation

    d. One drawback of the A-B design is that we don't know if the treatment worked as no data are systematically collected. Further, as your text notes, we can't be sure that the change in behavior is due to the treatment.

    e. In an A-B-A-B design one would first collect baseline data, then introduce the treatment, in this case reinforcement for participation, go back to collecting data without reinforcement and then reintroduce the treatment.

    f. One benefit is the increased validity of the design over an A-B design, or an A-B-A design. One drawback is that there is withdraw of the treatment and sometimes that is quite detrimental to the student's health or behavior, especially for serious behaviors. One way to combat the drawback is to employ a multiple baseline design.

g. One way to introduce more than one treatment (perhaps a type I reinforcement strategy (praise) and a type II reinforcement strategy (taking away groupwork Jessica might not want to do) is to introduce an alternating treatment design where sometimes the treatment is to praise while other times the treatment is to allow Jessica to not do group work in class but to do it independently.

h. Carryover effects are a drawback of alternating treatment designs. For example, it might be difficult to know if the participation behavior is because of the treatment today or the treatment yesterday.

Test-Like Event

1. a	6. a	11. c	16. c
2. b	7. b	12. b	
3. b	8. b	13. b	
4. b	9. c	14. b	
5. d	10. d	15. b	

Chapter 11   Descriptive Statistics

Chapter 11 Objectives

1. List the steps involved in scoring standardized and self-developed tests.
2. Describe the process of coding data, and give three examples of variables that would require coding.
3. List the steps involved in constructing a frequency polygon.
4. Define or describe three measures of central tendency.
5. Define or describe three measures of variability.
6. List four characteristics of normal distributions.
7. List two characteristics of positively skewed distributions and negatively skewed distributions.
8. Define or describe two measures of relationship.
9. Define or describe four measures of relative position.
10. Generate a column of 10 numbers, each between 1 and 10. You may use any number more than once. Assume those numbers represent scores on a posttest. Using these "scores", give the formula and compute the following (showing your work): mean, standard deviation, z scores, and Pearson r (divide the column in half and make two columns of five scores each).

Review the Terms

Provide a succinct definition in your own words for each of the following terms.

Statistic: _____
_____

Descriptive Statistics: _____
_____

Parameter: _____
_____

Tabulation: _____
_____

Coding: _____
_____

Measures of central tendency: _____
_____

Measures of variability: _____
_____

Measures of relative position: _____
_____

Measures of relationship: _____
_____

Mode: _____

_____

Mean: _____

_____

Median: _____

_____

Range: _____

_____

Quartile deviation: _____

_____

Variance: _____

_____

Standard deviation: _____

_____

Normal distribution: _____

_____

Skewed distribution: _____

_____

Negatively skewed distribution: _____

_____

Positively skewed distribution: _____

_____

Percentile rank: _____

_____

Standard score: _____

_____

z score: _____

_____

t score: _____

_____

Stanines: _____

_____

Parameter:_____

_____

For Your Own Review

Select the term below that describes the statements following. Write the letter of the term in the blank provided. Some of these answers will be used more than once while some answers may not be used at all.

a. mode
b. median
c. range
d. *z* score
e. mean
f. percentile rank
g. standard deviation
h. standard score
i. quartile deviation
j. stanine
k. Spearman rho
l. Pearson *r*
m. variance

1. The measure of central tendency most frequently reported _____
2. A basic standard score _____
3. The measure of central tendency that ignores extremely high or extremely low scores _____
4. The measure of variability appropriate for nominal level data _____
5. The measure of central tendency used for describing ordinal data _____
6. The measure of central tendency that represents the most frequently occurring score _____
7. The measure of relative position that indicates percentage of scores that fall at or below a given score. _____
8. The measure of variability appropriate when the median is an appropriate measure._____
9. The most stable measure of variability _____
10. The measure of central tendency used for describing nominal data _____
11 Most frequently used measure of association in education. _____
12. The measure of central tendency used for describing interval and ratio data _____
13. The measure of variability calculated as the difference between the highest and lowest score _____
14. The measure of relationship used with ordinal data _____
15. The measure of central tendency that represents the arithmetic average _____
16. Jim told his class he was surprised that nine students out of sixteen received a 90%. There were no other scores that had more than one student with that score. Jim is reporting the _____ to his class.
17. Razi is reporting the relationship between age and salary. He needs to report the _____
18. Min reported to her class that all of the test scores fell within 20 points of on another she was reporting the _____ to her class.

Other Sources for Review

The Rice Virtual Lab in statistics is a great website at http://www.ruf.rice.edu/~lane/rvls.html that provides online statistics books and links to statistics websites, case studies with real data to use to practice analyses and interpretation, and simulations and exercises that can help your conceptual understanding of statistics content. Visiting this site can greatly assist you in understanding and practicing the content for Chapters 11, 12 and 13.

Visit the Rice Virtual Lab specifically for Chapter 11 review. Go to http://www.ruf.rice.edu/~lane/stat_sim/descriptive/index.html and browse a bit. Not only does the 'lab' present the content in a new way, but also there is a simulation for central tendency that can help you review the content. This simulation allows you to modify the mean and median and visually see the effects on a histogram. This is an excellent exercise that shows the relationship between the median and the mode and skewed distributions.

Chapter 20 in your study guide also includes an additional dataset that contains some quantitative data. When you cover Chapter 20 you will have the opportunity to review content for Chapters 11-13 by entering and checking data as well as conducting descriptive and other statistical analysis.

Just for Practice

1. Given the following 20 scores on an attitude scale, complete the following exercise. You may check your answers in SPSS.

18	16	18	20
16	14	16	18
14	12	10	14
12	18	16	18
14	10	12	14

    a. Create a frequency distribution by hand on a separate sheet of paper. You can check your work with SPSS.
    b. What is the mean? _____
    c. What is the median? _____
    d. What is the mode? _____
    e. What is the range? _____
    f. What is the standard deviation? _____
    g. What is the approximate score of the person at the 85 percentile ranking? _____

Applying What You Know

Appendix A in this guide provides a dataset for the study designed in Chapter 5 and Chapter 9 activities. You may remember that Bruce is studying the benefits of different types of instructional materials for learning science content. Some research suggests that diagrams can be helpful to learning, but that often learners do not attend to them. Other research suggests that animations can be helpful to learning, but that they sometimes serve to distract the reader from important information.

Bruce randomly assigns students to one of three conditions. He collects demographic information (e.g., gender, class standing) and administers a 6 item, 3-point Likert Scale interest inventory that measures interest for science. Bruce sums the items for each person to give them an overall interest score. Learners were provided instructional materials commensurate with their condition for an hour-long learning session. After, they are immediately tested. Three outcome measures were used. A free recall test that required learners to remember and record everything that they could was scored as percentage correct. A multiple choice factual recognition test was administered and scored, again, as percentage correct. A problem-solving test was administered last. This test was scored with a 10-point rubric. Sixty-six students participated in the study and their data are presented in Appendix A.

1. Given each of the following variables, write in the blanks provided whether they represent *categorical* or *quantitative* data.

    a. Gender: _____
    b. Treatment condition: _____
    c. Major: _____
    d. Interest: _____
    e. Recall: _____
    f. Factual Recognition: _____
    g. Problem-solving: _____

2. Generate a code for each of the variables (those that are presented are arbitrary and can be changed if there is a different code that is more meaningful to you.)

3. This activity can be done by hand, but also it can be completed using SPSS, another statistics package, or database program. If you are going to use computer analysis, enter your data into a data file.

4. Double check your data entry against the data provided. If there is no one nearby to read it off for you, the computer voice on most machines can read it for you aloud and you can check it that way (Usually it will need to be in a word processing document to do this. If you are going to use this approach, it is best to enter the data as tab-delineated for easier transfer into another software package.)

5. Conduct descriptive statistics for <u>each of the variables</u>. Report the following from those analyses.

    a. Number of men and of women. Men _____ Women _____
    b. Frequency distribution of condition. Text _____ Diagram _____, Animation _____
    c. Mean and standard deviation for interest. Mean _____, standard deviation _____
    d. Range for interest _____
    e. For problem-solving: mean _____, median _____, mode _____, range _____ , standard deviation _____.

6. a Create a pie graph for class standing.
    b. Create a histogram for condition.

7. a. Without using an inferential test, on which of the outcome measures did students perform the best? _____

    b. Is this sample of students generally interested in science? _____
        How do you know? _____
        _____

Test-Like Event

Circle the best answer in each item.

1. Your text suggests that when scoring data a portion of the data should be checked for consistency in scoring. That portion should be approximately

    a. 5 %
    b. 10%
    c. 25%
    d. 50%

2. Of the following, which is NOT a measure of central tendency?

    a. Mode
    b. Median
    c. Range
    d. Mean

3. Of the following, which is NOT a measure of variability?

    a. Mean
    b. Range
    c. Standard deviation
    d. Quartile deviation

4. Ellen scored in the 72nd percentile on a standardized exam, what is her approximate z score?

    a. -2
    b. -1.5
    c. .5
    d. 1.5

5. Allie was so excited her son scored a 110 on the Wechsler Intelligence Scale. Which of the following is an appropriate conclusion regarding her son's score?

    a. He is below average.
    b. He is in the 4th stanine.
    c. His z score is positive.
    d. His percentile score is 85.

6. Mandy always brags about her Math SAT score. She got a 500. Which of the following is accurate regarding Mandy's score?

    a. She *z* score is positive.
    b. Her stanine score is 9.
    c. Her t score is 40.
    d. Her percentile score is 50.

7. On a test with a mean of 50 and a standard deviation of 10, the percentile score of a person who scores a 40 is approximately

    a. 2.
    b. 16.
    c. 34.
    d. 50.

8.-13.   Given a normal distribution with a mean of 75 and a standard deviation of 5, answer the following questions.

8. What is the approximate value of the median?

    a. 65
    b. 70
    c. 75
    d. 80

9. What score represents a score at the 50th percentile?

    a. 65
    b. 70
    c. 75
    d. 80

10. What is the T score of a person with a score of 80 on the exam?

    a. 45
    b. 50
    c. 55
    d. 60

11. Audrey scored a 60 on the exam. What is her stanine score?

    a. 1
    b. 2
    c. 3
    d. 4

12. Which of the following raw scores on the exam illustrates an approximate z score of –2?

    a. 60
    b. 65
    c. 70
    d. 75

13. Given this distribution, calculate the *z* score for Charles. He received a score of 78.

   a.   -.8
   b.   1
   c.   1.2
   d.   1.6

14.-18 Given the following distribution of scores, answer questions 14-18.

8	10
10	12
12	10
11	7
9	9

14. What is the mode?

   a.   7
   b.   9
   c.   10
   d.   12

15. What is the median?

   a.   8
   b.   10
   c.   11
   d.   12

16. What is the mean?

   a.   8.4
   b.   9.8
   c.   10.6
   d.   11.2

17. What is the range?

   a.   5
   b.   6
   c.   7
   d.   8

18. Given the following measures, what can one conclude about the data?

   a.   It is slightly positively skewed.
   b.   It is slightly negatively skewed.
   c.   It is bimodal.
   d.   It is trimodal.

19. The measure of central tendency that is appropriate for nominal data is

    a. mode.
    b. mean.
    c. standard deviation.
    d. range.

20. The measure of correlation appropriate for ratio data is

    a. Kendall Tau
    b. Spearman Rho
    c. Pearson *r*
    d. Gamma

Companion Website

For more practice on becoming competent in this chapter's objectives, go to the Companion Website that accompanies this text at www.prenhall.com/gay. This site includes:

Objectives with links to:
- more multiple-choice questions in Practice Quiz
- Applying What You Know essay questions
- relevant Web sites

Custom modules to help you:
- calculate statistical tests (see "Calculating Statistical Tests")
- do research (see "Research Tools and Tips")
- practice analyzing quantitative data (see "Analyzing Quantitative Data")
- practice analyzing qualitative data (see "Analyzing Qualitative Data")
- practice evaluating published articles (see "Evaluating Articles")

Chapter 11 Answers
For Your Own Review

1. e	17. l
2. d	18. c
3. b	
4. c	
5. b	
6. a	
7. f	
8. i	
9. g	
10. a	
11. l	
12. e	
13. c	
14. k	
15. e	
16. a	

<u>Just for Practice</u>

a.   frequency distribution:

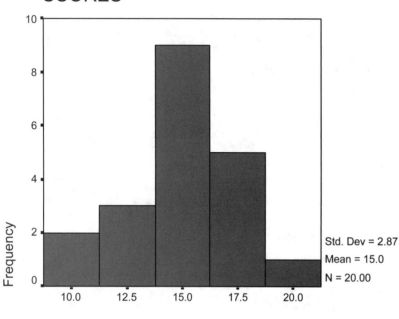

b.   mean: 15
c.   median: 15
d.   Bimodal 14, 18
e.   range: 10
f.   SD: approx 2.8
g.   Approximate score of person at 85 percentile ranking: approx. 18

<u>Applying what you know</u>

1.   a.   categorical
     b.   categorical
     c.   categorical
     d.   quantitative
     e.   quantitative
     f.   quantitative
     g.   quantitative

5.   a.   gender (53 female; 13 male)
     b.   condition (text, n=24; diagram, n=19, animation, n=23)
     c.   mean= 13.33; SD=2.48
     d.   range =10
     e.   mean=6.52, median=7, mode=8, standard deviation =1.98; range =8

6.   a.   Pie graph for class standing:

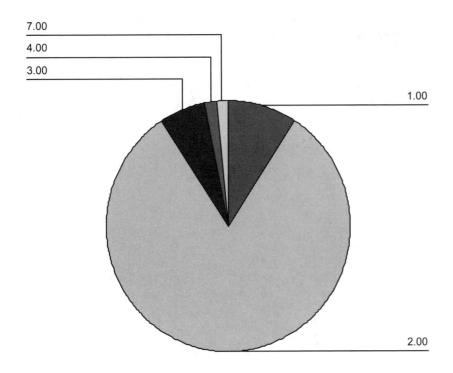

6. b.   Histogram for condition:

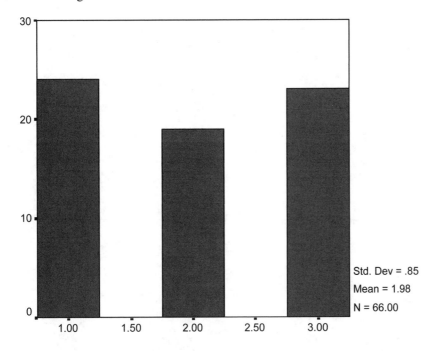

Std. Dev = .85
Mean = 1.98
N = 66.00

condition (1=text, 2=picture, 3 animation)

7. a.   Factual recognition –highest percentage correct

b. It really depends on your operational definition of 'generally interested.' I would say, "yes, kind of"; the mean for the sample was 13.33, and the median was 14 on an 18 point scale. The lowest score was an 8. Keep in mind, though, the possible range of scores for the instrument was a 3 to 18.

Test-Like Event

1. c
2. c
3. a
4. c
5. c
6. d
7. b
8. c
9. c
10. d
11. a
12. b
13. d
14. c
15. b
16. b
17. a
18. b
19. a
20. c

Chapter 12   Inferential Statistics

Chapter 12 Objectives

1. Explain the concept of standard error.
2. Describe how sample size affects standard error.
3. Describe the null hypothesis.
4. State the purposes of a test of significance.
5. Describe Type I and Type II errors.
6. Describe the concept of significance level (probably level).
7. Describe one-tailed and two-tailed tests.
8. Explain the difference between parametric tests and nonparametric tests.
9. State the purpose, and explain the strategy, of the *t*-test.
10. Describe independent and nonindependent samples.
11. State the purpose and appropriate use of the *t* test for independent samples.
12. State the purpose and appropriate use of the *t* test for nonindependent samples.
13. Describe one major problem associated with analyzing gain or difference scores.
14. State the purpose of the simple analysis of variance.
15. State the purpose of multiple comparison procedures.
16. State the purpose of a factorial analysis of variance.
17. State a purpose of analysis of covariance.
18. State two uses of multiple regression.
19. State the purposes of chi square.
20. Generate three columns of five one-digit numbers ("scores") and compute each of the following statistics (give the formula and show your work): state whether each result is statistically significant at alpha =.05, and interpret each result.
    a. *t* test for independent samples
    b. *t* test for nonindependent samples
    c. simple analysis of variance for 3 groups
    d. the Scheffe' test
    e. chi square (sum the numbers in each column and treat them as if they were the total number of people responding "yes," "no," and "undecided," respectively, in a survey).

Review the Terms

Provide an example for each of the following terms.

Inferential statistics: _____

_____

Standard error of the mean:_____

_____

Test of significance: _____

_____

Type I error: _____

_____

Type II error: _____

_____

Parametric test: _____

_____

Nonparametric test: _____

_____

t test: _____

_____

Two-tailed test: _____

_____

Degrees of freedom: _____

_____

t test for independent samples: _____

_____

t test for nonindependent samples: _____

_____

Simple analysis of variance (ANOVA): _____

_____

F ratio: _____

_____

Multiple comparison: _____

_____

Scheffe' test: _____

_____

Chi Square: _____

_____

Power: _____

_____

True category: _____

_____

Artificial category: _____

_____

For Your Own Review

1. State two of the assumptions of parametric tests.

    _____

    _____

2. When should a researcher use an independent samples t-test versus a nonindependent samples t-test?

    _____

    _____

    _____

    _____

3. Contrast statistic with parameter.

    _____

    _____

    _____

4. Contrast Type I and Type II error.

    _____

    _____

    _____

Other Sources for Review

Chapter 11 mentioned the Rice Virtual Lab as an excellent resource. As noted, this site contains many resources to assist you with your understanding of statistics content. One component of the site includes case studies with data that can be analyzed. For chapter 12 review, consider revisiting the site and accessing the case study on instructor reputation at http://www.ruf.rice.edu/~lane/case_studies/instructor_reputation/index.html to facilitate understanding of *t* tests (one-way ANOVA is also reviewed), and the physical strength and job performance case for correlation examples at http://www.ruf.rice.edu/~lane/case_studies/physical_strength/index.html

Another great website, SISA: Simple Interactive Statistical Analysis, facilitates understanding of basic statistical analysis by interactive examples. Access the site at http://home.clara.net/sisa/index.htm. This site allows you to modify outcomes by altering hypothetical (or real) data.

Chapter 20 has an additional dataset that you may use to practice both your hand calculations and your understanding of inferential statistics.

Just for Practice

These exercises are designed for you to practice some of your hand calculations. A calculator is suggested. You will need to work these on a separate piece of paper. Unless your instructor requires you to memorize the formulas, you may consult your text for the formulas and for the required critical values. Answers (and some benchmark answers along the way) are provided but you can also double-check your answers with SPSS.

1. Given a sample of 120 with a standard deviation of 10, what is the standard error of the mean?_____

2. Given the following data, calculate a *t* test for independent samples.

Group A	Group B
19	20
18	17
20	17
20	17
17	16
18	15
18	20
17	19
18	15
19	14

a. *t*= _____.
b. Is this a significant difference at *p*=.05? _____

3. Sixty sports fans were surveyed as to favorite sport (of those provided) to watch on television. It was expected that these sports fans would select equally the three sports. Calculate a Chi square test to determine if the observed frequencies significantly differ from chance.

Tennis	Soccer	Rugby
Observed 18	Observed 25	Observed 17
Expected 20	Expected 20	Expected 20

a. What is the chi square value? _____
b. Is this statistically significant? _____

4. Salim is curious if his student's content knowledge about driving rules increased after reading the drivers' manual that he gave them in class. He designed a twenty item multiple choice test that he gave them as a pretest. He then had them take an equivalent post test. He wants to determine if there are significant differences between their pre and post test. What test does Salim need to conduct on his data? _____. Yes, he needs to conduct a nonindependent t test. Below are his scores for the pretest and the posttest. Calculate the test by hand and then check your findings with SPSS.

12	15
14	16
11	17
9	12
15	18
20	20
17	20
16	18
10	11
14	15

a. What is the t value? _____
b. Is this value significant? _____

Applying What You Know

This exercise assumes that you have entered the dataset included in the appendix and have conducted the analysis for Chapter 11's "Applying what you know." If you have not done so, that activity should be done before you start this activity.

1. Create a scatterplot to examine the relationship between interest and problem solving. Estimate the relationship.

    _____

    _____

2. Compute the relationship between interest and problem solving. Is this a significant relationship?

    _____

    _____

3. Are there differences between male and female performance on the problem solving measure?

    _____

    _____

4. Are there differences in recall by condition?

    _____

    _____

Test-Like Event

1. What can we conclude about the standard error of the mean given the following two samples?
    A. Sample size of 150, standard deviation of 10
    B. Sample size of 100, standard deviation of 10

    a. The standard error of the mean is equal.
    b. The standard error of mean is smaller in sample A than in sample B.
    c. The standard error of mean is smaller in sample B than in sample A.
    d. We can't conclude any of the above given the provided information.

2. The standard deviation calculated on an entire population is referred to as a

    a. construct.
    b. statistic.
    c. parameter.
    d. variable.

3. The significance level selected determines

    a. the type I error.
    b. the type II error.
    c. both type I and type II error.
    d. neither type I or type II error.

4. In a *t* test, if a researcher rejects the null hypothesis and there really is a difference between the two groups' means then she has

    a. made a correct decision regarding the null hypothesis.
    b. made a type I error.
    c. made a type II error.
    d. committed both a type I and type II error.

5. Both Michele and Susan study learning statistics. If both women conduct similar studies from the same size samples from the same population and Michele sets her alpha at .05 and Susan sets her alpha at .001, of the following, what is the most reasonable conclusion regarding the researchers' chance of committing a type I error?

    a. Michele stands a greater chance of committing a type I error.
    b. Susan stands a greater chance of committing a type I error.
    c. They should have equal chances of committing a type I error.
    d. It cannot be determined from the provided information.

6. In Issam's study, on differences in test performance after a distributed review or a massed review, he found that students in the distributed review averaged 87% while students in the massed review averaged 76%. Those who didn't review at all averaged 67%. The differences between each of the conditions were significant. Which of the following is one thing that we can conclude from Issam's study?

    a. His study proves that distributed review is the best form of review.
    b. His study proves that review is important for learning.
    c. His study indicates no true difference between the massed and distributed practice.
    d. His study indicates that there appears to be a benefit for review.

7. Which of the following hypothesis allows for a two-tailed test of significance related to a research study that examines health differences between groups of children who either watch more than 7 or less than 2 hours of television a week?

    a. There are no differences in health between children who watch TV less than two or more than seven hours a week.
    b. Children who watch any amount of TV a week is worse than those who do not watch television.
    c. The health of children who watch less than two hours of TV a week is better than the health of children who watch more than seven hours of television a week.
    d. The health of children who watch more than 7 hours of television a week is worse than the health of children who watch less than 2 hours a week.

8. If a sample has a small standard error one can conclude that

    a. the sample mean does not estimate the population well.
    b. the sample mean does estimate the population well.
    c. the population distribution is very large.
    d. the population distribution is small.

9. Enrique conducted an independent *t* test with two groups. One group had 20 participants, the second had 24. The first group's average test score was 64 and the second group's average test score was 62. The formula for degrees of freedom for ANOVA is n1+n2-2. The degrees of freedom for Enrique's study, therefore, are

    a. 2.
    b. 20.
    c. 42.
    d. 64.

10. Leon is comparing different types of cooperative learning. In one group he used a Jigsaw II method, while for the other group he used Numbered Heads Together. After training and six weeks of experimental content, he assessed differences in amount students had learned. Of the following, which is the appropriate test of significance for Leon to use assuming random assignment and no pretreatment differences?

    a. Independent *t* test
    b. Dependent *t* test
    c. Difference scores
    d. ANOVA

11.-12. Nora's study addressed differences between three experimental conditions. In all three conditions, fifteen-year old children were given a multivitamin and a glass of orange juice. In addition, children in the first group were given sugar cereal for breakfast, in the second group children were given eggs and toast, and in the third condition, children were given a bagel and peanut butter. The children's blood sugar and confidence for learning were assessed at both 8:30 am and 11:30 am.

11. In Nora's study an independent variable is

    a. orange Juice.
    b. type of breakfast.
    c. blood sugar.
    d. children's age.

12. Which of the following tests of significance should Nora administer to analyze one of her research questions: Is there a difference in confidence at 11:30 am between learners given different breakfast meals?

    a. chi square
    b. *t* test
    c. ANOVA
    d. multiple regression

13. Given equal t and equal degrees of freedom, and a change from *p*=.001 to *p*=.05, the *t* value needed to indicate significant differences between groups will

    a. remain constant.
    b. decrease.
    c. increase.
    d. may either increase or decrease.

14. The statistical test that is used for prediction is

    a. ANCOVA.
    b. *t* test.
    c. multiple regression.
    d. chi square.

15. Jean's research examines variables that predict parental involvement in classrooms. She measures SES variables, prior education experience, and percentage of parents involved in PTO activities to determine which of these variables accounts for the most variance in likelihood to volunteer in a classroom. What type of analysis is Jean most likely going to use?

    a.   chi square
    b.   *t* test
    c.   ANOVA
    d.   multiple regression

16. An observed F value with 2 degrees of freedom within and 29 degrees of freedom between is 8.00. Given a significance level of *p*=.001, the corresponding table value is 8.85. Which of the following can be concluded?

    a. The researcher has proven that there are differences between groups.
    b. Differences between groups are not greater than those expected by chance.
    c. The researcher has proven that there are no differences between the groups.
    d. Differences between conditions are greater than those expected by chance.

Companion Website

For more practice on becoming competent in this chapter's objectives, go to the Companion Website that accompanies this text at www.prenhall.com/gay. This site includes:

Objectives with links to:
- more multiple-choice questions in "Practice Quiz"
- "Applying What You Know" essay questions
- relevant Web sites

Custom modules to help you:
- calculate statistical tests (see "Calculating Statistical Tests")
- do research (see "Research Tools and Tips")
- practice analyzing quantitative data (see "Analyzing Quantitative Data")
- practice analyzing qualitative data (see "Analyzing Qualitative Data")
- practice evaluating published articles (see "Evaluating Articles")

Chapter 12 Answers
For Your Own Review
1. Normal distribution, interval/ratio data, independent selection of participants, equal variances
2. A nonindependent *t* test is used when there is one group and a pre-post test, while an independent samples *t* test compares two groups.
3. A statistic is used for sample data while a parameter refers to population data
4. Type I error is an incorrect decision to reject the null. Type II error is the failure to reject the null hypothesis.

Just for Practice (see worked examples following)
1. .92
2. a. *t*=1.87   b.   no
3. a. 1.9   b.   no
4. a   t=4.61   b.   yes, p<.001

Just for Practice#1 handwritten solution:

(1.)

$$SE_{\bar{x}} = \frac{50}{\sqrt{N-1}}$$

$$SE_{\bar{x}} = \frac{10}{\sqrt{120-1}}$$

$$SE_{\bar{x}} = \frac{10}{\sqrt{119}}$$

$$SE_{\bar{x}} = \frac{10}{10.91}$$

$$\boxed{= .921}$$

Just for Practice #2 handwritten solution:

t test

①

Group A (X_1)	X_1^2	Group B (X_2)	X^2
19	361	20	400
18	324	17	289
20	400	17	289
20	400	17	289
17	289	16	256
18	324	15	225
18	324	20	400
17	289	19	361
18	324	15	225
19	361	14	196

$\Sigma X_1 = 184 \quad \Sigma X_1^2 = 3396 \qquad \Sigma X_2 = 170 \quad \Sigma X_2^2 = 2930$

$\bar{X}_1 = 18.4 \qquad\qquad \bar{X}_2 = 17$

$(\Sigma X)^2 = 33856 \qquad\qquad (\Sigma X_2)^2 = 28900$

$SS_1 = \Sigma X_1^2 - \dfrac{(\Sigma X_1)^2}{n_1} \qquad\qquad SS_2 = \Sigma X_2^2 - \dfrac{(\Sigma X_2)^2}{n_2}$

$= 3396 - \dfrac{33856}{10} \qquad\qquad = 2930 - \dfrac{28900}{10}$

$= 3396 - 3385.6 \qquad\qquad = 2930 - 2890$

$= 10.4 \qquad\qquad\qquad = 40$

T-test ②

$t = \dfrac{\bar{X}_1 - \bar{X}_2}{\sqrt{\left(\dfrac{10.4 + 40}{10 + 10 - 2}\right)\left(\dfrac{1}{10} + \dfrac{1}{10}\right)}} = \dfrac{18.4 - 17}{\sqrt{\left(\dfrac{10.4 + 40}{10 + 10 - 2}\right)\left(\dfrac{1}{10} + \dfrac{1}{10}\right)}}$

$df = n_1 + n_2 - 2$

$= 18$

$= \dfrac{1.4}{\sqrt{\left(\dfrac{50.4}{18}\right)\left(\dfrac{2}{10}\right)}}$

Table critical value
$p = .05$

2.101

$= \dfrac{1.4}{\sqrt{(2.8)(.2)}}$

NSig't because
$1.87 < 2.101$

$= \dfrac{1.4}{.75} \qquad \boxed{t = 1.87}$

Just for Practice #3 handwritten solution

$$X \qquad Y \qquad Z$$

$$\frac{18}{20} \qquad \frac{25}{20} \qquad \frac{17}{20}$$

$$\chi^2 = \sum \left(\frac{(f_o - f_e)^2}{f_e} \right)$$

$$\frac{(18-20)^2}{20} \; + \; \frac{(25-20)^2}{20} \; + \; \frac{(17-20)^2}{20}$$

$$= \; \frac{(-2)^2}{20} \; + \; \frac{(5)^2}{20} \; + \; \frac{(-3)^2}{20}$$

$$\frac{4}{20} \; + \; \frac{25}{20} \; + \; \frac{9}{20}$$

$$.2 \; + \; 1.25 \; + \; .45$$

$$\chi^2 = 1.9$$

Not Significant

$1.9 < 5.99$

df. C-1 = 2

Chi Square Critical Value

5.99 1

Just for Practice #4 handwritten solution

4.

$$t = \frac{\bar{D}}{\sqrt{\dfrac{\Sigma D^2 - \dfrac{(\Sigma D)^2}{N}}{N(N-1)}}}$$

X_1	X_2	D	D^2
12	15	3	9
14	16	2	4
11	17	6	36
9	12	3	9
15	18	3	9
20	20	0	0
17	20	3	9
16	18	2	4
10	11	1	1
14	15	1	1

ΣD 24 ΣD^2 82

Just for Practice #4 handwritten solution (continued)

$$\bar{D} = \frac{\Sigma D}{N} = \frac{24}{10} = 2.4$$

$$t = \frac{\bar{D}}{\sqrt{\dfrac{\Sigma D^2 - \dfrac{(\Sigma D)^2}{N}}{N(N-1)}}} \qquad \frac{2.4}{\sqrt{\dfrac{82 - \dfrac{(24)^2}{10}}{10(10-1)}}}$$

$$t = \frac{2.4}{\sqrt{\dfrac{82 - \dfrac{576}{10}}{10(10-1)}}}$$

$$t = \frac{2.4}{\sqrt{\dfrac{82 - 57.6}{10(10-1)}}}$$

$$t = \frac{2.4}{\sqrt{\dfrac{24.4}{10(9)}}}$$

Just for Practice #4 handwritten solution (continued)

$$t = \frac{2.4}{\sqrt{\dfrac{24.4}{90}}}$$

$$t = \frac{2.4}{\sqrt{.267}}$$

$$t = \frac{2.4}{.52}$$

ⓐ $t = ^- 4.61$

ⓑ $df = 9$
Critical t value = 2.26

yes 4.61 > than 2.26
this is a significant difference
Students' content knowledge is significantly
different (higher) after reading the
drivers' manual.

T-Test

Paired Samples Statistics

		Mean	N	Std. Deviation	Std. Error Mean
Pair 1	PRETEST	13.8000	10	3.39280	1.07290
	POSTTEST	16.2000	10	3.04777	.96379

Paired Samples Correlations

		N	Correlation	Sig.
Pair 1	PRETEST & POSTTEST	10	.875	.001

Paired Samples Test

		Paired Differences		
		Mean	Std. Deviation	Std. Error Mean
Pair 1	PRETEST – POSTTEST	–2.4000	1.64655	.52068

Paired Samples Test

		Paired Differences	
		95% Confidence Interval of the Difference	
		Lower	Upper
Pair 1	PRETEST – POSTTEST	–3.5779	–1.2221

Paired Samples Test

		t	df	Sig. (2-tailed)
Pair 1	PRETEST – POSTTEST	–4.609	9	.001

203

Applying what you know

1.

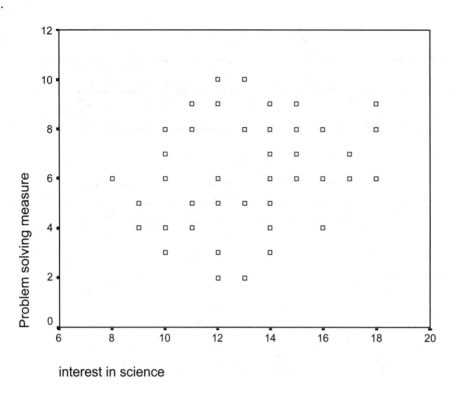

2. *r*=.28, *p*<.05—This is a statistically significant but perhaps not practically significant positive relationship.

3. This question can be answered with an independent *t* test, but the samples are rather different in size. Statistical adjustments can be made to control for unequal sample size. One way to answer this question is to simply compare the means, as noted from the printout below. I would probably look at these and conclude that there are no meaningful gender differences.

Report
Problem solving measure

gender (1=female)	Mean	N	Std. Deviation
1.00	6.5283	53	1.8770
2.00	6.4615	13	2.4364
Total	6.5152	66	1.9787

4. Are there differences in free recall by condition?

These analyses indicate significant differences between conditions on the free recall assessment with both groups outperforming the text-only condition but the diagram group and the animation group did not perform significantly different. To answer the question descriptive statistics for the dependent variable by condition are first presented. Second, a one-way ANOVA with free recall as the dependent variable and condition as the independent variable was conducted. This analysis indicated significant differences. Therefore, follow up Scheffe´ tests were calculated and indicated differences between pairs of conditions as reported above.

Multiple Comparisons
Dependent Variable: free recall task

Gender(1=F)	N	Mean	Std. Deviation
1.00	53	6.5283	1.8770
2.00	13	6.4615	2.4364
Total	66	6.5152	1.9787

Descriptives
free recall task

	N	Mean	Std. Deviation	Std. Error	95% Confidence Interval for Mean		Minimum	Maximum
					Lower Bound	Upper Bound		
1.00	24	38.17	15.41	3.15	31.66	44.67	24	78
2.00	19	51.37	15.53	3.56	43.88	58.85	29	91
3.00	23	60.43	12.06	2.52	55.22	65.65	38	88
Total	66	49.73	17.05	2.10	45.54	53.92	24	91

ANOVA
free recall task

	Sum of Squares	df	Mean Square	F	Sig.
Between Groups	5895.684	2	2947.842	14.280	.000
Within Groups	13005.407	63	206.435		
Total	18901.091	65			

Scheffe

(I) condition (1=text, 2=picture, 3 animation)	(J) condition (1=text, 2=picture, 3 animation)	Mean Difference (I-J)	Std. Error	Sig.	95% Confidence Interval	
					Lower Bound	Upper Bound
1.00	2.00	-13.20	4.41	.015	-24.26	-2.14
	3.00	-22.27	4.19	.000	-32.78	-11.76
2.00	1.00	13.20	4.41	.015	2.14	24.26
	3.00	-9.07	4.45	.134	-20.23	2.10
3.00	1.00	22.27	4.19	.000	11.76	32.78
	2.00	9.07	4.45	.134	-2.10	20.23

* The mean difference is significant at the .05 level.

Test-Like Event

1. b	5. b	9. c	13. b
2. c	6. d	10. a	14. c
3. a	7. a	11. b	15. d
4. a	8. b	12. c	16. b

Chapter 13   Postanalysis Considerations

Chapter 13 Objectives

1. List guidelines to be followed in verifying and storing quantitative data.
2. Explain how a rejected null hypothesis relates to a research hypothesis.
3. Explain how a null hypothesis which is not rejected relates to a research hypothesis.
4. Identify the major use of significant unhypothesized relationships.
5. Explain the factors that influence the interpretation of research results, including statistical, methodological, and significance.
6. Understand the role of power in significance testing.
7. Describe replication.

Review the Terms

For each of the following terms provide a definition in your own words.

Verification: _____

_____

Practical significance: _____

_____

Statistical significance:_____

_____

Research precision: _____

_____

Research accuracy: _____

_____

Replication: _____

_____

Statistical power: _____

_____

For Your Own Review

1. List two reasons to store your data.

   _____

   _____

2. List two methodological factors that can invalidate results.

   _____

   _____

3. Provide a potential limitation for a research study that examined differences between groups' preferences for academic tasks.

   _____

4. What two factors are necessary to make valid inferences about our population based upon our sample?

   _____

   _____

Checking What You Know

1. Given the following excerpt from a fictitious research report, indicate concerns that should have been noted during initial verification and coding of the study data.

   Children from a large urban elementary school participated in the after-school violence reduction program evaluated in this study (*n*=112). Most of the sample were boys *(n=89)*, however, several girls also participated (*n*=20). The majority of the students were African-American. Participants completed two outcome measures and a rating scale of the program. The first outcome measure was a definitions task, which required participants to provide definitions for 13 terms that were presented in the training. These items were scored correct or incorrect and a total score was taken. The second task was a problem-solving task that required students to apply the information presented in the training to a novel scenario. Scores on this measure ranged from 0-5 points. These two scores were combined to create a total outcome measure.

   The final measure, the rating was a single Likert scale item rating of the program that asked, "I think I learned valuable information in this violence reduction program" with a response of "1" representing Strongly Disagree and "5" representing Strongly Agree. Table 1 presents the means and standard deviations for the outcome measures.

   Table 1. Program outcome measures

	Mean	Standard Deviation
Definitions task	8	1.1
Problem solving task	2	.85
Total outcome	11	3.2
Rating	4	2.3

   List at least three concerns here:

   _____

   _____

   _____

2. A dataset was provided in chapters 11 and 12. If you did not note it during the analyses of that data, go back and examine the data. There is an error. What is the error and what is a plausible explanation?

   _____

   _____

Applying What You Know

Chapter 13 discusses the role of reporting hypothesized and unhypothesized findings. Consider the following example from a research report and answer the questions regarding the researchers' presentation and interpretation of their findings.

1. Refer to the article by Piotrowski, Botsko, & Matthews (2000) presented in Chapter 1.
   a. Were the researchers' hypotheses supported?_____
   _____

   b. Were findings consistent with previous research? _____ If so, briefly describe.
   _____
   _____

   c. Were there findings inconsistent with previous research, or unexpected findings? _____
   If so, briefly describe. _____
   _____

   d. If there were unexpected findings, was a plausible explanation presented as to why? _____
   If so, briefly describe._____
   _____

   e. Were any calls for future research based upon unexpected findings or findings in contrast to previous research included in the report? _____ If so, briefly summarize.
   _____
   _____

   f. Are the limitations of the study noted? _____ If so, briefly report those mentioned.
   _____
   _____

Practicing the Tasks

Task 7 in the text requires that you 'make up' data and generate a results section for your research topic. To practice this task, we will revisit the dataset used in chapters 11 and 12 Bruce's study of instructional materials in science learning. (This fictitious study was first introduced in Chapter 5's "Applying what you know" and revisited in Chapter 13's "Applying what you know.")

1. a. Although we know what happened in Bruce's study after completing the "Applying what you know" exercises in chapters 11 and 12, write a research hypothesis for his study:
   _____
   _____

   b. Determine the significance level for your tests of significance._____

   c. Select the appropriate test of significance. Report it here: _____. What is the reason why you chose this test?
   _____
   _____

d. Now compute it in SPSS. Print your SPSS output tables.
    Determine the statistical significance of your results. _____

e. Present your results in a summary statement and provide a table. Be sure to include if the findings relate to your test of significance.

Summary Statement: _____

_____

_____

_____

_____

_____

_____

_____

_____

_____

_____

_____

_____

_____

_____

_____

Test-Like Event

Circle the best answer for each item.

1. Gar conducted a study with developmental college students. He randomly assigned his 36 participants into one of two conditions. One group received study skills training and the other group received a motivation intervention. His hypothesis that the study skills group would perform better on end-of-semester GPA was not supported. Even though the study skills condition did perform better than the motivation group, the difference was not statistically significant. Which of the following should Gar consider when interpreting his findings?

    a. His dependent measure is nominal scale data.
    b. His Standard Error of Measurement is likely too small.
    c. His study may have too little power.
    d. His effect size is likely too large.

2. According to your text, one disadvantage of computer data analyses is that

    a. they are less accurate.
    b. they take longer.
    c. errors are hard to identify.
    d. they require many hand calculations.

3. In his experimental study on color preferences, Takeo stratified his sample selection so he had equal numbers of male and female participants. In his analyses, however, there are almost twice as many females as males. Which of the following errors is the most likely reason for his finding?

   a. computer
   b. analysis
   c. statistical
   d. entry

4. Wen found an old dataset on a floppy in his desk drawer. He has no idea what the numbers represent. Wen is most directly illustrating a(n)

   a. data entry error.
   b. verification error.
   c. storage error.
   d. analyses error.

5. Andrea calculated her chi square tests by hand with the help of a calculator. To examine the accuracy of her calculations, she should most specifically double check

   a. her data entry.
   b. the reasonableness of her results.
   c. her data collection procedures.
   d. her research hypothesis.

6. When reviewing a recent study that examined predictors of teen-age drug use in a 5400 participant sample, Roxanne noted that the participants' section of the report states that 48% of the sample were Caucasian, whereas in the results section it reports that 42% were Caucasian. This discrepancy is best described as a problem with research

   a. precision.
   b. accuracy.
   c. power.
   d. error rate.

7.-8   Caryll's thesis assessed gender differences in students' interest in physics.
She included 12 students in her sample and compared the six boys and six girls. She expected to find differences between the two groups, but did not.

7. What type of research did Caryll conduct?

   a. experimental
   b. descriptive
   c. correlational
   d. causal-comparative

8. What is your initial assessment of Caryll's findings?

    a. Her study did not have enough power to draw such conclusions.
    b. The small sample size and the lack of differences indicate that her conclusions are accurate.
    c. Previous research is likely flawed and Caryll is justified in her conclusions.
    d. Her instrument likely was not reliable and therefore is the reason her findings are different than previous research.

9. Regarding storage, computer-analyzed data should be

    a. discarded because only the raw data needs to be stored.
    b. printed and hardcopy only stored.
    c. saved to disk and stored electronically.
    d. saved to the hard drive but discarded after publication.

10. Alexandru's study addressed text processing differences between low and moderate readers. All previous work suggested that low readers process text more linearly. His findings did not support this expected difference. Of the following, which is the most appropriate course of reporting his findings for Alexandru to take?

    a. Report only those findings consistent with previous literature.
    b. State the lack of agreement and potential reason why.
    c. Modify his hypothesis to include this new finding.
    d. Report his findings without their relationship to previous work.

11.-12. Mimi and Herbert both study the relationship between self-concept and academic achievement. They both used the same standardized test to measure academic achievement and the same self-report measure of self-concept. The correlation in Mimi's study was a statistically significant r=.18. The correlation in Herbert's study was r= .28 and not statistically significant.

11. Of the following, what is one possible explanation for these results?

    a. Herbert's sample size was larger.
    b. Mimi's significance level was higher.
    c. Herbert's study had more power
    d. Mimi's sample size was larger.

12. In this example, one can interpret the correlations in the two studies as

    a. moderate to high correlations.
    b. of no statistical significance.
    c. of high practical significance.
    d. low to moderate correlations.

13. Micki just completed an ANOVA analysis on her study that compared student achievement in three different classrooms where the teachers were testing three different curricula. Of the following, which is the most immediate concern you might you have with the analyses Micki has conducted?

    a. With only three classrooms Micki doesn't have a large enough sample to do her analyses.
    b. By using pre-existing groups Micki likely violated the assumptions of her statistical test.
    c. Micki should have considered a correlational study to compare these groups.
    d. Micki is not able to test a null hypothesis given the study she conducted because she has no control group.

14. Sharise consulted power tables and did a power analysis prior to conducting her study to determine how many participants she needed. This strategy illustrates that Sharise is concerned with

    a. Type I error.
    b. Type II error.
    c. Type A error.
    d. Type B error.

15. Brent conducted a study that investigated differences in salary based upon geographic region. He is very excited that he found higher salaries for women than for men in two of the Urban centers in the midwest. This was an important finding although it did not relate to his research questions or hypotheses. According to your text, how should Brent proceed?

    a. He should report the finding since it is an important one.
    b. He should conduct another study to follow up this finding.
    c. He should modify his hypotheses to include this question and report the finding.
    d. Ignore the finding. If it wasn't hypothesized it isn't important enough to consider.

Chapter 13 Answers
For Your Own Review
1. Reasons to store data: A reviewer, an advisor, a different researcher, or you may want to do additional analyses with the data. The text suggests you might want to use the data for another study. In many cases this is considered unethical but there might be a case where you may want to consider different analyses for a given data set.
2. Ignoring measurement error, low statistical power, multiple comparisons
3. Some potential limitations include sample size or measurement error.
4. Sample must be representative; assumptions of statistical test must be met

Checking What You Know
1. There are clearly errors in this presentation of data that would have been caught by data coding and verification. First, the number of male and females in the study does not equal the total number of participants. Either this is an error or the researcher does not know the gender of all of the participants. If this information is unknown it should be reported as such. Second, the scores on the definitions task and the problem-solving task should add up to the outcome measures task. They do not. This may be a rounding error, but in APA style this information would be presented to two digits. Third, there is an error in the rating scores presented. It is not possible that there was a mean of 4 and a standard deviation of 2.3 when the answers were recorded on a 5 point scale. As your text notes, this is likely due to a coding error.
2. Case 20 has an error. This is might be a coding error but it is more likely a data entry error.

Applying What You Know
1. a. In this study, there were expectations but the null hypothesis was not tested as this work represents a descriptive survey study (see manuscript page 539.)

b. Yes, some. Some of the findings were consistent with previous research. Parents and teachers agreed on children being healthy and socially competent, parents placed a greater emphasis on academic skills, and preschool teachers had some higher expectations than did kindergarten teachers.

c. Yes, some. The authors also indicate that there are some unexpected findings that were inconsistent with previous literature. Two include that previous work indicated that less educated parents held higher expectations for their children regarding academic skills and that parents emphasized interest and curiosity over academic skills.

d. Yes, the researchers provide several interpretations as to why their findings are different. Sampling and measurement are suggested as plausible reasons.

e. Yes, see manuscript page 554. The authors do a nice job of providing additional unanswered research questions based upon their findings and they also note implications for practice and policy in the Discussion section as well.

f. The authors note several limitations in the study. For example, on manuscript page 553 the authors note that the findings cannot be generalized to parents who stay home with their preschoolers or for only Spanish-speaking parents. Also, the survey items were anchored to behaviors which limited the authors ability to ask parents about complex constructs. In addition, the authors note the study was conducted in a single school district.

Practicing the Tasks

1. a. Your research hypothesis might vary but one example hypothesis might be that learners who are exposed to science concepts with a labeled diagram will perform better on factual recognition test than those exposed to the text alone or with an animation. The null hypothesis, which will be tested by the analysis conducted, might be 'there are no differences in scores on a factual recognition test between learners who are provided a text, a labeled drawing, or an animation to learn science content.

b. The selected significance level might be $p=.05$. If the researcher was going to do a lot of analysis, the alpha level would, as you remember, be adjusted. Further, if the stakes for making an incorrect decision were high, there might also be an adjustment.

c. In this analysis, the independent variable, type of instructional material has three levels (text, labeled diagram, animation) and the dependent variable is a quantitative (interval level data) variable. We are interested in differences between groups and therefore would select an ANOVA test. Follow-up tests would need to be conducted as well. The text suggests the Scheffe' test to determine where differences between conditions exist if there are significant main effects.

d. To do this analysis in SPSS, go to the Analyze menu, drag down to the Compare Means and select the Factual Recognition Test as the dependent and the Condition as the independent variable and label groups as 1,3. Click the Post Hoc button on the bottom, select the Scheffe', and a $p=.05$, and click okay. The options button will allow you to obtain mean by condition and tests for the assumption of homogeneity of variance (an underlying assumption of the ANOVA test).

Below are the descriptive statistics from the analysis. These will be needed to create the table.

Descriptives
mc fact test

	N	Mean	Std. Deviation	Std. Error	95% Confidence Interval for Mean		Minimum	Maximum
					Lower Bound	Upper Bound		
1.00	24	68.9167	8.4438	1.7236	65.3512	72.4822	58.00	82.00
2.00	19	75.8947	12.0273	2.7592	70.0978	81.6917	52.00	92.00
3.00	23	81.9130	11.2892	2.3540	77.0312	86.7949	58.00	98.00

Total	66	75.4545	11.7907	1.4513	72.5560	78.3531	52.00	98.00

The test of homogeneity of variance follows and indicates there is not a violation that will cause concern with the ANOVA test.

Test of Homogeneity of Variances
mc fact test

Levene Statistic	df1	df2	Sig.
1.991	2	63	.145

The ANOVA table below should be familiar. This indicates that there is a difference between the conditions. The test reports a $p=.000$, which suggests that there is no chance that the differences between groups are not different. Of course there is always a chance and this finding would not be reported as $p=.000$, but as $p<.001$. It does indicate a difference of $p<.05$ and therefore we can reject our null hypothesis that there is no difference between the groups. It appears there is a difference. Now, we just need to determine where that difference is.

ANOVA
mc fact test

	Sum of Squares	df	Mean Square	F	Sig.
Between Groups	1988.915	2	994.457	8.890	.000
Within Groups	7047.449	63	111.864		
Total	9036.364	65			

Multiple Comparisons
Dependent Variable: mc fact test
Scheffe

(I) condition (1=text, 2=picture, 3 animation)	(J) condition (1=text, 2=picture, 3 animation)	Mean Difference (I-J)	Std. Error	Sig.	95% Confidence Interval Lower Bound	Upper Bound
1.00	2.00	-6.9781	3.2479	.108	-15.1208	1.1647
	3.00	-12.9964	3.0862	.000	-20.7338	-5.2589
2.00	1.00	6.9781	3.2479	.108	-1.1647	15.1208
	3.00	-6.0183	3.2789	.194	-14.2389	2.2023
3.00	1.00	12.9964	3.0862	.000	5.2589	20.7338
	2.00	6.0183	3.2789	.194	-2.2023	14.2389

* The mean difference is significant at the .05 level.

The Scheffe test indicates that there are significant differences between the text condition and the animation condition, but no differences between the labeled drawing and either of the other two conditions.

214

e.   It is customary to include a table of the means and standard deviations. Your APA manual can help you construct an appropriate table for your analysis.

1.00	24	68.9167	8.4438	1.7236	65.3512
2.00	19	75.8947	12.0273	2.7592	70.0978
3.00	23	81.9130	11.2892	2.3540	77.0312
Total	66	75.4545	11.7907	1.4513	72.5560

Results

(Note: The results section would likely also address other descriptive statistics and perhaps results of additional inferential tests for other hypotheses and variables. The paragraph most related to our hypothesis in a report would generally appear similar to the paragraph provided below. It is also critical to note that APA style would suggest that the results and the implications from the findings be more separate than those provided below. The implications or discussion of the findings generally appear in the discussion section not the results section.)

To determine if there were differences between conditions for the factual recognition test, a one-way ANOVA was conducted. It was expected that those learners who studied science concepts with labeled diagrams would perform better than those learners who were provided either a text or an animation. Results from the ANOVA test indicated that there were significant differences between conditions (F $(2,63)$=8.89, $p<.05$). Descriptive statistics for the factual recognition text by condition are presented in Table 1. Scheffe′ follow-up tests indicated significant differences between the animation and the text conditions but no differences between either the text and labeled drawing or the animation and the labeled drawing conditions. This finding is not consistent with the research hypothesis. Previous research had indicated mixed findings regarding the benefits of animation for learning science content. Some research indicated benefit for animations in learning (e.g., Mayer & Moreno, 2000) and other work suggested that animation can pose a distraction to effective learning (Rieber, 1996). In this study, due to the complexity of the text content and the importance of details in understanding a diagram, it was expected that the diagram would best support necessary understanding for performance on the outcome measure. While not consistent with our expectations, findings from the current study are consistent with previous work that suggests that animation can be an effective learning tool.

In the current work the labeled diagram did not facilitate understanding as well as did an animation. Future work should continue to examine the conditions under which animation is a helpful learning tool. The outcome tests in the current study were administered immediately after instruction. The benefits of the animation may decrease after a delay. Consistent with previous similar calls for research regarding graphic organizers (Robinson, 1998), future work that tests the efficacy of animation as an instructional tool for learning after a delay is needed.

Table 1 Means and standard deviations for the factual recognition test by group.

	Mean	Standard Deviation
Text (n=24)*	68.92	8.44
Labeled drawing (n=19)	75.89	12.03
Animation (n=23)*	81.91	11.29

* p<.05 between these two conditions.

(Note: Numbers are generally presented to two decimals in APA style; rounding rules apply.)

<u>Test-Like Event</u>
1.   c
2.   c
3.   d
4.   c
5.   b
6.   b
7.   d
8.   a
9.   c
10.   b
11.   d
12.   d
13.   b
14.   b
15.   b

Chapter 14   Overview of Qualitative Research

Chapter 14 Objectives

1. State the definition and purpose of qualitative research.
2. Describe the six steps in the qualitative research process.
3. Identify different qualitative research approaches.
4. Describe the characteristics of qualitative research.
5. State the definition of validity in qualitative research.
6. Describe strategies to address the trustworthiness (validity) of qualitative research.
7. Describe strategies to address the replicability (reliability) of qualitative research.
8. Describe the relationship between validity and reliability in qualitative research.
9. Describe the role of ethics in qualitative research.

Review the Terms

Provide a succinct definition in your own words for each of the following terms.

Qualitative research: _____

_____

Trustworthiness: _____

_____

Dependability: _____

_____

Confirmability:_____

_____

Credibility: _____

_____

Evaluative validity: _____

_____

Reliability: _____

_____

Validity: _____

_____

Descriptive validity: _____

_____

Interpretive validity: _____

_____

Theoretical validity: _____

_____

Triangulation: _____

_____

Generalizability: _____

_____

Interpretative research: _____

_____

For Your Own Review

1. List the six steps of qualitative research

    _____

    _____

    _____

    _____

    _____

    _____

2. List three of the common qualitative research approaches as presented in you text.

    _____

    _____

    _____

3. List three characteristics of good qualitative research.

    _____

    _____

    _____

4. Recall and describe two of types of validity in qualitative research.

    _____

    _____

    _____

Just for Practice

Given the following titles and abstracts, which qualitative approach(es) appear to be employed?

1. Prawat, R. S. (2000). Dewey Meets the "Mozart of Psychology" in Moscow: The untold story. *American Educational Research Journal, 37*(3), 663-696.

    Based on new evidence, I explore the likelihood that Vygotsky, who Toulmin refers to as the "Mozart of Psychology," met and exchanged views with John Dewey, the great American philosopher, during the latter's landmark trip to Russia in the summer of 1928. I also discuss a second kind of meeting that occurred around this time, a meeting of the minds between these two great scholars, unmistakably evident in Dewey's writings from 1925 on and in Vygotsky's writings towards the end of his life. The social and political context surrounding these two events, ironically enough, has not been adequately dealt with to date. A careful examination of the events leading up to and following the two hypothesized meetings calls into question a number of assumptions about Vygotsky's life and work--including Luria's popular, Cinderella-like account of how he came to the attention of the intellectual elite in Moscow.

(Copyright 2000 by the American Educational Research Association.)

Type of qualitative research _____

2. Quiroz, P. A. (2001). The silencing of Latino Student 'voice': Puerto Rican and Mexican narratives in eighth grade and high school. *Anthropology and Education Quarterly, 32*(3), 326-335.

Narratives of 27 Puerto Rican and Mexican students, written first in eighth grade then again as juniors in high school, address the important question of "Who am I?" and illustrate school-sponsored silencing, with students' critiques of their educational experience ignored by both the elementary and the high school. The narratives also provide a window into the high dropout rates of Latino children, the reasons behind students' academic decisions, and interventions needed to change negative schooling processes and outcomes. By giving witness to these voices, we as readers help ensure that through their writing, these Latino adolescents do not just speak but that they are heard.

Copyright American Anthropological Association Sep 2001

Type of qualitative research _____

3. Poveda, D. (2001). La Ronda in Spanish kindergarten classroom with a cross –cultural comparison to sharing time in the U.S.A. *Anthropology and Education, 31*(3), 301-310.

This article examines a common speech event in Spanish schools now as la ronda, in which children present oral narratives of their out-of-school experiences. I argue that the goal of this event is to allow the children and the teacher to build a sense of themselves as a moral community. Despite parallels in organization and content between la ronda and sharing time as described in U.S. literature, there are important cross-cultural differences that also are discussed as and interpreted here.

Copyright American Anthropological Association Sep 2001

Type of qualitative research _____

4. Shirin, A. D, & Kreimeyer, K. H. (2001). The role of interpreters in inclusive classrooms. *American Annals of the Deaf, 146*(4), 355-365.

A qualitative 3-year study followed three deaf interpreters in an inclusive school. Results of interviews indicated that, in addition to sign interpreting, the interpreters clarified teacher directions, facilitated peer interaction, tutored the deaf children, and kept teachers and special educators informed of the deaf children's progress. Differences in perception of the interpreter's role were also found. (Contains references.) (This abstract was modified slightly.)

Type of qualitative research _____

Checking What You Know

Which type of qualitative research appears to have been conducted by the following examples? The answer may be used more than once. Some answers may not be used at all. Write the qualitative approach on the line provided next to each description.

a.   Case study
b.   Ethnography
c.   Ethology
d.   Ethnomethodology
e.   Grounded theory
f.   Phenomenology
g.   Symbolic interaction

1.   Janet examined Mr. B's 11th grade chemistry class and described the characteristics of the class and the implementation of the new state curriculum in the class setting. _____

2.   Rich examined observational data, videotaped lessons, and interviews with parents, teachers, students, and the public in both Japan and the United States and addressed comparisons between the countries regarding hands-on experiences in the science curriculum. _____

3.   Tess is interested in the lives of children growing up in group homes for abandoned children. She videos their living setting, interviews them, and holds focus groups with the students so they can share their perspectives of growing up so Tess can better understand their experiences.

     _____

4.   Lucia investigated life at the Metropolitan Opera by observing the members for a year and interviewing them as they were available. She writes about the culture of the Met.

     _____

5.   Many states have Professional Development School initiatives but PDS appears very different depending upon the site where you examine it. Jaci examines how PDS 'works' at a local elementary school. _____

6.   Camelia studies the experience of Emotionally Behaviorally Disordered children who are fully included in a middle school setting by interviewing and observing them and analyzing their journals to better understand their school experiences. _____

7.   Linda is conducting a qualitative study of Teach for America. She studies the program through observations and interviews, and spends time in the school with three women placed in a one-year appointment with the program. The focus of her work is to understand the program from a site in which it has been implemented. _____

8.   Warren's work addresses the development of a theory of community reaction to school consolidation. He started with a few assumptions and has revised those assumptions as he has been informed by the data. _____

9.   David is concerned about the struggling readers in his third grade class. He perceives that they may not be reading enough. He poses the question, "What will the impact of more opportunities to successfully engage with text have on the struggling readers in my classroom?"

     _____

Practicing the Tasks

Task 8 in your text requires you to apply the six steps of qualitative research to develop a plan for your own qualitative research study.

Given the article, Hogan, J., & Corey, C. (2001). Viewing classrooms as cultural contexts for fostering scientific literacy. *Anthropology and Education Quarterly, 32*(2), 214-231, answer the following questions to practice aspects of Task 8.

1. What is the research topic of the study?

    _____
    _____
    _____
    _____

2. a. Describe the related literature presented in the article.

        _____
        _____
        _____
        _____
        _____

    b. How does the related research appear to have influenced the study?

        _____
        _____
        _____
        _____

3. How were the participants chosen?

    _____
    _____
    _____
    _____

4. How were data gathered?

    _____
    _____
    _____
    _____

5. Does the author provide information about how the data were analyzed? If so, briefly describe.

    _____
    _____
    _____
    _____

6. Describe the report. (For example, is this report narrative in nature? Is it written in the first person? Does it integrate the data in a form to the reader to support the conclusions drawn from the data?)

    _____
    _____
    _____
    _____

7. Given the description and characteristics presented in Chapter 14 of your text, in your opinion, is this a qualitative study? Why or why not?

    _____
    _____
    _____

Test-Like Event

Circle the best answer in each item below.

1. The type of qualitative research that asks the key question, "How do people construct meanings and shared perspectives by interacting with others?" is a

    a. case study.
    b. phenomenology.
    c. symbolic interaction.
    d. ethnomethodology.

2. Kendra's study addresses the role of childhood informal sport in Japanese, Russian, and the United States culture. Her work might best be categorized as which of the following?

    a. Case study
    b. Phenomenology
    c. Ethology
    d. Ethnography

3. Sherri is planning a qualitative study regarding intermediate mathematics classrooms. Of the following, which is the most likely primary data source for her study?

    a. Standardized test scores
    b. Instructional materials published by a textbook company.
    c. Observations of an intermediate class using manipulatives.
    d. A large-scale teacher survey that addresses how teachers use manipulatives.

4. Which of the following best illustrates data collection for a qualitative study that addresses computer-based technology usage?

    a. Gerald randomly selects 150 participants to answer a questionnaire on technology.
    b. Pauline uses test scores on a teacher-made test to assess computer-based technology skills.
    c. Arnold interviews children and parents about their use of technology for instruction in the home.
    d. Helga gives teachers an attitude survey on which they report willingness to use computer technologies in their classrooms.

5. After reading a peer-reviewed published report about three teachers' struggles working with non-native English speaking children in a rural school setting, Francis, also a teacher who works with non-native speakers, stated, "This isn't what working with these kids is like. This study is wrong!" The reason for Francis's statement is likely that the

    a. context of the study is different than the context Francis is familiar with.
    b. researcher did not collect accurate or valid data in his work.
    c. reliability of the data collection techniques the researcher used is suspect.
    d. researcher did not have enough participants to interpret their experience.

6. According to your text, regarding ethics one difference between quantitative and qualitative research is that

    a. qualitative research does not undergo IRB reviews.
    b. fully informed consent is easier in quantitative studies.
    c. confidentiality is not possible in qualitative research.
    d. research ethics only apply to quantitative researchers.

7. Adria is concerned with the stability of her data. This concern relates directly to which of the following validity criteria?

    a. Credibility
    b. Transferability
    c. Dependability
    d. Confirmability

8. Gretchen is a qualitative researcher concerned with the validity or trustworthiness of her data and findings. By addressing the objectivity and neutrality of her data, she is addressing which of the following characteristics of trustworthiness?

    a. Credibility
    b. Transferability
    c. Dependability
    d. Confirmability

9. When compared to quantitative reports, qualitative research reports are

    a. more objective.
    b. less interpretive.
    c. less biased.
    d. more reflexive.

10. Triangulation is a strategy that most directly affects the validity of the study through

    a. Credibility
    b. Transferability
    c. Dependability
    d. Confirmability

11. Tobari is a qualitative researcher studying the ways in which discussion is used as a teaching tool. He has identified his topic and conducted a review of the literature. According to your text, what is likely Tobari's next step in the research process?

    a. Collect data
    b. Select participants
    c. Analyze his findings
    d. Evaluate the research

Companion Website

For more practice on becoming competent in this chapter's objectives, go to the Companion Website that accompanies this text at www.prenhall.com/gay. This site includes:

Objectives with links to:
- more multiple-choice questions in Practice Quiz
- Applying What You Know essay questions
- relevant Web sites

Custom modules to help you:
- calculate statistical tests (see "Calculating Statistical Tests")
- do research (see "Research Tools and Tips")
- practice analyzing quantitative data (see "Analyzing Quantitative Data")
- practice analyzing qualitative data (see "Analyzing Qualitative Data")
- practice evaluating published articles (see "Evaluating Articles")

Viewing Classrooms as Cultural Contexts for Fostering Scientific Literacy
Kathleen Hogan
Catherine Corey
Institute of Ecosystem Studies

This article explores the sociocultural dynamics within an urban fifth grade science classroom in which we were teacher-researchers. We draw fine-grained portraits of our attempts to emulate the ideals of the collective culture of science within the classroom, and how students sought to reframe those practices. We argue that it is useful to think about students' approach to and deviations from the norms of scientific practices in terms of their contextual resources, interactive norms, and school-based cultural perspectives, rather than simply in terms of their cognitive development level.

Introduction

Educators on the leading edge of school reform over the past decade have become increasingly committed to shaping classroom work to mirror the authentic activities of scholarly disciplines (e.g., McGilly 1994; Schoenfeld 1999). Participating in the "ordinary practices" (Brown et al. 1989:34) of a scholarly community entails more than engaging in certain types of activities, however-it requires adopting a community's norms and ways of thinking, talking, and acting (Gee 1990). The notion is that adopting the culture of a scholarly discipline will enable students to acquire and use its tools (e.g., knowledge) more contextually and effectively.

Creating a classroom culture akin to the culture of disciplinary scholars is a complex endeavor. There are potentially vast differences between students and professionals within a discipline, including knowledge, age, experience, goals, motivations, rewards, and sometimes race and social class. Also, the school community itself is the predominant community of practice in which students participate when in school (Lave and Wenger 1991). Thus, learning in school is infused with schoolbased norms such as concern with reproducing rather than creating knowledge, or with getting better grades on tests than one's peers rather than excelling in performances that would be recognized as authentic by practitioners of the focal discipline.

Difficulties can also arise when the ideal norms and practices of a particular discipline that teachers are expected to teach are somewhat foreign to students' everyday practices. Sense-making in science, for instance, can differ from everyday sense-making according to what thinkers perceive to be problematic, their goals and methods for generating knowledge, their standards and processes for assessing the validity and quality of knowledge, and the structure of the resultant knowledge, with everyday knowledge structures being less internally consistent than the abstract conceptual frameworks of science (Reif and Larkin 1991). Science also has particular social conventions and modes of discourse and exchange through which knowledge claims are collectively generated and sanctioned, that differ from social interactions in everyday life (Hawkins and Pea 1987). Science education, then, can be a cross-cultural experience not only for racial and linguistic minorities who are underrepresented in professional science (Atwater 1994; Lee and Fradd 1998; Pomeroy 1994), but also for students within the demographic mainstream of our society, because everyday subcultures of peers and family differ from the subculture of science (Aikenhead 1996; Costa 1995).

Science education can thus be considered a process of enculturation that takes students beyond the boundaries of their own experiences to become familiar with new explanatory systems, ways of using language, and styles of developing knowledge (Driver et al. 1994). This is not a type of learning that happens spontaneously, but rather is an example of difficult learning that requires assistance to achieve. Therefore, science teachers are pivotal players in helping students appropriate the cultural practices of science. This study documents, however, how difficult it can be for even epistemologically savvy teachers to create the right conditions for inducting students into modes of scientific practice.

Reprinted courtesy of the American Anthropological Association from Anthropology and Education Quarterly 32(2): 214-233. Not for further reproduction.

Defining Norms for a Classroom Community of Scientists: Science as a Collective Endeavor

This article reports on our experiences and observations during a year in which we were guest science teacher-researchers within a classroom of fifth graders in an urban school. Our goal was to examine, in collaboration with the students' regular teacher, what happens as teachers work to create a scientific culture in their classrooms. This is a challenge being taken up by teachers across the United States in response to new science education standards.

We chose to emphasize one theme that pervades the National Science Education Standards (National Research Council 1995), namely a view of science as a collective endeavor. By emphasizing how science is constructed through argumentation and exchange among scientists, the standards reflect contemporary views of the nature of science that reject positivist accounts of science as a set of objective procedures carried out by lone researchers. For instance, studies of scientists at work in their labs (e.g., Pickering 1995; Traweek 1988) reveal that societal and individual values, personal relationships, social status, tactics of persuasion, and local contingencies of the research context each play a role in scientific productivity.

Our work was further informed by philosophers of science who take a contextual view of science (e.g., Longino 1990) by advocating that scientific methodology must be understood as a collection of social rather than individual processes. They depict scientific reasoning as a practice that takes place in participatory contexts and is evaluated with respect to particular goals, rather than as a disembodied set of computational rules. From this perspective, science progresses to the extent to which a scientific community maintains a critical, transformative dialogue that minimizes individual scientists' subjectivities in favor of the collective values of the whole community (Cole 1992; Longino 1990). This is not to claim that science is an objective reflection of the nature of phenomena but, rather, that it is a form of social knowledge that is collectively, rather than individually, specified.

Shaping a Composite Culture

Although it is necessary for teachers to take the step of embracing a particular epistemological perspective on the nature of scientific knowledge and its development, this is not in itself sufficient for guiding science teaching practices. Teachers must create a pedagogical package that reflects not just a philosophy of science, but also a philosophy of education, and which is adapted to the situational constraints of classroom life.

Teachers make pedagogical choices that support and constrain students' experiences of science, while the discipline of science in turn influences what is possible and desirable for a teacher to enact pedagogically. The teacher selects both scientific and pedagogical ideals to present to students (see figure 1). The term "composite culture" represents the classroom culture of science that students actually experience, which is a mixture of ideals of professional science practice (e.g., commitment to rigor in collecting and analyzing data; awareness of the influence of personal frameworks on data interpretation; ability to change prior ideas in light of new evidence or compelling alternative interpretations; integrity in collaborating, critiquing, and other sociointellectual activities) and pedagogical ideals (e.g., belief in learning science through interacting with natural phenomena and with people; attention to the social, emotional, and intellectual growth of each child; balancing student self-direction with teacher guidance via scaffolding to new planes of experience), as filtered through the realities of classroom life and scientific practice. An important point is that it is not the actual culture of professional science, but the composite culture that mediates students' experiences as science learners. Finally, students' perspectives feed back into shaping the composite culture of science in the classroom.

In this article, we focus primarily on tensions created and negotiated in the space traversed by the arrows between "Composite Culture" and "Students' Experiences and Perspectives" in Figure 1.

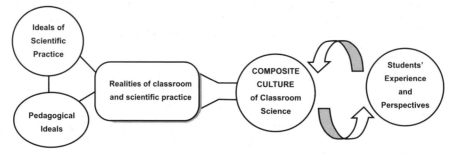

Figure 1

Study Overview

We depict a classroom culture by discerning the participants' collective sense of what is fair, desirable, and valuable in relation to the scientific practices being learned. The context for our analysis is four vignettes that portray how students approached four phases of doing a science project in the domain of ecology: achieving consensus on an experimental design, doing peer reviews, sharing responsibility for maintaining a controlled experiment, and interpreting experimental results. We found that students' reactions to and perceptions of these practices often ran counter to the scientific and pedagogical ideals that we were trying to enact. In particular, we call attention to the social and ideological dimensions of the students' engagement in scientific experimentation. We use these data to construct two main arguments. The first is that there is a core conflict between the individualistic culture of schooling to which students are acculturated and the collective nature of science as it was portrayed in our composite culture. The second is that in-depth portrayals such as we construct of the social and cultural aspects of children's immersion in learning scientific practices, are needed to counter-- balance portrayals of scientific reasoning as a purely in-the-head phenomenon (e.g., Kuhn et al. 1988). Students' reasoning proclivities generate social dynamics that in turn create conflicts, challenges, and dilemmas that teachers must face while guiding students to master new forms of reasoning. By revealing and illuminating these dimensions of classroom practice, we hope to contribute to the improvement of science education through emphasizing the necessity of attending to norms as well as to content when teaching science, and through illustrating the value of taking an anthropological perspective in research on how students learn the practices of a scholarly discipline such as science.

Participants and Setting

This study occurred with one class of fifth graders in a high-poverty urban school in New York state. There were 21 students in the class (eight girls, 13 boys; 16 African American, four Hispanic, and one Euro-- American).1 The teacher had chosen several of the boys to be in his class that year to prevent them from being tracked into special education for problems that he believed were more situational than psychological. The overall academic performance of the class was quite low, and the teacher was under enormous pressure to help the school raise its standing in the state's ranking of schools, based on students' standardized test achievement in reading, writing, and mathematics. Therefore, a large portion of the school day was dedicated to regimented direct instruction, practice, and drill in these subjects, imbued with reminders about tests and performances. When teaching subjects such as social studies, the teacher engaged his students in provocative moral discussions of issues such as religion and crime, so the students were used to sharing their opinions in open discussions and debates during some portion of the school day.

The teacher was an African American male who had taught for a number of years in city schools, and was an integral member of the community within which the school is located, including active leadership in a neighborhood church. For an entire academic year we were guest science teacher-researchers in the teacher's classroom, visiting two to three times per week to lead science activities. Catherine Corey was the primary guest instructor who also contributed to the research by writing daily reflective notes on classroom events and participating in data analysis. Kathleen Hogan was a participant-observer whose main role was to collect video and audio recordings of class sessions, take field notes, interview students, help design instructional activities, and lead the data analysis, but also to interact with students as a teacher during class sessions, especially during small-group work. The classroom teacher was a participant-observer who contributed spontaneously to the teaching of each science class, and contributed to research reflections. He also supervised the students' work on science projects between our visits.

Curriculum

The year-long theme for science lessons was ecology, with most investigations and activities drawn from a curriculum titled Eco-Inquiry (Hogan 1994) that addresses three core ecological topics: food webs, decomposition, and nutrient cycling. During the fall semester, students did basic explorative and comparative studies both inside and out-of-doors, as well as some simple, guided experiments. The curriculum also provides activities and discussion guidelines for explicitly addressing with students the nature of science (e.g., who scientists are, what they do, the nature and purpose of their collaborations and other interactions, etc.), and the transformation of their classroom into a research community. Thus, throughout the school year, the nature of science was a pervasive theme along with ecology, although more explicit activities on the nature of science occurred during the fall semester.

In the spring semester, students carried out a long-term experiment on plant growth with various kinds of compost (i.e., decomposed plant material). Controlled experimentation is a core practice of science that a process of national consensus building has determined all scientifically literate citizens should experience and understand (American Association for the Advancement of Science 1993; NRC 1995). Because preadolescence is widely held to be a stage when young people are beginning to consolidate their capacities for more abstract and complex reasoning, science education standards (NRC 1995) recommend that students in grades 5-8 are poised to learn how to design and conduct experiments by identifying and controlling variables, making systematic observations and accurate measurements to gather data, and using evidence to develop descriptions and explanations. We thus chose to focus throughout the spring on the practice of experimentation, given that it is a common component of the science curriculum for this age group. This article focuses on the spring semester.

Data and Analyses

All class sessions were videotaped. Additionally, there were a number of audio recorders in the classroom for recording small group interactions. Both Hogan and the students occasionally roved around the classroom to record informal interviews with students about the group work they were doing. Thus, we recorded both naturalistic and prompted interactions.

All students who returned permission forms (n = 16) also participated in formal interviews near the end of the school year. Interview questions tapped students' reflections on their science experiences, their interpretations of experimental results, and their ways of applying scientific reasoning to a new situation. We also collected written pre- and postdata on students' understanding of ecological concepts, but those data are not presented here.

Analysis procedures combined features of ethnographic microanalysis of interaction (Erickson 1992) with other qualitative data analysis traditions (e.g., Spradley 1980; Strauss and Corbin 1990). All tapes and fieldnotes were logged to create descriptive summaries of class episodes. From this large data base, we identified critical incidents in classroom interactions. We then transcribed those segments and began a process of coding both transcripts and fieldnotes to characterize important themes. In identifying incidents and themes we looked for elements that define group microculture, such as emotional tone, style, and modes; habitual acts; and the content of shared knowledge and behaviors (Fine 1987). Finally, we transcribed and coded student interviews and looked for conflicts and complementarity between students' individual perspectives and their behaviors and contributions during class sessions.

Enacting Science in a Fifth Grade Classroom

The following sections highlight key aspects of students' experiences with scientific inquiry during the spring ecology unit, using illustrative excerpts of classroom dialogue. Some students were more participatory during class discussions, so the excerpts of classroom talk reflect their voices. However, the responses of all students who were interviewed are also presented to broaden the portrayal of student perspectives. Within each of the following sections, we describe our interpretations of students' perspectives as well as our own objectives for their learning, and discuss our attempts to negotiate students' norms and the scientific and classroom norms we chose to emphasize.

"Why We All Got to Agree?" Community Consensus versus a Plant of One's Own

We began the spring ecology unit by introducing a study topic that built on students' prior experiences with and interest in plants, soil, and decomposition by having them examine compost made from leaves from three different locations: Their city, a forest, and a farm. We challenged them to discover whether the different composts would have different nutrient values, and therefore different effects on plants. Students decided that they would present this project as their contribution to the annual schoolwide Family Science Night, and thereby generated a practical purpose for finding out about the nutrient values of different composts: They would invite family guests to plant seeds to take home in cups of whichever compost the class had found to be the most nutritious.

We hoped that students would converge on the idea that an experiment could help them answer the question of which compost is better for plants. We also intended to help them see some advantages of doing one large experiment as a whole class. In addition to the traditional scientific benefits of having multiple replicates of experimental trials when doing an experiment as a whole class, we knew from prior experience that making experimental planning and procedures public and collaborative brings into the open many issues about experimentation that this age group finds problematic.

To see if the idea of experimentally testing composts would emerge from the students, we began with a discussion summarizing the lab in which they had inspected composts from the three locations. The following excerpt begins near the close of that discussion:

> Ms. Corey: We need to think about these three types of compost from the city, from the farm, and from (the forest) where I work. And Jermaine's sense is that they have different types of nutrients in them or different amounts. And how could we figure that out?

Students:	It's more nutritious.
Ms. C:	How do we know that?
S:	Get a nutrient machine.
Ms. C:	A nutrient machine? We could probably, but I don't have one, we can't test for nutrients in that way. What would be a way to indicate how nutritious something is?
Jermaine:	Oh, plant, you could plant seeds in it.
Ms. C:	Tell me more.
Jermaine:	You could plant the same amount of seeds in each one, and if like one grows faster than the other or if one lives more then you know which has more nutrients.
Ms. C:	I like that. (to class), What do you guys think about that?
Class:	Yes.
Jocelyn:	See which is the richest one, because if you plant a seed in there, and one the soils are richer then the plant will grow more and it will produce more seeds. (A discussion continues about what they would have to measure, and how they would need to keep a chart of how fast the plants grow.)
Ms. C:	So Jermaine thinks that compost will have an effect on plant growth. So I think we should test it out. And if you want to do an experiment, then I'm game.
Jermaine:	Yes, we want to do an experiment.
Ms. C:	Okay. So if I wanted to start doing an experiment (she writes "Question" on board, someone reads aloud, "Question"), right, I have to ask a question first. What is that question?

The class then refined a question together, settling on "What type of compost gives off more nutrients for plant growth?" Ms. Corey emphasized that the answer to their question was not one they would find in a book, so they really did have to do their own investigation.

Notice that although students had the general idea of growing seeds in the different composts, it was Ms. Corey who labeled this as doing "an experiment." Also, she led them directly to the first step of experimentation, which is refining a research question. So, although students came up with the basic idea of running a comparative study, Ms. Corey infused certain scientific protocols into their thinking.

Ms. Corey then brought out a box of materials to show students the resources available for setting up their experiments. When the students saw how well prepared we were to help them plan an experiment, some got suspicious about whose idea it really was to do an experiment. Aisha asked, "You knew we were going to do this experiment, didn't you?" Ms. Corey responded, "I did not ask Jermaine, I did not plant Jermaine in the audience to say that. I just assumed you guys would be thinking along these lines, so I brought everything I could think of and put it in a box."

Ms. Corey's response was an honest portrayal of our hope that students would come up with the idea of an experiment on their own. Students seemed comfortable with her explanation for the time being. However, once we proposed that the whole class should collaborate on one experiment by all addressing the same research question and agreeing to follow the same methods, a crack of dissention arose. Jermaine, the boy who had initially suggested the idea of an experiment, made the following comment, which was followed by Ms. Corey's rationale for why everyone should use the same procedures:

Jemaine:	What about we start our own project at home?
Ms. C:	Let's say, if we want to answer that question as a class (she points to the research question written on the board), is your home going to be exactly the same as the classroom?
D'wan:	Yes.
Ms. C:	D'wan, you know better.

Mr. Wilson:	(jokingly referring to D'wan's frequent after-school stays), He lives in the classroom. He lives right here. (Everyone, including D'wan, laughs.)
Ms. C:	So we also have to think about a fair test; if we want to do this to get a fair answer we have to do things fairly, which means you have to do things very much the same.
Makeeta:	How do we set up a fair test?
Ms. C:	So, Makeeta, you need to make it a fair test. If we want to test which type of compost grows plants the best, set up a fair test.
Makeeta:	Grow them at home.
Ms. C:	What are you comparing then? (Makeeta elaborates, inaudible.)
Jermaine:	That will still be a fair test.
D'wan:	No, it's not the same climate at home.
Ms. C:	So let's say you put Compost A in one cup, Compost B in another cup, and Compost C in a third cup and you grow the exact same seed under the exact same conditions, what variables are you testing?
Roland:	The different types of compost.
Ms. C:	That's exactly right. You're testing the different types of compost. That is the key, and that's what I think is a fair test; you're keeping everything the same and only changing one thing, and that is this type of compost. You're only changing the type of compost.

Ms. Corey took it as a given that all of the students would study the one question they had refined as a class, and thus her points about why they would not have a "fair test" (a notion the students had worked with in the fall) if people grew plants in different home conditions were related to the assumption that they would test one variable, which was compost. It was not clear at first whether Jermaine and Makeeta were not interested in the compost question itself, whether they did not accept the idea that it was necessary to control all other variables in order to answer the question, or whether they had some other concern, such as a reluctance to collaborate and share plant nurturing responsibilities with their classmates. But they were not alone in their concerns. Throughout the period, several other students brought up the idea of taking plants home to study. For instance, Dyrell said: "I think that each group, we should take one and mark it, and one of them take it home and water it, so one group take A home, one group take B home." (We had labeled the three composts as Types A, B, and C.) Interestingly, other students started to take on the teacher's voice and position about testing only one variable at a time. In response to Dyrell's comment, D'wan said, "We should take nothing home."

These tensions persisted as the experiment planning sessions progressed. For instance, in the following exchange, Makeeta brought up the idea of a control plant. At first, Ms. Corey was excited that Makeeta mentioned an important part of experimental design that they had learned about in the fall, but that had not yet emerged in the context of the compost experiment. But Makeeta's notion of a control plant was quite different from ours; she saw the control plant as somewhat of an extra plant, and thus one that perhaps she could take home.

Makeeta:	What about controls?
Ms. C:	Ahh, Miss Makeeta has a revelation, let her speak. (Makeeta smiles.)
Makeeta:	I was gonna say, if we all have our own control, one cup—
Ms. C:	Wait a minute, some of us don't know what a control is.
D'wan:	The control is what you don't do anything to. (Other students chime in to elaborate on this point.)
Ms. C:	So tell me how to set up a control cup. Makeeta thinks we should have a control, and remember we did that for the rest of our experiments, and maybe we should do that for this one, too. But I don't know how to set up the control.
Makeeta:	Okay, I think we all should have a control. Just put that in it, and we all bring our control cup home and see which one grows better. (Pandemonium erupts, as students speak at once in reaction against Makeeta's suggestion.)

Ms. C:	Shhh. Makeeta?
Makeeta:	We all should have our own control cup, bring it home, water it twice a week, and if one house is warmer than another house—(Students are still talking over her, so she pauses until others quiet down.)
Ms. C:	There's someone over here who is dying to disagree with you, so when you're finished Shalone will have a reply.
Makeeta:	Ummm, I think we should all take them home, water them twice a week, and if it grows, we'll know it only grows under certain conditions.
Ms. C:	So you think we should leave all of the treatment plants here and take the control plants home?
Shalone:	I don't think that's a fair test because this school is kind of cool, kind of cold in here and at home it might be hot.
Makeeta:	We always have a fair test, we should have an *unfair* test to see what happens in other people's houses.
Ms. C:	But if you don't have a fair test, how can you make any conclusions?
Makeeta:	Go to one person's house, and that conditions, we all know that's the growing condition.
Ms. Hogan:	How about we do that, too, and that will be a second experiment. Everybody will have a cup to take home, and then bring them back and compare them, and that will test your idea, which is which condition is the best, and that will be a second experiment.
Makeeta:	But without any compost.
Ms. H:	Yeah, without any compost.
Ms. C:	We'll have one control in the classroom, and one control that you bring home. Okay, is that a good compromise? (There is general agreement and affirmative head shaking, and the students ask Ms. Corey to take a plant home, too.)

So in response to Makeeta's and others' interests in doing an "unfair test," we introduced the compromise that they could also do an experiment with their own plants at home. Ms. Corey summarized by saying: "I'd like to get this experiment up and running so that you have some practice in how to set up an experiment so that if later you'd like to do one on your own, perhaps bring something home, or try a different method, then you'll know how to set up an experiment, because you've done it before." Thus we blended our agenda of focusing students on a common experiment with the desires of some of the students to do their own plant investigations at home.

Later, however, it became clear that it was not so much that Makeeta was anxious to pursue alternative questions at home, but rather that she wanted a plant to call her own:

Makeeta:	Are we going to have different controls, am I going to have my own control cup?
Jermaine:	Everybody's control cup is gonna be the same.
Makeeta:	I know, but will I have my own control cup?
Ms. C.:	Right, everyone will get their own control cup. And we'll talk about why it's good to have a bunch of control cups.

It is very common for students to want their own materials to work with during hands-on experiments, but when the materials are living things, young students' possessiveness takes on a particularly urgent edge. Something akin to "biophilia," a term coined to describe humans' seemingly innate affinity for other living things (Kellert and Wilson 1993), emerges as students make very personal connections with the plants or animals they are nurturing and observing. Our students expressed this affinity not just when planning their experiment, but throughout the experiment while caring for their plants. For instance, they could recount dramas and stories about the history and struggles of each plant they were growing, as well as who had done what to which plant. One boy, Malik, discarded the sterile labels of "Plants A, B, and C" by naming his three plants "Alpo," "Bobo," and "Coco." The plants were much more than experimental subjects to these students.

Recognizing students' desire to nurture their own plants, we introduced the idea that each person could care for their own plants within the classroom, rather than sharing plants as a group, so long as everyone followed the same procedures. This was in response not just to the desire of students like Makeeta to take care of their own plants, but also to hints that most students did not relish the idea of working together. Ms. Corey summarized our position: "So even if Alphonse just wants to do one cup and he just wants to work by himself, his cup will still have to be the same amount of seeds, the same type of layering in the cup as those who work in groups, so the experimental design still needs to be the same no matter if you want to work by yourself or work in a group." We wanted to maintain the requirement of sticking to a common experimental design so that later students would be able to see trends in a large data set.

We told students that they could choose whether to manage a complete replicate of plants as a group, or each have their own set of four plants. At first, only about half of the class decided to work in groups, and about half alone, but by planting day, all but a few of the students had decided to join groups. Interestingly, by the end of the experiment only one of the students who was interviewed had a sense that the reason we wanted the class to grow so many replicates of plants in each type of compost was so they could distinguish flukes from trends in the final results. D'wan said that many plants were needed so that if only one grown in a certain kind of compost died, then they would know that something was wrong with that plant, but if all of the plants grown in that type of compost died, then it was probably due to the compost. But when others were asked why we grew so many plants, two students said they did not know, and four said in case some of them died, got spilled, or tangled up, or someone made a mistake. Four others said that it was so that everyone could have their own plants to water and measure, and two saw it as kind of a contest to prove which group was better at taking care of plants.

In the final interview, students also responded to the question: "Would you have liked to keep some of the class experiment plants at home, or have each student do their own experiments at home or at school, instead of doing one big experiment in school?" Only three students still felt by the end of the experiment that it would have been better to do the whole thing at home. One of them just liked the idea of taking care of plants at home, one liked the idea of working on his own question, and the third, Makeeta, said that even if doing the experiment at home was not a fair test, it would be more interesting. Yet she also added that if students did the experiment at home, they should still pool their data to find out which compost was the best for plants, revealing that controlling all variables still did not seem necessary to her for drawing valid conclusions. The rationales of students who did support the whole-class experiment approach ranged from the need to keep conditions controlled, to the belief that plants would get better care at school than at home, to the advantage of having many minds focused on the same thing so that "nothing goes wrong," to the danger of getting mixed up if 21 different people all pursued their own questions. Thus, simmering beneath the surface of our class activities was a wide range of student perspectives on experimental design, some of which matched and some of which differed from our own.

Summary interpretations. The first row of Table 1 summarizes the scientific practice we were emphasizing during class sessions recounted in the preceding vignette, collaborative controlled experimentation, along with our pedagogical rationale and the students' reactions and perspectives. We had anticipated several educational benefits of having students design and do an experiment as a whole-class community, including that it would provide social support for tackling challenging cognitive work. However, we had not anticipated students' resistance to doing a common experiment.

The tensions that arose seemed to be rooted in a conflict between our long-range purposes as teachers and the students' immediate goals. We wanted the students to settle on a common design for technical as well as pedagogical reasons, knowing, for instance, that they would be able to draw more solid conclusions from multiple replicates of an experiment. However, technical issues were moot to the students in the face of compelling social and personal issues such as assuring individual ownership of plants and procedures. The students' moves to preserve their autonomy make sense on several levels, from personal-the desire to nurture a living thing of their own-to societal; traditional American school culture that promotes individual achievement and competition over a commitment to common progress (Jackson 1990; Sizer 1984). Although there certainly are strong elements of individualism within scientific culture as well, the desire to answer increasingly complex questions compels scientists to collaborate, often across disciplines, to plan and do their research (Goldenfeld and Kadanoff 1999). We were trying to emulate these collaborative practices of professional science in the classroom (as adapted within our composite culture to the comparatively artificial conditions of 21 people planning a simple experiment together), yet students understandably did not share anything similar to scientists' goals and motivations for collaborating.

Interpreting students' behaviors while learning science in terms of contrasts between their own and scientists' social and cultural contexts provides an alternative to traditional cognitive explanations (Kuhn et al. 1988) of students' difficulties with designing controlled experiments. Students such as Jermaine and Makeeta arguably understood how and even why to do controlled experiments, but they sought to reframe this practice, such as in terms of an "unfair test," to suit their personal needs and preferences. What counts as appropriate action depends on the norms and practices of a cultural group. Although we were promoting the norms of the macroculture of science that stem from scientists' commitments to theory development, students were acting sensibly in ways consistent with personal preferences and school-based norms for individual achievement and ownership. They were not being motivated to collaborate, as scientists are, by enhanced potential for making significant contributions to a disciplinary canon.

Peer Review: The Dreaded Dimension of Collaboration

Mr. Wilson had warned us that his students did not like peer reviews, which they had experienced primarily in writing workshops. They tended to dwell on the weaknesses in one another's work, so there was much anxiety and little trust between them.

Table 1

Summary of Themes from Classroom Vignettes

Scientific Practice Introduced to Students	Pedagogical Rationale	Student's Reactions and Perspectives
Collaboratively designing controlled experiment	To create a common focus and forum for working through the technical aspects of experimental design and to set up a need for ongoing interchange, sharing, and collaborative engagement	• Resistance to all participating in one experiment; multiple replicates not necessary except as back-ups or to give people their own plants • Desire to do an "unfair" test in which "controls" can be used flexibly • Preference to work alone, have own plants, not be accountable to one another
Engaging in peer review	To provide an opportunity for reflecting on study designs, and to give students the experience of strengthening a design based on feedback and pooled ideas	• Resistance to offering positive feedback and constructive criticism • Personal anguish, embarrassment when own design ideas are criticized
Maintaining a fair test	To help students learn that validity of results depends on following a consistent treatment protocol	• Being fair is a moral, not a technical issue • Cannot trust peer collaborators to carry out procedures competently
Pooling data to identify patterns and trends	To provide an opportunity for students to learn to use evidence to make warranted claims	• Focus attention only on own data, not whole class data • Single examples rather than overall trends more convincing • No need to rely on data to draw a conclusion since the correct result can just be demonstrated instead of tested • Confirming one's prediction is paramount

Anticipating the potential for peer review to be a negative experience for the students, yet still wanting to introduce the practice of peer review as central to doing science and as something that perhaps we could help students learn to do constructively, we decided to ask the students to look over each others' initial experiment plans to pick out one good idea from a peer's plans. Ms. Corey told them that she would make a list of all the good ideas on the board, and from that the class could construct a common experiment plan.

However, while we walked around the room during the peer review session, we noticed that many students were focusing on the weaknesses in others' plans. When we brought this to their attention, they pointed out that Ms. Corey had mentioned that scientists also look for things that could be better about another scientists' work. Indeed, they were calling us on our alteration of scientific norms for classroom purposes (i.e., the composite culture). Ms. Corey responded that although scientists point out both strengths and weaknesses during peer reviews, for our purposes of planning an experiment we only needed to work with good ideas. She continued:

> Ms. C: So I want to get an idea from people what they decided was the best point on the review. (She uncaps a marker, ready to write their ideas on a sheet on the board.) Jermaine, we don't have to have names, but in the proposal that you were reviewing, what was that person's best idea?
>
> Jermaine: That, ummm, I didn't really find one.
>
> Ms. C: So did you do the peer review, did you think about that person's proposal and what you thought was a good idea from the proposal?
>
> Jermaine: Yeah, most of the things that she had I disagreed with.

At this point Mr. Wilson intervened to ask Jermaine what made it a weak proposal, reluctant to let such a blanket dismissal of another student's work stand unsupported. This opened a floodgate of specific criticisms. Jermaine said that the proposal he reviewed was disorganized, not specific enough, used the term "radishes" instead of "radish seeds," and listed aluminum trays rather than the plastic cups which Ms. Corey had suggested they use as plant containers. Although both Mr. Wilson and Ms. Corey challenged Jermaine on some of his points and tried to alter the tone of his comments to be more constructive, the overall effect was a complete intellectual shredding of another student's proposal. The effect on Jermaine's unfortunate peer, Jocelyn, was clear. When Ms. Corey moved on with the comment, "So let's hear from some people who do have some good things to share," Jocelyn grabbed her paper back from Jermaine, put it into her folder, shut the folder, and began doodling, seeming to build a wall around herself for the rest of the period. Not only was Jocelyn publicly humiliated during peer review, but Jermaine also experienced disapproval from the adults for being negative when the directions were to be positive.

Summary interpretations. The second row of Table 1 summarizes the themes from this vignette. We had pedagogical and technical reasons for introducing peer review, just as we did when introducing collaborative experiment planning. We hoped to distribute the intellectual burden for experimental design across all class members, while creating an opportunity for them to learn from one another rather than only from an adult authority. We also hoped that the process of peer review would yield an experiment design that would help students successfully answer their research question. But once again, social issues came to the forefront as more salient to the students than our educational objectives.

The students' moves to point out the weaknesses rather than strengths of their peers' work make sense in light of traditions that are common in American schools. For instance, their norms for peer critique could stem from traditional school evaluation practices, such as norm-referenced assessments, in which one's high grades can depend on classmates' poorer performance (Wiggins 1993). Within such a system, students can come to believe that they can gain a competitive edge by pointing out the weaknesses in others' work.

Ironically, the way that peer review played out in this class was similar to how it can work in professional science where peer criticism can also become a game of one-upmanship, and often is not sensitively conveyed nor easily accepted. Many scientists comply with the unpleasant and demanding task of providing and responding to peer reviews, however, because of their epistemological commitments to how knowledge claims are constituted (Berkenkotter and Huckin 1995; Longino 1990). Unlike scientists, the students did not have larger commitments to making contributions to a disciplinary field, so from their perspective there were no long-term benefits of undergoing the anguish of peer review.

Clearly, our simple idea to have students point out positive aspects of their peers' work was insufficient to change some longstanding norms of interaction. But, in fact, some of Jermaine's points were quite insightful, such as that Jocelyn's plan did not specify adequate control of variables. We faced the dilemma then, of how to protect students' pride while also helping them learn how to craft a strong experiment plan. Our mistake, perhaps, was to include the objective of learning the scientific protocol of peer review, rather than simply giving students our own feedback on their plans. Or perhaps it would have been more effective not to restrict the peer reviews to positive comments, but rather to talk candidly beforehand with students about crafting balanced reviews, discuss why they had a tendency to be harshly critical of one another's work, and solicit their ideas for building trust. The cultural practices of professional science thus cannot be simply transferred to classroom settings, but rather must be adapted to suit the fundamental values that teachers hold, such as protecting students' self-respect, as well as to address the existing norms of the entire classroom community, and indeed of school culture as a whole. Students were understandably confused when we talked only about peer review as a scientific practice, rather than also about the need to attend to classroom norms and purposes.

The Moral Dimensions of Maintaining a Fair Test

Calling an experiment a "fair test" is a common way to introduce elementary school students to the practice of controlling variables. Although we used this terminology, we found that it was as much the moral as the technical aspects of being fair during experimentation that resonated with students.

During whole-class discussions it was clear that students understood why actions such as giving plants different amounts of water would constitute deviations from a fair test. Some students simply seemed not to care whether all planting cups were assembled identically, or if some plants got watered more than others, so long as they had a turn doing hands-on tasks. There were a number of students, however, who were quite concerned with breaches of responsibility for keeping the test fair. They were sure that if something went wrong with the experiment, it would be the fault of one of their peers. As D'wan said, "If one doesn't grow, then we'll know someone screwed up."

Whereas during the experiment planning phase the notion of a fair test was simply a technical design constraint, once the experiment was up and running students regarded keeping things fair as an ethical responsibility of each community member. Students were anxious to point fingers at violators of the experimental design. For instance, as soon as we entered the classroom one morning, Makeeta declared, "We don't have a fair test any more because people didn't water their plants." Another girl immediately chimed in to list the names of the students who did not fulfill their watering obligations. To diffuse the tattle-tale tone of this report, Ms. Corey remarked:

> In real-life experiments, these things happen. And so we try very hard to make it as equal as possible, but sometimes we just can't, so our test isn't as fair as we'd like it to be, and it's not as fair as it could have been, but that doesn't mean we should stop trying to water the same amount. We didn't water on Thursday the same amount, but we'll try to get back on task and water them the same amount from now on.

By introducing the idea that human error is a component of doing science, rather than by dwelling on the insinuation that some students were shirking their responsibilities, Ms. Corey sought to keep up students' morale and motivation to continue with the experiment, despite its flaws.

But we did use students' tendencies to think of fairness during experimentation as a moral issue to address a problem with mishandling plants. In their excitement to measure and care for their plants, students often handled them roughly or overwatered them. So we invited students to help us create a poster called "The Plant Speaks Out" by stating how they would want to be treated if they were plants. Appealing to their moral sense of being fair to plants engendered much animated discussion. Their suggestions for how to treat the plants included: "Equal like the other plants." "Like treat me the way you treat other people." "Umm, I would want to be taken care of." "I would say, treat me with respect." "Don't leave the plant where anyone will scare it or kill it." "Don't put me in danger." We used these comments as a springboard for discussing the biological needs of plants. In this way were able to tap into students' moral sensibilities to teach some relevant plant physiology.

Summary interpretations. The third row of Table 1 summarizes the themes from this vignette. Our goal in introducing the practice of maintaining a fair test (i.e., a controlled experiment) was to help students understand the connection between research procedures and the trustworthiness of results. Students did not seem to have a problem understanding the need to keep all variables consistent except for the variable being tested, which in their experiment was the type of compost. However, since maintaining the fair test was a community responsibility, social issues arose around failures of some individuals to fulfill their plant maintenance obligations. What prevented them from keeping variables controlled while actually doing the experiment thus was not limitations in reasoning capacities as other researchers have claimed (e.g., Kuhn et al. 1988), but rather social and motivational issues.

Moral issues regarding personal responsibility and treatment of other living beings resonated with these students and enhanced their learning of technical scientific procedures and information. Scientists, too, develop "a feeling for the organism" (Keller 1983), or an intuitive sensibility for their objects of study. Our observations of students' responsiveness to the affective dimensions of doing science concur with those of educators who have called for infusing humanistic and biocentric attitudes into science education (Solomon and Aikenhead 1994) to make the study of science both more authentic and more appealing to a broader range of students. This movement reflects the perspectives of feminist philosophers of science (e.g., Keller 1985) who propose an alternative vision of science as a practice that builds new forms of understanding through acknowledging humans' connectivity with the world at large. Thus, by exploring interpersonal responsibilities and the needs and rights of study organisms within the context of doing science, students' work was connected to a vision, if not always the practice, of professional science.

"It Turned Out Like I Said!"-The Shameless Link between Predictions and Conclusions, or the Importance of Being Right

When it was time to draw conclusions from the results of the experiment, it became clear that some students had expected a certain result all along, and so the data we gathered were not very interesting or important to them. In fact, from the beginning of the unit, the whole idea of setting up an experiment seemed moot to some students who already had strong ideas about which type of compost would be best for plants. For instance, on the day that students were generating ideas for how to set up an experiment, Alphonse suggested just growing seeds in the one type of compost that they already knew was best:

Ms. C:	Alphonse, what were you saying?
Alphonse:	We could take the compost that will help it grow more and just put it in one cup with the seeds.
Ms. C:	Okay, so you just want to do one, you just want to do one cup.
Alphonse:	Ain't three cups too much?
Ms. C:	By three cups I mean you put Compost A in one cup, Compost B in one cup, and Compost C in one cup.
Alphonse:	(inaudible)
Ms. C:	So you think you should just have one cup with the compost you think is best.
Alphonse:	Yeah, that's the one that makes it grow.
Ms. C:	The one that you predict will help it grow the best.
Alphonse:	Yeah.
Ms. C:	Okay, that's another idea.

Alphonse's approach to doing science was to demonstrate a phenomenon, not to test or explain it. Even in the postinterview, Alphonse and one other student stated that it was silly to have grown so many plants in different composts during the experiment when they only needed to grow a plant in the one compost that they knew would be best.

Although some of the other students had equally strong ideas about which type of compost would "win," they were more inclined than Alphonse to set up an actual test. We introduced the term "predictions" to describe students' opinions about which compost would be better for plants. We also encouraged students to articulate the personal theories underlying their predictions. Many of the students expressed the wellgrounded rationale that compost from sites with more decomposers and other animals would be richer because it would be more broken down and contain more scat.

However, when we sensed that students' ideas were becoming more like predetermined conclusions than predictions, we introduced the notion that a prediction does not have to be right in order to be useful. Ms. Corey stated, "Alright, so we made our predictions, and we're going to revisit them. And when you revisit them you might say, 'Oh, this wasn't right.' But don't erase it. Keep it, because that will help you trace your learning, help you figure out what you thought two or three weeks ago."

Ms. Corey's comment passed without reaction. But once the plants began to grow several weeks later, some students became intent on changing their predictions to match their observations of which plants were growing best, while others flaunted the fact that the plants in the compost they had predicted would be the most nutritious were indeed growing most vigorously. For instance, midway into the experiment, Makeeta and Aisha made it known to anybody whose attention they could get that their Compost B plant was growing best, just as they had predicted. They were proud, and acted as though they were winning a contest. However, as their control plant started to catch up to their plant growing in Compost B, Aisha became concerned that her original prediction might not be supported after all. Here is how she introduced her concern:

I have a question. If we were going to do another project, you know how we always do the predictions and stuff like that, but remember that time when we were writing the pros and cons of each one, I was wondering if next time when we do a project if we could write the things that might, A, B, C or control, write something for each one and why, like a pro or a con.

Ms. Corey did not understand what Aisha was getting at, so she asked her to elaborate, and other students chimed in to try to interpret what Aisha was saying. After some probing, Aisha finally said:

Yeah, but if you could write a prediction for each one, if we were to get one wrong, like the prediction wrong, and you wanted to do it over again or something like that, so if you could write a prediction for each one, and why you liked that prediction better than another one, because someone might like A and B, but they can only pick one.

Aisha wanted to hedge her bets by stating from the beginning some reasons why each of the growing mediums could turn out to be beneficial for plants. Her notion of articulating plausible alternative hypotheses was scientifically sound, but seemed to be motivated primarily by a social and perhaps school-trained need to be right, no matter how the experiment turned out.

On the day the class pooled all of the small groups' data, there was much suspense and anticipation as we averaged numbers and made bar graphs to show the effects of the different types of compost on plant growth. The experience of looking for trends in a large database was new to the students, and they were quite impressed with all of the numbers and charts. Ms. Corey exclaimed proudly: "This is your data, this is real science!" But as Ms. Corey continued to help the students draw conclusions, it became clear that not all students were inclined to base their conclusions on the class data:

Ms. C:	You did it, you measured it, that's all yours, that's all your hard work for the last months, up there for all of us to see. That's our evidence, and it's going to help us decide can we answer the question, which is, which compost helps plants grow best?
S:	B.
Ms. C:	Why do you say that, because when you look at height it's all the same, A, B, and C.
S:	Because the width.
Ms. C:	and…
S:	the color.
Ms. C:	Right. How come you're all so convinced?
Makeeta:	I thought B from the start because there are more nutrients and more animals in the soil.
Ms. C:	But A came from the farm, so they obviously have lots of soil animals, too. But in thinking about why you decided on B after looking on the evidence, why are you convinced of your decision now?
Makeeta:	Because our plants, B grew the best.
Ms. C:	So you're just looking at your observations, or are you looking at the data? Remember, we were supposed to lump all of our plants together. Lets bring them out here and see if our observations match the data.

We then brought out four trays of plants that we had reorganized prior to the start of class. Throughout the experiment, students had kept their own replicates together, but before class we had put all of the treatment A, B, C, and control plants together in separate trays. As soon as students saw the rearranged trays they immediately began searching for their own plants, ignoring the growth patterns that were dramatically visible when the plants were arranged according to treatment type. Clearly, whereas we were seeing the plants as clusters of data points, the students were seeing them as individual entities that they had nurtured.

Students' tendencies to pay more attention to the results of their own replicates than to the overall trends in the data was reflected in Makeeta's comment that her conclusion was based on the fact that her own group's plant B had grown the best. Makeeta also stated that she had known from the start how the experiment would turn out because of her knowledge about the origins of the different composts. Later, when Ms. Corey asked the class how they would communicate to their guests at Family Science Night which compost to use, Makeeta said that they would just have to tell them where each compost came from, and they would automatically pick Compost B because it was from a forest. Only after extensive prompting did one of the students suggest that they could present their data to the visitors to inform their choice of composts. Makeeta countered, however, that they should just put one illustrative plant next to the best compost, so that the visitors could see the results fo! r themselves.

Makeeta was not alone in her reasoning. In the postinterviews, when asked, "What would you do to convince another person that using compost to help plants grow was good advice?" eight students said they would just show them plants that had been grown with compost, or tell them to try that type of compost and see for themselves. One said that he would just tell people that he got rich by growing and selling plants grown in compost. Seven of the students did say, however, that they would do a comparative experiment and then show others their data.

In the postinterview we also showed students the final charts and graphs that the class had made, and asked them which compost they thought was best for the plants. Only two students completely disregarded the clear data patterns showing the superior growth, on average, of the plants grown in Compost B. One of them concluded that Compost A was better, and another that the control condition was the best, because those were the plants that were the healthiest in their own groups' replicates. However, several of the students who stated that Compost B was the best also were not basing their conclusions on all of the data. Makeeta emphasized that she knew Compost B was the best because her group's plant B grew the best, even though "for some groups their A or their C was best." Jocelyn said she based her conclusion on the fact that the largest plant in the classroom had been grown in Compost B, even though it was not one of her own group's plants. Only several students said th! at they based their conclusion on the outcome of averaging lots of groups' results, but it so happened that each of them had predicted that B would be the best from the start. Only one student conceded that B was the most nutritious compost given their data, even though he had originally predicted that compost A would be best. Overall, then, although there was fairly widespread (but not unanimous) agreement about the result of the experiment, students had divergent paths by which they had arrived at their personal conclusions.

Summary interpretations. The fourth row of Table 1 summarizes students' reactions to the scientific practice of pooling information to identify patterns in data. We had hoped to engage students in using a broad base of evidence to draw conclusions from experimental results. Instead, the students either found it unnecessary to rely on data at all for making claims, or they preferred to base their conclusions on the outcome of their own or another group's notable single replicate. They dutifully followed along as we pooled the class data, and seemed to understand what our final bar graphs meant. So their mode of interpreting their results did not seem to be because of a cognitive inability to see trends in data, but rather to epistemological perspectives on what counts as support for a knowledge claim.

Some students simply did not see the point in using data to make a claim about which compost was most nutritious for plants. Instead, they preferred to make a logical argument based on where the compost originated, and what factors they believed contribute to the richness of compost from a given locale, such as the presence or absence of animals and decomposers. This tendency has been called "knowing from theory," in contrast to "knowing from data" (Varelas 1996). Although theoretical knowledge is a crucial component of professional scientific practice, and indeed can sometimes blind scientists to alternative approaches or results (Kuhn 1970), the scientific community as a whole is committed to testing theories empirically (Longino 1990). In contrast, some students did not see a need for linking their theories with experimental or observational evidence.

Differences between students' and scientists' approaches to drawing conclusions reflect differences in their epistemological commitments (Hogan and Maglienti in press). Whereas in everyday life, conclusions need only to meet pragmatic criteria suited to immediate purposes (Hawkins and Pea 1987), in science, conclusions must meet the normative standards of an entire disciplinary community. Also, schools place a premium on being right, a norm that could have been the root for students' tendency to treat predictions as predetermined conclusions rather than as something that presented a risk of proving them wrong. Although individual scientists also share what seems to be a basic human need to be right and validated, and also are swayed by their prior theories when interpreting their data, the community of science as a whole recognizes that advancement in understanding can come from disproving hypotheses. The conflicts we observed between students' approach to drawing conclus! ions and the scientific ideals we were trying to promote can be understood in terms of the standards and epistemological commitments that reflect their different communities of practice, a point to which we will return in our concluding remarks.

The Cultural Dynamics of Learning Disciplinary Practices: Reflections and Implications

Four vignettes, drawn from various stages in the process of designing and doing a science experiment, revealed a variety of fifth-grade student perspectives and interactions within the context of the composite culture we created to blend our pedagogical goals and classroom constraints with a view of science as a collective enterprise. In the first vignette, in reaction to our agenda to create a whole-class experiment, students expressed preferences for working on their own, for doing an "unfair" test that would allow them to grow experimental plants at home, and for not considering each set of plants a replicate of a larger experiment. In the second vignette, we found that students tended to provide negative rather than constructive criticism during peer review, which had deleterious effects on those whose work was criticized. In the third vignette, the moral and ethical dimensions of caring for living things and of doing one's part in a collaborative project were clearly! more resonant with students than technical or epistemological motivations for maintaining a controlled experiment. Finally, when it came to drawing conclusions from experimental results in the fourth vignette, students showed a strong desire to confirm their predictions, and regarded their prior ideas and individual plants as a more compelling basis for drawing conclusions than the whole-class data.

Our premise is that although it is legitimate to think of these tendencies in students' scientific reasoning while planning, doing, and interpreting experiments as being rooted in their developmental stage or domain knowledge, it also is helpful to think of them in cultural terms. By regarding science learning, and indeed the practice of science, as extending beyond the cognitive structures of individual minds to include social norms, conventions, beliefs, and values, we see how engaging in a seemingly rational enterprise such as science is imbued with affect and cultural traditions.

The practices of a socioculturally defined group such as scientists or students are based on ideologies that frame how participants speak, think, and act, and therefore different cultural discourses can easily conflict with one another (Gee 1990). Appropriating new discourses and cultural practices can thus be more or less difficult depending on the ideological distance between one's own perspectives and those that are inherent in a new discourse.

We attribute our students' reactions to using some of the sense-making tools of science, as modified and presented within the composite culture of the classroom, at least in part to conflicts between individualistic-- oriented ideologies of school to which students are firmly acculturated, and the collective-oriented ideologies of the scientific community we chose to emphasize. Although it is impossible to distinguish whether students were reacting most strongly to the scientific ideals we were promoting or to our particular way of packaging them pedagogically, it is clear that students and scientists do science for different purposes and in radically different contexts. For instance, while scientists are acutely aware of the ultimate consequences that adherence to standards for research have for their ongoing participation in a community of practice, students do not have a contextual basis for understanding why certain methods would put them in a better position for maki! ng and defending knowledge claims to a larger community. Their accountability in school is usually only to a teacher, and often involves reiterating rather than challenging the established canon. The cultural model through which the preadolescents in this study approached scientific tasks seemed more rooted in concerns for personal preferences and positioning than in community accountability. Although at the end of the unit when students participated in pooling their data to draw conclusions, some of them began to see the larger purpose behind doing a collaborative experiment, the authentic context of sharing the fruits of their work with their families was not one that motivated a larger sense of accountability.

On a personal level or in small laboratory groups, scientists also can be competitive and concerned foremost with personal gains, as our students sometimes were (Cunningham and Helms 1998). However, in trying to emulate a scientific community of inquiry in the classroom as recommended by contemporary education frameworks, we adopted the standards of the macroculture rather than the microcultures of science. The constitutive values of science as an institution that establish what counts as acceptable scientific methods can differ from the personal, contextual values that individuals bring to practicing science (Longino 1990). But, ultimately, scientists who want to participate in the larger discourse of their community must accept its constitutive values.

It is the institution of science that has developed and upholds methods such as controls, replication, and peer review, along with norms such as a commitment to producing public knowledge (Brewer and Samarapungavan 1991). These core knowledge-building practices of a professional scientific community are more dispersed in time and space than they are when practiced within a classroom. We can thus view students' divergence from the methods and norms of science in terms of their lack of access to the distributed system and institutional advantages of professional science (Brewer and Samarapungavan 1991). This perspective differs quite radically from mentalistic views of what can make learning science difficult, especially those that emphasize individual students' cognitive roadblocks.

Implications for Classroom Practice and Research

Recognizing the cultural dimensions of both professional and classroom science points to the need to make norms and epistemological standards a more explicit part of science instruction. Although prospective and practicing teachers are becoming increasingly aware of the need to uncover what students do and do not already understand about science concepts as a foundation for instruction, recognition of the importance of finding out what students do and do not value as intellectual standards is not so widespread. As teachers and teacher educators gain this recognition and develop techniques for bringing norms and standards to the surface in classrooms, epistemological growth will become a more common targeted outcome of science instruction, which may be even more valuable to students in the long run than mastering conceptual material or gaining procedural proficiency in science. Researchers, too, can contribute to this effort by doing studies aimed at enhancing our relative! ly thin knowledge base about the range of epistemological perspectives among students of diverse ages and sociocultural backgrounds, and to find out if and how these vary according to the task and social contexts students are within at a given time.

An extremely important tool for airing different values and perspectives on scientific sense-making is classroom discourse. Discourse should be regarded as a science teaching tool whose value is on par with hands-on activities and investigations. Through open, mindful dialogue with students we can gain insight into their cultural and epistemological perspectives, then work toward creating learning situations that give them access to the tools of a specialized community of practice, while respecting the vitality and priorities that they bring to the cross-cultural exchange. Since recitation is still a predominant mode of classroom discourse, teachers, researchers, and teacher educators need to continue to explore the processes and results of alternative modes of discourse in science classrooms.

Finally, this study points to the need to draw teachers' and researchers' attention to the nature of the composite culture that shapes students' experiences of science. The particular aspects of the scientific enterprise that teachers choose to emphasize, and their pedagogical goals and methods, are two major elements of a composite culture that will vary widely across teachers and contexts. The extent to which teachers develop an explicit awareness of the interactions of these dimensions of their classroom culture will determine how easily they will be able to reflect on, adapt, and change them with experience. One of the major issues is how teachers negotiate the space between the composite culture and students' perspectives and capabilities that feed back to shaping that culture. One promising technique for orchestrating these negotiations is instructional scaffolding (Hogan and Pressley 1997), through which teachers diagnose the growing edge of students' capacities, t! hen model, coach, and assist them to reach a new plane of development. However, there are relatively few examples of how skilled teachers carry out instructional scaffolding in whole-class settings, so this is another area in which classroom-based research could greatly enhance our understanding of effective practices.

Conclusion

Our goal was to help students acquire an experiential understanding of the macrocultural ideals of a particular discourse (Gee 1990)science-- that happens to be a powerful one within our society. The time frame for judging the impact of our work with the students may need to extend beyond the one-semester period that we have described here. It is reasonable to expect the process of gaining cultural insights to unfold over years rather than months, whereas we recounted only an early stage in encounters among elements of scientific, classroom, and student cultures. This stage was full of tensions that perhaps would dissipate as teachers refine and adapt their construction of a composite culture, and as students begin to see science as a way of knowing that they can use for particular purposes, while maintaining the ability to critically assess its cultural norms and practices.

Acknowledgments. We thank the National Science Foundation (REC-9805825) and the Mary Flagler Cary Charitable Trust for financial support of this research, the results and conclusions of which reflect solely our own views, and JoEllen Fisherkeller, Kathryn Anderson-Levitt, and several anonymous reviewers for their insightful comments and suggestions on earlier drafts of this article. This article is a contribution to the program of the Institute of Ecosystem Studies.

1. The teacher's name and all students' names are pseudonyms. All of the students who are named and quoted in this article are African American. When a speaker's identity was not discernible on tape, the word "student" is used to denote the speaker.

Kathleen Hogan is an associate scientist, and Catherine Corey is a project coordinator, at the Institute of Ecosystem Studies in Millbrook, New York (hogank@ecostudies.org).

References Cited

Aikenhead, Glen S.

1996 Institute of Ecosystem Studies Science Education: Border Crossing into the Subculture of Science. Studies in Science Education 27:1-52.

American Association for the Advancement of Science

1993 Benchmarks for Science Literacy. New York: Oxford University Press.

Atwater, Mary M.

1994 Research on Cultural Diversity in the Classroom. In Handbook of Research on Science Teaching and Learning. Dorothy L. Gabel, ed. Pp. 558-576. New York: Macmillan.

Berkenkotter, Carol, and Thomas N. Huckin

1995 Genre Knowledge in Disciplinary Communication: Cognition/Culture/Power. Hillsdale, NJ: Erlbaum.

Brewer, William F., and Ala Samarapungavan

1991 Children's Theories vs. Scientific Theories: Differences in Reasoning or Differences in Knowledge? In Cognition and the Symbolic Processes: Applied and Ecological Perspectives. Robert R. Hoffman and David S. Palermo, eds. Pp. 209-232. Hillsdale, NJ: Lawrence Erlbaum Associates.

Brown, John Seeley, Allan Collins, and Paul Duguid

1989 Situated Cognition and the Culture of Learning. Educational Researcher 18(1):32-42.

Cole, Stephen

1992 Making Science: Between Nature and Society. Cambridge, MA: Harvard University Press.

Costa, Victoria B.

1995 When Science is "Another World": Relationships Between Worlds of Family, Friends, School, and Science. Science Education 79(3):313-333.

Cunningham, Christine M., and Jenifer V. Helms

1998 Sociology of Science as a Means to a More Authentic, Inclusive Science Education. Journal of Research in Science Teaching 35(5):483-499.

Driver, Rosalind, Hilary Asoko, John Leach, Eduardo Mortimer, and Philip Scott

1994 Constructing Scientific Knowledge in the Classroom. Educational Researcher 23(7):5-12.

Erickson, Frederick

1992 Ethnographic Microanalysis of Interaction. In The Handbook of Qualitative Research in Education. Margaret D. LeCompte, Wendy L. Millroy, and Judith Preissle, eds. Pp. 201-225. San Diego: Academic Press.

Fine, Gary Alan

1987 With the Boys: Little League Baseball and Preadolescent Culture. Chicago: University of Chicago Press.

Gee, James Paul

1990 Social Linguistics and Literacies: Ideology in Discourses. London: Falmer Press.

Goldenfeld, Nigel, and Leo P. Kadanoff

1999 Simple Lessons from Complexity. Science 284(2 April): 87-89.

Hawkins, Jan, and Roy D. Pea

1987 Tools for Bridging the Cultures of Everyday and Scientific Thinking. Journal of Research in Science Teaching 24(4):291-307.

Hogan, Kathleen

In press Comparing the Epistemological Underpinnings of Students' and Scientists' Reasoning about Conclusions. Journal of Research in Science Teaching.

Hogan, Kathleen, and Mark Maghenti

1994 Eco-Inquiry: A Guide to Ecological Learning Experiences for the Upper Elementary/Middle Grades. Dubuque, Iowa: Kendall/Hunt Publishing Co.

Hogan, Kathleen, and Michael Pressley, eds.

1994 Scaffolding Student Learning: Instructional Approaches and Issues. Cambridge, MA: Brookline Books.

Jackson, Philip W.

1990 Life in Classrooms. New York: Teachers College Press.

Keller, Evelyn F.

 1983 Feeling for the Organism. San Francisco: W. H. Freeman and Co.

 1985 Reflections on Gender and Science. New Haven, CT: Yale University Press.

Kellert, Stephen R., and Edward O. Wilson

 1993 The Biophilia Hypothesis. Washington, DC: Island Press.

Kuhn, Deanna, Eric Amsel, and Michael O'Loughlin

 1988 The Development of Scientific Thinking Skills. San Diego: Academic Press.

Kuhn, Thomas

 1970 The Structure of Scientific Revolutions. 2nd ed. Chicago: University of Chicago Press.

Lave, Jean, and Etienne Wenger

 1991 Situated Learning: Legitimate Peripheral Participation. New York: Cambridge University Press.

Lee, Okhee, and Sandra H. Fradd

 1998 Science for All, Including Students from Non-English-Language Backgrounds. Educational Researcher 27(4):12-21.

Longino, Helen E.

 1990 Science as Social Knowledge: Values and Objectivity in Scientific Inquiry. Princeton: Princeton University Press.

McGilly, Kate, ed.

 1994 Classroom Lessons: Integrating Cognitive Theory and Classroom Practice. Cambridge, MA: MIT Press.

National Research Council

 1995 National Science Education Standards. Washington, DC: National Academy Press.

Pickering, Andrew

 1995 The Mangle of Practice: Time, Agency, & Science. Chicago: University of Chicago Press.

Pomeroy, Deborah

 1994 Science Education and Cultural Diversity: Mapping the Field. Studies in Science Education 24:49-73.

Reif, Frederick, and Jill H. Larkin

 1991 Cognition in Scientific and Everyday Domains: Comparison and Learning Implications. Journal of Research in Science Teaching 28(9):733-760.

Schoenfeld, Alan H.

 1998 Looking Toward the 21st Century: Challenges of Educational Theory and Practice. Educational Researcher 28(7):4-14.

Sizer, Theodore R.

 1984 Horace's Compromise. Boston: Houghton Mifflin.

Solomon, Joan, and Glen Aikenhead, eds.

 1994 STS Education: International Perspectives. New York: Teachers College Press.

Spradley, James P.

 1980 Participant Observation. New York: Harcourt, Brace, Jovanovich.

Strauss, Anselm, and Juliet Corbin

 1990 Basics of Qualitative Research: Grounded Theory Procedures and Techniques. Newbury Park, CA: Sage Publications.

Traweek, Sharon

 1988 Beamtimes and Lifetimes: The World of High Energy Physicists. Cambridge, MA: MIT Press.

Varelas, Maria

 1996 Between Theory and Data in a Seventh-Grade Science Class. Journal of Research in Science Teaching 33(3):229-263.

Wiggins, Grant

 1993 Assessing Student Performance. San Francisco: Jossey-Bass.

Chapter 14 Answers
For Your Own Review
1. (See Figure 14.1)
    Identify research topic
    Review of research
    Selecting participants
    Collecting data
    Analyzing data
    Reporting and interpreting research

2. case study
    ethnography
    ethology
    ethnomethodology
    grounded theory
    phenomenology
    symbolic interaction
    historical research

3. Researchers spend a great deal of time with the participants and are immersed in the setting; Qualitative researchers avoid making premature decisions and remain open to alternative explanations; person to person interactions; data analyzed inductively; reports include detailed clear information and descriptions; informed consent is a critical ethics concern

4. descriptive validity, interpretative validity, theoretical validity, generalizability, evaluative validity for validity and credibility, transferability, confirmability

Checking What You Know

1. a	4. b	7. b
2. c	5. a	8. e
3. f	6. f	9. h

Just for Practice
1. Historical
2. Phenomenology
3. Ethology
4. Case study

Practicing the Tasks
Answers to questions about Hogan, K., & Corey, C. (2001). Viewing classrooms as cultural contexts for fostering scientific literacy. *Anthropology and Education Quarterly, 32*(2), 214-231:

1. The research topic is an examination of contextual scientific thinking in a fifth-grade class. The study might be classified as ethnography or case study. Aspects of several qualitative approaches are apparent.

2. a. The authors use related literature in many ways. They use literature to support the need for their study, to support the methods and curriculum used in the study, to support the data analysis techniques used, and to support their interpretations.

    b. The related literature facilitates a context for the study. The literature also informed analysis and interpretation as well as methodology used by the teachers' interactions with the students.

3. The participants were chosen because they were part of a selected class. Some students were also interviewed and were additionally selected based upon informed consent.

4.   Data sources included field notes, videotape, audiotape, informal interviews that were audiotaped, formal interviews, and additional data included content tests (not included in the analysis).

5.   The data analyses were described as including aspects of several qualitative data analysis traditions, ethnographic microanalysis—it is clear that some constant comparison method and a grounded theory approach were also employed. Contradictions in the data were sought out during analysis.

6.   The report is well written and in the first person and includes examples from the data integrated with interpretation and explanation. All main themes are supported with data and interpretation as well as critique of the processes used to collect data and limitations of the interpretations made.

7.   Yes, this is a qualitative study. It is a real world setting, the data are descriptive, and a holistic approach to the study was employed. The setting is carefully described and details of the data collection and interpretation are included. The meaning of the study is presented in the form of interpretation supported by participant narrative and examples from the data.

Test-Like Event
1. c
2. c
3. c
4. c
5. a
6. b
7. c
8. d
9. d
10. d
11. b

Chapter 15 Qualitative Data Collection

Chapter 15 Objectives

1. Define and state the purpose of qualitative data collection.
2. Identify the sources of qualitative data collection.
3. Identify specific qualitative data collection techniques and how they can be used in a qualitative study.
4. Describe the differences between unstructured and structured interviews.
5. Identify the threats to quality of observations and interview in qualitative research.

Review the Terms

Provide a succinct definition in your own words for each of the following terms.

Fieldwork: _____

_____

Structured Interview: _____

_____

Participant observer:_____

_____

Nonparticipant observer:_____

_____

Unstructured interview: _____

_____

Field notes: _____

_____

Observer bias: _____

_____

Observer effect:_____

_____

Artifacts: _____

_____

For Your Own Review

1. State the three primary qualitative data collection techniques.

   _____   _____   _____

2. List the types of participant observers.

   _____   _____   _____

3. Recall three of the guidelines for interviewing.

   _____
   _____
   _____
   _____

4. Recall three of the guidelines for constructing questionnaires.

   _____
   _____
   _____
   _____

Test-Like Event

1. Doug studies ecology education. His research team is going into the field to observe the characteristics of a summer ecology education program. Before they go, Doug provides them all with a common framework to use when taking their notes. This is referred to as a(n)

   a. protocol.
   b. interaction analysis.
   c. memo.
   d. analysis strategy.

2. Renee is studying the nature of young girls' gymnastics training. She goes to the gym lobby daily for six months and watches the 4 year old girls' practices but does not interact with the girls. Renee is displaying which of the flowing levels of observation?

   a. Nonparticipant observation.
   b. Active participant observation.
   c. Privileged active observation
   d. Passive observation.

3. Debbie is interested in the culture of a very successful high school marching band. She goes to the band's functions and observes. Since as an adult she cannot join the band, she obtains consent to observe and then she becomes a band booster club member to collect additional observational data regarding the band's culture. Debbie is best displaying which form of data collection?

   a. Participant observation
   b. Covert observation
   c. Nonparticipant observation
   d. Stakeholder observation

4. Hanna researches political beliefs of young Americans. She poses as an interested student and attends several Young Republican rallies and observes. Hanna is best illustrating

   a. external observation.
   b. nonparticipant observation.
   c. participant observation .
   d. covert observation.

5. Mike is interviewing teachers regarding their opinions of a new plan to require teachers to take a national competency exam. He audiotapes the interviews and carefully takes notes in the sessions. After, he types the audiotapes verbatim and then reads over them and makes some initial notes to himself. By typing the audiotapes verbatim he is

   a. memoing.
   b. transcribing.
   c. interpreting.
   d. categorizing

6. According to your text there are three main choices for collecting interview data. These include all EXCEPT which of the following?

   a. Take notes during the interview
   b. Write notes after the interview
   c. Audio- or video recording the interview
   d. Take notes before and after the interview

7. As a researcher who studies the strategies teachers use to effectively manage the inclusion of special needs learners within the general education classroom, you were recently observing a seventh grade history class. You noted that the teacher employed a cooperative learning strategy you had not seen before. At the end of class you asked him about the strategy and how effectively it works. In so doing you have illustrated which of the following types of interview?

   a. formal interview.
   b. structured interview.
   c. semi-structured interview.
   d. unstructured interview.

8. As a component of a study of teachers' use of technology in their classrooms. Kevin has participants use a frequency rating in response to how often they use each of a list of types of technologies available for classroom instruction within the district. He follows up on the ratings as part of his interview. The frequency ratings that Kevin employs best illustrate a(n)

   a. informal interview.
   b. semi-structured interview.
   c. a questionnaire.
   d. a structured observation.

9. Kevin sits down with a small group of teachers to discuss their struggles teaching with technology. He allows the conversation to go wherever the teachers take it, occasionally asking questions based upon what they say. This type of interview is best described as

   a. informal.
   b. structured formal.
   c. unstructured.
   d. spontaneous.

10. Bob is conducting a reading intervention in the schools that includes, as one component, the use of vocabulary training. Every time his graduate student Cindy works in the classrooms she finds that teachers spend most of their time on vocabulary training, even at the expense of other aspects of reading instruction. This is likely due to

   a. the halo effect.
   b. observer bias.
   c. observer effect.
   d. response bias.

11. Elaine is interested in a new self-determination training program. She believes the program can help students. She goes to a school that is implementing the program and observes the students' willingness to engage in difficult tasks, a skill taught in the program. She also observes students in schools that have not implemented the program. Given the situation, Elaine must be careful not to introduce

   a. response bias.
   b. observer bias.
   c. observer effect.
   d. negative case effect.

12. Darren studies perceptions of respect of administrative assistants at a small college and would like to interview several veteran staff members. Of the following, the most desirable location for Darren to conduct his interviews is

   a. in his office.
   b. in the campus library.
   c. in the staff offices.
   d. off campus at a coffee shop.

Companion Website

For more practice on becoming competent in this chapter's objectives, go to the Companion Website that accompanies this text at www.prenhall.com/gay. This site includes:

Objectives with links to:
- more multiple-choice questions in "Practice Quiz"
- "Applying What You Know" essay questions
- relevant Web sites

Custom modules to help you:
- calculate statistical tests (see "Calculating Statistical Tests")
- do research (see "Research Tools and Tips")
- practice analyzing quantitative data (see "Analyzing Quantitative Data")
- practice analyzing qualitative data (see "Analyzing Qualitative Data")
- practice evaluating published articles (see "Evaluating Articles")

Chapter 15 Answers
For Your Own Review
1. Observations, interviews, examining records
2. active participant observer, a privileged; active observer; passive observer
3. Listen more, talk less; follow up on what participants say and ask questions; avoid leading questions; don't interrupt; Keep participants focused and ask for concrete details; tolerate silence; don't be judgmental; don't debate with participants
4. Carefully proofread; avoid sloppy presentation; avoid a lengthy questionnaire; don't ask unnecessary questions; use structured items with a variety of possible responses; allow for other comments section; decide how you will track participants

Test-Like Event
1. a
2. a
3. a
4. c
5. b
6. d
7. d
8. c
9. c
10. c
11. a
12. c

Chapter 16 Narrative Research

Chapter 16 Objectives

1. Briefly state the definition and purpose of narrative research.
2. Describe the narrative research process.
3. Describe the different types of narrative research.
4. Describe the key characteristics of narrative research designs.
5. Describe narrative research techniques.

Review the Terms

Provide a succinct definition in your own words for each of the following terms.

Narrative research: _____

_____

Restorying: _____

_____

Narrative analysis:_____

_____

Analysis of narrative: _____

_____

Oral history: _____

_____

For Your Own Review

1. State one trend that has influenced the development of narrative research.

    _____

2. Recall the three steps in the restorying process.

    _____
    _____
    _____

3. Provide three of the key characteristics of narrative research.

    _____   _____   _____

Test-Like Event

1. Which of the following is NOT a type of narrative research?

    a. Oral histories
    b. Person-centered ethnographies
    c. Case study
    d. Narrative interviews

2. Regarding ethical standards, narrative researchers

    a. do not need informed consent.
    b. must undergo IRB review.
    c. generally undergo Category I review.
    d. rely on confidentiality.

3. Narrative research generally relies *primarily* on _____ for data collection.

    a. tests
    b. surveys
    c. existing documents
    d. interviews

4. Which of the following is a discipline that has a history of narrative research?

    a. Psychometrics
    b. Anthropology
    c. Kineseology
    d. Physiology

5. According to your text, of the following which is a trend that has influenced the development of narrative research?

    a. Increased school accountability
    b. Increased desire to understand student feelings
    c. Increased standardized testing
    d. Increased emphasis on teacher knowledge

6. One primary purpose in conducting narrative research is to _____.

    a. solve educational problems.
    b. assist in policy decisions.
    c. increase understanding of important issues.
    d. answer questions about accountability.

7. As a narrative researcher interested in the lives of newly immigrated high school students and the tension between working to help support family and staying in school; you have identified the purpose of your study and the phenomenon to explore. What is your next step?

    a. Pose initial narrative research questions
    b. Describe data collection methods
    c. Describe the researcher's role
    d. Select individuals to learn about the problem

8. As a narrative researcher you have established a relationship with Olivia to better understand the challenges of relearning after a brain injury. What is your next step?

    a. Pose initial questions
    b. Describe the researcher's role
    c. Describe data collection methods
    d. Complete the writing of the narrative account

9. Mimi is a narrative researcher interested in the challenges that LD learners face to navigate middle school. Of the following, who might be the best person to serve as an individual to learn about the problem?

    a. Maureen—an LD student's Mom
    b. Jillian—a first grade teacher
    c. Max—a principal in the middle school
    d. Jason—a middle school LD student

10. Regarding empirical data, narrative researchers _____.

    a. never rely on empirical data.
    b. interpret during data collection.
    c. collect empirical data before entering the field.
    d. use empirical data sparingly after they have left the field.

11. Which of the following is the most typical narrative researcher behavior?

    a. Establish a relationship with an individual.
    b. Comparing two teachers' individual styles.
    c. Collecting data via surveys.
    d. Consulting with stakeholders in the research setting.

12. Which of the following research topics is most conducive to narrative research?

    a. The relationship between increased testing and anxiety.
    b. Differences between boys and girls science knowledge.
    c. The benefits of a school-based intervention for attendance.
    d. The experience of junior year students applying for colleges.

Companion Website

For more practice on becoming competent in this chapter's objectives, go to the Companion Website that accompanies this text at www.prenhall.com/gay. This site includes:

Objectives with links to:
- more multiple-choice questions in "Practice Quiz"
- "Applying What You Know" essay questions
- relevant Web sites

Custom modules to help you:
- calculate statistical tests (see "Calculating Statistical Tests")
- do research (see "Research Tools and Tips")
- practice analyzing quantitative data (see "Analyzing Quantitative Data")
- practice analyzing qualitative data (see "Analyzing Qualitative Data")
- practice evaluating published articles (see "Evaluating Articles")

Chapter 16 Answers
For Your Own Review
1. increased emphasis on teacher reflection, teacher research, action research, and self-study in the past 15 years, increased emphasis on empowering teacher voices in the educational research process through collaborative educational research efforts

2. conducts the interview and transcribes the audio tapes, transcribes the data based upon the key elements that are identified in the story, organizes the story into a chronological sequence

3. focuses on the experiences of individuals, is concerned with the chronology of individual's experiences, focuses on the construction of life stories based on data collected through active interviews, uses restorying as a technique for constructing the narrative account, incorporates context and place in the story, narrative research is a collaborative approach that involves the researcher and the participants in the negotiation of the final text

Test-Like Event
1. c
2. b
3. d
4. b
5. d
6. c
7. d
8. a
9. d
10. b
11. a
12. d

Chapter 17 Ethnographic Research

Chapter 17 Objectives

1.   Briefly define and state the purpose of ethnographic research.
2.   Describe the ethnographic research process.
3.   Identify and describe the different types of ethnographic research.
4.   Describe the key characteristics of ethnographic designs.
5.   Describe ethnographic research techniques.

Review the Terms

Provide a succinct definition in your own words for each of the following terms.

Ethnographic research (ethnography): _____

_____

Culture: _____

_____

Critical ethnography: _____

_____

Ethnographic case study: _____

_____

Realist ethnography: _____

_____

Key informants: _____

_____

For Your Own Review

1. What are the three categories of participant observers?

    _____   _____   _____

2. Your text suggests one strategy to develop initial ethnographic questions. Please describe.

    _____
    _____
    _____
    _____
    _____

3. List primary data collection techniques used in ethnographic research.

    _____
    _____
    _____

Checking What You Know

Given the following scenario, describe how you could approach this study as an ethnographic research study. In a recent publication, several authors set about examining third grade teacher behaviors that relate to academic engagement. In their study they used several methods. Their abstract and reference follows. DO NOT use their study as a guide, but by using their topic area, walk through the steps and procedures addressed in chapter 17 of your text to more fully consider how you might conduct an ethnography. Consider the characteristics of ethnographic research as presented in your text as you think about the research processes you might engage in while conducting such as a study.

Sara E Dolezal, S. E., Welsh, L.M, Pressley, M., & Vincent, M. M. (2003). How nine third-grade teachers motivate student academic engagement. *The Elementary School Journal, 103*(3), 239-269.

Nine grade 3 teachers in 8 Catholic schools were observed and interviewed, and student work was collected to determine how the teachers motivated students. Engagement varied dramatically between some classes, covarying with motivating elements of instruction. Engaging teachers did much to motivate their students and little that might undermine academic motivation. Teachers were classified into 3 levels: low, moderately, and highly engaging. In the 3 classrooms characterized by low engagement, teachers were observed to use many practices that undermined motivation. The 4 moderately engaging teachers used many potentially motivating practices in their classrooms but assigned tasks that were low in difficulty. Teachers in the 2 highly engaging classrooms used many potentially motivating practices and required students to complete tasks that were appropriately, cognitively challenging (i.e., students could do them with some effort).

1. How might you do this study as an active participant observer, a privileged; active observer, or a passive observer. Describe each within the context of this potential study.

2. What steps might you take to gain entrée?

3. What is something you might erroneously do that might undermine rapport?

4. How long might you stay in the site? Justify your answer.

5. Pose some initial ethnographic questions for this study.

6. Include three things you might include in your field notes.

    _____

    _____

    _____

7. Given the vague field note "she welcomed the students to math class" create a detailed field note that might better describe how a third grade teacher might welcome children to math class (be creative!)

    _____

    _____

    _____

    _____

    _____

    _____

    _____

8. Given the study you have described here, what type of ethnographic research does this best match?

    _____

Test-Like Event

1. One commonly cited challenge of ethnographic research is that

    a. the data produced are not meaningful.
    b. the time to conduct such research is often lengthy.
    c. the findings are not accurate.
    d. the researchers are often overqualified.

2. Which of the following is NOT considered a type of ethnography?

    a. Life History
    b. Microethnography
    c. Biography
    d. Ethnographic novel

3. Which of the following is a characteristic of ethnographic research?

    a. Numerical data to show trends.
    b. Laboratory settings to collect data.
    c. Large numbers of participants
    d. Intimate interaction with participants.

4. Kent is doing a study on children's symbolic play. He gains entrée into a preschool classroom and observes the children's play for a month. He comes to the class daily and 'sets up' where he can watch the children and take notes. Kent is acting as which of the following types of participant observer?

    a. Nonparticipant observer
    b. Active participant observer
    c. A privileged; active observer
    d. A passive observer.

5. In qualitative research triangulation refers to

    a. Relying on one data source.
    b. Relying on several data sources.
    c. Creating your own data sources.
    d. Generating themes from your data sources.

6. It is important to write up your field notes

    a. as soon as possible.
    b. after you have had time to reflect.
    c. in complete sentences.
    d. so others may read them.

7. Jottings are used
    a. to augment field notes.
    b. instead of field notes.
    c. for others to confirm your thoughts.
    d. only by passive observers.

8. Your text suggests that there are several guidelines for field notes. Which of the following is NOT a guideline suggested.

    a. Separate description from interpretation and judgment.
    b. Select key informants to follow through the setting.
    c. Gather a variety of information to triangulate.
    d. Keep your own thoughts out of the notes.

9. Jacki is sure that she is not gaining full access to the teachers that she is observing. When they stop talking to one another, or leave the room to go do other tasks. While there may be many reasons why Jacki is having trouble, of the following, one reasonable explanation is that

    a. she is not collecting enough data.
    b. she has not established rapport.
    c. she does not triangulate her data.
    d. she is not conscientious enough.

10. Which of the following is NOT likely an ethnographic research data collection strategy.

    a. Observations
    b. Test Scores
    c. Interviews
    d. Collection of artifacts

11. Which of the following research topics is most likely a study that could be conducted using ethnographic research?

    a. The relationship between allocated school funds and instructional resources.
    b. The difference between higher-SES and lower-SES students' academic achievement scores.
    c. The nature of the middle school transition for children.
    d. The opinions of parents regarding the new school building.

12. Which of the following is a likely characteristic of ethnographic research?

    a. The researcher should control the experimental setting.
    b. The participants should be tested consistently.
    c. The participants are interviewed according to a strict protocol.
    d. The researcher should reflect about his role in the setting.

Companion Website

For more practice on becoming competent in this chapter's objectives, go to the Companion Website that accompanies this text at www.prenhall.com/gay. This site includes:

Objectives with links to:
* more multiple-choice questions in Practice Quiz
* Applying What You Know essay questions
* relevant Web sites

Custom modules to help you:
* calculate statistical tests (see "Calculating Statistical Tests")
* do research (see "Research Tools and Tips")
* practice analyzing quantitative data (see "Analyzing Quantitative Data")
* practice analyzing qualitative data (see "Analyzing Qualitative Data")
* practice evaluating published articles (see "Evaluating Articles")

Chapter 17 Answers
For Your Own Review
1. Active participant observer, passive observer, privileged active observer
2. Use who, what, when, where, why, and tell me a little more about that, to form your initial questions.
3. Participant observation, fieldnotes, interviews, collection of artifacts.

Checking What You Know
1. An active participant observer would likely be one of the teachers him or her self. A privileged active observer might be another teacher known to the classroom, a passive observer would have no instructional role in the classroom but would observe 'from a far' and not as part of the instructional setting.

2. To gain entry, you might already be a teacher in the school, know the school or teachers, and/or you would likely have to establish some credibility, you would likely have to obtain clearances to be in the school—regardless of whether you would be working with the children directly or not. The research site here would be the classrooms of these third grade teachers.

3. In school settings any judgments or comments viewed as judgments will decrease rapport. Further, disrupting the class or instruction by coming in while the teacher is talking, or something like that would surely undermine rapport. If the teacher felt that she was going to be 'ratted out' or talked about that would undermine rapport.

4. This is really unknown. Your text does indicate that it is often good to stay a cycle—in this case it might be a semester or a term or a school year.

5. Your answer may vary from the suggestions presented here and still be correct. Questions might include; "what words does the teacher use that might make a student interested? What words does the teacher use that students don't seem to react well to" Why would the teacher include this part of the lesson. Who is the teacher's words and actions directed to.

6. Your answer will vary but might include, a description of the room, a description of student behaviors, a description of teacher behavior or words she used, a description of the mood of the classroom, the activities planned or executed as part of the lesson, etc!

7. The range in responses possible is to great to provide a answer but your answer should be descriptive, should include details, such as the look on her face, any gestures, your note should have some identifying information, time etc, reflective field notes you might take would include any subjective thoughts you might have—such as I would have liked to be welcomed to math that way, or Ms. Smith doesn't look happy to be teaching today

8. Although your answer may vary, this study is likely a realist ethnography.

Test Like Event

1. b
2. c
3. d
4. d
5. b
6. a
7. a
8. d
9. b
10. b
11. c
12. d

Chapter 18 Qualitative Research: Data Analysis and Interpretation

Chapter 18 Objectives

1. Describe the purpose of qualitative research data analysis.
2. Identify the cautions to avoid premature analysis and action in qualitative research.
3. State approaches to qualitative data analysis.
4. Describe the processes involved in analyzing, and interpreting data.
5. Distinguish between data analysis and data interpretation.
6. Describe strategies for data analysis.
7. Describe strategies for data interpretation.

Review the Terms

Provide a description of the strategies used in each of the following aspects of data analysis and interpretation. For terms provide a succinct definition in your own words.

Data Analysis: _____

_____

Data Interpretation: _____

_____

Memoing: _____

_____

Describing: _____

_____

Classifying: _____

_____

Coding: _____

_____

For Your Own Review

1. List three of the several data organizing activities found in your text.

_____
_____
_____

2. There are many ways to interpret qualitative data. Your text suggests several guidelines. State and describe two.

_____
_____
_____

3. Compare and contrast data analysis and data interpretation.

_____

_____

Additional Sources for Review

Jan Armstrong at the University of New Mexico has a helpful website that provides resources and suggestions for writing qualitative research in education. The site http://www.unm.edu/~jka/qualres.html also provides links to software and updates on conferences where qualitative research is presented. There is also a piece on the site by Anthony Heath that provides a template for the components in a qualitative proposal that is helpful to those writing a qualitative thesis or dissertation.

Checking What You Know

Given the article, Hogan, J., & Corey, C. (2001). Viewing classrooms as cultural contexts for fostering scientific literacy. *Anthropology and Education Quarterly, 32*(2), 214-231 first introduced in Chapter 14 activities, answer the following related to the study.

1. a. Are the methods explicated in detail so the reader can judge whether it was adequate and makes sense? _____
    `b. Provide support for your answer._____

    _____

2. a. Are any assumptions stated? _____
    b. List one example.

    _____

    _____

3. a. Are the research questions stated? _____
    b. If so, restate here.

    _____

    _____

    c. Does the study answer the research questions? _____

    d. Does the study generate further questions? _____

4. a. Is the study reported in a manner that is accessible to other researchers, practitioners, and policy makers? _____

    b. Support your response. _____

    _____

    _____

5. a. Are observations (or data collection) made of a full range of activities over a full cycle of activities? _____

   b. Explain. _____
   _____
   _____

6. a. Are data collection strategies the most adequate and efficient available? _____

   b. What other data collection strategies might have been used? _____
   _____
   _____

Test-Like Event

1. Data analysis in qualitative research starts

   a. after all data are collected.
   b. prior to data collection.
   c. during the first interaction with participants.
   d. when all the data are transcribed.

2. Data analysis in qualitative research is _____.

   a. iterative
   b. objective
   c. pre-determined
   d. structured

3. Placing small pieces of data into more general categories is referred to as _____.

   a. memoing
   b. classifying
   c. Interpreting
   d. creating

4. Pemba is analyzing her data and she decides to use a strategy that focuses on the features of the organization. Which of the following strategies is she likely using?

   a. Concept mapping
   b. Asking key questions
   c. Organizational review
   d. Antecedents and consequences

5. Tomo is using a data analysis strategy that relies on creating a visual representation of the data. He is most likely using which of the following strategies?

   a. Concept mapping
   b. Asking key questions
   c. Organizational review
   d. Antecedents and consequences

6. Mike used graphs to help him organize and analyze his data. His friend Shiela told him that it was not an appropriate strategy to use. Which of the following is an accurate statement according to your text?

    a. Shiela is right. Graphs are a strategy used for quantitative data analyses.
    b. What Mike did was not an appropriate strategy because it is not interpretative.
    c. Using Graphs was fine. It allows for a display of the findings.
    d. Graphs should not be used as they limit the data to only what is recorded.

7. Suku is unsure how to next proceed with her data interpretation. She has analyzed the data but now is at a loss. Which of the following is her 'safest' data interpretation technique?

    a. Connect findings to her personal experience.
    b. Extend the data by raising questions.
    c. Turn to theory and tie the findings to existing theory.
    d. Use the existing literature as an external authority.

8. Of the following, according to your text and other cited sources, which is a question that a qualitative researcher might pose to guide their data analysis and interpretation?

    a. Is your research question still worth answering?
    b. Is your research question quantifiable?
    c. Is your research question tied to existing theory?
    d. Is your research question meaningful to others?

9. Which of the following is NOT one of the iterative steps of qualitative data analysis as presented in your text.

    a. Classifying
    b. Memoing
    c. Justifying
    d. Describing

10. Jana is ready to systematically analyze her data. She has collected all of her qualitative data in one place and is confident that she now can analyze and interpret the data. However, her first concern is that she can't place the notes in a systematic order. She can't tell which days she collected which information. Jana has best illustrated a problem in

    a. classifying.
    b. justifying.
    c. organizing.
    d. describing.

11. The stage of data analysis that addresses what is happening among the participants is the _____ stage.

    a. classifying.
    b. justifying.
    c. organizing.
    d. describing.

12. One reason that two different qualitative researchers might not produce the same categories when analyzing their data is

    a. Qualitative data are not reliable
    b. Qualitative data are not valid
    c. Qualitative researchers have biases.
    d. Qualitative researchers seek correct answers.

13. By placing your data on cards you most directly engaging in the _____ process.

    a. coding
    b. classifying
    c. justifying
    d. describing

14. By sorting the cards that contain your data you are most directly engaging in the _____ process.

    a. coding
    b. classifying
    c. justifying
    d. describing

Companion Website

For more practice on becoming competent in this chapter's objectives, go to the Companion Website that accompanies this text at www.prenhall.com/gay. This site includes:

Objectives with links to:
- more multiple-choice questions in Practice Quiz
- Applying What You Know essay questions
- relevant Web sites

Custom modules to help you:
- calculate statistical tests (see "Calculating Statistical Tests")
- do research (see "Research Tools and Tips")
- practice analyzing quantitative data (see "Analyzing Quantitative Data")
- practice analyzing qualitative data (see "Analyzing Qualitative Data")
- practice evaluating published articles (see "Evaluating Articles")

Chapter 18 Answers
For Your Own Review

1. Write dates on all notes, sequence notes with labels, label notes by type, make two photocopies of notes, organize computer files, make backups of all files, read through data to make sure it is complete and legible, begin to note themes and patterns that emerge.

2. Extend the analysis which is simply raising questions about the study and noting possible interpretations; connecting findings with personal experiences which is tying the findings to your experiences; Seeking advice of critical friends which means getting feedback from others; Contextualize findings in the literature, which means to tie findings to existing literature; Turn to theory, which means similarly to contextualizing in the

literature that can provide rationale and meaning; don't offer interpretation when you are uncomfortable doing so.

3.   Analysis is describing what is in the data and interpretation makes sense in what is in the data.

Checking What You Know

1.   a.   yes
     b.   A good description of collection, setting, data, and participants is provided. Four vignettes are described. It is not entirely clear how exactly these data are related to the scope of the full data collection that took place over the course of semester. The report provides a solid description of the researchers and their roles.

2.   a.   Some assumptions are stated. A model is provided.
     b.   These assumptions include, for example, those that relate to theoretical perspective and previous assumptions about relationships among knowledge and practice.

3.   a.   Not really research questions but a research topic.
     b.   An investigation of the role of scientific practice and thought emulated in educational settings with non-scientists.
     c.   The study describes how this topic was addressed very well.
     d.   Yes, further questions and directions for research are included. These include, for example, a section of recommendations for future research and practice. One suggestion is for research that addresses how skilled teachers scaffold class settings to develop a composite culture of science.

4.   a. & b.   yes, the study is easily read, supported by data, and interpreted in clear meaningful ways for both researchers and practitioners.

5.   a.   Data collection was over the course of a semester. The data presented was in the form of four vignettes. It appears it covered a cycle of activities. It is likely that the researchers had to limit their report to the data provided given the nature of their initial collection and the length of time of their data collection.

6.   a.   Data collection included both naturalistic and prompted classroom interactions through videotape, audio recordings, informal interviews. The researchers note that additional data was pre and post data on ecological concepts not presented in the current study. Additional data that might also have been collected in the current study include student journals, or research logs, more structured interviews, and perhaps additional information from the field notes which is likely available but not separately reported.

Test Like Event

1.	c	8.	a
2.	a	9.	c
3.	b	10.	c
4.	c	11.	d
5.	a	12.	c
6.	c	13.	a
7.	b	14.	b

Chapter 19 Mixed Methods Research:
Integrating Qualitative and Quantitative Methods

Chapter 19 Objectives

1. Define mixed methods research.
2. Distinguish between three types of mixed methods research designs.
3. Illustrate mixed methods research designs with a diagram that captures the priority and sequencing of data collection techniques.
4. Describe strategies for conducting mixed methods data analysis.
5. Use questions to help evaluate a mixed methods study.

Review the Terms

Provide a succinct definition in your own words for the following terms

Mixed methods research designs: _____
_____

QUAL-quan model: _____
_____

QUAN-qual model: _____
_____

QUAN-QUAL model: _____
_____

For Your Own Review

1. What are the three types of mixed methods studies as presented in your text?

    _____   _____   _____

2. What are the three salient differences between the three types of mixed methods studies?

    _____
    _____
    _____

3. Suggest two of the characteristics of a research report that can help the consumer determine if a study is a mixed methods design.

    _____
    _____

Test-Like Event

1. The Triangulation method of Mixed Methods Design is also known as

    a. qual-quan
    b. QUAL-Quan
    c. QUAN-Qual
    d. QUAN+QUAL

2. Mixed-methods research as presented in your text refers to studies that include both

    a. single subject and group designs.
    b. quantitative and qualitative data.
    c. within and between subjects designs.
    d. cluster and cohort designs.

3. Jocelyn studies the culture of coffee shops in academic communities. She goes to two of the local coffee shops and observes several times a week at various times for the course of a full year. She interviews patrons about the types of activities they engage in while at the coffee shop. She also asks three regulars to keep a brief journal regarding their experiences and what they accomplish at the coffee shop. Jocelyn is best illustrating

    a. qualitative research.
    b. quantitative research.
    c. QUAN-Qual research.
    d. QUAL-Quan research.

4. Kari is interested in the relationship between early exposure to the arts and later participation in community arts projects, such as theatre and musical events. She relies on some national data samples from surveys that examine the issue, surveys members of the audience at a local theatre production about their exposure as children, and follows up the survey with selected interviews. Kari is best illustrating

    a. qualitative research.
    b. quantitative research.
    c. QUAN-Qual research.
    d. QUAL-Quan research.

5. Kate is interested in the social relationships of children with developmental delays. She surveys the parents and teachers of several hundred children. She also administers standardized social skills assessments to many of the children. Kate is best illustrating

    a. qualitative research.
    b. quantitative research.
    c. QUAN-Qual research.
    d. QUAL-Quan research.

6. According to your text the exploratory mixed methods design is best described as

    a. qual-quan
    b. QUAL-Quan
    c. QUAN-Qual
    d. QUAN+QUAL

7. Mazi conducted a study that examined the role of homework in middle school students' lives. She starts by interviewing students and their families regarding their homework processes. She then conducts a survey and examines students test scores. Mazi's mixed methods design can best be described as _____.

    a. qual-quan.
    b. QUAL-Quan.
    c. QUAN-Qual.
    d. QUAN+QUAL.

8. One limitation of mixed methods designs is

    a. they generally don't provide enough data to draw conclusions.
    b. they generally lack reliability and validity and don't generalize.
    c. that it is difficult for one person to have expertise to conduct mixed methods designs.
    d. the findings between the methods are often disparate and require intense reconciliation.

9. According to your text quantitative research studies are good at establishing

    a. how.
    b. why.
    c. what.
    d. when.

10. When diagramming mixed methods designs the '+' indicates

    a. Sequence of presentation.
    b. Order of presentation.
    c. Data presentation.
    d. Concurrent presentation.

Companion Website

For more practice on becoming competent in this chapter's objectives, go to the Companion Website that accompanies this text at www.prenhall.com/gay. This site includes:

Objectives with links to:
- more multiple-choice questions in Practice Quiz
- Applying What You Know essay questions
- relevant Web sites

Custom modules to help you:
- calculate statistical tests (see "Calculating Statistical Tests")
- do research (see "Research Tools and Tips")

- practice analyzing quantitative data (see "Analyzing Quantitative Data")
- practice analyzing qualitative data (see "Analyzing Qualitative Data")
- practice evaluating published articles (see "Evaluating Articles")

Chapter 19 Answers
For Your Own Review
1. QUAL-Quan, QUAN-Qual, QUAN+QUAL
2. Priority given to data collection method, sequence of data collection, data analyis techniques used
3. Title includes terms that suggest mixed methods, both methods are used in the study, researcher describes the mixed methods applied, data collection section describes the data that are collected, purpose statement or questions indicate type of method used, questions are stated for both quantitative and qualitative approaches, researcher indicates preference given to qualitative or quantitative techniques, researcher indicates sequence of data collection, researcher describes how data were analyzed, the writing is balanced in terms of both methodologies

Test Like Event
1.	d
2.	b
3.	a
4.	c
5.	b
6.	b
7.	b
8.	c
9.	c
10.	d

Chapter 20 Action Research

Chapter 20 Objectives

1. State a definition of action research.
2. Describe the purposes of action research.
3. Describe the processes of action research.
4. Identify the four basic steps in conducting action research.
5. Describe the key characteristics of action research
6. Identify common data collection sources and strategies used to carry out action research.

Review the Terms

Provide a succinct definition in your own words for each of the following terms.

Action research: _____

_____

Reflective stance: _____

_____

Professional disposition: _____

_____

Reconnaissance: _____

_____

Critical action research: _____

_____

Practical action research: _____

_____

Dialectic action research spiral: _____

_____

For Your Own Review

1. List the four steps of action research.

   _____

   _____

   _____

   _____

2. What are the three levels of action research as identified in your text?

   _____

   _____

   _____

3.   List two of the several key characteristics of action research.

_____

_____

Other Sources for Review

There are many resources to review action research. One web site, http://www.parnet.org/ houses a research community of action researchers. Not all are educators as action research is used in other fields as well. Another http://www2.fhs.usyd.edu.au/arow/ in particular is a great place to start. This site, action research open web (AROW) contains definitions, action research projects, reviews of action research published articles, links to other related content, etc.

Checking What You Know

Answer the following questions regarding action research related to Hohenbrink, J., Johnston, M., & Westhoven, L. (1997). Collaborative teaching of a social studies methods course: Intimidation and change. *Journal of Teacher Education, 48*, 293-300 provided at the end of this chapter. The following questions were developed related to Chapter 20 activities.

1.   What is the research topic of the study? _____

_____

2.   What were the data sources used in the study? _____

_____

3.   Who provided these data? How were data gathered?_____

_____

4.   Describe the related literature presented in the article.

_____

_____

_____

_____

5.   How does the related research appear to have influenced the study?

_____

_____

_____

_____

6.   Does the author provide information about how the data were analyzed? If so, briefly describe.

_____

_____

_____

_____

_____

_____

_____

7. Describe the report. (For example, is this report narrative in nature? Is it written in the first person? Does it integrate the data in a form to the reader to support the conclusions drawn from the data?)

_____

_____

_____

_____

_____

_____

Applying What You Know

Related to task 9, and the chapter 20 content, consider the following scenario.

1. Cassandra is a high school chemistry teacher. She notices that the High School Science Club that meets after school on Thursday nights not only has a limited number of students but that some of her best students don't participate. In addition there are few girls or students of color in the club. This is concerning to her so she decides to look further into the program to get a better understanding. She consults with Dave who runs the program and asks if he is interested in investigating the participation concerns together. Dave bravely agrees. She and Dave first examine the attendance to ascertain if their initial perceptions are accurate. They seem to be.

    a. Your text indicates that the action research process includes identifying an area of focus. Succinctly state Cassanda and Dave's area of focus.

    _____

    b. The next phase of the action research process is to collect data. What type of data would you suggest that our action researchers, Cassandra and Dave, collect? Why?

    _____

    c. The next phase is data analysis and interpretation. Let's pretend that our researchers used a combination of interviews, that they analyzed qualitatively; and surveys, that they analyzed quantitatively, and their interpretations from these sources are the following: Not all potential students know about the science club. Those who know and are interested but don't attend are not participating because it is on Thursday nights. Thursday nights are the biggest homework night and nights in general are tough for many students who have other extra-curricular activities. Given these interpretations, the last phase of the action research processes is action planning. What do you suggest our researchers do?

    _____

2. Horatio was recently approached by a parent concerned about whether her daughter should be involved in extra-curricular activities. She is concerned that her daughter's grades will suffer so she asked Horatio his opinion. He thought about it a lot and decided to collect some data to better answer the question. He became curious about how students activities outside of school might be related to their in class performance. He collected some quick data survey to address this question as noted below. The first column is student number, the second column is how many activities, the third column is how much time is spent daily on homework and the last column is the math average for the last term. In preparation for Task 20 answer the following questions related to Horatio's study.

a. Write an area of focus statement.

_____

_____

b. Define the variables:

_____

_____

c. Develop data collection ideas:

_____

_____

1	0	40	90
2	2	40	88
3	1	30	84
4	2	50	94
5	3	20	72
6	1	10	70
7	5	30	86
8	1	30	84
9	2	40	90
10	2	60	96
11	2	20	74
12	6	20	76
13	4	10	72
14	2	50	95
15	4	20	78
16	3	30	80
17	3	20	75
18	1	40	92
19	0	30	86
20	4	30	84
21	0	20	80
22	2	40	88
23	3	30	82
24	2	50	94
25	3	40	90

Practicing the Tasks

Task 9 requires that you develop a design for an action research study to answer a school-based research question. Given your knowledge of action research imagine that you are working in a public school setting and that you have been frustrated by homework completion. Only about 25 percent of students appear to be completing their homework. Answer the following questions related to how you would approach this topic.

1. Given concerns about homework completion above, write an area of focus
    statement._____

2.   What two data collection methods will you might use to address this topic?

   a.   First source:_____   _____

   b.   Why did you select this data source?

   _____
   _____

   c.   Is this data source qualitative or quantitative? _____

   d.   Who will provide these data? _____
   _____

   e.   Second source: _____

   f.   Why did you select this data source? _____
   _____

   g.   Is this data source qualitative or quantitative? _____

   h.   Who will provide these data? _____
   _____

Test-Like Event
Circle the best answer in each item.

1.   Which of the following best illustrates action research?

   a.   A university professor reviewing research in a library.
   b.   Teachers attending a conference to learn new instructional strategies.
   c.   Teachers collecting data in classrooms and implementing strategies.
   d.   Principals instigating change in school policies based upon national trends.

2.   Which of the following is NOT one of the three levels of action research as presented in your text?

   a.   Individual teacher research.
   b.   Individual parent research.
   c.   Single department research.
   d.   School-wide research.

3.   Which of the following <u>best</u> illustrates a desired data collection strategy in an action research study of problem solving?

   a.   Judy observes her peers teaching problem-solving methods to gather data about practice at their school.
   b.   Kala looks at national trends in problem solving test scores to determine if more emphasis should be on problem solving in her school's curriculum.
   c.   Vijay examines the state based curriculum for strategies to implement to promote problem solving.
   d.   Arthur reads several books developed for teachers on how to promote problem-solving skills within a curriculum.

4. Action research in school-based settings is most often conducted by which of the following?

   a. School board personnel
   b. Students
   c. Teachers
   d. Parents

5. According to your text, which of the following is NOT necessary in action research?

   a. Consistency
   b. Change
   c. Collaboration
   d. Concern

6. The first issue related to identifying the research topic in action research is that the topic is

   a. important to practice.
   b. important to the researcher.
   c. important to theory.
   d. important to policy.

7. Of the following, which is likely <u>the best</u> research question for an action research study?

   a. Are low-SES students in our school likely to have higher drop-out rates?
   b. Are children of low SES struggling on our grade three standardized test scores?
   c. How can we support low-SES students in our classrooms to help keep them in school?
   d. How are national polices effecting the likelihood of high school completion for low-SES children?

8. One difference between action research in education and traditional research is that action research is usually

   a. conducted by trained researchers.
   b. conducted in controlled environments.
   c. done to generalize findings to other educational settings.
   d. done to promote change in specific environment.

9. Which of the following is a type of action research according to your text.

   a. Generalizable action research
   b. Validity based action research
   c. Practical action research
   d. Reliable action research

10. One focus of action research is for teachers to

   a. improve their own practice.
   b. develop standards of practice for other teachers.
   c. collect data for theory development.
   d. generalize findings from their study to other schools.

11. Action research projects should be

    a. broad to have the greatest application to practice.
    b. complex, to capture all pertinent variables.
    c. conducted to promote generalization of findings.
    d. related to a problem selected by the researcher.

12. Of the following, the most desired use of results from an action research study is that the results are

    a. used by legislators to initiate change in policy.
    b. examined by teachers to modify their practice.
    c. applied by superintendents to determine curricula.
    d. examined by researchers to develop theory.

13. Reflective stance refers to the ability is
    a. criticize authority.
    b. more effectively evaluate students.
    c. look critically at teaching.
    d. more adequately address reliability and validity.

14. Compared to other research methods, of the following, which is generally true of action research?

    a. Action research takes longer to conduct than qualitative research studies.
    b. Action research is smaller-scale than experimental studies.
    c. Action research is best conducted by teachers.
    d. Action research is concerned with teachers generalizing their findings.

15. Which of the following is a critical value of action research?

    a. Equitable
    b. Fault-finding
    c. Political
    d. Important

Companion Website

For more practice on becoming competent in this chapter's objectives, go to the Companion Website that accompanies this text at www.prenhall.com/gay. This site includes:

Objectives with links to:
- more multiple-choice questions in Practice Quiz
- Applying What You Know essay questions
- relevant Web sites

Custom modules to help you:
- calculate statistical tests (see "Calculating Statistical Tests")
- do research (see "Research Tools and Tips")
- practice analyzing quantitative data (see "Analyzing Quantitative Data")
- practice analyzing qualitative data (see "Analyzing Qualitative Data")
- practice evaluating published articles (see "Evaluating Articles")

Collaborative Teaching of a Social Studies Methods Course: Intimidation and Change

JOANN HOHENBRINK   MARILYN JOHNSTON   LISA WESTHOVEN
Ohio Dominican College   The Ohio State University   Worthington School District, Ohio

From *Journal of Teacher Education, 48,* 293–300. Copyright ©
1997 by Corwin Press, Inc. Reprinted with permission of Corwin Press, Inc.

In this article, we describe our initial apprehensions, difficulties of working across our differences, and changes in our understandings and teaching practice as we collaboratively taught a social studies methods course.

We began with stereotypes of each other implied by our university/school and professor/graduate student/classroom teacher roles. After 4 years of working together, we have come to understand our positions, knowledge, and expertise in different ways and as a result have changed our teaching.

We began our co-teaching experience as members of a Professional Development School (PDS) project. In this PDS, university faculty, graduate associates, school principals, and classroom teachers work closely to construct and evaluate the redesign of the university's elementary teacher education programs. One important aspect of this collaboration is co-teaching the methods courses for the Master of Education certification students in the program. Classroom teachers, doctoral students, and university professors make shared decisions about course syllabi, assignments, and evaluation to bring theory and practice into a productive dialogue.

Despite initial support for co-teaching the methods courses, both university faculty and classroom teachers were reluctant. Classroom teachers were uncertain about working with university faculty, about the time necessary for planning, and especially about leaving their classrooms for half a day each week. University faculty were hesitant to relinquish their autonomy and worried about the time required to team teach.

These hesitancies resulted in less concern about teachers' expertise in the subject area and more on their willingness to participate. Rather than participating in a formal selection process, faculty and teachers were asked to volunteer; decisions about which teachers would teach with which faculty were left to informal negotiations.

This article focuses on the co-teaching of a social studies methods course. We do not include practical descriptions of how we organized the social studies course, the students' evaluations of the course, or assessment of student learning. This is not to deny the importance of student outcomes that we discuss in other work in progress, but to situate this study within the literature on collaborative work and professional development.

Studies of teachers' professional development supported our interest in looking at our own learning and development. Traditionally evaluation of change initiatives have considered classroom instruction and student performance more than the teachers who managed the learning environments. Attention to teachers' growth and development has been slow in coming, particularly studies that include self-study and reflection.

Recently, researchers have been using case studies, collaborative methodologies, narrative forms, and feminist theories to look at the complexities and perspectives of teachers (Miller, 1990; Witherell & Noddings, 1991). Action research is enjoying a resurgence, and teachers are increasingly studying and publishing reports on their own teaching and beliefs (Bricher, Hawk, & Tingley, 1993; Nalle, 1993; Paley, 1989). Journals are increasingly including collaborative studies by teachers or between teachers and researchers (Gitlin, 1992; Hunsaker & Johnston, 1992). Greene (1988) argues that *stories—and myths, and diaries, and histories—give shape and expression to what would otherwise be untold about 'our lives'* (p. x). Multiple forms of expression help to reveal the complexities of personal lives as they are reflected in professional lives and development. These studies point to the value of teachers considering their own thinking and teaching as sites for reflection, inquiry, and change.

The authors (Lisa Westhoven, a classroom teacher; JoAnn Hohenbrink, a graduate teaching associate; and Marilyn Johnston, a professor) co-taught a two-quarter course for 2 years (1991–1993). Marilyn and Lisa co-taught the same course the following year, 1993–1994, and again in 1995–1996. JoAnn did her dissertation study on change in the first year of co-teaching (data collected 1991–1992). We extended what we learned in

Hohenbrink, J., Johnston, M., & Westhoven, L., *Journal of Teacher Education, 48,*
pp. 293-300, copyright © 1997 by Sage Publications
Reprinted by permission of Corwin Press, Inc.

85 the first year through continued conversations and self-reflection during the subsequent 3 years.

The changes we describe did not come easily. We were initially uncomfortable working together. Lisa and JoAnn felt intimidated; Marilyn was unclear how
90 to bring others into *her* class. We began the course using Marilyn's syllabus and reading materials because co-teaching arrangements were approved by the school district and university just before the quarter began. We had no time before class started to plan the course col-
95 laboratively or to talk about our apprehensions and differences.

We spent much time talking and planning throughout our co-teaching experience. Marilyn found planning took much more time than would have been re-
100 quired had she taught alone. Lisa had to plan for her substitute teacher as well as the methods course. We tried to deal directly with feelings of intimidation and imposition, which required building trusting relationships to support handling sensitive issues and criti-
105 cisms. Our attempts were necessarily partial. We could pursue only those things of which we were aware; we left undisturbed other issues and silences. We are nevertheless convinced that co-teaching has rich potential for prompting self-reflection for both university and
110 school-based participants. It led us to significant changes in our understandings and teaching practices and, most important, brought the limitations of the traditional separate roles of schools and universities in teacher education into stark relief.

Methodology

115 We used several theoretical positions in our research. First, we used interpretive/hermeneutic theories (Gadamer, 1984; Ricoeur, 1981; van Manen, 1990) to inform our interest in understandings. We were particularly interested in how our individual understand-
120 ings about teaching and learning, and about schools and universities, influenced our ability to collaborate. We were also curious to trace our construction of individual as well as shared meanings that might emerge from this experience.

125 Second, we depended on poststructural feminist theorists (Davies & Harré, 1990; Harding, 1986; Haraway, 1986; Lather, 1991; Weedon, 1987) to think about issues of language, positionings, and voice. Like interpretive theorists, poststructural feminists are interested
130 in the discursive and historical construction of meaning. Feminists, in addition, pay attention to the personal and political character of the self and the social context within which issues of power and control are ever present. In particular, we were interested in how our insti-
135 tutional contexts and socialization made interpretations of each others' meanings difficult. Our commitment to separate texts written to represent our different voices and perspectives is also supported, as well as problematized (Lather, 1991, p. 43), in feminist work.

140 We used audiotaped conversations over a period of 3 years (some 50 conversations), journal writing from 4 years, and the individual and group interviews conducted for the dissertation study as our major data sources. Periodically, we examined the data to look for
145 themes and changes in our understandings. These analyses became the focus of further conversations that in turn were data to be examined at a later point in time. This article is the collaborative result of 5 years of working and writing together.

Three Voices in a Dialogue

150 We write in three voices in order to capture our individual perspectives. We address the two themes of intimidation and change emerging from our study. The first theme addresses our beginning assumptions about knowledge that led to intimidation and apprehension.
155 In the beginning, we assumed that university knowledge is more important than school knowledge and valued theoretical/research knowledge over practical knowledge. From our present perspective, we would argue that such distinctions are not helpful because
160 they mask both teachers' theories and professors' practical knowledge. The second theme, change in teaching, describes our evolving understandings and teaching practices.

Whose Knowledge Counts?

We struggled continually with assumptions about
165 the different knowledge bases that we carried into our co-teaching experience. These assumptions, at times, led to feelings of intimidation and fears of imposition. These feelings are reflected in some of our journal entries during the first two quarters we worked together.

170 Lisa: I am very excited, very nervous, and very apprehensive—I am entering a world I know little about. What am I hoping to be able to offer? Social studies is not an area I would call my strength!! The conversations at Bernies [the deli where we had our morning planning
175 meetings] are quite intimidating. The other three [professor and two doctoral students] sit there and discuss things I've never heard of—'postmodern,' 'hermeneutic'—and they throw around authors' names. I could have been listening to a conversation in Japanese. That's when I
180 think—What am I doing here? (10-1-91)

JoAnn: I really am intimidated by Marilyn and how she thinks and how differently we come at things. She has had more interactions with the topics we are teaching—she has used them in classes before. I see her strug-
185 gling with not taking control of what has to be done. It must be frustrating for someone who has too much to do to take 2+ hours to plan something she has done so often.... Instead of backing away and thinking I may look stupid, I really need to take some responsibility so things
190 can be accomplished. (10-10-91)

Marilyn: JoAnn did the discussion of one of the assigned readings today and seemed uncomfortable. I've wondered whether I should leave when she's doing her part sometimes just to give her some space. She said she
195 doesn't feel comfortable sometimes because it's about social studies and I'm her advisor. Maybe she's trying to

do things in the way I would, but it's not how she would do it on her own. She runs a discussion in a very open way, asking students to respond to other students' ideas without focusing the questions. It made me think how much I try to get students to think through an issue (i.e., my issue) in a way that may not be responsive to their interests. I need to think about this. (1-13-92)

JoAnn: My part of class today was the assigned reading. I wanted students to be involved in discussion. Because of the time frame, I couldn't (or didn't feel I had time) to do the outline of the article. I was uncomfortable with Marilyn being there. I was in Marilyn's graduate social studies seminar and we worked on the same reading. I didn't want to put her on the spot, but I wanted her to talk about how she thought the example in the article was realistic. I remember her doing that in the seminar. I was uncomfortable not telling the students what I thought because I thought Marilyn expected that of me. It's not what I would do in my own class. Sometimes I just feel soooo wishy/washy. (11-13-91)

Marilyn: At this evening's planning session we had a difficult time talking about how much this is my class and how much ownership I should have or want. JoAnn clearly brings a level of expertise in social studies, but we have different perspectives about the goals. Lisa brings classroom expertise, but in ways that don't get well integrated into what we are doing in class. Maybe it's because she's teaching social studies in a different way than is espoused in class. Does this mean imposition of my way or university perspectives over what teachers typically do in their classrooms? Is this what co-teaching is all about? I keep asking myself how much of the course and my perspective I am willing to give away. (11-16-91)

Lisa: Doing small groups in class again makes me a little nervous especially when Marilyn asks if we need to generate questions together. Is that because she wants us all to do the same kind of thing, or is it that she isn't sure I understand the gist of what is to be covered? I hope she doesn't think that I won't move the conversation along and challenge their thinking. I don't really think that is the case. I think she would say something if she felt that way. (2-2-92)

JoAnn: I like what we planned for class. I like the book, 'White Teacher,' and I think having students reflect on their classroom experience will be good. Again Marilyn is handling the discussion of the reading. But, again, it's her topic. I'm glad we're using the video from Marilyn teaching in Lisa's classroom. (3-2-92)

Lisa: Next I think I need to write about Marilyn's visit to teach in my room. At first I worried about what her first impressions of my room would be. Once she got there, I worried about what she would think of my kids. What would she think about the way I handle my kids? Her lesson went very well especially for not knowing the kids. It made me feel good because I thought she asked the same kinds of questions I ask them. I think the lesson went similar to the way it would have gone if I had known how to do it. I guess I thought she would have every child sitting on the edge of his/her seat and they would all be wrapped around her finger. (3-6-92)

Marilyn: I've puzzled a bit about why it's the eighth week of the quarter and I'm just getting out to Lisa's classroom to do some teaching. It's clear from our discussions that coming to her classroom bothers her. I get set up as the authority and therefore a critical eye. But then, I feel like I'm under scrutiny having co-teachers in my class. I often wonder what they think, what doesn't make sense, how my biases appear to them. There's rarely any negotiation that suggests I'm doing it wrong and that it ought to be more like how Lisa is teaching. There are differences between my philosophy and Lisa's, but it always seems like she's changing to accommodate my point of view rather than the other way around. Is this imposition from the power of one knowledge base over the other? (3-6-92)

Joint Reflections on "Whose Knowledge Counts?"

Our worries as we started our co-teaching experience were clear. Lisa was apprehensive about entering the university world with its new vocabularies and expectations. Her strength as a teacher was not in social studies; in fact, she did not like social studies much at all. She had signed up to teach language arts, but at the last minute, the professor decided not to take a co-teacher, and Lisa joined us. JoAnn was *intimidated* by Marilyn because she was her adviser. In addition, they had differences of opinion about what should occur in a social studies methods course. She was also apprehensive about looking uninformed if she did things more to her liking. Marilyn was committed to co-teaching in principle but unsure about how to keep some integrity to what she wanted in the course and still share the decision making. Underlying all of this was the assumption that the university knowledge exemplified in Marilyn's attitudes and purposes had higher value than what a graduate student or teacher might bring to the course.

Throughout the two quarters of co-teaching, we worried about what each of us thought about each other. We talked a lot about issues of power and role and the ways they interfered with making our work together more genuinely collaborative. We made decisions to work in ways that would push against the stereotypic expectations we held for each other and that students held as well. We decided never to let Marilyn begin class so that students would see Lisa and JoAnn as equally in charge of the announcements, assignments, and evaluation issues discussed at the beginning of each class. We tried to share different aspects of the class and defy expectations when we could. Rather than Marilyn leading discussions about the readings, we shared this responsibility. Rather than Lisa doing all the talking about a videotape of her classroom, we discussed it ahead of time and shared in the class discussions. We divided different sections of each class session so that each of us had equal responsibility for setting up activities or beginning discussions. We set time periods for each section so that Marilyn's tendency to go on and on about something would not infringe on what Lisa and JoAnn had prepared to do in class. These arrangements were symbolically important to us even if the students did not always recognize them.

It was easy, however, to fall back into stereotypic

279

power relations and role definitions. Lisa countered this by pushing hard for her fair share and for a sense of equality. We nicknamed her our *watchdog of hierarchy*. It was extremely helpful that she was willing to say when she thought that Marilyn and JoAnn were usurping more than their share of time. Marilyn and JoAnn tried also to do their share of asking questions about procedures and responsibilities. We were continually amazed at how easy it was to fall back into familiar patterns and expectations. The hours we spent the first year talking into a tape recorder for JoAnn's dissertation helped us to continually keep these issues in front of us.

Changes in Understanding Teaching

Change occurred for each of us as a result of this co-teaching experience. We have made changes in our teaching and readjusted our goals for teaching the social studies methods course. Although change occurred for all of us, the character of the change was different. How we changed is related to the problems and demands of our institutional contexts and our backgrounds and personalities. These influences are reflected in our separate accounts of change written after a second year of co-teaching together.

Lisa: I could probably fill a book if I were to describe all the changes that have taken place in my classroom and in myself since becoming a part of the co-teaching team. I have questioned my whole approach to teaching. Because change demands time, thought, planning, and risk taking, I have only begun to make the changes I want. I have gone from being a very traditional teacher who was very teacher centered, and moved to a classroom where children are more involved in their own learning. I now focus less on facts and more on critical thinking, inquiry, and process. I make fewer classroom decisions without first having a conversation with the class in order to have a better understanding of students' wants and needs. For example, at the beginning of this school year instead of having the room setup when students walked in, we discussed the physical arrangement of our classroom and what makes one way work better than the next. Students were involved in the decision about the room. I was wondering lately what the kids think about our community-building time, so I asked them to write about it:

Jeff: I learned we can work things out as a group and the teacher doesn't make all the decisions by herself.

Jane: What you can learn is how to solve problems.

Mary: I think it is worthwhile because it helps you think about your problems and we solve class problems together. Working together is better than working alone.

I was pleased to find that this kind of classroom is making a difference in their thinking. Their responses have encouraged me to plan more group cooperative work and less individual isolated work. These changes have not always been easy and I find myself much more unsure about what I'm doing than when I was the teacher and this is what we're going to do. I'm never sure if I am giving too much input and therefore having too much influence. I'm also not sure exactly when to step in and be

'the teacher.' These emerging ideas, like shared classroom ownership and openness to children's input, make my job less predictable and more ambiguous. In many ways I feel like a first year teacher again; I have more questions than answers.

JoAnn: When I think about how I have changed based on my co-teaching experience, I reflect especially on my attitudes and beliefs. First, I would say that I thought of teaching as a one-person job and of myself as the one who has the knowledge that students need to learn. This was based on my own experience in elementary school and college. How could it be any different? What I found out is that it could be very different. I experienced a classroom situation that was filled with ideas. I became aware of the socio-cultural nature of learning as I co-taught with others whom I knew and respected. I was continually aware of how much I was learning from our conversations both in class and during planning. In turn, I realized that the students in our class were also learning from one another, and us from them. Was it because there were more 'teachers' with ideas that students felt they could share their ideas as well? We used cooperative learning groups to generate ideas. We encouraged students to speak from their own perspectives, and to value other points of view. Co-teaching was definitely not a hierarchical experience of teaching and learning for me.

Because of my co-teaching, I have taken a much different view of my teaching now that I am a college professor on my own. Instead of having college students focus on me as a teacher, I have students sit in a way that they can see and talk with each other. I try to encourage them to take an active part in class believing now that there are always as many teachers and learners as there are participants in the room.

Through this experience, I came to understand how isolating teaching is and the problems isolation can create. Only by doing the teaching differently was I able to understand better my previous experiences. I also experienced how this isolation kept me from seeing different options. For example, I used to think that each student should be assigned an individual field placement. Now I see the importance of students working in pairs in their fieldwork because of the social learning that takes place as they discuss their experiences together.

Co-teaching challenged me to think about how others see issues and teaching. Seeing other perspectives has helped me to examine my own, and, as a consequence, I have changed my mind about some things and expanded my thinking about others. I have not adopted someone else's perspective, but rather used their ideas to extend my own thinking and teaching practice.

Marilyn: Initially, I thought I could best facilitate collaborative teaching by helping my co-teachers become more like me and my becoming more like them. I thought if I gently shared what I knew with them and spent time in classrooms with them, we could both benefit. I knew the practical examples I used in my courses needed updating, but I wasn't sure that I had anything particularly new to learn. I had been a classroom teacher for 15 years. I always thought my courses were practical because I brought in lots of classroom activities. I thought that Lisa could offer fresh examples because she was in a classroom every day and by being around her and her classroom I could gather some 'fresh' examples as well. I

440 knew I would change in some ways because I'm always looking for new ideas and like a good debate about issues. Nevertheless, deep in my heart, I thought Lisa and JoAnn had more to gain from this experience than I did. Lisa kept asking me how I was changing. She was full of
445 stories about how her classroom was changing and was convinced that a test of genuine collaboration would be that I was also changing. It was clear that the course was different. There were three of us contributing, we expressed our different points of view, and we handled
450 class situations and student questions in different ways. I could see the students were benefiting from this diversity. This was not the kind of change Lisa was looking for. It took a while for me to see the impact co-teaching was having on my own understandings. Rather than thinking
455 we would all become the same, I came to see how much we were learning from our differences. It was from the differences that I was learning about my own ideas. Rather than imparting knowledge that I assumed others needed, their questions were helping me to think better
460 about my own conceptions of social studies. Many times my commitment to a particular point of view came into question as Lisa and JoAnn asked questions. Sometimes the questions came from Lisa's immediate classroom context; sometimes the questions were more abstract.
465 Lisa and JoAnn were more sophisticated with issues than the preservice students in our classes and so their questions pushed harder at the core of my beliefs. I saw much more clearly how complicated some of these ideas are and the ways in which they can be easily misunderstood.
470 For example, I used to rant and rave about the shortcomings of textbooks for social studies instruction. Lisa and JoAnn helped me to see the ways in which I made students feel guilty about using them especially as first year teachers. That was not what I intended. As they helped
475 me to see the consequences of my position, I could work on ways to make my point, but not debilitate new teachers. We now talk about textbooks as 'springboards' rather than 'platforms.' The students have benefited and so have I.

480 The question of whose knowledge counts gradually disappeared; rather the conversations became three people working together to understand better what we were trying to do together. Whether it was a theoretical or practical issue became a useless distinction. We
485 were working to understand each other and our different ideas. Each of us at times had questions that helped us understand something new. We eventually trusted each other enough to take risks, expose our ignorance, and test our ideas before they were well formed. It was
490 exciting rather than intimidating. We worked hard to understand that we each had different/helpful things to offer in the conversation.

Joint Reflections on Change

As Lisa and Marilyn begin a third year of co-teaching, things again changed considerably in the
495 course. It seemed less important to work against typical expectations. Marilyn started class if it made sense for her to do so. Lisa discussed a videotape from her classroom because she best knew what had happened. We no longer felt it necessary to put time limits on sections

500 of class designated to a particular person. Rather, we decided who would be responsible for moving from one topic to another and let the flow of the class determine the time spent on a particular issue.

The major change in the course, however, was not
505 as obvious as these changes in course structure. It concerned our growing appreciation for each other's knowledge and expertise. This moved us beyond an appreciation for differences that developed during the first year. Appreciating another person's knowledge
510 and expertise came to mean seeing a potential for others to contribute to our own thinking and our shared project. This involved an acknowledgment that we needed another's ideas and expertise, that there will be times when their ideas will be better than our own, and
515 that they will legitimately claim the right to their fair share of authority and decision making. Intimidation is less likely when both parties respect the other's knowledge and expertise, especially in the context of a trusting relationship. In such a context, challenge becomes
520 a way to learn rather than a means to intimidation; differences of opinion provide options rather than conflict.

Appreciating each other's knowledge and expertise took time. We needed to know about each other's in-
525 stitutional contexts and background. We needed to understand each other's commitments and concerns. We needed to build some shared understandings. What we have come to share is as important and valuable as our differences. For example, Lisa has recently come to
530 understand how the differences in expectations in schools and universities influence how people talk to each other.

Lisa: It took awhile but I have come to recognize that in different contexts (my school and the university) different types of discourses are used. At the university,
535 multiple perspectives, divergent thinking, and the questioning of ideas are encouraged. Schools typically socialize teachers to accept ideas, ask questions only to clarify, and keep quiet when we disagree with the perceived majority. When teachers act at school in the same
540 manner as university-based teachers do at their institutions, they are thought to be negative or 'trouble makers.'

With different expectations inherent in our separate institutional contexts, it is no wonder that university-
545 and school-based practitioners have difficulty talking to each other. We are used to different ways of dealing with ideas and conflicts. In our co-teaching, we needed to understand these different norms and positionings (Davies & Harré, 1990) and how they influenced our
550 interactions as we worked together.

Change came slowly. We may be slow learners, but I think not. There are many barriers to be overcome, many understandings that must be constructed, and levels of trust that must be nurtured. Expecting imme-
555 diate changes in minds or institutional structures seems to us to be naive. Collaboration across the significant differences of schools and universities is challenging,

and change for us took commitment, empathy, and good will.

Conclusion

560 In the beginning of our co-teaching experience, we could do little more than articulate our differences. Although we started in contradictory positions, we have influenced each other's thinking and have found new ways to help students negotiate the differences

565 between what research says and the realities of classrooms. But, of course, we have not resolved all potential conflicts. And the possibility of intimidation from university folks and passive resistance from school participants is as likely as not. Working together does

570 not guarantee better feelings or avoid all intimidation. There are issues of role, beliefs, and personality that must be considered and taken into account. None of this is easy, but when it works, it can be very rewarding.

575 Most school-based and university-based educators acknowledge, along with the popular press and national commissions reports (Carnegie Forum, 1986; Holmes Group, 1990), that the lack of cooperation between schools and universities is counterproductive. How to

580 work against the stereotypes and hierarchies that interfere with more genuinely collaborative relationships is unclear. How to resolve the differences in purposes and institutional rewards is uncharted territory. How to construct situations where we learn to appreciate our

585 different expertise and work toward common goals presents a clear challenge. We found the weekly interactions and joint decision making of a co-teaching situation to be a rich context to discuss and surmount some of these challenges.

References

Bricher, R., Hawk, M., & Tingley, J. (1993). Cross-age tutoring for at-risk students. *Teaching and Change, 1*(1), 82–90.

Carnegie Forum on Education and the Economy. (1986). *A nation prepared: Teachers for the 21st century.* New York: Author.

Davies, B., & Harré, R. (1990). Positioning: The discursive production of selves. *Journal for the Theory of Social Behavior, 20*(1), 43–63.

Gadamer, H. (1984). *Truth and method* (G. Barden, & J. Cummings, Trans.). New York: Crossroad.

Gitlin, A. (1992). *Teachers' voices for school change: An introduction to educative research.* London: Routledge.

Greene, M. (1988). Forward. In C. Witherell & N. Noddings (Eds.), *Stories lives tell* (pp. i–xi). New York: Teachers College Press.

Haraway, D. (1986). Situated knowledges: The science question in feminism and the privilege of partial perspectives. *Feminist Studies, 14*(3), 575–599.

Harding, S. (1986). *The science question in feminism.* Ithaca, NY: Cornell University Press.

Holmes Group. (1990). *Tomorrow's schools: Principles for the design of professional development schools.* East Lansing, MI: Author.

Hunsaker, L., & Johnston, M. (1992). Teacher under construction: A collaborative case study of teacher change. *American Educational Research Journal, 29*(2), 350–372.

Lather, P. (1991). *Getting smart.* New York: Routledge.

Miller, J. (1990). *Creating spaces and finding voices: Teachers collaborating for empowerment.* Albany: State University of New York Press.

Nalle, K. (1993). Democratic processing of children's classroom concerns. *Teaching and Change, 1*(1), 91–97.

Paley, V. (1989). *White teacher.* Cambridge: Harvard University Press.

Ricoeur, P. (1981). *Hermeneutics and the human sciences: Essays on language, action, and interpretation* (J. B. Thompson, Trans.). Cambridge: Cambridge University Press.

van Manen, M. (1990). *Researching lived experience: Human science for an action sensitive pedagogy.* Albany: State University of New York Press.

Weedon, C. (1987). *Feminist practice and post-structuralist theory.* London: Basil Blackwell.

Witherell, C., & Noddings, N. (1991). *Stories lives tell: Narrative and dialogue in education.* New York: Teachers College Press.

About the Authors: JoAnn Hohenbrink is assistant professor at the Ohio Dominican College, Columbus. Her specializations include teacher education and social studies education.

Marilyn Johnston is associate professor at The Ohio State University, Columbus. Her specializations include school/university collaboration, collaborative research, and social studies/social foundations.

Lisa Westhoven is a teacher and clinical educator at Worthington School District, Ohio. Her specializations include classroom research and social studies.

Chapter 20 Answers
For Your Own Review
1. Identifying an area of focus, data collection, data analysis and interpretation, action planning.
2. Individual teacher research, small teacher groups or teams in a single school or a single department, and school wide research.
3. Persuasive and authoritative, relevant, accessible, challenges the intractability of reform of the educational system, not a fad.

Applying What You Know
1. a. Your answer will vary here but mine is: Why is attendance in the science club not larger. Are there interested students who are not participating? If so, why?
    b. Your text suggests that action researchers often use qualitative methods. In this case I have decided that I would use surveys that have Likert scales so I can get information from a broad number of students. I also am going to suggest interviews since this will allow Cassandra and Dave to specifically target students that they think might be interested but who are not participating. Your strategy might have been different.
    c. My suggestion is to move Science Club to two mornings a week before school. It then won't interfere with other after school activities or a heavy homework load. There are drawbacks to this solution, I am sure. Your answer might be different—and Cassandra and Dave might have even a different answer yet

2. a. The purpose of the study is to examine the extra curricular activities in the context of school achievement.
    b. The variables of interest include number of extra curricular activities, types of activities, homework completion, and grades among others.
    c. I would collect interview data with families and children that were and were not involved in one or more extra-curricular activities. As noted in the scenario, one might also be interested in grades, how much time spent on homework, and number of activities a week.

Checking What You Know
1. The topic of the study is teachers' changes in teaching practice and reflection of collaborative teaching over time.

2. Data sources included audio taped conversations (50 conversations), journals (4 years), some interviews.

3. The teachers provided these data.

4. The related literature supports the need for the study and methodology (page 170 right column), Theoretical stance (page 171, left column), and some support for the conclusions drawn (page 175, left column)

5. The related research appears to have influenced the study from a theoretical stance. There is also literature cited that supports the methodology and value of teachers reflecting on their own practice. The conclusions are also tied to some related literature.

6. There is not clear discussion in this report about how the data were analyzed. The manuscript states that the data were examined periodically to look for themes and changes in understandings. These analyses became the focus of future conversations.

7. The report is narrative and describes support for four aspects of the theme: Change in teaching directly from the data (conversations).

Practicing the Tasks
Your answers to this exercise will vary. Sample answers and rationale are provided.

1. The research topic should include a question that is within the scope of expertise of those working in the school and one that can be conducted given the time constraints of school personnel. It should begin with "why", "how", or "what" and should not be answerable with a "yes" or "no". Examples might include "How can we support students by implementing "X" strategy to facilitate their homework completion?" or " Will reviewing homework before they leave for the day help students to complete their homework?"

2.   To answer this question review the data collection sources presented in our text..
    a.   Teacher journaling might be a good data source. Teachers could record the characteristics of the assignment they gave for homework, why they assigned it, the skills necessary for the students to complete it, how long they think it should take the students, and then include relative completion of the assignment in their journal.
    b.   Teacher journaling might be a good source because it could help the teachers examine what they are giving as homework and cause them to reflect on the nature of the assignment. Perhaps teachers are giving homework that takes too long, or that is too difficult for the students, or is perceived as unrelated to class by the students. These aspects of the 'homework' situation can be investigated by this data source.
    c.   Qualitative
    d.   The teachers would provide this data.
    e.   A second source might be student or parent feedback tools. A questionnaire, a brief interview might serve as this data source. An open class discussion might also serve as a student feedback tool.
    f.   There may be a number of reasons why children are not completing homework. Perhaps it is not perceived as relevant to learning. Perhaps the parents do not know that homework is assigned or perhaps they struggle to support homework completion but don't know how to help. It could be students even believe that homework is optional. Without knowledge of how homework is currently perceived it is difficult to instigate any change.
    g.   This source could be either quantitative or qualitative.
    h.   The students and parents would provide this data.

Test-Like Event
1. c
2. b
3. a
4. c
5. a
6. b
7. c
8. d
9. c
10. a
11. d
12. b
13. c
14. c
15. a

Chapter 21 Preparing a Research Report

Chapter 21 Objectives

1.   Identify and briefly describe the major sections of a research report.
2.   List general rules for writing and preparing a research report.

Review the Terms

Instead of providing definitions for Chapter 21 terms, write one component generally contained within a section of a research report next to each section title listed below. For example, *characteristics such as age and SES of the sample* would be an answer for "Participants".

Title page: _____

_____

Acknowledgments page: _____

_____

Table of contents: _____

_____

List of tables and figures: _____

_____

Abstract: _____

_____

Statement of the problem: _____

_____

Review of the literature: _____

_____

Statement of the hypothesis: _____

_____

Significance of the study: _____

_____

Participants: _____

_____

Instruments: _____

_____

Design: _____

_____

Procedure: _____

_____

Results: _____

_____

Discussion: _____

_____

References: _____

_____

Appendix: _____

_____

Other Sources for Review

Chapter 21 addresses the production of a research report. One aspect of producing a research manuscript is referencing.   Although other style manuals are used, the *Publication Manual of the American Psychological Association*, 5th edition, is a common style manual used for research reports in education, psychology, and other fields. It is a good idea to buy the manual so you can add all your own notes, "stickies", and "dogears" to it. A website, www.apastyle.org/elecref.html, is also available online from APA. The site has examples of appropriate referencing, helpful information on referencing, and information for other important components of producing research manuscripts, such as eliminating bias in your language.

In writing your thesis or dissertation, your institution as well as your college, program, and your advisor will all have unique expectations for the characteristics of your document. Chapter 21, however, provides very helpful general guidelines for the document. Another resource is a website by S. Joseph Levine at Michigan State University titled *Writing and Presenting Your Thesis or Dissertation.* This source provides extensive helpful information and advice for most everything needed for a thesis or dissertation from start to finish http://www.learnerassociates.net/dissthes/ . Bobbi Kerlin at Queen's University also has extensive information on preparing research proposals and reports http://kerlins.net/bobbi/. She includes very helpful information and numerous resources specifically for qualitative research

Your university or college requirements are a very valuable resource as well. Many institutions now post them online. One such example is New Mexico State University. Their guidelines are found at http://gradschool.nmsu.edu/Guidelines/index.html.   It is also very important to look at other theses and dissertations from your program or department, college, as well as those produced by other students of your advisor. Each study will be slightly different so it is important to examine not one, but several, so that you can develop a general sense of the expectations.

Practicing the Tasks

Task 10 requires you to produce a research report that includes the components commonly found in thesis or dissertation. Theses and dissertations are often substantially large documents, too large to reproduce and example here. However, as noted, your library is an excellent source for theses and dissertations from your institution. To obtain full text copies of theses and dissertations on-line, one resource is http://wwwlib.umi.com/cresearch/main, a service called current research@. This service coordinates with many institutions to have theses and dissertations published and available for a cost, or free of charge if your institution is enrolled.

1.   A condensed example of a student research proposal for a thesis is provided to support your efforts for Task 10. This proposal, written by Dan McCollum, appears at the end of this chapter and provides all of the components generally found in a thesis proposal. Dan is now a faculty member at the University of Houston-Clearlake. This task example is different from the Task 10 example criteria in that the results and discussion of the study are not provided here.

2.   Loujeania Bost's research competency is another example to support Task 10. Her program of study requires, as part of the students' competency exam process, that students conduct a study from start to finish under the support of their committee but primarily independently. The task is very similar to a mini-dissertation. Loujeania agreed to share her survey study as support for Task 10; it appears at the end of this chapter. This study not only filled a competency requirement, but also as the pilot study Loujeania conducted for her dissertation. Loujeania finished both the proposed research found here and her dissertation and now is at Clemson University.

3.   Unlike the first two proposals, the third example for Task 11, is a report of research by Joel D. Galbraith. Joel is a doctoral candidate at Penn State in Learning and Performance Systems. This is a research project he did for one of his classes. He will be modifying this class paper for publication. Joel will be relying on the APA manual to assist him with these modifications.

These three proposals can provide scaffolding for the graduate student researcher. Dan's study is primarily quantitative, Loujeania's study represents an example of descriptive survey research, and Joel's study includes a mixed methods design and has elements of both quantitative and qualitative research.

Test-Like Event

Circle the best response for each item.

1.   Which of the following examples illustrates the appropriate use of numbers in text?

   a.   150 students enrolled in the study as part of class procedures.
   b.   Participants included 8 learning disabled students in a self-contained classroom.
   c.   The study participants included one hundred and twenty three fourth graders.
   d.   Thirteen children were included in the study.

2.   Marcelle proofread Jeremy's research report. The report was well organized, the headings and structure were appropriate, however, there were many spelling and grammatical errors. Jeremy's research report illustrates

   a.   structure and format errors.
   b.   style errors.
   c.   format errors.
   d.   style and format errors.

3. In a research report prepared in APA style, which of the following is accurate?

    a. The manuscript is single-spaced.
    b. The manuscript is double-spaced.
    c. The first level headings are underlined.
    d. The first level headings are in all capital letters.

4. In a typical research report, the participants section is located in the

    a. preliminary pages.
    b. introduction.
    c. method.
    d. results.

5. In a typical research report, the hypotheses are located in the

    a. preliminary pages.
    b. main body.
    c. method.
    d. results.

6. Jamar studies cooperative learning. He trains students to use a specific cooperative learning strategy. The training he conducts should be described in detail in which section of his research report?

    a. Preliminary pages
    b. Introduction
    c. Method
    d. Results

7. Katherine conducted a survey study that addressed parent's perceptions of the benefits of field trips for their children's education. Her advisor required her to include the cover letter that she used to recruit parents for the study in her dissertation report. Where should Katherine include the letter?

    a. Preliminary pages
    b. Introduction
    c. Discussion
    d. Appendixes

8. Operational definitions of terms used in the study are generally found in which of the following components of a research report?

    a. Preliminary pages
    b. Introduction
    c. Method
    d. Results

9. Alya's report of her qualitative study contains an extensive section describing the participants and setting in her study. This information is most likely included in which section of her report?

    a. Preliminary pages
    b. Introduction
    c. Method
    d. Results

10. Yuki assigned groups of students to three different treatment conditions in a crossover design. The way she assigned students to groups should be presented in which of the following components of a research report?

    a. Design
    b. Participants
    c. Procedures
    d. Instruments

11. Jamila's dissertation was difficult. In her ethnographic study she traveled to several different regions of primarily rural America to examine the phenomenon of current one-room schools. She would like to recognize the efforts of both her family and a local foundation that supported her research. Where should this be placed in her dissertation report?

    a. Preliminary pages
    b. Introduction
    c. Appendix
    d. Abstract

12. According to APA guidelines, the text in a report should be written

    a. as single-spaced.
    b. in the past tense.
    c. in the first person.
    d. in Times font.

13.-16. Alan did a study of 124 low achieving second- grade learners' preference for instructional method in mathematics and is preparing the report. In one group, math concepts were initially introduced using manipulatives. In the other group, the same concepts were initially introduced through instructor-led presentation. Both before and after instruction learners' understanding of the concepts were assessed with a set of math problems. His research hypothesis was that those who were initially taught through instructor-led presentation would perform better than those initially taught through the use of manipulatives. He found no differences between the groups.

13. The content describing "124 low-achieving second grade learners" would be placed in which of the following sections of Alan's report?

    a. Preliminary pages
    b. Main body
    c. Method
    d. Results

14. The research hypothesis--those who were taught through instructor-led presentation would perform better--would be placed in which of the following sections of Alan's report?

    a. Preliminary pages
    b. Main body
    c. Method
    d. Results

15. The description of the math problems would be placed in which of the following sections of Alan's report?

    a. Preliminary pages
    b. Main body
    c. Method
    d. Results

16. In independent variable in this example is

    a. second-graders.
    b. math problems.
    c. low-achieving.
    d. instructional method.

17.-20. A. J. conducted a study on the typical strategies of emerging writers. He interviewed about a dozen writers and analyzed writing samples from each over the course of three years.

17. A.J.'s study best illustrates

    a. qualitative research.
    b. evaluation research.
    c. quantitative research.
    d. basic research.

18. In which section of his study is A.J. likely to include a description of the writers?

    a. Introduction
    b. Main body
    c. Methods
    d. Results

19. In which section of his report is A.J. likely to include a description of the techniques he used to score the writing samples?

    a. Introduction
    b. Main body
    c. Methods
    d. Discussion

20. A.J.'s written report will likely be written

    a. in a narrative form.
    b. in the second person.
    c. in the future tense.
    d. in the present tense.

21.-24. Gemma is conducting a survey study that addresses teachers' and principals' opinions regarding split-level classrooms. Split classrooms contain children from two grade levels within the same class. For example a classroom might contain both first and second or both third and fourth grade learners in one room with one teacher. Several schools in the State have introduced these classrooms.

21. Given Gemma's study, a description of the survey used in the research will be found in

    a. Preliminary pages
    b. Main body
    c. Method
    d. Results

22. Given Gemma's study, a description of the current trends in education related to multi-age classrooms would be found

    a. Preliminary pages
    b. Main body
    c. Method
    d. Results

23. A description about the years of experience of the participants would be found in the

    a. Preliminary pages
    b. Main body
    c. Method
    d. Results

24. In the study, it appears that teachers and principals may have different opinions regarding the use of split-level classrooms. Further, younger teachers seem more accepting of the practice. This information would be reported in the

    a. Preliminary pages
    b. Main body
    c. Method
    d. Results

Companion Website

For more practice on becoming competent in this chapter's objectives, go to the Companion Website that accompanies this text at www.prenhall.com/gay. This site includes:

Objectives with links to:
- more multiple-choice questions in Practice Quiz
- Applying What You Know essay questions
- relevant Web sites

Custom modules to help you:
- calculate statistical tests (see "Calculating Statistical Tests")
- do research (see "Research Tools and Tips")
- practice analyzing quantitative data (see "Analyzing Quantitative Data")
- practice analyzing qualitative data (see "Analyzing Qualitative Data")
- practice evaluating published articles (see "Evaluating Articles")

Chapter 21 Answers
Test-Like Event
1. d
2. b
3. b
4. c
5. b
6. c
7. d
8. b
9. c
10. c
11. a
12. b
13. c
14. b
15. c
16. d
17. c
18. c
19. c
20. a
21. c
22. b
23. c
24. d

Research Proposal:

Constructing the Motivational Components of Foreign Language Achievement Scale

Daniel L. McCollum

Educational Psychology Program

Department of Educational and School Psychology and Special Education

Pennsylvania State University

Introduction

Achievement motivation has been described as one of the most important factors in students' success (Covington, 2000). Across several decades of research, motivation has been demonstrated to be a complex, multidimensional construct and new dimensions of motivation continue to be identified and developed. Given this complexity, a single, comprehensive definition of motivation has been elusive. One definition that allows for the incorporation of the many constructs that have come to be identified as components of motivation was formulated by Wentzel (1999). She refers to motivation as a process and defines motivational processes: "a set of interrelated beliefs and emotions that direct behavior" (p. 76). The research proposed here will approach motivation according to Wentzel's (1999) definition.

In educational research, theories of motivation have continued to be conceived and revised as new constructs related to motivation have been identified. However, in educational research focused on foreign language learning, a social psychological theory of motivation has been dominant for over two decades (Dornyei, 1994). The theory can be traced back to Gardener and Lambert (1959), when the primary components of what is now the socio-educational model of motivation were introduced. The initial components of the model were two motivational orientations – instrumental and integrative. An instrumental orientation refers to people learning a foreign language because it will give them a practical advantage of some kind. An integrative orientation refers to people studying a foreign language to become a greater part of the second-language group. However, the instrumental and integrative orientations are not the same a motivation (Gardener, 1985).

In 1985, Gardener described three components of motivation to learn a foreign language. The three components are: effort towards a goal, desire to learn the language and satisfaction with studying the language. Considering these motivational components, the socio-educational model posits two groups of variables that influence motivational components. The groups are integrativeness (attitude toward the group speaking the desired language) and attitude towards the learning environment. The Attitude/Motivation Test Battery (AMTB) is an instrument designed to assess the three motivational components and the two groups of attitudes (Gardener, 1985). The AMTB and the theory of motivation underlying the instrument are not up to date with the theories of motivation in educational psychology.

Recently, researchers and educators of foreign language learning have suggested that motivation considerations in foreign language learning should become more oriented to theories addressed in educational psychology (i.e., Dornyei, 1994; Noels et al., 2000). The theorist who developed the dominant model of motivation in foreign language also encourages further exploration to develop a better understanding of motivation to learn a foreign language (Gardener and Tremblay, 1994). Several researchers have begun moving foreign language learning towards this goal and they have successfully contributed to a better understanding of motivation in the foreign language-learning context (i.e., Dornyei, 1994; Noels et al., 2000).

The research proposed here for the creation of a new instrument to measure motivational constructs will capture some of the dimensions of motivation from educational psychology research that have recently been investigated by foreign language researchers. The instrument will also incorporate constructs that are prevalent in the motivation research in educational psychology, but not addressed in foreign language learning. Thereby, the proposed research is for the development of a measurement instrument that incorporates goal orientation, persistence, effort, self-efficacy, prosocial behavior and self-worth.

Review of Literature

Goal Orientation

The early work on goal orientation theory led to the derivation of two types of goal orientation - mastery orientation and performance orientation (Dweck & Leggett, 1988). Mastery oriented students are interested in developing greater competence and appreciation for the material they are learning. On the other hand, performance oriented students are concerned with gaining positive judgments of their behavior (i.e., good grades). Building on the initial goal orientation dichotomy, Elliot, McGregor & Gable (1999) developed a goal orientation trichotomy that includes mastery orientation, performance-approach orientation (formerly performance) and performance-avoidance orientation. Students characterized as performance-avoidance seek to avoid negative judgments of their performance. Performance-avoidance oriented students tend to be less successful than mastery oriented and performance-approach oriented students. Furthermore, in research on the trichotomous achievement goal framework, Elliot et al. (1999) revealed that mastery and performance-approach goal orientations predicted greater effort and persistence than a performance-avoidance goal orientation.

The MCFLAS incorporates mastery and performance-approach goal orientation, thereby utilizing the components of goal orientation that have been positive predictors of academic success. Mastery goal orientation is

294

defined as a set of reasons for pursuing an achievement goal, centered on developing one's competence and appreciation for the material being learned. Performance goal orientation - defined as a set of reasons for pursuing an achievement goal, centered on gaining positive judgments for their achievements.

Willingness to make an Effort and Willingness to be Persistent

Prior to goal orientation research, Bandura (1982) and Covington (1984) also presented evidence that students who are motivated and successful tend to make greater efforts to achieve and tend to persist when faced with obstacles. As mentioned above, the more successful mastery oriented and performance-approach oriented students (opposed to performance-avoidance oriented students) demonstrate the behaviors of effort and persistence (Dweck & Leggett, 1988; Elliot et al., 1999). Thus, the pertinent research supports the inclusion of willingness to make an effort and willingness to be persistent variables, in a measure of motivational components. In the MCFLAS willingness to make an effort is defined as one's perception of the likelihood that they will take actions to achieve a goal and willingness to be persistent is defined as one's perception of the likelihood that they will continue towards a goal when faced with unexpected events and obstacles.

Self-efficacy

Self-efficacy refers to one's perceived capability to produce a specific outcome or attain a specific goal. One's self-efficacy impacts one's motivation and behavior (Bandura, 1982). It is important to realize that self-efficacy is considered a context-specific phenomenon, rather than a trait that is stable across situations. Thus, in the proposed research I will confine the construct of students' self-efficacy to the endeavor of learning a foreign language.

Willingness to be Prosocial

Willingness to be prosocial refers to one's perception of the course of actions they would take in a social-academic context (i.e., participating in group work). The prosocial component of motivational processes comes partly from the finding that mastery oriented students tend to be more successful in developing relationships with their peers; they develop more relationships and relationships that last longer (Dweck & Leggett, 1988). More recently, it has been revealed that prosocial goals and achievement have a strong, positive relationship (Wentzel, 1999). Furthermore, Covington (2000) posits that academic goals and social goals are strongly connected.

Although there is evidence of a relationship between prosocial behavior/goals and achievement goals, the nature of this relationship is relatively unexplored, therefore not fully understood. With limited research pertaining to student achievement in relation to prosocial behavior, leading researchers of achievement motivation are advocating more research into the prosocial goals-achievement goals area (i.e., Wentzel, 1999). Although the nature of the relationship of prosocial behaviors to academic achievement is relatively underdeveloped, it will be included in the MCFLAS.

Desire for Self-worth

While all of the aforementioned components of motivational processes are addressed often in the motivational research or are becoming increasingly addressed, self-worth has fallen outside of the mainstream of ongoing motivational theories. Despite some movement away from the considering self-worth in motivational theories, Covington's (1984) self-worth theory will be addressed in the proposed research because at the very least it has been shown to have a positive correlation with the effort and persistence components of motivation (Covington, 1984). The self-worth theory posits that one's desire for a sense of worth is one's motive for achievement. In the proposed research, desire for self-worth is addressed in a way that the level of one's desire for academically related self-worth is one component affecting one's motivation. In this research, desire for academically related self-worth is defined as one's desire to increase or maintain positive feelings about their competence in an academic context.

Summary

Considering past research, it is clear that motivational processes include an elaborate relationship among constructs such as goal orientation, persistence, effort, self-efficacy, prosocial behavior, and desire for self-worth. The relationship between these variables has been made apparent in multiple research efforts (i.e., Bandura, 1982; Covington, 1984; Dweck & Leggett, 1988; Elliot et al. 1999; Wentzel, 1999). The proposed research will incorporate all of the abovementioned components of motivational processes, except for performance-avoidance goal orientation. A performance-avoidance variable is being excluded from the initial version of the instrument due to the large number of constructs already being measured.

Purpose of Proposed Research

The purpose of the proposed research is to develop a scale for measuring the multiple components of motivational processes - as identified in educational psychology research - in the context of foreign language learning. The scale, titled Motivational Components of Foreign Language Achievement Scale (MCFLAS), has been developed to measure seven related constructs: desire for self-worth (e.g., Covington, 1984), mastery and performance goal orientations (e.g., Dweck & Leggett, 1988), self-efficacy (e.g., Bandura, 1982) willingness to be prosocial (e.g., Wentzel, 1999), willingness to make an effort and willingness to be persistent (e.g., Bandura, 1982; Covington, 1984; Elliot et al, 1999; Dweck & Legget, 1988). The primary psychometric objectives in the development of the MCFLAS are assessing the reliability of the subscales and providing evidence of the subscales' validity.

Method

Participants

Participants will consist of approximately 130 undergraduate students, enrolled in German language courses, from Pennsylvania State University. There are two data sources being used in this study - an existing data set and new data being gathered. All of the approximately 130 participants' come from classes that have identical grading criteria; this ensures the comparability of the criterion measure (class grade) between classes.

Design of the MCFLAS

I created the 42 items in the seven subscales of the MCFLAS (see Appendix B for definitions of constructs measured by the seven subscales and see Appendix C for items). Educational measurement and foreign language experts reviewed the items. Items are worded to assess the level of presence of each component. Responses to items indicate level of agreement on a Likert scale of 1 to 5, with 1 being strongly disagree and 5 being strongly agree. Higher scores on a subscale indicate more presence of the component it measures. Half of the items are reverse worded to help prevent acquiescence.

Social Desirability Scale

A shortened version of the Marlowe-Crowne Social Desirability Scale (Strahan & Gerbasi, 1972) is built into the MCFLAS to check for social desirability in responses.

Analysis

Scoring

Scores for the 42 items, seven subscales and the overall MCFLAS will be obtained using ITEMAN software (see Appendix C for items on the subscales and direction of scoring). Scoring of the MCFLAS will be done by calculating an average score for each subscale – dividing the score on each item by the total number of items on the subscale. By adding all of the average subscale scores, a composite score can be obtained. Higher scores on a component will indicate more presence of that component, and lower scores will indicate less presence.

Statistics, Reliability, Validity

All analyses will be conducted with SPSS version 10.0. First, descriptive statistics, including skewness and kurtosis of item scores, will be obtained. Second, exploratory factor analysis will be conducted; image extraction with oblimin rotation will be used because image extraction is good for scale items and the factors are expected to be oblique. Factor analysis will be used as to search for evidence of factorial and discriminant validity. Third, reliability will be determined using coefficient alpha. Fourth, predictive validity will be estimated by correlations between subscale scores and final class grades, as well as item scores and class grades. Fifth, item correlations with the social desirability scores will be determined.

Social Desirability

MCFLAS items that are substantially correlated with social desirability will be considered for exclusion from the scale (DeVellis, 1991).

Predictive Validity

Final course grades, which will act as the criterion measure in this study, will be obtained from participants' teachers at the time they complete the MCFLAS. Since grades are being obtained after the MCFLAS is completed, they will serve as a predicted criterion.

Factorial and Discriminant Validity

Evidence of factorial validity can be provided by items from the same conceptual subscales loading on the same factors in the exploratory factor analysis. Evidence of discriminant validity can also be provided through the factor analysis, such that items from conceptually different subscales load on different factors.

Summary of Proposal

The MCFLAS incorporates the motivational components of goal orientation, persistence, effort, willingness to be prosocial, self-efficacy and self-worth. The MCFLAS measures all of these components of motivation in a foreign language context. Therefore, the instrument is unique in two important ways. First, no existing instrument measures all of the constructs that the MCFLAS purports to measure, so there is also no instrument that measures all of the constructs in a foreign language context. The creation of the MCFLAS can be valuable to foreign language educators and researchers, who have called for incorporating motivational theories from educational psychology into foreign language learning. The MCFLAS will offer foreign language educators and researchers a comprehensive tool for measuring multiple components of motivational processes put forward in educational psychology.

Timeline

Creating the MCFLAS will require several steps. The steps of developing the materials – test items and informed consent form, acquiring IRB approval and collecting data have already been completed as part of a pilot study. Next, the analyses of the data will be completed; this will take approximately one month. Finally, the write-up of the results, discussion and conclusions will be completed; this will also take about one month.

Appendix A

Literature Search Plan

The literature search for the proposed research was conducted using PsycINFO and ERIC. Search terms included combinations of the following: achievement motivation, motivation, goal orientation, self-efficacy, self-worth, classroom prosocial behavior, prosocial goals, second language learning and foreign language learning.

Appendix B

1. Self-efficacy - defined as one's perception of their own capabilities to take actions necessary for attaining a specific outcome

2. Mastery goal orientation - defined as a set of reasons for pursuing an achievement goal, centered around developing one's competence and appreciation for the material being learned

3. Performance goal orientation - defined as a set of reasons for pursuing an achievement goal, centered around gaining positive judgments for their achievements

4. Desire for academically related self-worth - defined as one's desire to increase or maintain positive feelings about their competence in an academic context

5. Willingness to be prosocial - defined as one's perception of the course of actions they would take in a social-academic context (i.e., participating in group work)

6. Willingness to be persistent - defined as one's perception of the likelihood that they will continue towards a goal when faced with unexpected events and obstacles

7. Willingness to make an effort - defined as one's perception of the likelihood that they will take actions to achieve a goal

Performance Goal Orientation (4)

1. It will be satisfying to pass my foreign language class, even if everyone else does better than me. (-)
8. I am learning a foreign language because I want to show people how cultured I am.
16. My grade in my foreign language class is of little importance to me. (-)
37. Learning a foreign language is important because in a global job market employers may see me as more valuable.

Self-Efficacy (7)

2. I am confident that I can learn the material in my foreign language class.
3. Regardless of my efforts, it is unlikely that I will do well in my foreign language class. (-)
14. Learning a foreign language is too difficult for me to do. (-)
21. I am capable of learning a foreign language.
28. Whatever difficulties students in my foreign language class may have, the difficulties will be even worse for me. (-)
31. I have some serious doubts about my ability to learn a foreign language. (-)
40. I believe I have the ability to learn a foreign language.

Willingness to make an Effort (5)

10. By completing required tasks, I will succeed in my foreign language class.
18. It is unimportant to make an effort to learn the material in my foreign language class. (-)
25. By making an effort I will learn the material in my foreign language class.
29. The effort I make will have a significant effect on how well I do in my foreign language class.
36. Working hard in my foreign language class will have little effect on my level of success in the class. (-)

Willingness to be Prosocial (6)

4. It is important to me to provide a positive contribution to group work in my foreign language class.
7. I would want to help a peer in my foreign language class if they were struggling with the class.
13. It is annoying to work together with peers in my foreign language class. (-)
22. I consider it valuable to make friends in my foreign language class.
32. Feeling like part of the group in my foreign language class is of very little importance to me. (-)
38. There is little value for me to develop friendly relationships with people in my foreign language class. (-)

Willingness to be Persistent (6)

5. I will compensate for any setbacks that I may encounter in order to perform well in my foreign language class.
12. Distractions will eventually stop me from learning a foreign language. (-)
15. I would keep trying my best in my foreign language class even if I were doing poorly.
20. When obstacles arise in my foreign language class, I will still do what I can to get my work done.
27. It is highly unlikely that I will be able to overcome difficult events on my way to learning a foreign language. (-)
42. I would stop trying to do well in my foreign language class if I started to have many difficulties with the material. (-)

Self-Worth (6)

6. Considering myself a competent student is unimportant to me. (-)
9. I feel like an adequate student even when my performance in school is less than I hoped for. (-)
17. I like to do my best in school because it makes me feel like a good student.
24. I value myself less when I do poorly in school.
39. Feeling good about myself has very little to do with how well I do in school. (-)
34. I consider it important to think of myself as a competent student.

Mastery Goal Orientation (8)

11. I dislike the challenge involved in learning a foreign language. (-)
19. My desire to understand a foreign language is the reason I am taking this class.
23. Getting a good grade without developing an appreciation for the foreign language will be disappointing to me.
26. I am learning a foreign language mostly for the sake of learning something new.
30. The only reason I am taking a foreign language class is to fulfill a requirement towards my degree. (-)
33. Enrolling in a foreign language class had very little to do with my appreciation for foreign languages. (-)
35. Getting a good grade in my foreign language class is far more important than truly learning the language. (-)
41. I am learning a foreign language because it is interesting.

Note: Items with a (-) are reversed scored.

References

Bandura, A. (1982). Self-efficacy mechanism in human agency. American Psychologist, 37(2), 122-147.

Covington, M.V. (1984). The self-worth theory of achievement motivation: Findings and Implications. The Elementary School Journal, 85(1), 1-20.

Covington, M. V. (2000). Goal theory, motivation and school achievement: An integrative review. Annual Review of Psychology, 51, 171-200.

Dornyei, Z. (1994). Motivation and motivating in the foreign language classroom. The Modern Language Journal, 78, 273-284.

Dweck, C. S., & Leggett, E. L. (1988). A social-cognitive approach to motivation and personality. Psychological Review, 95(2), 256-273.

Elliot, A. J., McGregor, H. A., & Gable, S. (1999). Achievement goals, study strategies, and exam performance: A mediational analysis. Journal of Educational Psychology, 91(3), 549-563.

Gardner, R. C. (1985). Social psychology and second language learning: The role of attitudes and motivation. London: Edward Arnold.

Gardner, R. C., & Lambert, W. E. (1959). Motivational variables in second language acquisition. Canadian Journal of Psychology, 13, 266-272.

Gardner, R. C., & Tremblay, P. F. (1994). On motivation, research agendas, and theoretical frameworks. The Modern Language Journal, 78, 359-368.

Noels, K.A., Pelletier, L.G., Clement, R., & Vallerand, R.J. (2000). Why are you learning a second language? Motivational orientations and self-determination theory. Language Learning, 50(1), 57-85.

Strahan, R., & Gerbasi, K. C. (1972). Short, homogenous versions of the Marlowe-Crowne social desirability scale. Journal of Clinical Psychology, 28, 191-193.

Wentzel, K. R. (1999). Social-motivational processes and interpersonal relationships: Implications for understanding motivation at school. Journal of Educational Psychology, 91(1), 76-97.

Teacher Familiarity and Use of Reading Comprehension Strategies With Students With Learning Disabilities

Loujeania Williams Bost

Department of Educational and School Psychology and Special Education

The Pennsylvania State University

Spring 2002

Abstract

Data were analyzed from 158 survey respondents to examine (1) general and special education teachers' familiarity and teaching of 11 reading comprehension strategies proven to be effective for students with learning disabilities and (2) the contextual variables related to the sustained use of reading comprehension strategies. Overall, findings revealed that many teachers report that they are unfamiliar with these comprehension strategies. The findings also indicate that although familiarity with strategies is fundamental to strategy teaching, familiarity alone does not account for all the variability associated with strategy use. Following regression analyses, findings concluded that continuing to teach reading strategies, teaching reading strategies while teaching content, receiving mentoring and coaching in the classroom, and observing benefit for the students contributed significantly to strategy use. However, the relationship between those variables changed between general and special educators and across grade level assignments.

Background

Learning to read is one of the most important things children accomplish in elementary school because reading is the foundation for most of their future endeavors (Kameénui & Carnine, 1998; Stevens, Slavin, & Farness, 1991). Reading skills acquired in the early elementary grades should emphasize mastery of basic components of reading such as phonemic awareness, segmenting, and decoding (Adams, 1999). However, beginning in the upper elementary grades and middle school the emphasis of reading should move to emphasize comprehension (Armbruster, Anderson, & Ostertag, 1987).

Most students learn to read fluently and demonstrate good comprehension skills. However, many students in elementary and secondary schools show serious deficits in reading (National Assessment of Educational Progress, 1998; National Partnership in Reading, 2001). Students with LD have more difficulty comprehending what they read than do students without disabilities, even when controlling for the level of decoding (Englert & Thomas, 1987; Taylor & Williams, 1983). They have problems remembering facts and details of text materials, locating and identifying main ideas, clarifying, interpreting, making inferences, and summarizing information (Gajria & Salvia, 1992; Malone & Mastropieri, 1992). A major reason many children with LD experience poor comprehension is due to a failure to read strategically and to spontaneously monitor their understanding of what is being read (Englert & Thomas, 1987; Kameénui & Carnine, 1998; Paris, Wasik, & Turner, 1991; Stevens, 1999).

Strategy instruction can help students improve these weaknesses. In the past two decades, several strategies have proven to be effective in facilitating reading comprehension in students with LD. Examples of these strategies include (a) self-monitoring (e.g., Graves, 1986), (b) summarizing the key points in a paragraph (Jenkins, Heliotis, Stein, & Haynes, 1987), (c) asking questions that stimulate activation of relevant background knowledge (e.g., Billingsley & Wildman, 1988), (d) extracting main ideas (Graves, 1986; Wong & Jones, 1982), (e) self-questioning (Wong & Jones, 1982), (f) paraphrasing (Schumaker, Denton, & Deshler, 1984), (g) using text structures (Bakken, Mastropieri & Scruggs, 1997; and (h) promoting visual imagery (Clark, Deshler, Schumaker, Alley, & Warner, 1984).

Because of the success of these intensive studies, general and special education teachers are being asked to teach reading comprehension strategies to students with LD. To teach reading comprehension strategies to students with LD, teachers must be able to teach the specific strategy steps and assist the student to understand when and how to use the strategy with flexibility. Teachers must also balance strategy instruction and content learning while motivating students to engage in the learning process (Scanlon, Deshler, & Schumaker, 1996).

However, teachers vary considerably in the extent to which they teach reading comprehension strategies to students with LD (e.g., Englert & Tarrant, 1995; Gersten, Morvant, & Brengelman, 1995; El- Dinary & Schuder, 1993; Klingner, Vaughn, & Schumm, 1998). Often, teachers do not teach or encourage the use of these strategies at all. A great deal of attention and discussion has ensued regarding ways to increase and sustain the use of reading comprehension strategies by general and special educators. Yet, research in this area has been slow to emerge. As a result, we do not know what teachers know about reading comprehension strategies, which strategies are being taught to students with LD, or what variables or combination of variables are likely to sustain the use of these strategies in classrooms.

Review of Relevant Research

Explanations are cited in the literature as to why teachers generally do not implement research-based interventions in their classrooms. Most of these explanations are in the form of perceived beliefs. As such, they are speculative, unverified, and do not form a scientific basis for intervention. Similarly, explanations about sustained use of reading comprehension strategies exist primarily in the form of self-reflective essays (Abbott, Walton, Tapia, & Greenwood, 1999; Fuchs and Fuchs, 1998; Gersten, Chard, & Baker, 2000; Pressley & El – Dinary; 1997). However, there are four data based studies on strategy familiarity and use: three studies examining general education teacher familiarity and use of strategies and one examining sustained use of reading strategies by general and special educators. These studies are reviewed below.

Familiarity and Use of Reading Comprehension Strategies

Often teachers do not teach comprehension strategies to students with LD or encourage their use. One assertion made in the literature is that teachers have not been taught these strategies and therefore, cannot teach them (Malouf & Schiller, 1995; Manzo, 1991; Vadasy, Jenkins, Antil, Phillips, & Pool, 1997). Manzo (1991) posits that even a cursory analysis of teacher preparation practices would support the presumption that training in reading comprehension strategies is minimal rather than optimal and that many veteran teachers had not even heard of earlier strategies because the strategies did not begin to appear in textbooks until the early 1980's. Research appears to confirm this assertion in the three studies examining teacher familiarity of reading comprehension strategies by general education teachers. The results of these studies revealed that approximately 40% of the teachers surveyed were unfamiliar with strategies [e.g. Know -Want to know – Learned (K-W-L), Survey, Question, Read, Recite, Review (SQ3R)] recommended in the professional literature (Howe, Grierson, & Richmond, 1997; Nichols, Rupley, & Mergen, 1998; Spor & Schneider, 1999). Spor and Schneider, (1999) also reported that teachers with 5 years of experience or less, who were recently certified, appeared to be more familiar with strategies than teachers with between 6 and 10 years of experience.

Another assertion in the literature is that even when teachers are presented with innovative practices designed to support the learning of students across a range of achievement levels, they do not necessarily use them (Gersten, Vaughn, Deshler, & Schiller, 1997; Malouf & Schiller, 1995). The four studies examined in this review appear to confirm this assertion. The results of these studies revealed that many teachers who are familiar with reading strategies, still do not use them. Teachers reported use of general reading strategies (e.g., guided reading, guided writing, fix up strategies, journal writing, prediction, and setting purpose) rather than strategies like self-questioning, graphic organizers, and comprehension monitoring.

Using analysis of variance procedures, Spor and Schneider, (1999) found that teachers who had received recent training during reading workshops or college coursework reported more strategy use than those not receiving training. However, they found no relationship between strategy use and years of teaching experience. Although recently certified teachers reported more strategy use than did more experienced teachers. The latter finding is consistent with Manzo's (1991) explanation that strategy instruction was not a part of many veteran teachers repertoire of skills because the strategies did not begin to appear in college textbooks until the early 1980's.

Contextual Variables

Another assertion in the literature is that teachers' use of reading comprehension strategies is affected by contextual factors. These factors include demands on teacher time, training, mentoring and support, administrative directives, and the extent to which the strategies fit within the overall context of the classroom affect teacher (Abbott, et al. 1999; Gersten et al. 1997; Malouf & Schiller, 1995; Pressley & El Dinary, 1997; Vaughn, Klingner, & Hughes, 2000). These factors were thought to singularly or in combination influence teacher decision-making about the sustained use of reading comprehension strategies.

To test a number of these explanations, Klingner, Vaughn, Terjero, & Arguelles, (1999) examined the extent to which teachers who had participated in a yearlong professional development program had sustained and /or modified three instructional practices. The study followed the teachers over a three year period to determine: (a) how often they had continued to use three reading strategies; (b) the ways in which teachers had adapted or modified the three strategies; (c) the reasons for adapting or modifying the practices; and (d) the factors teacher perceived to have facilitated or impeded their implementation of the practices.

The extent to which teachers maintained the practices over time was assessed by classroom observations during which researchers took extensive notes about the types and quality of the interactions between students and teachers and among students and specific information about the ways in which teachers adapted the practices. Observations were scheduled at times convenient for the teacher and teachers were aware of the purpose of the observations.

Results from the study indicated that all but one teacher had maintained one or more of the practices at high levels. Unfortunately the practice implemented least was Collaborative Strategic Reading (a multi- reading comprehension strategy). In addition, teachers in the study were most likely to sustain the practices when: (a) they were part of a support network that enabled them to discuss the practice and get ideas about its continued implementation; (b) they received ongoing administrative backing for instructional practices; (c) their students benefited from the practice and/or like the practice; and (e) the teacher had in-depth knowledge of the practice and how the practice helps students learn. Teachers also identified time to implement the practice, concerns about content coverage, mandated curriculum requirements, and preparing students for the high-stakes assessments as factors affecting sustained use of the practices. Not surprisingly, teachers also reported that their own personal instructional styles affected their use of the practices.

The results of these studies suggest that teachers may not teach reading comprehension strategies because they are unfamiliar with them. In addition, even when teachers are familiar with strategies, they may not use more effective strategies. These studies also identified contextual variables that teachers report as affecting their use of reading comprehension strategies. The extent to which the findings of these studies will generalize to working with students with LD is unknown as is the accuracy of the teachers' perceptions about the contextual variables that sustain reading comprehension strategy use over time. The purposes of this study were to examine (1) general and special education teachers' familiarity and teaching of reading comprehension strategies to students with learning disabilities and (2) the contextual variables related to the sustained use of reading comprehension strategies.

Method

A Cross- sectional survey design was utilized to investigate the research questions. An instrument entitled Reading Comprehension Strategy Questionnaire (RCSQ) was used to survey the selected sample of participants. Specific information relative to the design of the survey instrument, selection of the survey sample, collection of data and data analysis is presented next.

Instrumentation

Instrument development. The RCSQ was developed specifically for this study and used to elicit quantitative data about teachers' reported familiarity of reading comprehension strategies, the types of students to which these strategies were taught, and contextual variables related to sustained use of research validated reading comprehension strategies. The RCSQ consists of three sections and contains 25 closed format questions that allowed quick collection of detailed information from large numbers of individuals.

The first section contains seven questions to ascertain demographic information related to group membership [i.e. years of teaching experience, grade level assignment, area(s) of instruction, type of setting, highest degree attained, area of certification, and teaching routine]. The second section consists of 14 questions intended to ascertain teachers' familiarity and use of reading comprehension strategies. Eleven strategies were real and three were bogus strategies added to assess veracity of responses (Gall, Borg & Gall, 1996; Wiersma, 2000). The list of reading comprehension strategies was compiled from a review of the literature that included PsycINFO and ERIC citations, research reviews (Gersten, Fuchs, Williams, & Baker, 2001; Mastropieri, Scruggs, Bakken, & Wheadon, 1996), current college textbooks (Carnine, Silbert, & Kameénui, 1999; Deshler, Ellis, & Lenz, 1996; Mercer & Mercer, 2001), and proceedings from the National Reading Panel Report (National Institute of Child Health and Human Development, 2000).

Each strategy was rated on two dimensions. The first dimension required respondents to rate their familiarity of and use of each strategy on the following 3-point scale. One "Never heard of it"; 2 "I have heard of it"; 3 "I can teach it". Respondents were required to circle the applicable choice in the column marked "Familiarity".

The second dimension required respondents to identify the students to which each reading comprehension strategy was taught. Respondents used the following codes: 1 "I teach this strategy to all my students"; 2 "I teach this strategy to my students with comprehension problems"; 3 "I teach this strategy to my students with IEPs"; 4 "I do not teach this strategy"; and 5 "I used to teach this strategy but no longer do so". For each strategy previously rated 1 "never heard of it", the respondents were asked to place a check in the N/A column.

The third section of the questionnaire consisted of four closed questions to examine the contextual variables were related to the sustained use of a learning strategy (see for example, Gersten et al. 2000; Gersten et al. 1997; Malouf & Schiller, 1995; Pressley & El Dinary, 1997; Rogers, 1995; Vadasy et al. 1997; Vaughn et al. 2000). The first question asked where respondents learned strategies and if that source of learning had influenced them to teach strategies. A list of eight sources was provided (undergraduate course work, graduate coursework, state or national conferences, peers and colleagues, district or state sponsored training, professional journals, and textbooks or curricula guides). Respondents chose one of three response options for each applicable source (learned, learned and influenced, and influenced). Respondents could indicate more than one source.

The second question asked the respondent's to select from an array of factors (e.g., support from colleagues and administrators, student benefit, personal use of a strategy, parental request) those factors that prompted their teaching of each reading comprehension strategy. Respondents could select as many factors as applicable. Respondents were also given the option to indicate if they once taught a strategy but stopped. If the respondent selected this option, they were requested to answer questions three and four.

The third question asked the respondent to select from an array of factors (e.g., lack of support of colleagues and administrators, lack of student benefit, strategy complexity, inability to teach while teaching content, lack of time) those factors that impeded or were barriers to their teaching of strategies. Respondents could indicate more than one source.

The final question asked the respondent to select from an array of factors (e.g., mentoring and coaching, administrative support, student benefit, time, part of school curriculum) those factors that would encourage them to resume teaching strategies if they once taught strategies and stopped. Respondents could indicate more than one source.

Instrument validation. As a confirmatory step in the refinement process, a draft of the survey was submitted to six experts in reading comprehension strategies, learning disabilities, or survey research. Each expert was asked to review the survey's content for completeness, clarity, and relevance. Feedback from these experts was incorporated into the questionnaire.

The questionnaire was modified and pre- tested using 20 general and special education teachers who were similar to the target populations. The questionnaire was reformatted to provide extra space where teachers could comment about each question's clarity and relevance. Teachers were also asked to state what they thought each question meant. The responses from the field test were incorporated into the final version of the RCSQ.

Sample Selection

Participants. Participants were general and special education teachers, teaching fifth through twelfth graders with LD in Pennsylvania public schools. Teachers who did not teach students with LD were not included in the sample. Potential participants were identified through the following procedures. First, two rural and two non-rural intermediate units (IU) were randomly selected from the 9 intermediate units in western Pennsylvania. These IUs served urban, suburban, and rural school districts and one suburban charter school. Second, school buildings housing at least three learning support classes for fifth - through twelfth - grade students with LD were identified from the statewide database maintained by the Pennsylvania Department of Education. Two hundred nineteen school buildings with 1800 teachers were identified. Third, school buildings were randomly selected electronically until 100 general education teachers and 100 special education teachers were chosen. The final sample included 70 teachers from six urban schools, 66 teachers from six suburban schools, and 64 teachers from six rural schools.

Data Collection Procedures

The four intermediate unit directors and the special education coordinator of the charter school were contacted to ascertain their willingness to allow the administration of the survey during required fall (2001) in-service training sessions sponsored by the intermediate units and the charter school. All directors agreed to allow 30 minutes at the beginning of the training sessions and to assign potential participants together to facilitate the administration. Six training sessions were held on three different days.

The investigator attended the in-service and followed these procedures. First, the RCSQ and a cover letter were distributed, the study was explained, and participants completed consent forms. Next, the participants completed the surveys. Total administration time for the survey, including oral directions, ranged from 15 to 20 minutes. The researcher remained in the room, collected the completed surveys, and left the training site. Finally, the surveys were checked for completeness, numbered, and coded for data analysis.

Results

One hundred eighty – four completed surveys (92 %) were returned from general and special education teachers. Twelve questionnaires completed by special educators were dropped (i.e., 5 special educators taught in lower grades; 4 special educators were administrators without student caseloads; and 3 special education teachers were emotional support teachers). Eight questionnaires completed by general educators were dropped (i.e., 3 educators were principals without student caseloads; three taught in lower grades; and 2 did not teach students with LD). One of the aforementioned questionnaires was dropped because the respondent reported the use of bogus strategies. Six questionnaires were discarded because of preservative responses, (i.e., responses did not vary and were judged to have been made in all likelihood without reading the stem; 4 of which also reported familiarity and use of bogus strategies). Therefore, 158 surveys were included in the data analysis.

Sample Demographics

The participants included in the data analyses were 86 (54%) general education teachers and 72 (46%) were special education teachers. The mean number of years of teaching experience was 15.5 years (with range of 1 to 34 years). Fifty-nine percent (n = 94) of respondents had earned graduate degrees. One hundred and ten respondents (69.6%) held certification in general education and 73 (46%) held certification in special education. Twenty-five (16 %) of these teachers (one general education teacher and 24 special education teachers) were certified in both general and special education. Three subject areas were identified most frequently: English, language arts, and math. Fifty-three respondents (33.5%) reported teaching in other areas, 18 (34%) were teachers of reading.

Question 1: What Reading Comprehension Strategies Do Teachers Report Enough Familiarity To Teach?

Responses to the question about familiarity were first tabulated, and means and standard deviations calculated. Teachers report some familiarity with all strategies. Teachers report the most familiarity with main idea (M = 1.88), summarization (M = 1.79), and prior knowledge (M = 1.80) strategies. Teachers report least familiarity with K-W-L (M = 1.30), question generation (M =1.46), and comprehension monitoring (M =1.50) strategies. Closer inspection of the means indicate that teachers are often unfamiliar with validated reading comprehension strategies.

Question 2: What Reading Comprehension Strategies Do Teachers Report Using?

Responses to the question about the strategies taught by teachers were tabulated, and means and standard deviations calculated. As shown in Table 2, teachers reported teaching all strategies to at least some students, primarily those with comprehension problems or IEP objectives. Mean scores for teacher use range from zero (I do not teach this strategy) to 2 (I teach this strategy to all my students). A score of 1.0 indicates that the teacher reported teaching the strategy to students with comprehension problems or students with IEP objectives. The strategies likely to be taught to most students were main idea ($M = 1.57$), prior knowledge ($M = 1.50$), and summarization ($M = 1.48$). The strategies least likely to be taught were K-W-L ($M = .92$), visual imagery ($M = 1.14$), and question generation ($M = 1.17$). Inspection of the means, indicate that teachers report more familiarity than use of comprehension strategies, indicating even when teachers are familiar with strategies, they do not always teach them.

Question 3: Is There A Significant Difference Between Teacher Familiarity And Teacher Use?
To determine if a significant relationship existed between strategy familiarity and strategy use, familiarity and use scores were computed for each respondent by summing the ratings across all strategies. Familiarity and use scores were rank ordered and Spearman Rank Order correlation was computed. A high positive correlation ($r = .70$, $p < .01$) was found between strategy familiarity and strategy use. Further analysis revealed significant differences in strategy familiarity ($F = 10.97$, $p < .001$) and strategy use ($F = 15.67$, $p < .001$) between middle and high school general education teachers. Similarly; differences in strategy familiarity ($F = 10.20$, $p < .001$) and strategy use ($F = 11.94$, $p < .001$) were found between high school general and special education teachers; and in strategy use ($F = 12.24$, $p = .001$) between middle school general and special education teachers. Significant differences were not found between middle and high school special educators.

Question 4: What Contextual Variables Contribute To Teacher Use Of Research Validated Reading Comprehension Strategies?

Preliminary testing of the data found no significant correlations based upon years of experience, highest degree attained, or area of certification. However, the literature is clear that elementary and secondary educators differ in their approaches to teaching, as do general and special educators. Therefore, four parallel stepwise multiple regression analyses were performed (middle school general education teachers, high school general education teachers, middle school special education teachers, and high school special education teachers). In the analyses, strategy use was the criterion variable and ten contextual variables identified in the literature on sustaining research-validated interventions served as predictors. Variables were entered into the system when correlations were significant at $F \leq .05$ and removed when the variable no longer contributed at $F > .15$.

Middle school general education teachers. The solution to the stepwise multiple regression analysis for middle school general education teachers was reached at step three. Predictor variables contributing to general education teachers were familiarity of strategies, student benefit, and teaching while teaching content. Familiarity of strategies accounted for the greatest amount of the variance (57 %). Next was student benefit (13%), followed by teaching while teaching content (8%). These variables, all made significant contributions in accounting for the variance in strategy use ($p < .001$, $p < .001$, $p < .001$ respectively). These predictor variables accounted for approximately 78% of the variance associated with strategy use ($R = .88$, $SE = 2.62$), leaving approximately 23 % accounted for by other variables. These results infer that strategy familiarity, student benefit, and the ability to teach strategies while teaching content are significant contributors to strategy use for middle school general education teachers. Table 3 contains the results of the analysis in more detail.

High school general education teachers. Table 4 contains the solution to the stepwise multiple regression analysis for high school general education teachers was reached at step two. Predictor variables contributing to general education teachers were familiarity of strategies and mentoring and coaching. Familiarity of strategies accounted for the greatest amount of the variance (43 %) and mentoring and coaching accounted for 9 % of the variance with strategy use. These variables, all made significant contributions in accounting for the variance in strategy use ($p < .001$, $p = .049$ respectively). These predictor variables accounted for approximately 52 % of the variance associated with strategy use ($R = .72$, $SE = 5.64$), leaving approximately 48 % accounted for by other variables. These results infer that strategy familiarity and receiving mentoring and coaching to teach strategies are significant contributors to strategy use for high school general education teachers

Middle school special education teachers. The solution to the stepwise multiple regression analysis for middle school special education teachers was reached at step three. Predictor variables contributing to middle school special education teachers were familiarity of strategies and continuing to teach strategies, and teaching strategies while teaching content. Familiarity of strategies accounted for the greatest amount of the variance (23 %). Next, continuing to teach strategies accounted and for approximately 14 % of the variance and teaching strategies while teaching content accounted for 7 % of the variance. These variables, all made significant contributions in accounting for the variance in strategy use (p = .001, p = .003, p = .024 respectively). These predictor variables accounted for approximately 45 % of the variance associated with strategy use (R = .69, SE = 4.91), leaving nearly 55 % accounted for by other variables. These results infer that strategy familiarity, continuing to teach strategies, and the ability to teach strategies while teaching content are significant contributors to strategy use for middle school special education teachers. Table 5 contains the results of the analysis in more detail.

High school special education teachers. As shown in Table 6, the solution to the stepwise multiple regression analysis for high school special education teachers was reached at step two. Predictor variables contributing to high school special education teachers were familiarity of strategies and teaching strategies while teaching with content. Familiarity with strategies accounted for the greatest amount of the variance approximately (29 %) and teaching strategies while teaching with content accounted for approximately 16 % of the variance. These variables, all made significant contributions in accounting for the variance in strategy use (p = .006, p = .025 respectively). These predictor variables accounted for approximately 45 % of the variance associated with strategy use (R = .67, SE = 3.97), leaving nearly 55 % accounted for by other variables. These results infer that strategy familiarity and the ability to teach strategies while teaching content are significant contributors to strategy use for high school special education teachers.

Discussion

The purpose of this study was twofold: (1) to examine the extent to which general and special education teachers are familiar with and teach students with learning disabilities (LD) to use research validated reading comprehension strategies; and (2) to examine contextual variables related to the sustained use of research validated reading comprehension strategies. In examining the findings of this study, certain inferences can be drawn and possible explanations can be discussed relative to the research validated reading comprehension strategies taught by general and special education teachers to students with LD. These are addressed here, in the order they were identified in the study.

Familiarity of Reading Comprehension Strategies

Both general and special education teachers report some familiarity with reading comprehension strategies found to be effective in improving students with LD's comprehension skills. However, several of the strategies included in this study remain unfamiliar to teachers. For example, over forty percent of the teachers reported that they had never heard of K-W-L, comprehension monitoring, and question generation strategies. In addition, nearly 30% of the high school general educators reported that they had never even heard of the strategies with which other high school teachers reported were most familiar (i.e., identifying main ideas, prior knowledge, and summarization). These findings are consistent with previous research conducted with elementary and secondary general education teachers. Several researchers (Howe, et al. 1997; Nichols, et al. 1998; Spor & Schneider, 1999) found that teachers often reported that they were unfamiliar with reading comprehension strategies recommended in professional literature. The findings in this study extend these findings to special education teachers working with students with LD. That teachers are not familiar enough to teach these strategies to students with LD is cause for great alarm because of the demonstrated effectiveness of these strategies on the academic achievement of students with LD. This alarm is particularly heightened at the high school level where students with LD are expected to learn difficult content in general education classrooms.

Use of Reading Comprehension Strategies

The high correlation ($r = .67, p < .01$) between familiarity of strategies and strategy use in this study indicated that teacher familiarity and teacher practice are inextricably linked. Essentially, teachers teach strategies that are most familiar to them. For example, special education teachers reported that they were most familiar with strategies for main idea, prior knowledge, summarization, and clarifying. These teachers also reported teaching these strategies to more students. General educators reported that they were most familiar with strategies for main idea, prior knowledge, summarization, and text structure and reported teaching these strategies to more students as well.

While teachers reported teaching some reading comprehension strategies to students with LD, the results of this study indicate that there is a significant difference between the strategies teachers report they can teach and the strategies they teach. This finding is consistent with previous research conducted with elementary and secondary general education teachers (Howe, et al. 1997; Nichols, et al. 1998; Spor & Schneider, 1999). It is also consistent with findings from an empirical study (Klingner, et al. 1999) and self reflective essays by special education researchers (Abbott, et al. 1999; Gersten et al. 2000; Gersten et al. 1997; Mastropieri & Scruggs, 1998) indicating that even when teachers are familiar with research validated reading strategies, these strategies are often not taught to students with LD.

Contextual Variables Related to Teaching Reading Comprehension Strategies

The results from this study indicate that although familiarity with strategies is fundamental to strategy teaching, familiarity alone does not account for all the variability associated with strategy use. In the regression analysis conducted to identify significant contextual variables that contributed to strategy use, four contextual variables emerged as predictors for the teachers in the sample: teaching reading while teaching content, student benefit, continuing to teach strategies, and receiving mentoring and coaching.

Teaching while teaching content. Teaching reading while teaching content was a predictor variable for all groups except high school general education teachers. It was anticipated that this variable would emerge because of the strong positive correlation found with strategy use ($r = .53$, $p < .01$), and the belief by some teachers that strategy instruction and content instruction are not concurrent events. This finding is consistent with findings of previous research on professional development (Vaughn, et al. 2000). Vaughn, and colleagues (2000) found that general and special education teachers prefer instructional practices that are feasible to implement within the general education context and are relevant for most, if not all, students. Vaughn, and colleagues (2000) also report that comprehension strategy takes time for teachers and students to learn, particularly when students lack basic reading skills and are lost with content text. As such, this finding further supports the importance of integrating strategy instruction into content learning.

Student benefit. A significant and encouraging finding was that student benefit emerged as a predictor variable for general education teachers in middle schools and accounted for over 13 % of the variance associated with strategy use. This group was the only group in which student benefit emerged as a significant predictor of strategy use. This finding implies the value of student benefit as a variable influencing teachers sustained teaching of reading comprehension strategies. This finding may also account for the significant difference in strategy use for this group of teachers as compared with the other three groups. This finding is consistent with that of Klingner and her colleagues (1999) in which a critical determinant toward teachers adopting new practices was whether the practice led to demonstrable gains in student achievement.

Receiving mentoring and coaching. Receiving mentoring and coaching was a significant predictor of strategy use for high school general education teachers. This variable accounted for
9 % of the variance associated with strategy use for this group. It is also noteworthy that the mean strategy use by this group of teachers was significantly less than the mean for high school special education teachers. Although, this variable emerged as a predictor in only one group, this finding is significant because of the way in which the question was posed in the survey questionnaire. The final question in the survey asked the respondent to select from an array of factors (e.g., mentoring and coaching, administrative support, student benefit, time, part of school curriculum), those factors that would encourage them to resume teaching strategies if they once taught strategies and stopped. This finding may infer that providing mentoring and coaching to high school general education teachers may increase strategy use.

This finding is also supported by previous research conducted in sustaining research-based interventions. For example, Gersten et al. (1995) and Englert and Tarrant (1995) both found that effective teaching behaviors were increased by coaching and mentoring. Gersten's point that teachers require technical and conceptual support to understand and implement comprehension-strategies instruction, including mentoring and coaching in the classroom may well be evidenced in this finding.

Continuing to teach strategies. Continuing to teach strategies was a significant predictor of strategy use for middle school special education teachers. This variable accounted for 14 % of the variance associated with strategy use for this group. That special education teachers in the middle grades did not stop teaching strategies is encouraging given the very nature of special education instruction with students with LD. Although the regression coefficient (R) was lower for middle school special education teachers, the predictors in this model emphasizes the combined significance of being familiar enough with reading comprehension strategies to teach them, integrating the strategies with content, and task persistence.

Conclusions

Results of the study indicate that teachers in the survey fall into three groups: those who are unfamiliar with the strategies; those who are familiar enough with the strategies to teach them, but do not do so; and those who are familiar enough to teach the strategies and teach some of them. Results also indicate that variables that make significant contributions to teacher use of reading comprehension strategies can be predicted. Although, variables predicted differently across the sample by type of teacher and grade level assignment, familiarity of strategies, teaching while teaching content, student benefit, continuing to teach strategies, and receiving mentoring and coaching were found to have significant relationships to sustained teaching of reading comprehension strategies for students with LD.

Limitations

However, a number on limitations of this research affects the extent to which the findings may generalize to other teachers. First, as with all correlational research, the findings establish a relationship between the variables explored and are in no way asserted to be causal. Further experimentation is needed to ascertain causality of these variables on strategy use. Second, the current study was limited to general and special education teachers in western Pennsylvania. Teachers in other regions of the state and elsewhere may not have the same responses to a similar survey. Further studies would be needed to address familiarity and use of research validated reading comprehension strategies by teachers in other geographic regions of the state and the country. Third, a limitation inherent in all survey research, the researcher must assume that the respondents are responding truthful to the survey items. There is no way to verify the accuracy of the reported data. Bogus strategies were added in the survey to identify and minimize this limitation. The five respondents reporting familiarity and use of the bogus strategies were omitted from the data analysis. A final limitation to the study is that even where respondents are truthful, there is no way of knowing if the strategies the teachers believe they are teaching are taught as intended by the researchers. There is a concern with implementation fidelity that must be examined and addressed to ensure that students with LD are receiving maximum benefit from strategy instruction. Further research is needed in this area.

Implications for Practice

The following implications derived from the findings and conclusions of this study, suggests possible improvements in practice. First, as suggested by the lack of familiarity of reading comprehension strategies reported by teachers, students with LD are not provided access to these powerful strategies. Obviously, teachers are unable to teach these strategies to students if they them selves do not know them. Teacher preparation programs, district and state sponsored professional development activities, and other training entities must develop ways to make sure that teachers have both conceptual knowledge of and facility with teaching these strategies. Second, key variables emerged in this study that predict contextual variables that influence decisions to use strategies. School administrators, especially building principals and curriculum directors, should select textbooks and instructional materials that incorporate strategic learning of content and that enable teachers to teach strategies while teaching content. A final implication is that researchers, practitioners, and policymaker alike must begin to emphasize the benefit of teaching all students to use strategies to gain information from text. The importance of this benefit cannot be over emphasized. If students with LD are to acquire greater reading proficiency they must acquire reading comprehension strategies from their general and special education teachers.

References

Abbott, M., Walton, C., Tapia, Y., & Greenwood, C. (1999). Research to practice: A blueprint for closing the gap in local schools. *Exceptional Children, 65(3), 339- 352.*

Adams, M. J. (1999). *Beginning to read: Thinking and learning about print.* Boston, MA: The MIT Press.

Armbruster, B. B., Anderson, T. H., & Ostertag, J. (1987). Does text structure/ summarization instruction facilitate learning from an expository text? *Reading Research Quarterly, 22, 331-346.*

Bakken, J. P., Mastroperi, M. A., & Scruggs, T. E. (1997). Reading comprehension of expository science materials and students with learning disabilities: A comparison of strategies. *The Journal of Special Education, 31*(3) 300-324.

Billingsley, B.S., & Wildman, T.M. (1990). Facilitating reading comprehension in learning disabled students: Metacognitive goals and instructional strategies. *Remedial and Special Education, 11*(2), 18- 31.

Carnine, D., Silbert, J., & Kameenui, E. J. (1997). *Direct instruction reading* (3rd ed.). Columbus, OH: Merrill.

Clark, F. L., Deshler, D., Shumaker, J., Alley, G. R., & Warner, M. M. (1984). Visual imagery and self-questioning: Strategies to improve comprehension of written material. *Journal of Learning Disabilities, 17,* 145-149.

Deshler, D., Ellis, E., & Lenz, K. (1996). *Teaching adolescents with learning disabilities: Strategies and methods* (2nd ed.). Denver, CO: Love.

El-Dinary, P. B., & Schuder, T. (1993). Seven teachers' acceptance of transactional strategies instruction during their first year using it. *Elementary School Journal, 94,* 207-219.

Englert, C. S., & Tarrant, K. L. (1995). Creating collaborative cultures for educational change. Remedial and Special Education, 16, *325-336.*

Englert, C. S., & Thomas, C. C. (1987). Sensitivity to text structure in reading and writing: A comparison between learning disabled and non-learning disabled students. *Learning Disability Quarterly, 10*(2), 93-105.

Fuchs, D., & Fuchs, L. S. (1998). Researchers and teachers working together to adapt instruction for diverse learners. *Learning Disabilities Research and Practice, 13*(3),126-137.

Gall, M.D., Borg, W.R., & Gall, J.P. (1996). *Educational Research: An introduction.* (6 th ed.). Columbus, OH: Merrill.

Gajria, M., & Salvia, J. (1992). The effects of summarization instruction on text comprehension of students with learning disabilities. *Exceptional Children, 58*(6), 508-516.

Gersten, R., Chard, D., & Baker, S. (2000). Factors enhancing sustained use of research based instructional practices. *Journal of Learning Disabilities, 33*(5), 445 - 457.

Gersten, R., Fuchs, L., Williams, J., & Baker, S. (2001). Teaching reading comprehension strategies to students with learning disabilities: A review of research. *Review of Educational Research, 71*(2), 279 - 320.

Gersten, R., Morvant, M., & Brengleman, S. (1995). Close to the classroom is close to the bone. *Exceptional Children, 62,* 52- 67.

Gersten, R., & Woodard, Vaughn, S., Deshler, D., & Schiller, E. (1997). What we know about translating research based practices. *Journal of Learning Disabilities, 30*(5), 446-476.

Graves, A. W. (1986. Effects of direct instruction and metacomprehension training on finding main ideas. *Learning Disabilities Research, 1*(2), 92-100.

Howe, Mary E., Grierson, Sirpa, T, & Richmond, Mark G. (1997). A comparison of teachers' knowledge and use of content area reading strategies in primary grades. *Reading Research and Instruction*, 36(4), 305 – 324.

Jenkins, J. R., Heliotis, J., Stein, M. L., & Haynes, M. C. (1987). Improving reading comprehension by using paragraph restatements. *Exceptional Children, 54,* 54-59.

Kameénui, E. J., & Carnine, D. W. (1998). *Effective teaching strategies that accommodate diverse learners.* Upper Saddle River, NJ: Merrill.

Klingner, J. K., Vaughn, S., & Schumm, J. S. (1998). Collaborative strategic reading during social studies in heterogeneous fourth-grade classrooms. *Elementary School Journal, 99*(1), 3-22.

Klingner, J., Vaughn, S., Tejero, N., & Arguelles, M. (1999). Sustaining research-based practices in reading. *Remedial and Special Education, 20*(5), 263-274.

Malone, L. D., & Mastropieri, M. D. (1992). Reading comprehension instruction: Summarization and self-monitoring training for students with learning disabilities. *Exceptional Children, 58*(3), 270-279.

Malouf, D.B. & Schiller, E.P. (1995). Practice and research in special education. *Exceptional Children, 61*(5), 414-424.

Manzo, A. V. (1991). Training teachers to use content area reading strategies: Description and appraisal of four options. *Reading Research and Instruction, 30*(4), 67-73.

Mastropieri, M. A., Scruggs, T. E., Bakken, J. P., & Whedon, C. (1996). Reading comprehension: A synthesis of research in learning disabilities. In T. E. Scruggs & M. A. Mastropieri (Eds.), *Advances in learning and behavioral disabilities* (Vol. 10, Part B, pp. 201-223). Greenwich, CT: JAI Press.

Mercer, C., & Mercer, A., (2001). *Teaching Students with Learning Problems.* (6 th ed.). Upper Saddle River, NJ: Merrill/ Prentice Hall.

National Center for Educational Statistics. (1999). *NAEP 1998 readings: A report card for the nation and the states.* Washington, DC: U. S. Department of Education.

National Reading Panel (2000). Teaching children to read: *An evidence- based assessment of the scientific research on reading and its' implications on instruction.* Washington, DC: National Institute of Child Health and Human Development.

Nichols, W., Rupley, W., & Mergen, S. (1998). Improving elementary teachers' ability to implement reading strategies in the teaching of science content. In Elizabeth Sturtevant, G. (Ed); Dugan, JoAnn (Ed). *Literacy and community*: The twentieth yearbook: A peer reviewed publication of the College Reading Association 1998. (pp. 188-213). Carrollton, GA: U. S. College Reading Association.

Paris, S.C., Wasik, B.A., & Turner, J.C., (1991). The development of strategic readers. In R. Barr, M. L. Kamil, P. B. Mosenthal, & P. D. Pearson (Eds.), *Handbook on reading research* (Vol. 2, pp. 805-840). New York: Longman.

Partnerships for Reading. (2001). *Bridging scientific evidence to learning.* National Institute for Literacy. National Institute of Child Health and Human Development. Washington, DC: U. S. Department of Education.

Pressley, M., & El- Dinary, P. B. (1997). What we know about translating comprehension research into practice. *Journal of Learning Disabilities, 30*(5), 486-495.

Rogers, E. (1995). *Diffusions of Innovations.* (Fourth ed.). New York, New York: The Free Press.

Scanlon, Deshler, D. & Schumaker, J. (1996). Can a strategy be taught and learned in secondary inclusive classrooms? *Learning Disabilities Research and Practice, 11*, 41-57.

Schumaker, J. B., Denton, P., & Deshler, D. (1984). *The paraphrasing strategy.* Lawrence: The University of Kansas Press.

Spor, M.W., & Schneider, B.K. (1999). Content reading strategies: What teachers know, use, and want to learn. *Reading Research and Instruction, 38*(3) 221- 231.

Stevens, R.J., Hammann, L., Balliett, T. (1999). Middle school literacy instruction. In R. J. Stevens (Ed.), *Teaching in American Schools,* (pp. 221- 244). Upper Saddle River, N.J.: Prentice Hall.

Stevens, R. J., Slavin, R.E., & Farnish, A.M. (1991). The effects of cooperative learning and direct instruction in reading comprehension strategies on main idea identification. *Journal of Educational Psychology, 83*(1), 8 -16.

Taylor, M. B., & Williams, J. P. (1983). Comprehension of learning-disabled readers: Task and text variations. *Journal of Educational Psychology, 75*, 743-751.

Vadasy, P. F., Jenkins, J. R., Antil, L. R., Phillips, N. B., & Pool, K. (1997). The research-to-practice ball game: Classwide peer tutoring and teacher interest, implementation, and modifications. *Remedial and Special Education, 18*(3), 143-156.

Vaughn, S., Klingner, J., & Hughes, M. (2000). Sustainability of research-based practices. *Exceptional Children, 66*(2), 163-171.

Wiersma, W. (2000). *Research methods in education.* (7 th ed.). Needham Heights, MA: Allyn and Bacon.

Wong, B. L., & Jones, W. (1982). Metacomprehension in learning disabled and normally achieving students through self-questioning training. *Learning Disabilities Quarterly, 5,* 228-240.

Table 1
Means and Standard Deviations of Strategy Familiarity and Strategy Use by Middle School Teachers (*n* = 100).

Strategy	General Education Teachers				Special Education Teacher			
	Familiarity		Use		Familiarity		Use	
	M	*SD*	*M*	*SD*	*M*	*SD*	*M*	*SD*
Main idea	1.95	.22	1.81	.57	1.98	.15	1.68	.62
K – W – L	1.69	.64	1.44	.90	1.49	.78	.91	.86
Comprehension monitoring	1.66	.63	1.51	.84	1.60	.68	1.23	.81
Question generation	1.54	.75	1.31	.93	1.55	.75	1.23	.84
Clarifying	1.50	.77	1.36	.91	1.72	.62	1.40	.80
Textual graphics	1.90	.30	1.70	.70	1.72	.50	1.21	.91
Text skimming	1.76	.57	1.68	.97	1.55	.65	1.17	.90
Summarization	1.90	.36	1.78	.59	1.79	.51	1.32	.81
Text structure	1.85	.36	1.69	.70	1.68	.56	1.26	.77
Visual imagery	1.73	.58	1.53	.84	1.58	.58	1.00	.86
Prior knowledge	1.82	.53	1.86	.47	1.85	.36	1.45	.72

Table 2

Means and Standard Deviations of Strategy Familiarity and Strategy Use by High School Teachers (*n* = 58).

| Strategy | General Education Teachers | | | | Special Education Teacher | | | |
| | Familiarity | | Use | | Familiarity | | Use | |
	M	*SD*	*M*	*SD*	*M*	*SD*	*M*	*SD*
Main idea	1.58	.75	1.06	.99	1.96	.20	1.76	.52
K – W – L	.88	.85	.36	.78	1.12	.64	.64	.86
Comprehension monitoring	.97	.84	.52	.87	1.68	.56	1.36	.91
Question generation	1.03	.95	.73	.98	1.72	.33	1.48	.77
Clarifying	1.28	.85	.75	.95	1.88	.33	1.52	.82
Textual graphics	1.42	.83	.88	.99	1.60	.65	1.12	.88
Text skimming	1.39	.86	.94	.97	1.84	.47	1.48	.77
Summarization	1.51	.71	1.12	. 99	1.91	.28	1.75	.61
Text structure	1.48	.76	1.12	.96	1.72	.54	1.24	.83
Visual imagery	1.21	.82	.64	.89	1.76	.44	1.40	.82
Prior knowledge	1.40	.79	.97	.98	1.92	.28	1.64	.64

Table 3

Step-Wise Multiple Regression Analysis for Middle School General Education Teachers

(n = 57).

Variable	Beta	F	p
Step 1		73.520	
Familiarity of strategies	.753		< .001
Step 2		23.68	
Familiarity of strategies	.611		< .001
Student benefit	.391		< .001
Step 3		18.508	
Familiarity of strategies	.569		< .001
Student benefit	.180		< .038
Teach while I teach content	.359		< .001

Note: R = .881: R = .777 for Step 3

316

Table 4

Step-Wise Multiple Regression Analysis for High School General Education Teachers ($n = 25$).

Variable	Beta	F	p
Step 1		18.126	
Familiarity of Strategies	.656		< .001
Step 2		4.322	
Familiarity of Strategies	.601		< .001
Mentoring & Coaching	.090		.049

Note: $R = .721$: $R = .520$ for Step 2.

Table 5

Step - Wise Multiple Regression Analysis for Middle School Special Education Teachers ($n = 46$).

Variable	Beta	F	p
Step 1		13.655	
Familiarity of strategies	.482		.001
Step 2		10.142	
Familiarity of strategies	.372		.007
Stopped teaching strategies	- .399		.003
Step 3		5.466	
Familiarity of strategies	.372		.007
Stopped teaching strategies	- .145		.374
Teach while I teach content	.364		.024

Note: $R = .721$: $R= .520$ for Step 2.

Table 6

Step - Wise Multiple Regression Analysis for High School Special Education Teachers.
($n = 23$).

Variable	Beta	F	p
Step 1		9.061	
Familiarity of Strategies	.540		.006
Step 2		5.867	
Familiarity of Strategies	.383		.040
Teach while I teach content	.423		.025

Note: R = .668 and R = .446 for step 2.

Appendix A.

READING COMPREHENSION STRATEGY QUESTIONNAIRE

(This questionnaire is designed to assess teacher familiarity and use of reading comprehension strategies. The questionnaire takes approximately 10 - 15 minutes to complete.)

SECTION 1- Demographic Information: Fill in the information that best describes you. Where ovals are presented, please make sure they are completely filled in.

1. I have _____ years of teaching experience

2. My grade level assignment this year is _____.

3. Area(s) of Instruction: *FILL IN ALL THAT APPLY*

      O English   O History   O Language Arts   O Math   O Science

      O Social Studies   O Other _____

4. Setting: *FILL IN ALL THAT APPLY*

      O I have students with LD in my class
      O I do not have students with LD in my class
      O I am a general education teacher
      O I am a special education teacher

5. Degree: *FILL IN Highest Degree and Year Received*

      O Bachelors _____O Masters _____   O Doctorate _____

6. Certification Area: *FILL IN ALL THAT APPLY*

      O General Education O Special Education O Other

7. Teaching Routine:

      O In my classroom, I am responsible for student learning
      O In my classroom, the student is responsible for student learning
      O In my classroom, student learning is shared responsibility

---

Please Continue on Next Page

READING COMPREHENSION STRATEGY QUESTIONNAIRE

SECTION 2. <u>DIRECTIONS: USING THE CODES BELOW RATE EACH STRATEGY TWICE.</u>

A. <u>FIRST RATE YOUR FAMILIARITY WITH EACH STRATEGY. CIRCLE YOUR CHOICE IN THE COLUMN MARKED "FAMILIARITY".</u>

<u>CODES:</u> 1 = Never heard of it.   2 = I have heard of it. 3 = I can teach it.

********** FOR EACH STRATEGY YOU RATED <u>1= NEVER HEARD OF IT,</u> PLACE A CHECK IN THE <u>N/A</u> COLUMN FOR THAT STRATEGY AND <u>DO NOT</u> Circle A RESPONSE IN THE COLUMN MARKRD "<u>USE</u>" **********

B. <u>NEXT, RATE YOUR TEACHING OF EACH STRATEGY USING THE FOLLOWING CODES:</u> CIRCLE your choice in the column marked "Use"

<u>CODES:</u>
1= I teach this strategy to all my students;
2 = I teach this strategy to my students with comprehension problems
3 = I teach this strategy to my students with IEPs
4= I do not teach this strategy
5= I used to teach this strategy but no longer do so.

Strategy	Familiarity (1-3)	N/A	Use (1-5)
EXAMPLE	(1) 2 3	✓	
8. Identifying Main Ideas	1 2 3		1 2 3 4 5
9. Know-Want to Know-Learned (KWL)	1 2 3		1 2 3 4 5
10. Comprehension Monitoring (including self questioning)	1 2 3		1 2 3 4 5
11. Question Generation	1 2 3		1 2 3 4 5
12. Clarifying	1 2 3		1 2 3 4 5
13. Textual graphics, organizers, and concept maps	1 2 3		1 2 3 4 5
14. Text skimming, previewing, and surveying	1 2 3		1 2 3 4 5
15. Heuristic generation	1 2 3		1 2 3 4 5
16. Summarization (including paraphrasing)	1 2 3		1 2 3 4 5
17. Comprehension conferencing	1 2 3		1 2 3 4 5
18. Text Structure (e.g. compare/contrast, problem/solution, description)	1 2 3		1 2 3 4 5
19. Visual Imagery	1 2 3		1 2 3 4 5
20. Prior Knowledge of concepts and vocabulary	1 2 3		1 2 3 4 5
21. Detailed sequencing	1 2 3		1 2 3 4 5

Please Continue on Next Page

READING COMPREHENSION STRATEGY QUESTIONNAIRE

SECTION 3. For each question below, <u>COMPLETELY</u> fill in the oval that best describes you.

22. Fill in the oval next to "Learned" to indicate how you learned about reading comprehension strategies and fill the oval next to "Influenced" if you were influenced to use them. Fill in <u>both</u> if both apply.

Undergraduate coursework	O Learned	O Influenced
Graduate coursework	O *Learned*	O *Influenced*
State or national conferences	O Learned	O Influenced
Peers /colleagues	O Learned	O Influenced
District/state sponsored training	O Learned	O Influenced
Professional journal	O Learned	O Influenced
Textbooks or curricula guides	O Learned	O Influenced
Other _____	O *Learned*	O *Influenced*

23. I teach reading comprehension strategies because: *FILL IN ALL THAT APPLY*

    O I have support of colleagues
    O I have support from administrators
    O My students benefit from strategy instruction

    O Strategies are part of my school's curriculum.
    O I personally use the strategies I teach

    O Strategies are consistent with my other teaching approaches
    O   Parents requested it
O Other _____
    O I used to teach strategies, but I stopped

******** <u>PLEASE COMPLETE THE REMAINING QUESTIONS, ONLY IF YOU USED TO TEACH STRATEGIES AND STOPPED TEACHING THEM</u> ********.

Please Continue Next Page

READING COMPREHENSION STRATEGY QUESTIONNAIRE

24. I do not teach reading comprehension strategies because of: *FILL IN ALL THAT APPLY*

    O lack support of colleagues

    O lack support from administrators

    O My students did not benefit from strategy instruction

    O Strategies are not part of my school's curriculum.

    O I do not personally use strategies

    O Strategies are not consistent with my other teaching approaches

    O Other _____

25. I would teach reading comprehension strategies, if: *FILL IN ALL THAT APPLY*

    O I had more time to teach these strategies

    O I had mentoring or coaching was available to help me

    O Strategies were consistent with my other teaching approaches

    O Strategies were less complex

    O I could teach them while you teach content

    O Administrators supported teaching strategies

    O Parents requested it

    O Other _____

THANK YOU FOR COMPLETING THIS QUESTIONNAIRE! Do not forget to complete your entry for the drawing.

Understanding the Nature of Self-Regulation Behavior of Learners Using

Variable Speed Playback in Digital Video-Based Instruction

Joel D. Galbraith

INSYS 574

Understanding the Nature of Self-Regulation Behavior of Learners Using

Variable Speed Playback in Digital Video-Based Instruction

Abstract

Scores of inexpensive products and services are on the market today that facilitate the simple creation and distribution of media-rich presentations for instruction and training purposes. The control affordances of these instructional offerings vary greatly, impacting self-regulation strategies employed by learners. This grounded theory study sought to better understand the regulatory practices of learners using variable speed playback (VSP) functionality in a media-rich accounting course. All participants employed quite effective self-monitoring and regulation strategies. VSP seemed to play an important early role in their regulatory behavior. Once the highest comfortable speeds were found, other control affordances became more dominant. The recording of Galvanic Skin Response data was piloted as an observation tool with limited success. It is hoped the study will help individual learners and instructional technologists proceed more knowledgeably when deciding how to begin using VSP functionality.

Statement of the Problem

Variable Speed Playback (VSP) functionality, or a user's ability to dynamically control the playback speed of multimedia presentations, was previously available only through specialized software or hardware. Today, however, this ability to control the playback speed of digitized audio and video is available to learners on two of the three largest media players on the market. Learners can now listen to audio/video-based instruction at their desired speed, regardless of whether the instructor, designers, or developers ever intended the materials to be accelerated. This does not inherently present a problem, but research to be discussed later in this paper does suggest that above certain speeds, comprehension dramatically falls off for most people. On the other hand, users able to moderately accelerate presentations have reported increased attentiveness and comprehension. From an instructional design and development perspective, it would be helpful to understand the motivations behind learner's use of VSP, and how learners might be using VSP to support their learning or, unwittingly inhibit it. Perhaps, one might even discover what constitutes appropriate or wise VSP use in given settings. While this study will not likely answer the latter question, it does seek to generate hypotheses on the nature of self-regulated learning (SRL) behavior of students using variable speed playback functionality in a digital video-based course.

Researcher Identity

Let me start by stating my epistemological stance (Creswell, 1998, 2003). I favor the existence of objective "reality", but also maintain a belief in the "realities" perceived and constructed both individually and socially, that to varying degrees approach objective reality. It is these constructed realities that largely define our mortal experience, the ones we deal with on a day-to-day basis, and it is these that I investigate in this study—that is, how do learners perceive, report and self-regulate their study behaviors with regard to using variable speed playback functionality, in this course. In describing the researchers role in phenomenological research, Van Manen (1997) states,

> To establish a strong relation with a certain question, phenomenon or notion, the researcher cannot afford to adopt an attitude of so-called scientific disinterestedness…To be strong in our orientation means that we will not settle for superficialities or falsities (p.33).

To be sure, I am no "disinterested" or objective observer. My interest in this topic is personal. It springs from many of my own experiences and observations that I will describe in the following paragraphs. In the spirit of full disclosure, I was the chief designer of the software used to deliver the instruction some three years prior to this study. There were no financial incentives of any kind for my pursuing this research, nor was I directly affiliated with any ongoing software or course development. Even more relevant, this study was not a formative evaluation of the courseware, nor a summative effectiveness study; Instead, it hoped to focus on learner processes by looking at usage patterns, self-monitoring abilities and regulating practices/strategies of learners. While the participants may not have been affected by my having created their course materials—because this was not disclosed, this is not to say that the research as a whole is unaffected. As researcher, I found it difficult at times to stay out of the usability testing mode, and remain focused on my primary research question. My focus, unlike in previous studies, and on other projects, was no longer looking for ways to improve the product or software, but rather to understand the learner. The differences remain subtle, and I reflected on them in a journal entry as I traveled home from gathering my data:

> I wish I knew then about qual[itative] research, what I know now. It would've been so helpful…I guess while every tester should be a qual researcher, it may not go the other way around. I was worried that I might keep slipping into product eval[uation] mode, because it seems so close to what I've been doing the last few days…As long as I mentally focused more on the study questions (SRL) and the learner as I asked my questions, I was ok, and not thinking ahead about the programming necessitated to fix what they were complaining about…Both that looking forward[to future software updates] and looking back[at what we'd developed] were hard to avoid due to my previous intimate involvement with the project.

Description of the Problem

I have long held that instruction can be both inhibited and promoted with the use of technology. Some of this is due to features of the technology itself, with other variables being dependant on the learner. That is, people's perceptions and attitudes towards technology can be equally inhibiting or facilitative to learning. In this semester-length accounting course, my participants were not required to come to class on a regular basis. They are provided with multimedia instructional materials on six CDROMs or one DVDROM. A course schedule, including regular online quizzes, exists to help students manage their time, but by and large, students are expected to "personally activate and sustain behaviors, cognitions, and affects, which are systematically oriented toward the attainment of learning goals" (Schunk, 2004 p.355). According to Schunk, this is the process of self-regulated learning.

One technological innovation that I have worked with in the last few years is, Variable Speed Playback (VSP) as applied to video-centric, multimedia presentations for instruction and learning. Today's VSP technology allows one to speed up and slow down audio and video presentations without pitch distortions. It has recently experienced a resurgence in both availability and popularity and is included now by default in Microsoft's Windows Media Player in Windows XP.

In my five years as a professional non-linear video editor I learned the value of being able to swiftly navigate and view--"speed read"--vast amounts of media at high speeds while still being able to comprehend the content. In my later years as an instructional media designer/developer I built VSP functionality into a video-centric hypermedia course allowing students to dynamically control the playback rate or speed at which the instructional presentations (audio, video, graphics and animation) played. It is important to note that prior to introducing VSP to the multimedia course, student surveys indicated quite positive attitudes toward the course. The single biggest frustration, however, was that the professor spoke too slowly, and repeated himself too often. I recall some students directly asking--pleading--for a way to speed him up. As the courseware developers, I and my team were personally all too aware of the student's sentiment. We had just spent months videotaping, digitizing, editing, programming, testing, and revising the course materials and knew first hand of what they spoke! A solution to accelerate the hypermedia lectures was identified and integrated midway through the second semester that the multimedia course was offered. Course feedback and positive ratings skyrocketed that semester—we were on to something, but were not sure what. We had struck something valuable, but did not understand its properties nor its effects.

As the designer, I was very pleased that since introducing VSP functionality, student frustration levels had subsided, and I hoped now that motivation and comprehension might also increase, and that students would use acceleration responsibly. I feared, however, that the positive response might have been simply due to the fact that they could "whip" through the material faster than before. I was left with questions as to when, where, how and why students might use VSP technologies to support their learning. In an earlier survey study following the integration of VSP into the accounting course (Galbraith & Spencer, 2001), students reported regularly accelerating through instructional presentations up to 2.5 times (2.5x) the normal playback speed over the course of a semester. At the same time, a few students choose to use no, or very little, acceleration. Their self-reported motivations for speeding through the material varied widely from the individual's familiarity with the content, to needing to catch a bus. In light of this information, and the rather high average speed reportedly used by students, I was concerned about whether students were sufficiently capable of self-monitoring and regulating their use of VSP to support their learning. Was the allure of "getting through" the material at a faster rate--even at the expense of learning--just too enticing? How was this tool being used, and what were students' perceptions of its utility?

All the literature I had come across on accelerated audio focused primarily on listener comprehension of accelerated speech, or the effectiveness of various speech compression algorithms, but not the usage patterns--and certainly not couched in the context of self-regulated learning. I found one usability study published by Microsoft that evaluated such technology in a modified version of their media player, then called "Netshow" (Omoigui, He, Gupta, Grudin, & Sanocki, 1999). Like other studies, it did not assess learner intent and motivation--why users were motivated to adjust speeds? but it did record and report on how their viewers interacted with 5 video samples that varied in content and duration, over the period of a couple days of viewing.

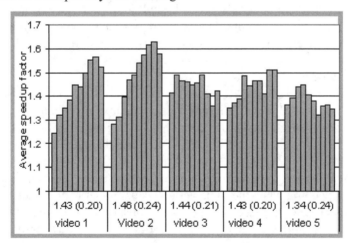

Figure 1--Chart from Orr et al. study (1999)

Figure 1 shows how the researchers tracked average speeds of users for every 10% segment of the video. Of their observations, they noted, "...we clearly see that the subjects are watching them faster as they get deeper into the video. There is some slowdown right at the end, an area that corresponds to the concluding remarks" (Omoigui et al., 1999, p.5). I was generally impressed with their study and with the detailed observation data they were able to collect, but it was the last line about an implied, but not corroborated, connection between viewing habits and concluding or summary remarks that really stood out to me. During another project's usability testing, a sight-impaired student came and tested one of our online courses using a popular screen reader software employed by many blind students on campus to read web pages and other online documents. He revealed how blind students--according to him--employ similar "reading" techniques to accomplished speed readers. From a selection of synthetic computer voices, their software reads screen text at very rapid rates (up to 10x times normal speed), and they rarely read entire passages or texts. He had learned "by necessity" to skim texts, jumping to the beginnings and ends of paragraphs to get the gist of what authors were saying—often disregarding the whole middle sections of paragraphs. The tools he used facilitated this behavior.

I was intrigued by his account and demonstration on how blind learners commonly navigated text on computer screens and self-regulated or modified their navigation behavior based on comprehension. Because screen readers can navigate text non-linearly, convert text to audio, and play the audio at a very rapid pace, I saw many correlations to the accounting hypermedia course used in this study. Incidentally, and contrary to my expectations, this individual was not at all impressed with the control affordances of our accounting courseware. While it did not require reading a textbook and allowed him instead to hear an instructor's voice, and it did allow for acceleration, and non-linear random access, it did not, in his view, facilitate the easy navigation, or jumping from the beginnings to ends of the instructor's spoken paragraphs that his screen reading software did with text. It was a humbling moment (or week?) for this designer to discover he had missed a small but important audience he was hoping to have served.

To understand how sighted students were using the courseware, I knew that I wanted similar kinds of data to the Microsoft study. It would help us understand first *how*—and only thereafter, *why* users were interacting with course features the way they did (specifically VSP functionality). Moreover, as the instructional designer, I desired to understand how conscious they were of their motivations and usage patterns, and what they did with that awareness. This study aimed at exploring these questions.

It is important to note that VSP use is not an isolated event. The slider control that is used to adjust acceleration is integrated into an interface which includes numerous other ways to control the media. Other controls include play, stop, pause, "jump back 10 seconds" buttons, and a detailed index or "table of contents" hyperlinked to various portions of the media.(See appendix E) These other controls are important, because they play a facilitative role in how students use VSP. For example I often observed students clicking the "jump back 10 seconds" button. During interviews they discussed using this button frequently if they were momentarily distracted by a room mate or a non-course related thought. Because they proceeded swiftly through the material, the "jump back 10" button was often used in tandem with acceleration. There were other less relevant course features like a calculator and glossary that will not be discussed here.

Thick, descriptive answers to the self-regulation behavior questions of this study, are critical for instructional designers and technologists designing video-centric course materials. They are not easily obtained through the surveys, and focus groups commonly used for gathering feedback in instructional development contexts. These methods usually fail to describe self-regulated learning behavior and usage patterns adequately.

In 1971, Gilbert Ryle first introduced the notion of thick description as a means of differentiating between what is really happening when the same action occurs under different circumstances. I too was interested in trying to understand processes behind similar observable outward behaviors. Are there different motivations behind similar actions? (i.e. the act of accelerating a presentation). Clifford Geertz (1973) extended Ryles notion by emphasizing the importance of understanding intent and meaning behind the culture's signs and that descriptions are always multilayered. Ricki Goldman-Segall (1998) suggests additional descriptive layers in adding the affordances of digital media. In digital form, her thick descriptions integrated fieldnotes, video, audio, text, documents, images, and perhaps most importantly, participant-generated points of viewing—their comments, annotations, constructions and reflections on the researcher.

Our whole body is a learning system, and our physical bodies are believed to both reflect and influence our behavior, our feelings and thoughts by way of more "covert" processes (neural, cognitive, autonomic and affective). My courseware design and development experience in higher education has illustrated to me how few college learners are skilled at self-monitoring, and how unaccustomed they are to "think aloud" activities, and to analyzing their highly routinized behaviors and learning strategies for researchers. Thus, additional methods of gathering data--observing--are required--methods that help learners be more self-aware and better equipped to describe and critique the instructional products they use, such as VSP. This qualitative study employed a combination of research techniques to help participants more fully reflect on their VSP use experiences in relation to their learning.

Through my graduate studies I have gained a greater appreciation for the notion that not all learning and behavior is conscious. The exploratory use of Galvanic Skin Response (GSR) data in this study as a form of observation data was perhaps uncommon but not unprecedented in either educational or qualitative studies (see Clariana, 1990, 1992). Qualitative research in nursing and care-giving has long valued quantitative data such as heart rate, blood pressure and blood sugar in service of better understanding their patients and the quality of their health. In this study, the quantitative GSR data was to also serve the qualitative process by providing talking points during the interviews. For the researcher, GSR observations can be made of more covert, automatic and fleeting processes in the learner. For the learner, the GSR data was to help promote deeper reflection and self-monitoring. During interviews, it was hoped that a joint review of learner GSR data might trigger new awareness, or memory of previously subtle or forgotten thoughts and feelings regarding the participant's regulatory habits vis-à-vis the interface and the content. It was to act as a form of member check or triangulation.

The ability to self-monitor and report one's attentiveness and level of activation is a characteristic of a self-regulating learner. As early as 1907, Carl Jung claimed that "verbal responses do not tell all" and that electrodermal activity, such as GSR "revealed the secrets of mental life" (Stern et al, 2001 p. 206). Some research suggests that subjective reports of arousal, stress or anxiety seldom correspond with physiological measures (Glynn, Christenfeld & Gerin, 1999). Admittedly, GSR is anything but clearly interpreted. Nevertheless, it has had a relatively long, stable history and is a good measure of emotional response and some cognitive processes—more specifically, attention, arousal, anxiety and stress levels (Stern et al, 2001; Clariana, 1990,1992; Reeves et al., 1989; Schwartz & Shapiro, 1973). As GSR is reflective of a host of physiological and emotional conditions the data alone is not useful to this study. Thus only in combining the data with my observations and subsequent collaborative interpretation with my participants, could the data be made useful and relevant. Unfortunately, although good GSR data was collected, being able to bring that data into the interview with participants, in conjunction with video from the observations, proved to be unwieldy and impractical given the technology and time available to me in this study, and was therefore dropped early in the data collection process.

Gaining Access

The participants in this study came from a large and fairly unique introductory accounting course (Accounting 200) at Brigham Young University (BYU). I arranged access to the students through the instructor, with whom I had worked closely in the past to develop instructional tools. Importantly, the video-centric course employed the Variable Speed Playback (VSP) technology, which made it an ideal setting for my study. By way of reminder, unlike many large 200 level college courses, this course does not meet regularly in a classroom. Instead students study course materials on their own presented in the form of interactive multimedia lectures. The mode of instruction arguably requires a good deal more self-regulation than traditional face to face classes.

Applications to IRB offices at both BYU (study site) and Penn State (my location) were required to help ensure the rights and safety of research study participants before gaining access to the site. The site was undeniably selected, but not wholly, because of existing trustful relationships with the instructor. In the future, I would likely explore similar questions with students in other contexts using other tools, but for the time being, I was delighted with the opportunity to more deeply understanding this context. Perhaps noteworthy, I chose not to disclose to students that I had been the designer of the software they were using. This was a conscious decision on my part because I did not want that information to unduly influence their conversations with me. I believe that most student simply perceived me as I had been introduced to them—a former alumnus of BYU, currently pursuing a Ph.D. at Penn State, now at the BYU campus to conduct a research study.

<u>Participants</u>

Eleven participants were selected from among a host of volunteers. Volunteers responded to either an announcement made in class by their instructor, or to the same announcement posted on their course website. In volunteering, they were to indicate the following through email. 1) when they generally studied-what days, what time, what environment? and 2) How often they adjusted speed controls (hardly ever, sometimes, a lot). I quickly received over 100 volunteers, and knew I could only ever deal with up to 10 participants. I removed my announcement from the website confident that my research questions could be adequately addressed from those who had already volunteered. I set about building a participant pool by contacting volunteers to gauge how my research topic aligned with the potential participant's experience (Seidman, 1998). Generally, I attempted to get a variety of cases that would likely generate, to the fullest extent, as many diverse properties of the categories as possible (Glaser & Strauss, 1967 p.49).

As I was dealing with limited time, I was not able to arrange all my participants in this fashion. When I had "down time" between scheduled observation/interviews, I ended up "trolling" the computer labs on campus for prospective participants. As the course enrolls over 1,200 students each semester, finding students in this manner presented no significant challenge. At any given time of day, the large labs I visited had at least two-six people working on the accounting course.
The final result with regard to study participants was

- Observations and interviews with ten students
- Interviews (no observations) with one student and two accounting lab TAs,
- Numerous ad hoc discussions (no formal observations) with accounting students in various campus computer labs.

As an interesting side note, on March 31st I wrote this in my journal:

Today (3/31/04) one Acc lab TA I talked to mentioned that I should contact evening TAs as it is they who deal with students who may have procrastinated trying to prepare for and take quizzes that are due by midnight (every Tuesday and Thursday night). Interestingly, it is those very students who might not have time to talk to me, and they would be an interesting group to include. I did not seek out people who were early birds, but sure seem to have found people that were staying well ahead of the game with the exception of only one I think.

As I noted in my journal, there was a group of students--procrastinators? whom I did not talk to who might have been struggling with self-regulatory practices and whose perspective would certainly have added to this story. Ecological validity was important for me. That is, it was important for me to observe participants in the environments that they commonly used to study. Of the student participants, one observation/interview took place in an apartment (student's bedroom), one in a parent's home (student's bedroom), one at the individual's office (during working hours), three in various general campus computer labs and five in the accounting computer lab. In my journal, I recorded some of my thoughts on three of my participants whose names I have changed.

Dave was an interesting find. I overheard that he was an accounting major, and was surprised because of the amount of questions he asked of the acc TAs in the lab. He also seemed to be struggling with simple concepts. It was later when I approached him that I learned he was an accounting major. I also observed that he was viewing materials at 1.2 and 1.5x [comparatively slow]. Again, surprising since he was a major and should be getting this stuff. While speed use is no race, I was surprised to see a major proceeding so slowly and deliberately. It is good to see a tool that is so flexible, and can accommodate many different types of learners and their self-regulation practices.

Chris was also of particular interest to me. Chris is a handsome trendy looking young man. I had run into his father on campus, an old casual acquaintance of mine. His father told me of how Chris was taking the class for the second time and that Chris was diagnosed as having ADD--but was currently not taking any medication. Since failing is so hard to do in this class, [in my opinion] and since his ADD would be an interesting case in relation to self-regulation, I was interested in his story and arranged to observe and interview him at his home the next day.

Troy was anxious to talk to me. In response to my recruitment email, he said he had opinions on the course, and had taken many distance education and technology courses. I thought his perspective might be an interesting… for one, simply because he seemed so anxious to talk to me! I expected to get an earful!, and not necessarily about the topic of my research. Troy was a 40+- year old professional considering an executive MBA program. He seemed eager to continue his education, perhaps to secure a more stable life. Because I had followed a career path similar to his, and sought some stability for my family, perhaps I am projecting my rationale onto him. We'll see.

These were all interesting people to say the least, and I wish I had captured my thoughts and initial impressions on the others as well. I don't get the sense that these are extreme cases, but that everyone in the class--all 1,200 of them probably has equally interesting backgrounds and stories that bring them to this course. I felt extremely privileged to be let into these participants minds and their study time.

Collecting Data

While this is a Grounded Theory study, data collection on self-monitoring and self-regulation as well as on software usage habits is at its core, a largely phenomenological process--getting at the lived experience of learners involved in certain activities (Van Manen, 2001). The study's "grounded theory-ness" comes more from data analysis processes than from its data collection processes. In order to understand those lived experiences more fully, participant observation (Laurier, 2003) in the field was a must, as it is in many qualitative research studies. Participant interviews would of course also be necessary and Seidman (1998) suggests a "three interview series" (p.11) for such data gathering processes. 1) a focused life history, 2) the details of the experience, and 3) reflection on the meaning. Furthermore, he makes stipulations on interview durations (90 mins.), spacing (3-7 days) and on adhering to the sequence and structure of the interview series.

Despite the admonition to use distinct interviews, I combined interviews 1 and 2 due to time constraints and have thereby arguably reduced a potential source of richness in my study. The result is hoped to be minimal. As mentioned, data was collected through three main activities: 1) Direct observation, 2) post-observation interviews and 3) physiological measurements (GSR). During the participant observation periods, I took notes on the environment-the space—the individuals, and of course their regulatory behaviors while interacting with the lesson materials. To these latter observations, I also wrote down the time of the observed activity. I generally sat beside and behind participants as they worked on the computers. I was aware that they were aware of my presence, and accordingly tried to avoid distracting behaviors like obvious note taking and large body movements. This awareness was supported by the GSR data. In one of a handful of such instances, I inadvertently dropped my pen. As I leaned forward to pick it up, I noted the time in my observation log. Later when viewing the GSR data, an obvious spike was evident at that moment, and the participant confirmed being distracted by my actions at that time. While I had no delusions about being a fly on the wall, I did not intentionally try to be obtrusive. In an attempt to be reflexive (Rossman and Rallis, 2003), I chose to directly discuss my presence with participants during the interviews.

Speaking to my role as researcher/observer, Laurier (2003) would suggest that my intimate experience with the course and tools used by participants could be considered a strength. I certainly feel that this was the case. For example, I was aware of the multiple ways to repeat a lesson section. I therefore found the idiosyncratic ways participants went about repeating sections interesting and of possible importance—I was able to discern nuances that would go perhaps unnoticed by a less vested observer. I avoided the temptation to make assumptions or "read meaning" into observed behaviors by discussing them with participants during interviews.   I had also planned on videotaping all observations for more careful coding and analysis, but after reviewing the first three videotapes, I realized the futility of that effort. There was simply insufficient observable activity to merit videotaping in my judgment. Anything that needed to be observed was easily noted along with a timestamps in my observation log (See appendix D for a sample log). In addition, using the video during interviews to refer to particular participant on-screen activities, proved to be logistically awkward and slow—and was therefore discontinued.

Similarly, my plan for using the GSR data also ended up deviating from the original plan. The GSR capture device was a small, lightweight, wireless armband worn on the upper arm. Physiological data (GSR) was recorded and graphed on a laptop computer present at the interviews. During interviews, the data was downloaded from the armband and displayed on the screen along a timeline. By way of "eyeballing" it, I suspect some 95% of events accounted for in my observation logs, also appeared on the GSR graph. There were however some instances on the GSR timeline for which I had no time-stamped observations in my notes. I also had no clear way to precisely (within milliseconds) tie observed GSR events to specific observed behaviors. That is, GSR events and those observed in my notes occurred simultaneously—as far as my relatively unsophisticated method of timing could tell. What this meant was that I could not use the GSR data to infer motivation for any observed self-regulation behavior. Of course, any such inferences would have been subject to participant corroboration. In any case, this aspect of the study needs additional work, but still holds promise in my mind.

I felt the interviews went much better once I stopped taking notes. I was able to listen and feel secure that my recorder was picking up the interview. I stopped my note-taking after the second interview and found I was able to listen better during the rest of the interviews and was better able to focus my attention on my participants when I trusted my digital recorder to capture their comments for later analysis. I could still not avoid glancing down every now and then to make sure the recorder was still working and that the batteries hadn't run out.

 The only things I really wrote down anymore were any additional questions that came to me during observations and the interviews.

Observations and interviews took quite a while, on average about 90-100 minutes. The time felt about right. After about 40 minutes, observations weren't yielding anything new, and interviews seemed to saturate at around 50 minutes. Some observations were a bit shorter due to students finishing their assigned lessons. Certainly more could be discussed, but out of respect for the time of the participants I ended the interviews and asked if I might contact them again with follow-up questions to which they all agreed.

Document analysis was fairly minimal in the course. It seemed that analysis of test scores was not likely to reveal anything too insightful, and furthermore that it might overshadow other more nuanced findings. Some of my participants took their quiz right after our observation period. Upon submitting their quiz, scores were immediately posted on the screen, including those from all previous quizzes and exams. No one objected to me seeing their exam scores, and in some cases I asked a question or two about them. I asked a couple participants to look at their scores over the semester, and see if they could make any correlation between the scores they were getting and their study habits or speed use. Answers revealed a variety of reasons for particularly low scores and they usually reflected simply not having enough time that particular day or week to view the course materials. Other document analysis included a brief review of the student's notebooks. Student notebooks, purchased through the bookstore, included key frames from the graphics and animations presented with the video lessons. There were six frames per page with three blank ruled lines beneath each image for notes, much like the "handouts" page in Microsoft's PowerPoint (See appendix C).

I was curious as to how and whether they were taking notes. Here too, within my participants, there was great variety. Some took heavy notes in and around the key slides, most marked up the notes moderately circling key terms, underlining sections, adding their own thoughts, while one made nary a mark on his pages. Interestingly, despite the differences in note-taking, all participants had the notes open and in front of them while viewing the multimedia lectures, and only two of them appeared to stop the presentations now and then expressly for the purpose of note taking. It is unclear what relevance the note-taking has to self-regulated learning and VSP usage at this point of analysis, but at the time it seemed like an important facet of the experience to capture.

Findings

As mentioned, the qualitative grounded theory approach looked to be an appropriate method to explore the nature of student VSP use and self-regulation behaviors. It was a way to help the implicit emerge and become explicit; a way to generate theory or make hypotheses from social research data that is systematically obtained and analyzed (Glaser & Strauss, 1967). In this section, I will begin to describe what appears to be emerging from the data--a preliminary description of some major themes found in the interviews. It is not, however, reflective of the more thorough data analysis processes included in open, axial, and selective coding recommended for such a study by Strauss & Corbin (1998).

Students in general appeared to be quite good at self-monitoring—and quite deliberate about how they used VSP. Controlling the speed seemed to play an important early role in their regulatory behavior of all the participants. But, once comfortable speeds were identified fewer speed adjustments were made within lessons and other control affordances such as repetition, became more dominant. They did not adjust very often,(not dynamically) and chose instead to repeat sections rather than slow down. I wondered out loud with one participant if perhaps an acceleration foot pedal might be a nice device to have for speed control—sewing machine like. Would such a device encourage more dynamic and frequent use of VSP? The worst case scenario for use of VSP controls dictated that one participant set aside their notes from off their lap, lean physically forward, clear a space on the desk for the notes, put their pen down, grab the mouse, navigate to the VSP controls and then make an adjustment. It was not an easy and natural task, yet most participants situated themselves such that regulating playback speed in relation to their comprehension, took far less effort.

Another recurring theme was regarding attentiveness and concentration. "Speeding up helps me stay focused and keeps my attention better than normal speed" said Susie. "It saves time" said one participant.

"I mean the quicker I can get through the lesson the better. But I also want to understand it, you know. At first when I started doing it, I started at normal speed but that just drove me nuts because it just seemed so slow. So then I put it on double speed and that worked good for a while and then it just seemed like it was too slow too, so I sped up to about 2.2 and that seemed to work out good. Also, like, it forces me to focus and to concentrate be cause it's going so fast that if I don't--like if I doze off or something I'll miss so much. Whereas if it's just on normal speed, it's kind of monotonous, it's easy to not focus your thoughts, so I think it does kind of help you to focus when its going faster.

Repeating (replaying) phrases became a more dominant way of regulating comprehension, but this still all occurred at higher than normal (1x) speeds. Jack mused that he expected his mind wandered less at higher speeds and that it actually reduced the number of times he'd have to rewind and repeat phrases or thoughts. This sentiment seemed universally held although a couple did relate equal mind wandering when viewing too fast. Both points are borne out in the literature. (See Harrigan 1995, 2000; Gutenko, 1995; and King & Behnke, 1989 for a discussion on these issues.)
In either case, when participants felt they missed particular content, they chose more often to repeat a few lines rather than adjust speed. This of course, does not shed light on the speed adjustments that did occur. Two of my three female participants, Laura and Trisha, adjusted speed a couple different times during the lesson for related reasons. Laura started out her lesson in the accounting lab by setting her speed at 2.0x (2 times normal speed –or double speed).

Figure 2--Accounting lab where 5 of 11 participants were observed

After about a minute, she released the mouse and sat back in her seat, listening with her course packet notes (see appendix C) open in front of her. She jotted down notes now and then, seemingly following along with the lectures. After about six minutes she leans forward and increased her speed to 2.1x, and sits back to view and write again. In about another eight minutes she slowed down the presentation noticeably to 1.7 times normal speed for about 1 minute, after which she accelerated back up to 1.9x. Never did she stop or replay sections. When asked what motivated her to slow down the audio, she said that the content was complicated, and she wasn't getting it—so she slowed down. Her lack of distraction was especially noteworthy to me since at one point the lab TA approached me and attempted persistently to engage me in conversation about what I was doing. I tried without success for what seemed like minutes to communicate that I was busy and didn't want to chat. In interviews Laura recalled the distraction, but ignored it. Laura and I were both wearing headphones. It's an interesting idea that the use of headphones by all the participants, except those studying their materials at home, helped them manage and regulate their attention. Participants never said as much, but common sense would suggest it did help them concentrate and minimize distractions particularly in noisy lab setting like the accounting lab where TAs consulted with students and study groups met regularly and talked out loud (see figure 2).

Trisha also started her lesson out at 2.0x. She yawned repeatedly during the lessons. After one big yawn, she reached over and tried unsuccessfully to accelerate the presentation above 2.0x, but the control was maxed out. I chuckled inside. Since I was listening simultaneously with her, I knew what she was going through. Having not even had the background of this lesson, I understood the material and was ready to pick up the pace and wished (as did she apparently) that the presentation could have been accelerated at that point. Her particular computer configuration did not allow higher speeds than 2.0x. Rather than skip ahead and risk missing something, Trisha relied strictly on VSP and acceleration to pick up the pace. When she ran into a more challenging section, she, like Laura slowed down to 1.8x for about 4 minutes. Her "slow" period in contrast to Laura, was interrupted with numerous short section replayings—of course still at the relatively high speed of 1.8x.

Todd employed VSP in a unique way. He chooses to not adjust speeds during lessons sometimes even during the boring parts, instructor stories, or content he's familiar with. "During slow times, I'll get up and get some other things done…make me a sandwich and stuff." He said. "I like to keep the sound running so I don't miss stuff, but can still get other things done until I get to new material, and then I come back." He even described slowing lessons down a bit further, so he could get more other tasks done at the same time.

When I posed the question about what got in the way of her learning in this course, Laura stated emphatically "The instructor's examples! I think he waaaay over-explains things, way! And it bugs me cuz I still have to go through it." She also felt the need to accelerate through materials rather than skip ahead. This fear of skipping ahead is probably related to the medium of video. Video cannot be skimmed in the same way or as efficiently as text. The use of VSP to accelerate presentations, as described by our blind evaluator, acts as a speed-reading tactic for learners.

Overall, course control affordances seem to facilitate SRL (see appendix B for a list of controls available to the learner). All my participants were ahead of schedule in their course, rather than procrastinating. They hadn't painted themselves into a corner—forcing themselves to go faster than they should have, just to meet course deadlines--although remember that a TA had mentioned that some class members did fall prey to that scenario. Students loved the flexibility of the course. Its asynchronous nature helped them manage their study time both in this class as well as in their other, less flexible, classes. Jack's words represent the feelings of all the participants in this regard:

> I like being able to do it on my own time. I'm able to listen to the cds and what not, and also you can get ahead. You can kinda plan your weeks out...If you have a lot of homework in your other classes one week, you can look ahead—and get ahead in the accounting lessons, and if that week gets too hectic for ya, you don't have to worry about it.

An interesting aspect of student's self-regulation is that despite their limited time, participants will wind up viewing far more material than they ever would have received in the face-to-face class. They choose to view everything. They view all the remedial lessons, and helps that were designed for struggling students. Most participants believed that because accelerated, they must be saving time. There were approximately 25 hours of additional instruction recorded for this course above and beyond what a student would have encountered in the face-to face version of the course. This fact, combined with the amount of replayed segments that I observed, was not likely compensated for by student acceleration rates.

The course quiz structure is not conducive to self-regulated learning, making it difficult to be learning for the right reasons. Perhaps out of necessity in such a large class, scores, and not qualitative feedback are continually being fed to students, instead of qualitative forms of feedback that might prompt deeper self-reflection (Corno & Randi, 1999). Yet, here too, students seem to be taking responsibility for their learning and not just studying to perform well on the quizzes. Elliott & Dweck (1988) found in a study with 5th graders that when children using performance goals (i.e. must score high on quiz), failure and challenges are more likely to provoke a helpless response. But when children were instead focused on learning goals, failure and challenges were more likely to "provoke continued effort" (p.17). It would appear that in learning environments such as this multimedia accounting course, students that scored low seemed to feel like they just needed to study harder, slow the video down or study more effectively. One TA spoke to this issue when he described helping people in the accounting lab. "A lot of students will come to me and say, 'hey I didn't get any of this." And I'll ask, 'what speed did you watch it at?' The majority of the time they listened to it at an accelerated pace, so I usually tell them to go back and listen to it again, slower."

Rather than blame their intelligence, abilities or the teacher—the course seems to be structured to support self-regulatory practices and encourages students to take responsibility for both their learning as well as for the study strategies they employ. This is perhaps due to the "independent study" nature of the course and the levels of user control built into the course interface. As the designer of the technological aspects of the course (media and interface, but not pacing, assignments, course schedule or syllabus) it was my intent to build in a great deal of flexibility into a medium (video) not commonly known for its user-control affordances.

Conclusions

Additional research is needed to explore the relationship between control affordances and self-regulated learning. It is clear that SRL cannot occur without a certain level of learner autonomy and control. This course, as it is implemented, appears to provide learners with sufficient controls, allowing them to develop and exercise a variety of self-regulation behaviors. Of the available controls, variable speed playback appears to play a central regulatory role with these learners in this multimedia accounting course. VSP is pervasive in so many of the participant's SRL strategies, coloring the way they view and interact with their course materials. It's influence even carries over into their traditional lecture courses where some lamented not having the ability to accelerate all their university instructors in like manner.

Reflections

First I feel the need to defend what I've created here. The process of doing this paper, specifically letting the emic perspective (Rossman & Rallis, 2003) show through has been short circuited. I don't feel, I have done my participants or the data any sort of justice yet when it comes to data analysis. Now that that is off my chest, I can continue.

I feel I've incorporated many of my reflections already in the paper, but some other points stand out that are not appropriate for inclusion in the paper that I will mention here. Firstly, qualitative research is fun! I think I say this because it appears to be much more meaningful and human to me, and not because its mechanics are all that much more fun than other ways of conducting research. I thoroughly enjoyed my interviews despite the long hours, and was excited every day to get out and talk to more people.

I have only begun really listening to my interviews, and practice-coding one interview. The procedures are obviously new to me, and I still feel quite lost. Some of the themes presented in the paper may not be as emergent as I think, and felt quite forced for the purposes of the assignment. I was even uncomfortable trying to come up with them for fear that they would stick too strongly in my mind before I knew how they really reflected the data. It's funny how strongly I think I am (mankind is?) driven to find answers. It takes a good amount of effort to not jump to solutions, or jump prematurely to answers or conclusions when looking at the data. This process requires patience, but I feel the process will lead to a state of satisfaction that one has done justice to the data, and exercised due diligence in trying to understand what participants were saying.

Obviously, I need to understand GSR data a bit better, and may need more sensitive analysis software. I'll have to spend some time sorting that out over the summer. I'm encouraged by it, but need some better logistical protocols to make it work right. Some additional points or lessons learned are listed below:

- I should have gone to the lab at 11:30 p.m-midnight to get the "procrastinators" I was too lazy/tired to head back in to campus after a long day, and am still kicking myself about it.
- This takes time! I was able to schedule 4 on one day, But knew that I couldn't keep up that pace. Luckily I only had a few days to collect all my data.
- I found that my planned questions often dropped from any sort of order and became much more fluid with time. I'm sure I will still sound very stilted once I start listening to the interview recordings.
- Don't interview next to a water cooler. I should have known better from my video days, but I rendered some audio largely useless as a result—but not too much of it
- Be open about everything, ask about your influence on them during observation period. There's no hiding the elephant in the room!
- Listen! Don't take notes to remember, but rather for follow up questions (record the interview and listen to that later)
- Get better at asking the right kinds of questions—no matter how open ended your question are, it's what you ask that gets answered. Be aware of what you're asking, and NOT asking.
- Coming home at night with my digital interviews in hand reminded me of my old photography days where after a shoot out on the town, I wanted to get my film back so bad from the lab to see my images that I could taste it!—I now sit here wanting to get my data transcribed, knowing that there's no way I can do it all myself---so it sits, and I sit frustrated. I'll think of something.
- I admittedly took pleasure in coming up with new (but not very creative) names for my participants—not any name would do, it had to be one that suited my memory of them.

This has really been an eye-opening activity that has let me look upon research more favorably.
-Joel Galbraith

References

Dweck, C.S. (1999). *Self-Theories: Their role in Motivation, Personality and Development*. Philadelphia, PA: Psychology Press

Clariana, R. B. (1990). Gender and ability differences in galvanic skin response during pair and individual computer-assisted math instruction. Journal of Computing in Childhood Education, 2(1), 69-82.

Clariana, R. B. (1992). Media research with a galvanic skin response biosensor: Some kids work up a sweat! Presented at the annual meeting of the Association for Educational Communications and Technology (AECT), Washington, DC, February, 1992. (as ERIC Document Reproduction Service: ED 381 141)

Corno, L. & Randi, J. (1999). A design for classroom instruction in self-regulated learning.. Ch 13 In C. M. Reigeluth (Ed.), *Instructional-Design Theories and Models: A New Paradigm of Instructional Theory, vol. II*. Mahwah, NJ: Lawrence Erlbaum Associates.

Creswell, J.W. (2003). *Research Design: Qualitative, quantitative and mixed method approaches*. Thousand Oaks, CA: Sage.

Galbraith J., & Spencer, S. (2002). Asynchronous Video-Based Instruction with Variable Speed Playback: Is Faster Better? Proceedings of the World Conference on Educational Multimedia, Hypermedia & Telecommunications(ED-Media), Denver, Colorado.

Geertz, C. (1973) *The interpretation of cultures*. New York: Basic Books

Glaser, B. G. & Strauss, A. L. (1967). *The Discovery of Grounded Theory*. Chicago: Aldine Publishing Company.

Glynn, L. M., Christenfeld, N. and Williams, G. (1999). Gender, Social support, and cardiovascular responses to stress. Psychosomatic Medicine. 61, 234-242

Goldman-Segall, R. (1998). *Points of viewing children's thinking: A digital ethnographer's journey*. Mahwah, NJ: Lawrence Erlbaum Associates

Gutenko, G. (1995). Speed: "Run"- Time Compressed Video for Learning Improvement and Digital Time Compression Economy. Retrieved March 24, 2003, from the World Wide Web: Eric Document, ED384 341.

Harrigan, K. (1995). The SPECIAL system: Self-paced education with compressed interactive audio learning. Journal of Research on Computing in Education, 27(3), 361-370.

Harrigan, K. (2000). The SPECIAL system: Searching time-compressed digital video lectures. Journal of Research on Computing in Education, 33(1), 77-86.

King, P. E., & Behnke, R. R. (1989). The Effect of Time-Compressed Speech on Comprehension, Interpretive and Short-Term Listening. Human Communication Research, 15(3).

Laurier. E. (2003). Participant Observation, in Research Methods in Human and Physical Geography, ed. Nick Clifford & Gill Valentine, London: Sage

Omoigui, N., He, L., Gupta, A., Grudin, J., & Sanocki, E. (1999). Time-Compression: Systems Concerns, Usage, and Benefits. Paper presented at the CHI 99, 1999, Association for Computing Machinery, Pittsburgh, PA.

Reeves, B., Lang, A., Thorson, E., & Rothchild, M. (1989). Emotional television scenes and hemispheric specialization. Human Communication Research, 15(4), 493-508.

Rossman G., Rallis, S. (2003). *Learning in the field: An introduction to qualitative research*. Thousand Oaks, CA: Sage

Ryle, G. (1971). Collected Papers Vol.2. New York: Barnes & Nobles.

Schunk, D. H. (2004). *Learning Theories: An Educational Perspective*. (4rd Edition). Upper Saddle River, NJ: Prentice-Hall Inc.

Seidman I. (1998). *Interviewing as qualitative research*. New York (2nd ed): Teachers College Press

Strauss, A. & Corbin, J. (1998). *Basics of qualitative research: Grounded theory procedures and techniques*. Thousand Oaks, CA: Sage

Stern R., Ray, W. & Quigley, K. (2001). Psychophysiological Recording. New York: Oxford University Press.

Van Manen, M. (2001). *Researching lived experience*. Ontario, Canada: Althouse Press

Appendix A (sample interview questions)

Note: Not every question below was asked of each participant. Some questions emerged during one interview, and were then also asked of subsequent participants.

Primary Research Question: What is the nature of student self-monitoring and self-regulation when using variable speed playback (VSP) technology in a video-centric course?

1. What had you heard about this course (good and bad) before you took it?
2. Tell me generally how you use the speed controller (VSP)?
3. What kinds of things motivate you to adjust (or not) the speed of presentations (faster and slower)?
4. How do you use the other presentation controls (pause, rewind, stop, play, table of contents) with the VSP controller?
5. Why do you NOT use the speed controller?
6. Do you leave settings consistently fast, but stop and replay sections for better comprehension?
7. If so, do you repeat certain types of sections more than others?
8. Do you play the beginnings and ends of lessons slower or repeat them?
9. Do you play lecture summary statements made by the instructor slower, faster or repeat them?
10. Do you play the instructor's examples/stories different ways than other parts of lectures?
11. Do you play the instructor's "problem" sets and "walk-throughs" (answers) differently than other parts of lectures?
12. Have you ever viewed course materials on a computer without the VSP functionality? Tell me about that experience.
13. How might your particular study habits, learning strategies and/or usage patterns be motivated by your use of the VSP technology?
14. How do you think your speed control behavior might influence how you learn—on your study patterns? (does it make procrastinating easier?—you'll just watch the next section faster)
15. Do you ever feel your use of the speed control might be hurting your learning?
16. If so, do you do anything to compensate?
17. Is this how you usually study? (what time of day generally, why?)
18. Why do you study in this location? (apt. lab, library?)
19. Why do you go through all the walkthroughs? You got all the answers correct!

20.   How aware were you of me? (The camera? The arm band?, my note–taking?)

21.   Do you ever view the CDs with someone else? Why, why not?

22.   How do you think you learn best? How do you use or control the course features to support that?

23.   What things here [gesturing at course screen] get in the way of your learning?

24.   Has this course helped you discover anything about how you learn? Or don't learn?

25.   Do you recall moments when your mind wandered in this section? What were you thinking about (if you don't mind me asking?)

26.   Were any parts/concepts particularly challenging to understand?

27.   *[looking at GSR data] Here, here and here (pointing to spots on GSR data timeline) is where you adjusted presentation speed. What do you notice, and would you explain the GSR data in relation to how you adjusted presentation speed? (assuming any patterns exist)

28.   *[looking at GSR data] look at this "spike" OR "gradual in-/de-creasing trend" OR "pattern" here in the GSR data. Yet, according to my observations, here you did NOT adjust speed or stop. Can you recall what this data might reflect? Lets look at the video at this point to see what part of the lesson you were on. (challenging content, frustrating concepts, poor explanation, going too fast, going too slow, just saw my girlfriend walk in the lab etc.)

29.   *How do you think looking at this (GSR) data and having this discussion together might influence your study habits or awareness of how you use the VSP tool?

* Question area dropped due to logistical impracticalities.

Appendix B (control affordances)

The accounting course affords the following learner control:

1. Control over presentation *playback speed* (VSP)

2. Control over material *sequencing* (although a linear sequence is suggested for those with no background in the field)

3. Control over *how often to repeat* or replay content.

4. Control over within lesson pacing or playback controls; stop, play, pause, jump back 10 seconds, slider with position indicator for current segment of instruction.

5. Control over which media to watch (video and/or supporting graphics and animations can be viewed/stepped through independently or in synchronized mode)

6. Control over what supplementary materials to view and work through.(step-by-step problem solutions, hints, additional problem sets)

7. Control over *when* to interact with course content (weekly quizzes help "force" students to stay on track-although quizzes may all be taken early)

8. Control over *where* to view course materials (home, campus labs, work)

9. Students may opt to get additional help from upper level TAs in an accounting lab.

Control or choices not given to students include:

1. Software only works on the Microsoft Windows platform or on emulators such as Virtual PC on the Macintosh platform. This can cause significant anxiety for many users not familiar with the MS Windows environment, although none of our participants were affected in this way.

2. Students have no alternative method of taking the course (i.e. no traditional face-to-face section exists) although a textbook and study outline exists for students desiring such an alternative.

3. As discussed, students are given regular and frequent quizzes to help them avoid getting too far behind in the course. Students cannot choose to get too far behind without hurting their grades, but may elect to complete the course early.

4. Students are not given control over the learning goals or objectives of the course, that is, outside of being able to personally choose how they respond to the given or prescribed course objectives. This is generally antithetical to notions of self-regulated learning in the field (Corno & Randi, 1999)

340

What would the 12/31/X5 adjusting entry have been if the allowance account had actually had a debit balance before adjustment, meaning that the writeoffs must have totaled $1,280 rather than $920, and therefore the 20X4 estimate would have been underestimated rather than overestimated?

Allowance for Uncollectible A/R

		1,100	12/31/X4
Writeoffs	1,280		
Underestimated	180		
		?	12/31/X5 Adjustment
		2,352	(8% x 29,400)

Bad Debt Expense	2,532	
Allowance for Uncollectible A/R		2,532

Bad Debt Expense should be overstated in 20X5 to compensate for the $180 understatement in 20X4.

31.

Alternative approach to estimating uncollectible accounts receivable.

Aging of Accounts Receivable: (Using different %'s for aged categories)

		Est. % Uncollect.	
Current:	$ 15,000	5%	$750
Past Due:			Amount
0 - 30 days	8,000	8%	640
30-60 days	3,000	10%	300
60-90 days	2,000	15%	300
90 + days	1,400	20%	280
	29,400		2,270

32.

Allowance for Uncollectible A/R

		1,100	12/31/X4
Writeoffs	1,280		
Underestimated	180		
		?	Adjustment
		2,270	12/31/X5

Bad Debt Expense ($2,270 + 180)	2,450	
Allowance for Uncollectible A/R		2,450

33.

Credit Card Sales

Customer agrees to pay charges from card use.

Credit card issued upon credit approval.

34.

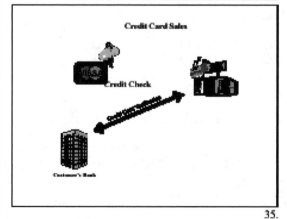

Credit Card Sales

Credit Check

Customer's Bank

35.

Credit Card Sales

Bank credits restaurant's account.

Bank charges fee to restaurant.

Customer's Bank

Restaurant's Bank

36.

Appendix D (Sample observation log)

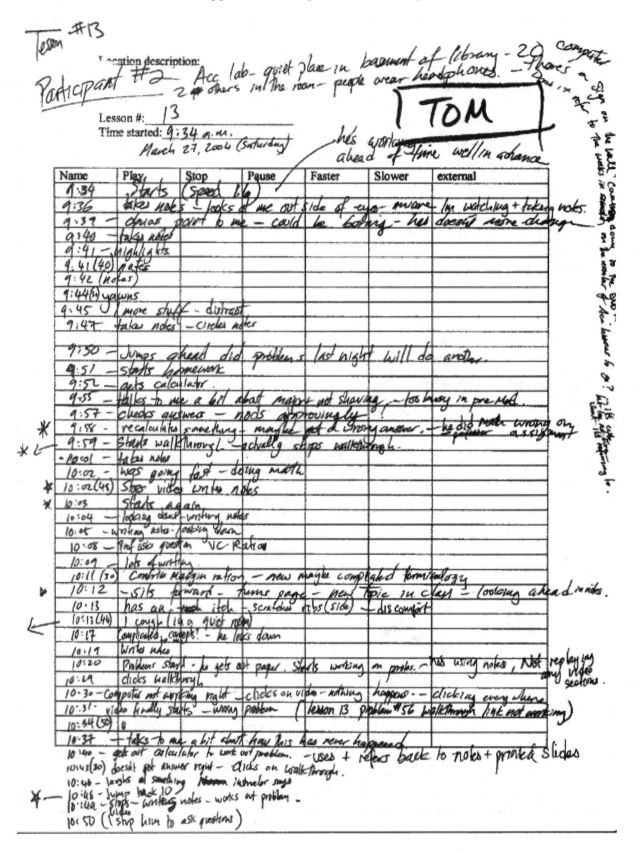

Appendix E (accounting course and VSP interface)

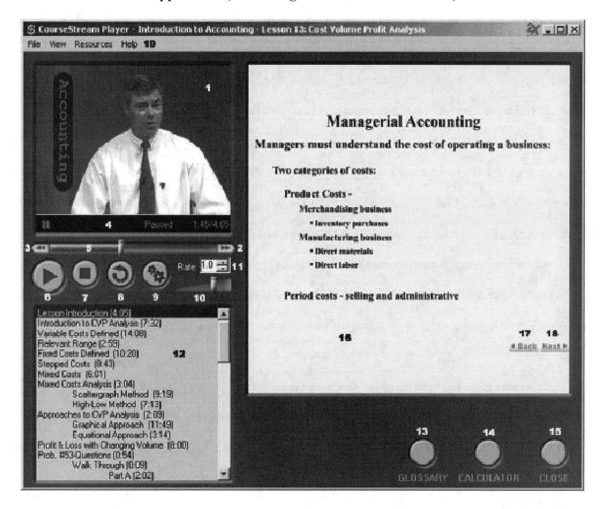

1. **Video Window** — This is the video portion of the lesson. This window now has the ability to double in size. To change the video to double size, Click "View" and then click "Double size video."

2. **Fast Forward** — This button fast-forwards the video at about 10 times the original speed (NO audio).

3. **Fast Rewind** — This button fast rewinds the video at about 10 times the original speed. (NO audio)

4. **Video Status Window** — This section now provides better video information. The status window tells the user the present state of the video and the video now counts in real-time.

5. **Time Bar** — The time bar is now much more advanced and responsive over the previous version. The time bar now moves in real-time as the video plays. The user can also manipulate the time bar with greater ease.

6. **Play/Pause Button** — The play and pause button are now combined.

7. **Stop Button** — This button stops the video and returns the time bar to the beginning of the video segment.

8. **Ten Seconds Back button** — This button moves the video back ten seconds. We changed this button from five seconds to ten seconds because most students move through the material at 2X the original speed and five seconds was simply not enough time.

9. **Synch Button** — This button synchronizes the video with the current slide

10. **Volume Control Slider** — This slider controls the volume of the presentation.

11. **VSP (Variable Speed Playback) Module** — This integrated module allows the user to increase or decrease the presenter's rate of speech without distorting the pitch of the voice. This module only works properly in Windows XP and functions much like the Enounce 2xAV plug-in. This integrated module and the Enounce plug-in can be used simultaneously to achieve combined playback rates faster than four times the original speed. This integrated module can be turned off in the Settings menu causing the Enounce 2xAV plug-in to be the sole VSP engine. We strongly suggest that when a student watches the lessons for the first time they do so at rates lower than or equal to 2.5X the speed. If a student chooses to review the material for a test or exam then it may be appropriate to watch the lessons at a faster rate.

12. **Table of Contents** — This is an outline of the content in the lesson.

13. **Glossary Button** — (see below for more information about the glossary).

14. **Calculator** — This button loads the internal program calculator. If you desire, you can set the program to load the default Windows calculator in the settings menu when you click this button.

15. **Close** — This button shuts down the program.

16. **Slide Window** — This is the flash animation window.

17. **Back Button** — This button causes the slide window to show the previous slide.

18. **Next Button** — This button advances the slide window to the next slide.

19. **Menu System** — Please refer to "Menu System" below for an explanation.

Chapter 22 Evaluating a Research Report

Chapter 22 Objectives

1. For each of the major sections and subsections of a research report, list at least three questions which should be asked in determining its adequacy.
2. For each of the following types of research, list at least three questions which should be asked in determining the adequacy of a study representing that type:

    Descriptive research
    Correlational research
    Causal-Comparative research
    Experimental research
    Single-subject research
    Narrative research
    Ethnographic research
    Mixed-methods research
    Action research

Review the Terms

Instead of providing definitions for Chapter 22 terms, given the following sections of a research report, or the following types of research reports, indicate one <u>question</u> you should ask yourself when you evaluate a report.

Problem : _____

_____

Review of literature: _____

_____

Hypothesis: _____

_____

Participants: _____

_____

Instruments: _____

_____

Design and procedures: _____

_____

Results: _____

_____

Discussion: _____

_____

Abstract:_____

_____

Qualitative research: _____

_____

Observational studies: _____

_____

Descriptive research: _____

_____

Interview studies: _____

_____

Causal-comparative research: _____

_____

Experimental research:_____

_____

Correlational studies: _____

_____

Prediction studies: _____

_____

Ethnographic research: _____

_____

Mixed methods: _____

_____

Narrative research: _____

_____

For Your Own Review

1. What are two questions that one should pose when reviewing general qualitative research studies?

   _____

   _____

2. List two questions to pose regarding the internal validity and two regarding external validity of a study.

   _____

   _____

   _____

   _____

Applying What You Know

1. Use the provided criteria to write an abstract for Loujeania Bost's study (Don't use hers!) presented in Chapter 21. The abstract you create should be less than 150 words.

     _____
     _____
     _____
     _____
     _____
     _____
     _____
     _____
     _____
     _____
     _____
     _____
     _____
     _____
     _____
     _____
     _____
     _____

2. Given Dan McCullum's proposal (introduced in Chapter 21) use the following questions to critique his Problem Statement.

    a. Is there a statement of the problem? If so, what is it?

        _____
        _____
        _____

    b. Is the problem researchable? _____

    c. Does the problem have educational significance? _____

3. Refer to the Pajares (2001) article at the end of Chapter 1 and answer the following questions related to the conclusions the author draws from his findings.

    a. Is each result discussed in terms of the original hypothesis or topic to which it related?

        _____

    b. Are generalizations consistent with the results?

        _____

    c. Are the possible effects of uncontrolled variables in the results discussed?

        _____

    d. Are recommendations for future action made?

        _____

4. Given Joel Gailbath's study shared in Chapter 21, answer the following questions.

    a. Is the method used to record responses described?
    _____

    b. Is the interview guide included? _____

    c. Does the interview guide indicate the type and amount of prompting and probing that was permitted? Explain._____
    _____

Test-Like Event

Circle the best answer for each item.

1. When reviewing a recent article, Kenya noted that several subscales of an instrument were used in the study. A description of the scales used was likely reported in the

    a   literature review.
    b. hypothesis statement.
    c. methods section.
    d. results section.

2. Stanley conducted a qualitative study and is writing up his report. Which of the following is of importance to his research report?

    a. Is the criterion variable well defined?
    b. Was an appropriate experimental design selected?
    c. Is the study replicable?
    d. Has he examined the possibility of personal bias?

3. After reading a recent report, you finished the article and were unsure if the hypothesis was supported. This illustrates a flaw in the

    a. introduction
    b. method
    c. results
    d. discussion

4. Of the following, which question should be considered when reviewing the abstract of an article?

    a. Is related literature addressed to show relevance?
    b. Is the scope of the study conveyed?
    c. Are the number and type of subjects described?
    d. Is the validity of the instruments used presented?

5. In writing the report for his dissertation study, Derek includes a section that explains in detail the qualifications of his interviewers. He notes, for example, that they are all experienced administrators and had all taken qualitative research methods courses. Derek included this information in the _____ section of his report.

    a. Abstract
    b. Procedure
    c. Introduction
    d. Instruments

6. In reviewing the survey that was used in a previous report on the benefits of extra-curricular activities for children, David notes that several of the questions in the survey include 'ands' and actually are asking two different questions. David has noted a flaw in which of the following components of the report?

    a. Abstract
    b. Introduction
    c. Procedure
    d. Instruments

7. Maurice has conducted an intervention study that examines a specific four-step strategy to increase learning disabled children's problem-solving. He uses a pre-post design and uses standardized achievement test scores at the end of the year to determine if students have learned the strategies. Identify the flaw that Maurice has included in the instruments' section of his study.

    a. His dependent measure should be norm-referenced.
    b. His dependent measure should be criterion-referenced.
    c. His dependent measure should be a longer test.
    d. His dependent measure should have greater test-retest reliability.

8. Amanda was surprised when reading a recent article on perfectionism. There appeared to be several references to sources unrelated to the topic. What was really interesting is that they all had the same author last name. With which of the following sections of the article is this concern most directly related?

    a. Summary
    b. Introduction
    c. Review of the literature
    d. Discussion

9. Lisa failed to obtain IRB permission but conducted a study regarding students' opinions about laboratory practicals as a requirement to admission to the engineering masters program. This illustrates a flaw in the _____

    a. Design and procedures.
    b. Participants.
    c. Results.
    d. Review of the literature.

10. Cynthia failed to mention in a recent presentation of her work that she used a 100 point scale, and not a Likert scale, in her pilot study. Cynthia's omission is a weakness in the

    a.   Participants.
    b.   Design and Procedures.
    c.   Instruments.
    d.   Results.

11. In reading a recent report of a structural equation study, Molly notes errors in some of the basic descriptive statistics. She is concerned that the authors may not have the skills needed to conduct the study that they have presented. Your text indicates that this is a question to address in the

    a.   Introduction.
    b.   Method.
    c.   Results.
    d.   Discussion.

12. In writing up the report for his recent study that examines animation, Dan notes all of the research that supports the use of animation but does not include the studies that have indicated no benefit or animation in learning. This is a flaw most directly related to the _____ section of the report.

    a.   introduction
    b.   method
    c.   results
    d.   design and procedures

13. Of the following questions one might ask when critiquing a research study, which is a concern for the design and procedures section?

    a.   Is the relevancy of the references explained?
    b.   Are the size and characteristics of the sample described?
    c.   Are generalizations consistent with the results?
    d.   Are control procedures applied?

14. Of the following, which question is relevant when critiquing an action research study?

    a.   Are the characteristics that differentiate the groups clearly defined or described?
    b.   Was the area of focus something that the researcher was passionate about?
    c.   Were any control procedures applied to equate the groups on extraneous variables?
    d.   Are sources of invalidity associated with the design identified and discussed?

15. Dave is writing up his within-subjects study on his work that addresses the change over time in reading rates of students reading Web-based text. Of the following the most important question Dave should answer in his report is

    a.   Were efforts made to overcome observer bias and observer effect?
    b.   Were control procedures applied to equate groups on extraneous variables?
    c.   Was the questionnaire pretested?
    d.   Was an appropriate experimental design selected?

16. Peggy is reviewing a manuscript for a teacher practitioner journal. The study is somewhat interesting but the authors don't illustrate how it is relevant to teachers in the field. In her review, Peggy indicated that the authors should focus on revisions to the

    a. results.
    b. method.
    c. introduction.
    d. procedures.

17. Recently Shannon was reading a study that addressed the measurement of motivation in reading. The study indicated that the MRP was used in a study with high school students. Shannon found that odd as the MRP is a measurement tool generally used with elementary school learners. Shannon may have identified a weakness in the _____ of the report.

    a. problem statement
    b. literature review
    c. hypotheses
    d. method

18. Which of the following questions should be considered in a casual-comparative study?

    a. Is the independent variable clearly defined or described?
    b. Was the resulting prediction equation validated with another group?
    c. Were the sources of data related to the problem mostly primary?
    d. Is a rationale given for selection of predictor variables?

19. Christopher conducted a regression analysis for his dissertation. He is most concerned about addressing which of the following questions in his report?

    a. Are the sources of data related to the problem mostly primary?
    b. Is a rationale given for selection of predictor variables?
    c. Was the appropriate sampling method used to form the groups in his study?
    d. Was a coded recording instrument used?

20. Sampling technique used in a study should be included in the _____ section of a research report?

    a. Results
    b. Instruments
    c. Participants
    d. Design and procedure

Companion Website

For more practice on becoming competent in this chapter's objectives, go to the Companion Website that accompanies this text at www.prenhall.com/gay. This site includes:

Objectives with links to:
- more multiple-choice questions in Practice Quiz
- Applying What You Know essay questions
- relevant Web sites

Custom modules to help you:
- calculate statistical tests (see "Calculating Statistical Tests")
- do research (see "Research Tools and Tips")
- practice analyzing quantitative data (see "Analyzing Quantitative Data")
- practice analyzing qualitative data (see "Analyzing Qualitative Data")
- practice evaluating published articles (see "Evaluating Articles")

Chapter 22 Answers
For Your Own Review
1. Three are numerous answers. See page 1116 and 1117 of your text to check your response.
2. There are numerous answers. See page 1121 and 1122 to check your response.

Checking What You Know
1. Check the abstract that you wrote for these elements.
    - Is the problem restated?
    - Are the number and type of subjects and instruments described?
    - Is the design identified?
    - Are the procedures described?
    - Are the major results and conclusions restated?

2. a. The problem is stated and some research supports the need for the study and relevance of the topic.
    b. This is a research topic that can be answered with data.
    c. The problem has educational significance for those teaching second languages.

3. a. The conclusions of this article are brief. (My experiences with this journal are that page restrictions do exist.) Some of the recommendations from this data are subtle but there. They are posed for future consideration and research. Dr. Pajares has posed, in essence, that to understand our phenomenon of study, we need to examine a broader context.
    b. yes
    c. yes, one place these are evident is in the limitations presented.
    d. Yes

4. a. yes, he recorded and also tape recorded
    b. yes, a lengthy protocol is provided.
    c. Joel discusses this point in his lessons learned section.

Test-Like Event

1.	c	5.	b	9.	a	13.	d	17.	d
2.	d	6.	d	10.	c	14.	b	18.	a
3.	d	7.	b	11.	a	15.	d	19.	b
4.	c	8.	c	12.	a	16.	c	20.	c

Appendix A: Dataset

Dataset for SPSS exercises for Chapters 14 and 15.

ID	CONDITIO	INTEREST	CLASSYR	GENDER	RECALL	FACTUAL	PROBLEMS
1	1	10	2	1	25	64	4
2	1	11	2	1	24	64	5
3	1	11	2	1	26	62	4
4	1	14	2	1	27	60	3
5	1	12	2	2	31	68	2
6	1	12	2	1	28	60	5
7	1	9	2	1	78	82	4
8	1	10	2	1	54	74	3
9	1	13	1	2	28	62	2
0	1	14	1	2	27	60	5
11	1	11	3	1	41	68	5
12	1	12	2	1	50	72	3
13	1	10	2	1	61	74	8
14	1	17	2	1	70	82	7
15	1	8	2	1	29	58	6
16	1	11	2	1	34	64	5
17	1	12	2	1	36	72	6
18	1	12	2	1	35	70	6
19	1	10	2	1	54	80	6
20	1	10	7	1	30	60	6
21	1	9	2	1	24	58	5
22	1	11	3	1	26	80	8
23	1	13	2	2	31	82	8
24	1	14	2	1	47	78	7
25	2	14	2	2	54	60	6
26	2	14	2	1	43	52	8
27	2	15	2	2	47	84	8
28	2	16	2	1	50	86	6
29	2	12	2	1	52	90	10
30	2	11	2	1	58	88	9
31	2	10	1	1	84	68	7
32	2	17	1	1	51	78	7
33	2	18	1	2	46	90	8
34	2	14	1	1	39	92	4
35	2	14	2	1	40	84	9
36	2	13	3	1	29	66	8
37	2	11	4	1	34	60	8
38	2	15	2	2	36	72	8
39	2	16	2	1	58	78	6
40	2	14	2	1	91	88	5
41	2	13	2	1	48	68	5
42	2	11	2	2	64	70	4
43	2	15	2	1	52	68	8
44	3	14	2	1	48	58	9
45	3	18	2	1	68	80	9
46	3	16	2	1	56	70	4
47	3	12	2	1	67	90	9

48	3	17	2	1	84	96	6
49	3	18	2	1	45	98	8
50	3	14	2	1	64	88	8
51	3	14	2	1	56	66	8
52	3	15	2	1	52	62	7
53	3	14	2	1	54	74	5
54	3	13	2	1	58	88	5
55	3	10	2	2	64	92	8
56	3	15	2	1	49	94	6
57	3	14	2	1	38	90	7
58	3	13	2	1	67	88	10
59	3	14	2	2	88	94	8
60	3	15	2	2	57	70	9
61	3	14	2	1	62	80	9
62	3	14	2	1	49	74	9
63	3	18	2	1	56	80	6
64	3	17	2	1	68	80	7
65	3	16	3	1	62	82	8
66	3	16	2	2	78	90	8

References

Aleksic, M. (2001). Questioning as a method of improving illustration processing, learning, and student interest. Proposal awarded the "Graduate students Alumni Society Research Initiation Grant, December 2001-December 2002, The Pennsylvania State University.

American Psychological Assocation (2001). *Publication Manual of the American Psychological Assocation*, 5th ed. Washington, DC: American Psychological Association.

American Psychological Association (2002). APA style. Retrieved June 2002 from the World Wide Web: www.apastyle.org/elecref.html

American Statistical Association Section on Survey Research (1998). What is a survey? Retrieved June 2002, from the World Wide Web: http://www.stat.ncsu.edu/info/srms/surveymail.pdf.

Armstrong, J. Qualitative research Home Page, Retrieved June 2002, from the World Wide Web: http://www.unm.edu/~jka/qualres.html.

Bochna, C. (2002). Treating Autism: An Investigation of the Young Autism and TEACCH Projects. Unpublished manuscript.

Bost, L. W. (2002). Teacher Familiarity and Use of Reading Comprehension Strategies With Students With Learning Disabilities. Unpublished manuscript.

Buros Institute of Mental measurements. Test Locator. http://www.unl.edu/buros/

Cattell, R. B. & Horn, J. L., & Sweney, A. B. (1964). Motivation Analysis Test.

Duke University's Medical center: Research ethics: Education and resources. Retrieved June 2002, from the World Wide Web: http://researchethics.mc.duke.edu/clinethics.nsf/webpages/home

ERIC clearinghouse on Assessment and Evaluation. Survey research in Education. Retrieved June 2002, from the World Wide Web: http://ericae.net/faqs/Surveys/survey_research.htm.

Gambrell, L. B., Codling, B. M., Mazzoni, R. M., Anders, S. (1996). Motivation to Read Profile (MRP).

Gambrell, L. B., Martin, B., Codling, R. M., & Mazzoni, S. A. (1996). Assessing motivation to read. *The Reading Teacher, 49(7), 518-533.*

Ganesh, T. G. [Webmaster] (Update May 2002). The AERA Special Interest Group (SIG) on Communication of Research Website. Retrieved June 2002, http://aera-cr.ed.asu.edu/links.html.

Gottfried, A. E. (1982). Children's Academic Intrinsic Motivation Inventory.

Hogan, K, & Corey, C. (2001). Viewing classrooms as cultural contexts for fostering scientific literacy. *Anthropology and Education, 32*, 214-233.

Hohenbrink, J., Johnston, M., & Westhoven, L. (1997). Collaborative teaching of a social studies methods course: Intimidation and change. *Journal of Teacher Education, 48*, 293-300

Hughes, I. University of Sydney Australia Action Research on the Web. Retrieved June 2002, from the World Wide Web: http://casino.cchs.usyd.edu.au/arow/links.htm#AROW

Lane, D. (2001). Rice Virtual Lab. Retrieved June 2002, from the World Wide Web: http://www.ruf.rice.edu/~lane/rvls.html.

Lane. D. (2001) Rice Virtual Lab simulations. Retrieved June 2002, from the World Wide Web: http://www.ruf.rice.edu/~lane/stat_sim/index.html.

Lane, D. (2001). Rice Virtual lab descriptive statistics simulation. Retrieved June 2002, from the World Wide Web: http://www.ruf.rice.edu/~lane/stat_sim/descriptive/index.html

Levine, S. J. Writing and presenting your thesis or dissertation. Retrieved June 2002 from the World Wide Web: http://www.learnerassociates.net/dissthes/.

Lovett, M.W., Lacerenza, L., & Borden, S. L. (2000). Putting struggling readers on the PHAST track: A program to integrate phonological and strategy-based remedial reading instruction and maximize outcomes [Abstract]. *Journal of Learning Disabilities, 33*, 458-476.

Lovett, M. W., Lacerenza, L., Borden, S. L., Frijters, J. C., Steinbach, K. A., DePalma, M (2000). Components of Effective Remediation for Developmental Reading Disabilities: Combining Phonological and Strategy-based Instruction To Improve Outcomes [Abstract]. *Journal of Educational Psychology, 92*, 263-283.

Ma, X (2001). Bullying and being Bullied: to what extent are Bullies also victims [Abstract]. *American Educational Research Journal, 38*, 351-370.

Mayer, R. E., & Moreno, R. (1998). A split attention effect in multimedia learning: Evidence for dual processing systems in working memory. *Journal of Educational Psychology, 90*(2), 312-320.

McClellan, S. (2002). The effects of technology resources on achievement in statistics. Unpublished manuscript.

McCullum, D. (2002). Constructing the motivational components of foreign language achievement scale. Unpublished manuscript.

National Institutes of Health (NIH). Human Participant Protections: Education for research teams. Retrieved June 2002, from the World Wide Web: http://cme.nci.nih.gov/.

Oregon State University. Educational/Research Ethics. http://www.orst.edu/instruct/coun510/ethics/educat.htm. Maintained by B. Scott Christie and last accessed June 2002

Ortiz, C., Arnold, D. H., & Stowe, R. M. (1997). A Brief Rating Scale of Preschool Children's Interest in Shared Picture Book Reading [Abstract]. (ERIC Document Reproduction Service No. ED421247).

Pajares, F. (2001). Toward a positive psychology of academic motivation. *Journal of Educational Research, 95*, 27-35.

Perry, J. A. (2001). Fifth-graders' mathematical communications: Lessons from the field [Electronic version]. *The Educational Forum, 66*(1), 71-75.

Piotrowski, C. S., Botsko, M., & Matthews, E. (2001). Parents' and teachers' beliefs about children's school readiness in a high-need community. *Early Childhood Research Quarterly, 15*, 537-558.

Pollard, C. K. (2002). e Effect of Review Options on Computerized Test Scores. Unpublished manuscript.

Poveda, D. (2001). La Ronda in Spanish kindergarten classroom with a cross –cultural comparison to sharing time in the U.S.A[Abstract]. *Anthropology and Education, 31*(3), 301-310.

Prawat, R. S. (2000). Dewey Meets the "Mozart of Psychology" in Moscow: The untold story[Abstract]. American Educational Research Journal, 37, 663-696.

Quiroz, P. A. (2001). The silencing of Latino Student 'voice': Puerto Rican and Mexican narratives in eighth grade and high school[Abstract]. *Anthropology and Education Quarterly, 32*, 326-335.

Rieber, L.P. (1996). Animation as a distractor to learning. *International Journal of Instructional Media, 23*(1), 53-57.

Robinson, D. H. (1998). Graphic organizers as aids to text learning. *Reading Research and Instruction, 37*(2), 85-105.

Russell, G., Williams, J. P., Fuchs, L, Baker, S., Koppenhaver, D., Spadorcia, S., Harrison, M. (1998). Improving reading comprehension for children with disabilities: A review of Research. Final Report (ERIC Document Reproduction Service No. ED 451650)

Saracho, O. (1986). The Development of the Preschool Reading Attitudes Scale [Abstract]. *Child Study Journal; 16*, 113-24.

Schunk, D. H., & Rice, J. M. (1992). Influence of Reading Comprehension Strategy Information on Children's Self-Efficacy and Skills [Abstract]. (ERIC Document Reproduction Service No. ED403534).

Shirin, A. D, & Kreimeyer, K. H. (2001). The role of interpreters in inclusive classrooms[Abstract]. *American Annals of the Deaf, 146*, 355-365.

SPSS (2001). SPSS Student Version 10.0, Version 4.

Syrett, K. L., & Rudner, L. M. (1996). Authorship Ethics. (ERIC Document Reproduction Service No. ED410318).

Uchiyama, K., Simone, G., & Borko, H. (1999). Publishing Educational Research: Guidelines and tips. AERA.Net Electronic Publications. http://www.aera.net/epubs/howtopub/index.htm.

Uitenbroek, D. G. (1997). *SISA Binomial.* Southampton: D.G. Uitenbroek. Retrieved Februrary, 2001, from the World Wide Web: http://home.clara.net/sisa/index.htm.

Wigfield, A. (1996). A Questionnaire Measure of Children's Motivations for Reading. Instructional Resource No. 22 [Abstract]. National Reading Research Center, Athens, GA.; National Reading Research Center, College Park, MD [Abstract]. (ERIC Document Reproduction Service No. ED394137).

Wright, M. L. (2002). Effects of mental imagery training combined with visual literacy training on reading comprehension of third grade elementary students. Unpublished manuscript.